TEACHERS FOR OUR NATION'S SCHOOLS

❖   ❖   ❖

John I. Goodlad

❖   ❖   ❖

TEACHERS FOR OUR NATION'S SCHOOLS

❖　❖　❖

Jossey-Bass Publishers • San Francisco

Substantial discounts on bulk quantities of Jossey-Bass books are available to corporations, professional associations, and other organizations. For details and discount information, contact the special sales department at Jossey-Bass Inc., Publishers. (415) 433-1740; Fax (415) 433-0499.

For sales outside the United States, contact Maxwell Macmillan International Publishing Group, 866 Third Avenue, New York, New York 10022.

Manufactured in the United States of America. Nearly all Jossey-Bass books and jackets are printed on recycled paper that contains at least 50 percent recycled waste, including 10 percent postconsumer waste. Many of our materials are also printed with vegetable-based ink; during the printing process these inks emit fewer volatile organic compounds (VOCs) than petroleum-based inks. VOCs contribute to the formation of smog.

Library of Congress Cataloging-in-Publication Data

Goodlad, John I.
    Teachers for our nation's schools / John I. Goodlad.—1st ed.
      p.   cm.—(The Jossey-Bass education series) (The Jossey-Bass higher education series)
    Includes bibliographical notes and index.
    ISBN 1-55542-270-5 (alk. paper)
    ISBN 1-55542-663-8 (paperback)
    1. Teachers—Training of—United States. I. Title. II. Series.
III. Series: The Jossey-Bass higher education series.
LB1715.G53   1990
370'.71'0973—dc20   90-53090
                                      CIP

FIRST EDITION
HB Printing   10 9 8 7 6 5 4 3   *Code 9085*
PB Printing   10 9 8 7 6 5 4 3 2 1   *Code 9459*

A joint publication in
The Jossey-Bass Education Series
and
The Jossey-Bass
Higher Education Series

❖　❖　❖

Contents

❖   ❖   ❖

Preface

❖　　❖　　❖

Few matters are more important than the quality of the teachers in our nation's schools. Few matters are as neglected. Most parents exercise considerable care in deciding who should baby-sit for their children. But the doors to teaching are unlatched; if the front door is locked, one enters through the back. Those who want to teach in our schools are required to meet no tests of character or commitment.

This grievous situation is the fault of a society whose values are confused. We give scant recognition to teachers, teaching, and teacher education, while extolling the importance of education and schools. We make little effort to attract the best and the brightest into teaching and reward poorly even the best of those who do choose to teach (despite the slings and arrows of all those who eschew a teaching career—while admitting that *someone* must educate their children). Throughout the history of our public educational system, making sure that we had enough teachers has taken precedence over making sure that we had good ones. Yet most of the time we have managed to maintain a more dedicated corps of able teachers than could have been expected in light of the prevailing conditions and circumstances.

A central thesis of this book is that there is a natural connection between good teachers and good schools and that this connection has been largely ignored. During successive eras of school reform, insufficient attention has been paid to the recruitment, education, and support of the men and women who are essential to school renewal. Excellent teachers do not in themselves ensure excellent schools. But it is folly to assume that schools can be exemplary when their stewards are ill-prepared.

Teacher education may have been neglected, but it has certainly not been ignored. On the contrary, it has been harnessed and prodded almost to death, yet given little nourishment. Most of all, teacher education has suffered from superficial scrutiny and consequently from inadequate understanding. So imperfectly have we understood what is needed to attract, educate, and retain able, committed individuals to teach our children, that simplistic prescriptions have appeared and reappeared in reform reports ever since the 1890s. If the diagnoses behind those prescriptions had been correct, the teacher education enterprise would be in good health today. It is not. After repeated doses of essentially the same medicine, teacher education appears to be more the victim of neglect and faulty diagnoses than the object of tender loving care.

Background

These and other disturbing conclusions stem from a comprehensive inquiry into the education of educators for our nation's schools that several colleagues and I conducted over a five-year period. We carefully selected sample settings to represent six types of colleges and universities that prepare teachers. The data on which this book is based were drawn from documents sent to us from each of the settings; questionnaires filled out by thousands of future teachers near the end of their preparation programs and by a broad sample of faculty members; notes and impressions gleaned from visits to each site by two teams of experienced educational researchers; and case histories of the institutions, which were prepared by several educational historians associated with us in this work. The hundreds of hours of interviewing presidents, provosts, deans, faculty members, students, and selected individuals in nearby school districts provided rich insights, particularly into the patterns that began to emerge early on and became increasingly marked.

The inquiry into teacher education reported on in *Teachers for Our Nation's Schools* arose out of an earlier inquiry into schools. This latter, described in *A Place Called School* (1984), four books by colleagues, and a clutch of technical reports and articles in journals, revealed many less-than-satisfactory educational practices and the apparent persistence of these year after year. What future teachers experience in schools and classrooms during their years as students profoundly shapes their later beliefs and practices. As teachers, they follow closely the models they have observed. Mental stereotypes developed over years of observing their own teachers are not challenged or fundamentally changed, apparently, by their experiences in formal teacher preparation programs. Why?

Our study of this and other questions began in 1985, just as the nation was plunging into still another orgy of school reform. Once again, there was no clear recognition of the ecological relationships among schools or of the array of circumstances impinging on teachers' performance. Had there been recognition and understanding, surely reformers would not have prescribed once again that old bromide: Have today's teachers mentor tomorrow's. Schools and teachers are not very effective, said report after report. Yet according to the conventional wisdom, the best way to ensure a competent teaching force is to place neophytes in those same schools with those same teachers. Surely we can come up with better remedies than this.

The teacher education enterprise reveals layer on layer of complexity. Despite its low status, it is linked to the quality of our schools, to which, in turn, the health of our economic system is tied. Teacher education (although it forms part of higher education—the most prestigious level of our educational system) suffers from chronic prestige deprivation. Although generally equated with schools and colleges of education, most of the education of teachers is conducted elsewhere. Though restricted by state regulations in a way no other academic or professional endeavor is, teacher education manages to survive. It is here to stay; it must be improved.

Overview of the Contents

Teachers for Our Nation's Schools seeks to unpeel these layers of complexity. Chapter One describes the changing circumstances in the recent history of the United States that have outrun and overwhelmed policies and strategies intended to restructure our schools. Clearly, these circumstances place enormous demands on teachers, who are now called upon to design schools capable of compensating for the erosion of families, religious institutions, and communities. Such teachers require preparation that goes far beyond immersion in the school, current classroom practices, and the subjects they will teach. Chapter One also describes the research methods my colleagues and I employed in our efforts to study teacher education and the institutional and regulatory context in which it is conducted. In effect, Chapter One sets the stage for a description of the conditions of teacher education, to which details are added in Chapters Four through Seven.

Chapter Two sets forth a conception of the role of schools and teachers in a democratic society—one that, in my judgment and that of my colleagues, should provide the beacon to guide the conduct of teacher education programs. I argue that teaching in schools is a special case, in which generic principles of teaching are empty unless disciplined by moral purpose and sensitivity. Teaching as an occupation cannot lay claim to professional status and recognition solely on the basis of scientific knowledge, or it is doomed to failure. Chapter Two concludes with nineteen presuppositions regarding the conditions that will need to be in place if able, dedicated men and women are to be attracted into schoolteaching, well prepared for the challenges they will face, and induced to stay with teaching as a career. We believe in these so strongly that we referred to them throughout our inquiry as postulates.

Chapter Three presents a sobering picture of the neglect that has characterized teacher education over the 150 years since the founding of the first normal schools—institutions deliberately created to recruit and educate teachers. It is a debilitating legacy that has been handed down. The question of central importance now is whether dynamic faculty groups seeking to confront the problems of our schools and to prepare teachers to address them can arise when circumstances are more likely to arouse anxiety and self-doubt than self-confidence and forthright action.

This question is always near the surface also in Chapter Four. There I examine both the university context and the school of education context, in which the health of teacher education is rarely robust. In Chapter Four, I also examine the regulatory context, which almost invariably ensures a continuing existence for teacher education programs, but always within narrowly defined boundaries. By the end of the chapter, it becomes clear to what degree current practice exerts virtually tyrannical control over neophyte teachers and, consequently, considerable influence over their teaching performance later in their careers, as well. Unfortunately, the practices learned during student teaching are as likely to have been established by administrative fiat as they are to represent the views of experienced teachers or teacher educators.

Chapters Five and Six report primarily on the perspectives of faculty members in the colleges and universities we studied and on the students enrolled in their teacher education programs. Although the institutional context—whether that of a liberal arts college, a regional university, or a flagship university—influences faculty views, the differences are more of degree than of kind. Similarly, the programs described in Chapter Seven are not significantly different in kind, whatever the institutional setting. All of those we visited were characterized, for example, by disconnectedness of the component parts. The parts are not even loosely coupled; they are not linked at all.

The myriad problems are not the work of delinquent or irresponsible actors, though teacher education, like all human enterprises, is marred by a few of those. Teacher education is simply, as I stated earlier, one of our nation's neglected enterprises. A great deal of commitment, energy, creativity, and support will be required to revitalize it.

Chapters Eight and Nine are devoted to redesign and renewal. In Chapter Eight, the postulates introduced in Chapter Two become the organizing framework for summarizing the conditions and circumstances of educating teachers in the settings studied. I recommend alternatives after each of the nineteen postulates and identify the people who should play a key role in efforts to implement them. The alternatives would further the mission of education, schools, teachers, and teacher education in a democratic society, which depends heavily on an educated citizenry.

In Chapter Nine, to combine the recommended alternatives

in an integrated whole and to portray the political, social, and technical processes of change that unfold during any serious effort to redesign and renew, I tell a fable in which the characters are caught up in a long-term effort to redesign teacher education at an imaginary public regional university. Although Dean Harriet Bryan is the catalyst, what she manages to accomplish could not have occurred without the support of the president of the university and an array of other individuals—along with the serendipity that can be only hoped for. Those who have been deeply involved in long-term reconstruction of an educational institution or program will recognize the degree to which the account reflects reality.

A significant message in Chapter Nine is that fundamental programmatic or institutional change is a long-term venture. Movement during the first two or three years is minuscule; there is some acceleration during the next two or three. In the fable, eight years elapse between the time that Dean Bryan makes her first major move toward revitalizing the teacher education program at Northern State University and the graduation of the first class.

This time span is more the norm than the exception in such ventures. Yet many policymakers and administrators, in particular, call for evidence of positive results to be provided within two or three years. Not surprisingly, the road to educational improvement is littered with good ideas that never got a fair hearing. Unfortunately, the burden of blame is almost invariably placed on the ideas and on those who were sufficiently daring to give them an initial trial. It is exceedingly difficult to restore to active duty either the ideas or the reformers now languishing by the wayside.

The story of renewal at Northern State is a fable in two senses: First, it is fictitious; second, everything runs pretty smoothly. Dedicated individuals bring off what they set out to do and are allowed enough time and a modicum of the support necessary to accomplish their aims. Something of educational significance happens. Many real-life events of such significance must occur in the years immediately ahead if educational reform in the United States is to stem the tide now overwhelming our educational system.

The study described in these nine chapters also embraced inquiry into the preparation of teachers to deal with children and adolescents considered to require specialized educational services (some of the findings are reported in Technical Report 10—see Appendix A), as well as the preparation of principals for elementary and secondary schools. Initially, I had planned to devote chapters to both topics in *Teachers for Our Nation's Schools*, but I later decided not to. It became increasingly apparent that doing so would unduly increase the length of this book and endanger its symmetry and its focus on the education of teachers. Furthermore, both subjects deserve more comprehensive treatment than space constraints allow.

Consequently, my colleagues and I are planning to develop these themes at some later point more comprehensively than the restraints would have permitted. I do not yet know precisely how this project might unfold. Undoubtedly it will involve the collaboration of individuals not now associated with the Center for Educational Renewal. An important assumption can be made, however: If the mission set here for teacher education is sound, it is equally sound for the guidance of programs for the education of specialists and principals for our schools.

Seattle, Washington John I. Goodlad
August 1990

To teachers and teacher educators everywhere,
with special thanks
to those who assisted us in our work

Acknowledgments

❖ ❖ ❖

In 1985, my colleagues and I launched not only the study described in *Teachers for Our Nation's Schools* but also two closely related projects, which taken together involved many people. These individuals are listed in groups in Appendixes B and D. With the exception of four or five of them, they are or were part-time (and usually short-term) employees of the Center for Educational Renewal. The other contributors were advisers or authors of commissioned papers.

I am glad to have an opportunity to thank here all those who served on the center's staff, gave advice as members of our National Advisory Board, wrote position papers or technical reports, or advised on an ad hoc basis. My colleagues and I at the center are particularly appreciative that everyone identified to such a degree with our goals and helped so unstintingly.

We enjoyed the support of several philanthropic foundations. The John D. and Catherine T. MacArthur Foundation provided the financial support for writing and publishing *The Moral Dimensions of Teaching* (Goodlad, Soder, and Sirotnik, eds., 1990). A grant from the Spencer Foundation enabled us to inquire into the evolution of the teacher-preparing programs in the colleges and universities in our sample, an inquiry that resulted in *Places Where Teachers Are Taught* (Goodlad, Soder, and Sirotnik, eds., 1990).

We extend appreciation also to the foundations that supported other parts of our effort: to the Danforth Foundation for its help in pioneering school-university partnerships (especially for improved preparation programs for school principals); to the Ford Foundation for a grant to maintain our National Advisory Board and to promote more equitable practices in schools; to the William and Flora Hewlett Foundation for supporting our efforts to promote and evaluate school-university partnerships; to the Joyce Mertz-Gilmore Foundation for ensuring the center's continuing existence as an entity; and to the Southwestern Bell Foundation for funds to help plan a five-year effort to improve teacher education that is to follow the initial five-year period of research and development.

Most of the planning for the study reported in this book and all of the subsequent data gathering and analyses were made possible by a series of grants from the Exxon Education Foundation. I could not and would not have entered into these years of hard work and tiring travel without the encouragement of Scott Miller. Sincere thanks are extended to him, his colleagues, and the foundation. My thanks go also to Clark Kerr, president emeritus of the University of California, who urged me not only to undertake the study but also to explore the matter of financial support with the Exxon Education Foundation.

Finding and working with a publisher can easily ruin the final year of a project such as the one reported on here. We were truly fortunate to establish at the outset a most gratifying relationship with Lesley Iura, education editor, and her colleagues at Jossey-Bass and to sustain it throughout. The three books referred to above benefited enormously from the constructive suggestions and superb editing. Yet the authors' prerogatives were respected with unfailing sensitivity.

In acknowledging the people associated with me in the work leading to a book I wrote several years ago, I spoke of my good fortune in being associated over the years with exceptional colleagues. The good fortune continues. Kenneth A. Sirotnik, Roger Soder, and I joined in creating and naming the Center for Educational Renewal. We have shared every important decision since. We traveled together every other week for nearly nine months of data gathering. This alone might have strained the relationship; it served only to strengthen bonds of friendship and collegiality. We coedited *The Moral Dimensions of Teaching* and *Places Where Teachers Are Taught*. Although I take full responsibility for *Teachers for Our Nation's Schools*, the concepts, findings, conclusions, and even recommendations are products of their minds as well as mine. Thanks to them, the final manuscript is much different and much better than it was in earlier versions. Ken and Roger would be embarrassed by lavish praise. To both, I extend my thanks, not just for their extraordinary contributions to the whole but for the sensitive way in which they made this old warrior (spell it *worrier,* if you will) their peer.

In the manuscript, I refer to two research teams, one visiting each setting a week or two after the first. The second of these comprised Jan DeLacy (on leave from the Bellevue, Washington, School District), Phyllis Edmundson (on sabbatical leave from Boise State University), and Zhixin Su (for the first half of our visits) from the center's staff. Their diligence, intelligence, and contributions are noted here with deep appreciation.

The pages of this manuscript have been through many revisions and many hands. The fingerprints appearing most often are those of Paula McMannon, for whom, to use her own words, this book has been her special baby. She has typed and retyped, corrected misspellings and grammatical errors, caught mistakes missed by everyone else, and rechecked what I thought already had been checked enough. If I have perused every page ten times, she has perused each at least twenty times. To her go much credit and appreciation for a level of dedication and performance rarely encountered.

Once again, Jordis Young of the College of Education provided superb editorial counsel, especially during the early stages. Zhixin Su, already mentioned for her other contributions, checked out every one of the references (listed by chapter at the end of the book). Joan Waiss followed Kathleen Olson in sustaining the necessary connections with the colleges and universities in our sample. Pamela Keating, a faculty colleague, worked closely with our National Advisory Board in seeking good advice at several important stages once the study was launched. My thanks go to these associates for their contributions.

For reasons of confidentiality, we are unable to list the persons at the sites we visited who made this study possible. They are recognized collectively in the dedication. Very special thanks go to the site coordinators, as we referred to them, who arranged the details of our visits, setting dates, sending documents, scheduling interviews, distributing and recovering questionnaires, handling crises, and more. The fact that everything seemed to work is due largely to them.

Thanks and apologies to my wife, although equally appropriate, would sound hollow. She has represented over many years of projects, books, and associated sacrifices a kind of commitment and support that is little heralded in our culture. To Evalene (her given name), Len (the family abbreviation initiated by her younger brother), Lynn (the name used by friends), and Irving (conferred for no apparent reason by Paula and Stephen, our children)—who has both contributed and endured enough for four individuals—I offer my love.

J.I.G.

The Author

❖   ❖   ❖

John I. Goodlad is professor of education and director of the Center for Educational Renewal, University of Washington. Born in Canada, he has taught at all levels, from kindergarten through graduate school. He served from 1967 to 1983 as dean of the Graduate School of Education, University of California, Los Angeles. He holds a B.A. degree (1945) in history and an M.A. degree (1946) in history and education, both from the University of British Columbia; a Ph.D. degree (1949) from the University of Chicago in education; and honorary degrees from nine universities in Canada and the United States.

Goodlad's research interests are in educational change and improvement and have been reported in more than twenty books and hundreds of other publications. An extensive study of schooling resulted in *A Place Called School* (1984).

The conceptual underpinnings and historical context of the research reported on in *Teachers for Our Nation's Schools* are developed in two companion books: *The Moral Dimensions of Teaching* and *Places Where Teachers Are Taught* (both Goodlad, Soder, and Sirotnik, eds., 1990). Goodlad's plans for the future include a large-scale effort to implement the recommendations contained in *Teachers for Our Nation's Schools*.

TEACHERS
FOR OUR
NATION'S
SCHOOLS

❖   ❖   ❖

Chapter One

A Nation Awakening

❖ ❖ ❖

Everybody wants to have education available. Everybody wants it paid for by taxes. But nobody has a kind word for the institution that was only the other day the foundation of our freedom, the guarantee of our future, the cause of our prosperity and power, the bastion of our security, the bright and shining beacon that was the source of our enlightenment, the public school.

—*Robert M. Hutchins*[1]

This nation is slowly awakening to the realization that circumstances are overwhelming its system of schooling. The call for restructuring that arose in the late 1980s and had not abated by the 1990s is evidence of that awakening. But ours is the awakening of a child, as yet largely innocent of the circumstances in which it finds itself.

Universal schooling—our Great American Schooling Experiment—"is as radical an idea as Americans have embraced."[2] That ideal encompassed at the beginning of the twentieth century a common school, comprising only the elementary grades, in which the

1

fundamentals of reading, writing, spelling, and figuring were to be taught to all our children. But "all" meant primarily immigrants pouring in from Europe and their cousins already here; it conveniently left out Native Americans and involuntary immigrants. That ideal nearly 100 years later is a common secondary school education for all, encompassing a considerable understanding of mathematics, science, technology, history, literature, and civics in preparation for an increasingly interdependent world. And what does "all" mean now? When the chief school officers of the fifty states proclaimed the goal of high school graduation for virtually all by the year 2000, they did not have in mind the exclusion of any.[3] The goal is truly universal even if the present reality is not.

The circumstances to which the nation is awakening so slowly are these. First, this nation of minorities provides an extraordinarily heterogeneous student body for the schools charged with achieving the ideal outlined above. Teaching the young has never been easy. But once upon a time, not so long ago in the history of our nation, teaching the young in schools was very much easier than it is today, largely because the school and its surrounding community were joined in common values and expectations and only a small percentage of boys and girls went beyond the elementary school.

Second, schools grown accustomed to a humbler task cannot meet the challenge of today simply by doing better what they have always done. Educators must rethink what education is, what schools are for; and they must examine and rework the structures and practices that have always been out of sync for some students and are now revealed to be inappropriate for many. The catchword of the late 1980s for this necessary renewal was *restructuring*.

Third, the designation of schools as a major, if not *the* major, instrumentality in solving our social and economic problems in the short run is unrealistic and dysfunctional. Schools can only educate. It is appropriate and sufficient to expect them to do this well. Yet so long as we fail to address today's critical problems through political action directed at economic and social restructuring, schools will continue to be burdened with inappropriate, excessive demands; to disappoint us; and to serve as scapegoats for our incompetence and inadequacies in both domestic and international arenas.

This nation has not yet awakened, however, to a fourth set of circumstances—circumstances that liberal causes have failed to redress: the growing poverty, malnourishment, and lack of education among millions in this country and around the world.[4] The social dynamite in these circumstances is heated dangerously by the growing disparity between these people and those who are wealthy, well fed, and much schooled.

This is a book about teacher education. Clearly, the leverage it can exert on these four sets of circumstances is modest. The problems embedded in these circumstances are far too complex to respond to singular solutions, or even singular sets of solutions. What we need is an *array* of initiatives, with each component honed in such way as to be maximally effective. This array must tackle, among other things, the teacher education enterprise, which is not effective. It has been neglected for a long time.

We do not know how much the exemplary education of schoolteachers would ameliorate the nation's problems, especially when education exerts only indirect leverage and schools are only part of our total educational delivery system. Nonetheless, we are probably on the right course in believing that elementary and secondary schools providing superb education do and will make a significant contribution over the long haul. The conduct of such schools presupposes a large corps of very well educated and trained teachers and administrators.

During successive eras of educational reform, the reform of schools and the reform of teacher education have rarely been connected. In fact, the latter has received much less attention generally; because of this, it has been referred to as an "unstudied problem."[5] James B. Conant, former president of Harvard University, followed his critical study of secondary schools in 1959 with a comprehensive look a few years later at the ways of preparing teachers in colleges and universities.[6] But the school reform effort surging to national proportions in the 1960s paid scant attention to his or any other recommendations regarding the preparation of those who teach.

A central thesis of this book and the study on which it is based is that the education of teachers must be driven by a clear and careful conception of the educating we expect our schools to do, the conditions most conducive to this educating (as well as the conditions that get in the way), and the kinds of expectations that teachers must be prepared to meet. Further, the renewal of schools, teachers, and the programs that educate teachers must proceed simultaneously.

The context in which schools function is in a constant state of change and presses in on schools, particularly through those they are designed to serve. In recent years, this context has all but overwhelmed schools accustomed to responding to directives but unaccustomed to self-directed renewal. There have been directives, to be sure, but so many, so conflicting, and often so far afield from daily exigencies that many teachers—ill-equipped to begin with—have become benumbed. Half quit before completing five years in the classroom.

The problem is one of preparing teachers to confront and deal with the daily circumstances of schooling *while redesigning their schools.* They are not now prepared for this; nor can they do it alone—nor can they do it while employed only to teach. Unfortunately, the policies and directives within which they are called upon to function are not enlightened by public awareness of what we should expect of schools or of the crises schools face. The loss of innocence must come soon.

Toward the Loss of Innocence

Those who have been most denied access to schools and knowledge for the longest period of time are most aware of the degree to which our schools have failed to catch up to the nation's educational aspirations and ideals. In trying to come to grips with inequities rooted in prejudice, Conant described this country as having been born with a congenital defect—the slavery of its black people. In the early 1960s, he described the schools of the suburbs as getting more and those of the inner cities as needing more and getting less.[7]

During the 1960s and 1970s, the most promising solution to inequality, supported by the Supreme Court *Brown* v. *Board of Education* decision of 1954, was the deliberate, planned integration of schools. Legal action by blacks to gain access to white schools became, along with busing, the means to integration. Neither the

Supreme Court decision nor subsequent legal action stood up well with the passage of time. Consider, for example, the case of Mary Ellen Crawford, a black girl who filed her case in the Superior Court of Los Angeles on August 1, 1963. Twenty years later, the all-white school to which she had sought access was still segregated; it enrolled only Mexican American boys and girls! By the time her case was settled, she was a grandmother. Additionally, many black students who were bused to integrated schools found themselves in segregated classes. Some black educational leaders challenged conventional wisdom by suggesting that the desegregated schools black children were attending were not worth being bused to.

The issue of equal access then broadened to the more complex issues of equal access to knowledge and to the amenities that foster growth. In many ways, the pioneering research and robust, informed opinions of a black scholar named Ronald Edmonds drew attention to what are still today's educational challenges:[8] Minority children must do as well as white children in school. But it is not enough for all races and ethnic groups to do equally well in existing schools. They must do equally well in much better schools. Edmonds's belief that schools could make a difference rekindled the aspirations of educators who had interpreted the work of James S. Coleman and Christopher Jencks to mean that there was not much schools could do to overcome the limitations brought from their pupils' homes into classrooms.[9] The resulting "effective schools movement" inspired many principals to believe that they and teachers had an important role to play in improving the quality of their schools.

The black experience over several decades of this nation's clambering toward universal schooling was not an uplifting one. De facto segregation in the cities outran all efforts to effect smooth integration of the races in schools. On reaching integrated schools, minority students in classes for the disadvantaged in elementary schools and the poorly served lowest tracks of secondary schools experienced an inferior education paralleling that of economically disadvantaged whites.[10] Successive waves of reform reports during the 1980s conveyed the message that the schools into which minorities were to be absorbed were not up to the quality of schools in other countries of the industrial world.[11]

An equally or perhaps even more troubling message has not yet been fully deciphered by many of the most successful black leaders and most of the white leaders who sincerely want success in good schools for all children. An insightful anthropologist, an immigrant from Africa named John Ogbu, has been observing "the American natives" in selected communities over several years. He sees clearly what our obsession with the schools we created out of a myopic vision of "all" has obscured: Large numbers of black children and, in particular, youths—many of them bright and of high academic potential—want no part of the school that "whitey" created to serve white purposes and benefit white children. These youths choose to excel in athletics rather than academics; and if schoolwork comes easily, they seek to disguise this fact by becoming class clowns.[12] The relatively small corps of black parents with Ph.D. degrees despair and puzzle over the unwillingness of some of their own offspring to pursue advanced degrees.

The puzzling, sometimes heartbreaking, and always complex cycles of learning that have resulted in considerable disillusionment and loss of innocence among our black citizens have been to considerable degree paralleled among the diverse array of people too conveniently grouped by such words as *Hispanic* and *Latino*. The parallels lie primarily in their struggle to gain equal access to knowledge and to appropriate support systems in their effort to advance in schools. They also face an insulting put-down in the insensitive white expectation that they (and all other minorities) shed rich, evocative languages and cultural traditions to blend innocuously into the culture of the school and community.

In states such as California, with the population of Spanish- and Portuguese-speaking immigrants growing rapidly, the schooling response of the 1960s and 1970s was "compensatory education." The language and cultural characteristics of these immigrants were widely regarded as shortcomings to be compensated for in children coming to school and ultimately—the sooner the better—to be replaced by a new first language and alternative cultural artifacts. The intriguing prospect of all children becoming fluent in two languages was pursued by only a few forward-looking projects.[13] Instead, Mexican American children, for example, were caught and often savaged between the language and expectations of the school and those of the home. One of the things we know is that children benefit immensely when home and school join in their education. This was not the experience of Mexican American and other immigrant groups during this period. They were expected to adjust to existing schools, not join in redesigning schools to adapt effectively to changing communities and changing student populations.

One commonly held but false assumption that plagued Mexican American students in the era of compensatory education was (and to a considerable degree still is) that all are progeny of migrant farmworkers. Ignored was the fact that many—particularly those living in such states as Texas, New Mexico, Arizona, and California—were descendants of families whose roots in this country predate those of other European settlers. They were not recognized as citizens of the United States and, like foreigners, were told by surprised peers and teachers, "You sure speak English well."[14] Such insensitivity contributed to poor academic achievement as well as to serious unraveling of the fabric of a nation still rapidly evolving.

During the 1960s and 1970s, I watched sadly as those who were determined to ameliorate the circumstances—most of whom were themselves Hispanic—sought solutions. "All will be well," they said, "when our own people are in positions of leadership." Yet their hopes faded when, for example, cousins became school principals in Los Angeles but nothing changed. Now, I was told, the problem was that the rules governing schools still came down from people who did not understand the particular needs of Mexican American children.

One solution proposed and attempted was a curriculum for these children designed by those who most understood and cared for them. The Mexican American Commission to the Los Angeles Board of Education, for example, sponsored a program in the mid 1970s in the teaching of reading designed specifically for Mexican American children in the primary grades. Alas, it was nothing more than an approach to teaching reading organized around behavioral objectives. I reluctantly declined to lend my support to the endeavor (offering instead a more complex and comprehensive initiative that did not interest the commission at that point). Two years after implementation of their program, reading scores of the target group of children had improved only 3 percent a year. The program was soon abandoned.

The development of my views over the next few years on efforts to effect change favoring the circumstances of Mexican American children in California schools was influenced by my understanding of the work of Ronald Edmonds and his belief that minorities must do as well *in the best schools* as their white counterparts. It was becoming increasingly apparent that efforts designed to bring Mexican American children into the mainstream of schooling would ultimately be judged according to the sole criterion of whether the results warranted the effort. And did they? The answer was not definitive. However, reform reports clearly said that the schools in which minorities sought a congenial, supportive haven were overdue for comprehensive overhaul and redirection. Why not, then, unite all groups in the necessary reconstruction of schools for *all* of this nation's children and youths? As goes the school best designed for all, so go the educational interests of that diverse array of minorities that make up the United States of America. The efforts conducted up to now to design schools according to the specialized interests of minority and other groups have benefited neither them nor our nation.

On the other hand, designing a common school to embrace all pushes us up against one of the central educational questions we keep avoiding: "What do the special characteristics of this person or group of persons require of the intervening process to enable this person to function with adequacy and satisfaction?"[15] Our eyes have been so narrowly focused on achievement test scores, for example, that we believe Asian students to be well taken care of in schools to which they have adapted well. They are often referred to as "model students" because of their consistently high levels of academic achievement and obedient behavior.[16]

Increasingly, however, research is showing that many Asian students pay a price; academic achievement may mask unhealthy levels of anxiety. Japanese American and Chinese American college students, compared in a study with mainstream students, exhibited more somatic complaints and family conflict. Similar results have been reported for third-generation Japanese American high school students.[17] Teachers have difficulty perceiving anxiety in children (of any race) who perform well on what achievement tests measure, and they often fail to realize that the creative potential of these strong achievers may be underutilized. This problem is accentuated for Asian children, whose parents expect much.[18]

The American people have tranquilized themselves into believing that most of the shortcomings of the schools can be accounted for by cultural shortcomings in the families of minority students. The loss of innocence that the American public must undergo demands full realization that this belief blinds us to the fact that schools created to serve expectations and student populations quite different from those now prevailing—and modified only a little—are not up to today's demands. Their shortcomings—most severe in their impact on minorities—transcend race and ethnicity, although they are exacerbated by prejudice and ethnocentricity.

Because minority groups have suffered most from these shortcomings and have seen their hopes dashed even as doors appeared to be opening, they seem to be more aware of things askew in the rooms beyond. Their gains in securing access have served to accentuate the gap between what they sought and what they got. I recall the words of Oscar Wilde in *Lady Windermere's Fan,* Act Three (thought by some critics not to be original with Wilde): "In this world there are only two tragedies. One is not getting what one wants, and the other is getting it. The last is much the worst, the last is a real tragedy!"

The tranquilizer shared by the white majority and minorities alike has been a belief in the American educational credo stipulating "that the schools constitute the ultimate promise of equality and opportunity; that they enable American society to remain somehow immune from the inequities and social afflictions that plague the rest of mankind; that they, in short, guarantee an open society. . . . The school is our answer to Karl Marx—and to everything else."[19] As I said before, education cannot be a substitute for economic and social reform. These issues must be addressed head on. To expect schools to educate well is to expect a great deal of them; but it is to expect what is reasonable. It also is to expect what is reasonable of this nation's teachers.

Part of the national awakening, then, must be to the realization that our schools do *not* educate well. They never did, in part because they left out too many people. But this point of history is relevant only if it reminds us that we dare not make this mistake again. Edmund Gordon properly stated our challenge: "The national problem posed by a concern with equity is that of making educational and social development, and ultimately social/political/economic participation and survival, independent of the backgrounds from which differential status group members come."[20]

Learnings and Stirrings

The nation's leaders have a responsibility to alert the people to threats to their well-being. During the 1980s, they did a good job of convincing large numbers of us that economic developments beyond our shores were threatening our way of life at a level comparable to engagement in war. Indeed, the 1983 report of the National Commission on Excellence in Education, *A Nation at Risk*, was an educational call to arms. It used a good deal of military language, beginning with the statement that the thrusting of our educational system upon us by a foreign power would have been regarded as an act of war.

The warnings brought no mobilization of an army and no commitment of resources to fight "the enemy," however. In "A Parable from War," Theodore Sizer provides a description of what was said and done in the aftermath of *A Nation at Risk* that would be hilarious if the stakes were not so high. His commentary on the parable hits the mark: "To expect the army of American teachers to wage a war to lessen the nation's risk without an investment in new and appropriate weaponry and in exhaustive research and development on how it can be effectively deployed is demonstrably silly. And yet that is what this country is doing."[21]

President Reagan appeared enormously pleased with what his commission had brought forward. Although the nation was at risk, the war was to be fought from sea to shining sea by teachers armed with axes and shovels, by local school boards, and by administrators in all the towns and villages. Education is a *local* affair, he said.

Yet, these local clutches of board members, teachers, and administrators stirred scarcely at all.[22] Nor did those who prepare the people who work in schools. The apparent lethargy in the face of calls for school reform continued even as the reports—most generated at the state level—came to number into the hundreds. Why?

There are no clear answers. Even though the beast was now blown up to mammoth proportions, there had been many cries of "wolf" before. After all, kicking the schools is more often in than out of fashion. Teachers have grown accustomed to hearing alternating blame and praise. The words of condemnation had been particularly harsh this time, however, and some educators sulked. There were still in the trenches, too, those veterans of innovation in the 1960s who were not about to be "suckered in" one more time.

But there were also in the schools and in teacher-preparing programs a good many educators who were well aware of how difficult it is to effect educational change, especially in schools experiencing the effects of momentous social upheavals: breakdown of the traditional family, mobility, literally dozens of first languages other than English in student populations, widespread use of drugs and alcohol among the young, unprecedented violence in schools, the increasing dominance of noneducational values expressed in acquisitiveness, and more. Just to cope was to be reasonably successful. Somehow, recommendations of a longer school day and year, more homework, and tougher standards for grade-to-grade promotion and graduation did not connect with life in schools and classrooms.[23] Further, *A Nation at Risk* and many later reports said that teachers deserve greater respect and more pay. There was a flurry of recognizing the best teachers of the year and some outstanding schools (the criteria for which were rather vague), but more pay was withheld pending measurable results.

I am convinced that many educators were benumbed in seeking to connect their personal circumstances to the extraordinary feats that they, their colleagues, and their schools were to perform—and with little more than rhetorical support. The incumbent in the White House exhorted them; his second appointee to the post of secretary of education berated them. Yet the indictment of over 100 appointees to offices of the federal administration on various charges of malfeasance blunted the moral imperatives of the teachers' role in the educational component of the American Dream. The continuing downslide in the capability of American corporations to produce the automobiles, appliances, and audiovisual equipment that teachers and others wanted at affordable prices —a downslide often blamed on declining educational standards— did not appear to be closely connected to what children were doing in school. After all, those making the key decisions in Detroit, Chicago, and New York were educated in earlier schools that were "the cause of our prosperity and power" and surely should be performing better.

Nonetheless, there were two loosely connected school reform efforts during the second half of the 1980s. The first was politically driven. The momentum was in and among the states; only at the end of the decade were state and federal concerns and initiatives beginning to unite. A loose alliance of governors, corporate executives, heads of professional organizations, and well-positioned educators was coming together around a set of not-yet-jelled and not fully compatible notions of the educational reforms required.[24] Except in a few states, very little of what went on within and around this alliance connected directly with the structures and infrastructures that support professional educators beyond the office of state superintendent of schools or commissioner of education. Local superintendents of schools dutifully brought the messages back to their districts, but there the words lost their urgency and faded away.

The second effort was diffuse, sporadic, and local. It was less a response to the specifics of state and national proposals than it was to provocative ideas hanging around the fringes of conventional practice that have repeatedly been dusted off and revisited in reform eras. To old concepts such as individualized instruction, continuous progress, and nongrading were added newer ones of cooperative learning, site-based management, and teacher power. Their common link was an underlying philosophy that butted up against ongoing demands for improved test scores.

The failure of both the politically driven initiatives and the more grassroots stirrings to connect was becoming painfully apparent toward the end of the decade. What caught on most with teachers and principals—not surprisingly—was an idea that had begun to pick up support in the late 1960s and into the 1970s but had then faded with general lack of interest in school reform: the individual school as the unit or center of change. Analyses of the general failure of top-down reform to penetrate schools during the 1960s and of the resistance of the school culture to countervailing initiatives from outside were being discovered at last by educators.[25] Although educational reform eras are always ahistorical at the outset, earlier efforts to create within the culture of the school the mechanisms and processes of continuing renewal were also rediscovered.[26] There were then, however—by the second half of the 1980s—stirrings to suggest that some educators in schools were interested in getting more involved in improvement if somebody else was not standing over them, always telling them what to do.

So by the late 1980s there was much talk of a "second wave" of reform, this one to be more attentive to the educational workforce: The school had to be restructured—whatever *that* means— and the hope lay in empowering teachers at the site and infusing the whole with concepts of efficient management drawn from the business world. The signals conveyed regarding freedom and control were ambiguous and often contradictory.

Nonetheless, it was the idea of effecting change at the level of the school, with greater power and autonomy for teachers, that began to connect the two reform movements. This idea was particularly attractive to philanthropic foundations. Providing funds for a clutch of schools to innovate and becoming closely involved with their efforts had a tangible appeal to corporate foundations, in particular. This was good public relations, and it promised visible results. The concept appealed to governors and legislators as well. Several states made funds available on a competitive basis for "schools for the twenty-first century" or "schools for the year 2000 and beyond."

The Education Commission of the States, active particularly in sustaining the interest of governors in educational reform, expanded the work of Theodore Sizer and his Coalition of Essential Schools into an implementation effort (known as Re:Learning) in several states. Sizer had designed what he called "an experiment for Horace," in which a group of invited secondary schools committed themselves to the development and testing of nine principles put forward in an updated version of his book, *Horace's Compromise*, first published in 1984.[27] With a ring of associated junior and senior high schools added, the Coalition network reached into the major regions of the United States.

Almost simultaneously, the National Education Association (NEA) launched its Mastery in Learning Project, under the direction of Robert McClure, and the American Federation of Teachers (AFT) attacked the problem of urban schools. Individual schools in the former effort were networked with one another and with schools now coming together in other networks. (The network existed for several years before being connected by a computer-based system, which is still very much in a developmental stage.) Marsha Levine of the AFT diligently reviewed previous efforts—in both practice and conceptual work—in order to put together the various elements of fundamentally restructured schools. The work of William Spady, earlier focused on the specification of attainable outcomes, broadened into rather comprehensive attention to the components of school programs needing to be refined and integrated in order to achieve results.[28] A few school districts with a relatively long history of decentralizing authority and responsibility to the local school were stimulated and encouraged to intensify these efforts. The concept of the school as the center of change was being increasingly legitimated in both educational practice and theory.[29]

There was growing recognition, too, that the quality of the teachers entering schools might affect the quality of education provided there—strangely, a connection rarely made in eras of school reform. After visiting a dozen essentially graduate schools of education and noting the low status and near absence of teacher education in them, an insightful critic from abroad, Harry Judge, left unanswered his question as to what such entities are for.[30] If his prickly conclusions stirred these schools and others like them, the ripples failed to go beyond the campuses of the major universities of which they were a part. Teacher educators and professors of education generally remained silent, even in the immediate aftermath of *A Nation at Risk.*

It is reasonable to believe that both *A Nation at Risk* and Judge's provocative analysis contributed to the coming together of the provosts and deans of education of some of the nation's top universities in a historic meeting. The members of this Holmes Group (named after a former dean of Harvard's Graduate School of

Education) set out to find ways that they could improve teacher education programs in universities such as their own.

The second draft of a Holmes Group document designed to refine this goal suggested a broader one: Direct attention to the health of elementary and secondary schools. The published, later version (1986) of this draft addressed the twin goals of the reform of teacher education and the reform of the teaching profession but fell short of connecting these to a simultaneous attempt to effect school reform.[31] This is perhaps a realistic stance, given the resources of universities and especially the nature of prevailing faculty reward systems in them. The Holmes Group did, however, connect the teacher education function of these institutions to selected "professional development schools," where teachers and university faculty members would join in doing research, improving practices, and educating teachers. At the time this book is going to press, such schools had become the centerpiece of the Holmes Group agenda, albeit with considerable accompanying debate.

The report of the Carnegie Forum on Education and the Economy, published almost simultaneously, called for both redesigned schools and substantially higher standards for the teachers who would teach in them.[32] This report joined that of the Holmes Group in recommending greater command of academic subjects. The former came out for a bachelor's degree in the arts and sciences as a prerequisite for the professional study of teaching; members of the Holmes Group split on this issue. In spite of the push of both reports toward postbaccalaureate preparation programs for teachers, the stance of the Association of American Colleges three years later made it clear that the role of undergraduate programs was alive and well and would remain so into the 1990s.[33]

Another development of the late 1980s also helped lay the groundwork for the conjunction of school reform and the education of teachers prepared both to cope with existing conditions and to effect renewal. Although there is now a massive body of research relevant to learning and teaching, it had not previously been connected to the tasks teachers face and the decisions they must make. There had been no agreement among teacher educators over what knowledge (from the mass of research data available) was most likely to empower teachers. Now, however, both the American Association of Colleges

for Teacher Education and the Association of Teacher Educators have
brought together compendia of the knowledge base believed by scholars to be of high value.[34] (The task of codifying that knowledge base
according to taxonomies of teaching behavior remains. Such codification must be characterized by responsiveness to continuing inquiry
into learning and teaching.)

The 1990s began, then, with encouraging signs that the educational reform effort launched with great fanfare in the 1980s and
periodically infused with blasts of alarm might settle down into the
long-term effort necessary to attaining our expectations for excellence and equity. The educational agenda in President Bush's 1990
State of the Union speech was devoid of particulars, but at least part
of it addressed what schools are for: "Every child will start school
ready to learn. The high school graduation rate will be 90 percent.
U.S. students will be the first in the world in math and science.
Every school will be drug free. Every adult American will be skilled
and literate. By the year 2000."[35]

Perhaps lofty goal setting is all we should expect from the
plans and budget presented by the president to the people each
January. The effort to achieve these and other goals offered by Bush
was presumably to be sustained at state and local levels. But Congress, too, was stirring in response to growing awareness of the
magnitude of the educational tasks still lying ahead. Just as the
final decade of the twentieth century was beginning, Senators
Kennedy and Pell were promoting two bills (S. 1675 and S. 1676)
designed to put federal dollars into teacher recruitment, particularly
of minorities, and model teacher education programs directed toward the development of promising classroom practices.

Despite these favorable signs, however, the educational reform effort begun in the 1980s was, at the beginning of the 1990s,
very close to the point at which that of the 1960s (following the
launching of Sputnik) sputtered and died. The nation's resources
had not yet been mobilized and focused and the American people
were not yet ready to make the sacrifices necessary. Were they at least
somewhat more knowledgeable about the nation's educational malaise? We must hope so. The stakes are too great for us to lull ourselves into believing that we will have still another chance.

but it most certainly has an underachieving curriculum. Only 15 percent of our students enroll at the high school level in advanced mathematics; only 3 percent pursue a full calculus course. The mathematical yield of U.S. high schools is among the lowest of any advanced industrialized country in the world.[38] In general, the mathematics curriculum of our K–12 school system lags about a year behind that of other industrialized countries for students who graduate from high school. The question going unanswered, of course, is the degree to which some of these countries might adopt a less demanding curriculum were they, too, to set as a goal 90 percent graduation from secondary schools. Opportunity to learn is the single factor with the greatest explanatory power in accounting for differences among students, schools, and countries.[39]

International comparisons aside, a barrage of surveys during the late 1980s caused educators and citizens generally to worry about revelations of widespread ignorance in the young: inability to name major land masses on a map, locate on a map the largest cities in the United States, explain the cause of seasons, recognize the names and areas of contribution of the nation's most famous citizens, identify the major branches of government, distinguish between the Senate and the House of Representatives, and on and on. Added to such findings were horror stories regarding the poor performance of some schoolteachers on state-administered tests of basic literacy. Not surprisingly, a book with long lists of what every American should know received widespread attention at this time.[40]

Slight gains in verbal and mathematical scores during the late 1980s on National Assessments of Educational Progress tests administered nationwide since the 1970s were encouraging, but students' performance in problem-solving failed to improve. Growth over the four years from the thirteen-year-old to the seventeen-year-old groups in such important abilities as writing coherent paragraphs and deriving meaning from printed materials continued to be disappointing. Equally disappointing: By the end of the decade, the gap between the performance of white students and both black and Latino students, though slowly closing, was still substantial.

The most discouraging statistics to come out of the 1980s vividly portrayed our general failure to recruit from these minority groups more than a trickle of the individuals required to provide

tomorrow's professional, business, political, and civic leaders. The
very small pool of minority students with high scores on the
Scholastic Aptitude Test (SAT) fueled gloomy predictions regarding tomorrow's supply of black and Hispanic professors, doctors,
lawyers, and business executives, even as universities and corporations continued their recruitment efforts as though there were able
candidates "out there" somewhere.

Major universities announce the desirability of high scores
on the SAT or comparable tests of academic attainment. Let us
assume that these universities decide that they are interested in admitting only students scoring in the top fifth on the SAT. Using
1988 data, this would translate into a minimum combined score of
about 1,150 (550 on the verbal section and 600 or more on the mathematics section). That year, about 147,000 white students nationwide
achieved at these levels. In contrast, only 3,826 blacks scored over
550 on the verbal section and only 3,129 met the 600-level criterion
in mathematics. The number of Latinos was 3,823 and 4,263, respectively. For Native Americans, the corresponding numbers were 771
and 967. (See Table 1.)

When we consider higher levels of performance, the comparisons become even more stark. For example, 7,414 whites and 1,877
Asians scored 750 or more on the mathematics section of the SAT in
1988, but only 64 blacks, 120 Latinos, and 30 Native Americans did so.

We have a problem. Most of its roots are in the social and
economic inequities of our culture. For the rest, we must look to our
schools. We will direct our attention to neither if we continue to
believe that the answer lies in more intensive recruitment practices
based on the belief that minority candidates for top executive posts
and professorships are progressing successfully through our schools.

It is appropriate to look into school practices generally for
explanations. Large percentages of minority students (other than
Asians) admitted to colleges soon find themselves on academic probation. The SAT scores of these probationary students often fail to
meet college admission requirements but are accepted anyway, in
line with the argument that these tests discriminate against minorities. Yet these students' school transcripts generally reveal satisfactory grades. Why this discrepancy between SAT scores and grades?
A look back into secondary schools reveals that students of low

Table 1. Scholastic Achievement Test (SAT) Scores, 1988.

	≥ 550 Verbal	≥ 600 Math
Native Americans	771	967
Mexican Americans	1,496	1,668
Puerto Ricans	510	582
Other Latin Americans	1,817	2,013
Blacks	3,826	3,129
Asians	10,475	20,118
Whites	138,266	157,301
Other	2,117	2,295
Total (all those who answered the race/ethnicity question)	159,278	188,073
Those unidentified by race/ethnicity	10,202	11,615
Grand total (national)	169,480	199,688

economic status—disproportionately from minorities, of course—
are grouped into the lowest tracks. In these tracks, the opportunities
to learn the high-status subject matter required for success in college
are usually decidedly inferior to the opportunities available in the
highest tracks. This is one of several reasons why 55 percent of black
students and 51 percent of Latino students who enter college do not
have a college degree twelve years later. The figure for white students is 33 percent.

We must go back further, however, to many of the questionable assumptions and practices of the primary grades that are perpetuated year after year in grade after grade. And even more
powerfully determining factors lie outside of schools. Not to look
beyond schools as well as into schools for explanations of the academic conditions cited above (reported over and over in recent years)
is to be blind to both the schools' and the nation's formidable agendas. The crises we face are crises of us all.

Using the recent but now anachronistic definition of *family*—a married couple, one male and one female, and their children,
living together—there are more nonfamily households than family
households in the United States. There are over fifteen million children living with one parent—the mother in over 90 percent of the
cases. Nearly two million children live with neither parent. Of the

children living with just their mother, 50 percent of white children are with a mother who is divorced, 54 percent of black children are with a never-married (and therefore nonalimonied) mother, and 33 percent of Hispanic children's mothers have not married. The average annual income for female households with children is just over $11,000; the average for married couples with children is above $36,000.[41]

Today 40 percent of the poor are children. Over 35 percent of the children born last year are of minorities; more of these were born poor than was the case the year before. In just a few years, they will carry their nutritional and other developmental disadvantages into schools ill-prepared to take them from where they are. Most will be in the least advantaged schools, where they will be less likely to be taught by the most able teachers and where class registers of pupils turn over two or three times in the course of a year. In many settings, a large percentage of those children coming to school for the first time will experience their first lessons in being regarded as stupid and in feeling stupid. The tests they will fail in kindergarten—Pestalozzi's garden for children—will constitute the first precursors of a self-fulfilling prophecy.

The words of the eminent philosopher Alfred North Whitehead come to mind: "When one considers in its length and breadth the importance of a nation's young, the broken lives, the defeated hopes, the national failures, which result from the frivolous inertia with which [education] is treated, it is difficult to restrain within oneself a savage rage."[42] Were Whitehead alive today, he would surely expand his lens to encompass conditions beyond education that are treated with inertia—conditions that confound teachers and seriously impede the effectiveness of schools.

Individual Schools. To say that the schools are out of sync with the circumstances described above and no longer enjoy either values commonly shared in the surrounding community or the support of stable families and other institutions is a gross understatement. In regard to the potency of schools, I have advanced two arguments. First, they cannot compensate adequately for what has been lost. Second, add-ons to meet first this and then that exigency not only fail, they doom the school as a whole. Yet it is the *whole* that must renew so as to be maximally educational for all. I closed my report on a comprehensive study of elementary and secondary schools in the late 1970s and early 1980s as follows: "Education is as yet something more envisioned than practiced."[43]

The rising chorus of dissatisfaction with schools following World War II was heard not because schools suddenly were doing things differently or worse. Rather, the perpetuation of ways becoming fully legitimated by an increasingly bureaucratized system of schooling was increasingly seen to be inadequate and dysfunctional. The problems to be remedied and adjustments to be made laid out in research-based reports published almost simultaneously with *A Nation at Risk* have been extensively cited in still more reports, but little heeded.[44] Their contents are still valid, and probably more poignantly so. To say that we are already fully aware of everything in the short summary that follows is to indict us all for not acting upon such awareness. I select only a few of the conditions begging attention.

Most schools function in accord with the bizarre assumption that students are to be uniformly ready for whatever custom dictates that they are to be ready for—from the day of their arrival until the day of their departure from the system. The question of what this child is ready for provides a perspective sometimes discussed in preservice and in-service teacher education classes and workshops, but it has nothing to do with the "real world." Rather, conventional wisdom tells us that explanations for the failure of a child not ready for the first grade to master the work of the first grade are to be found within the child—as are the explanations for his or her later failure to master the work of the fifth grade even after repeating the work of the fourth.

Policies regarding promotion and nonpromotion from grade to grade go in and out of fashion while an extraordinary body of research on individual differences among children that could enlighten the whole lies undisturbed on the shelves of university libraries. Every now and then, solutions to the educational management of inevitable individual differences in learning, such as individualized progression through nongraded schools—introduced in a few settings in the 1930s, rediscovered in the 1960s, and now emerging once again—are dusted off and tried on a small scale.[45]

But this and other innovations with substantial validation behind them lack the appeal of novelty. They are readily rejected for the contradicting reasons that they are neither new nor adequately tried. Effecting change in the face of this rationale is a bloody challenge, a British military officer might say.

The grouping of children in the primary grades into low, middle, and high groups—particularly for reading and arithmetic—is as alive and well today as it was fifty years ago. The emergence of an impressive body of research showing that such practices not only exacerbate the spread of individual differences, further disadvantaging the lowest groups, but also deter individual diagnosis and remediation has not influenced these practices one whit.[46] Pupils carry their accumulated deficiencies into the upper grades, experiencing grade failure once or twice in the process, and predominate in the enrollment of low-track classes in secondary schools. The accommodation of individual differences through grouping arrangements has blocked progress in the use of curricular and instructional interventions likely to advance the learning of all students.[47]

The most obvious educational response to the nonlearning of students, one would think, is to try a different instructional approach. Research shows, however, that all but a small part of the time spent on teaching and learning involves a great deal of teacher talk and very little student interaction.[48] Activities calling for student initiative are rare. Students are largely passive and, at least by the time they reach the upper elementary and secondary school grades, appear to assume that passivity is what best fits the nature of school. They even come to dislike disturbances of their passivity. This ethos seems to accommodate well the flaccid curriculum of homogenized classroom topics and textbooks.[49] Ironically, this is the characteristic of schools least likely to excite criticism from the community. Thus we are forced to ask ourselves how eager we are, both inside and outside of schools, to foster critical thinking and creative nonconformity.

The health of a school is largely determined from the comparative scores of its students on standardized achievement tests. This measure is probably about as useful as reading a thermometer to determine the health of a patient; the thermometer diagnoses only a fever, not heart disease and cancer. Largely as a result of being called upon to use this measure excessively, schools have no inventories of their students' encounters with humankind's knowledge and ways of knowing. Further, they lack an overall guiding conception of the depth and breadth of knowledge that students *should* possess—a conception against which to evaluate a student's curricular "takings" to date. One course offering begins to look about as good as another. In addition, forces outside the school (the state legislature, for example) demand that their concerns be addressed in the classroom. The school must be all things to all people. The ultimate result is an incredibly incoherent curriculum and a shopping mall high school.[50]

Enough already! The indictment is fair: All of the above is familiar and has been so for far too long;[51] progress toward change is made with glacierlike slowness. It is convenient to beat on teachers for school-based educational deficiencies, and they must be held responsible for some, to be sure. But others are imposed on them and clash with the wisdom that teachers possess about how to deal with the school and classroom circumstances they face.[52]

It is fair to ask teachers to put their knowledge to work in redesigning their schools and to integrate with it relevant additional knowledge largely ignored. A few faculty groups have struggled against all odds in creating practices and schools that deviate—and they have usually suffered the slings and arrows of being different. The redesigning necessary to bring about many such schools will require time and resources not now available in the context of schooling. To employ teachers for 180 days of teaching each year is to ensure 180 days of teaching and not much of anything else—most certainly not the restructuring of schools.

And to ensure 180 days of *good* teaching no doubt requires different and better education and training than today's teachers received. To guarantee that teachers and principals possess the knowledge and skills required to renew their schools undoubtedly requires components not present in today's preparation programs. Educating educators better and differently means that we must abandon the commonsense clichés of reform that inevitably prevail when we lack an understanding of what is wrong.

Teacher Education. Recommendations in reform reports on teacher education throughout the century have been repetitious and superficial: Recruit the best and the brightest, enroll them for four years in an arts and sciences curriculum, keep them away from "Mickey Mouse" methods courses, and mentor them to a practicing teacher.[53] The first recommendation obviously makes sense; it has simply not proved to be practical; the competition of higher-paying work in other professions and industry is simply too intense. The prospect of low pay and slow advancement deters large numbers of top teacher candidates, and those top candidates who choose teaching even though other doors are open are obviously not drawn by the money. Some undeterred by low pay who start out to become teachers change their minds on becoming fully aware of the restraints and shabby conditions under which they would be required to work.

Nobody denies the importance of future teachers' having a thorough understanding of the subjects they will be called upon to teach. The largely unexamined problem is that graduation from a college of general studies with a major in a subject discipline provides no guarantee that the desired knowledge has been obtained. Most of today's colleges, like most comprehensive high schools, might aptly be called shopping malls. There is no assurance that freshmen and sophomores preparing to teach make sound choices; there is rarely a pre-education program, in the sense of premedicine, to guide them. Further, in many universities, teaching is no longer the primary mission. Future teachers in college are thus at least as likely as they were in high school to observe teaching methods that should not be replicated.

Some teaching methods courses, like some courses in most fields, are a waste of time. The solution is to improve them, not to encourage students to avoid them. The latter course simply ensures that future teachers will not encounter research that is highly relevant to teaching in schools and that is not now generally possessed by practicing teachers.

The suggestion that mentoring stands virtually by itself as the way to make students knowledgeable about and expert in teaching defies comprehension. Yet this is largely what the president of the United States, some governors, and some members of Congress appear to have in mind when they propose "alternative certification." The findings regarding how teachers teach now reported in the various reports cited above—very similar to findings reported over a long period of time—have not been challenged. Indeed, the testing and other restraints imposed on schools and teachers since publication of *A Nation at Risk* appear to have reinforced the didactics of lecturing, workbooks, and textbooks—the diet that made the patient sick in the first place.[54] This is what we wish to mentor future teachers into?

By the end of the 1980s, segments of the nation were slowly awakening to the realization that the ritualistic repetition of unexamined "commonsense" answers to the complex problems of educating teachers well made no sense. One of the learnings in these stirrings is that the education and training of teachers and principals must be closely tied to both the realities of schools and the conditions necessary to their substantial improvement. "Substantial improvement," in turn, means much more than tinkering around the edges of what we now have. It means changing our schools in profound ways; the schools of tomorrow must be highly deviant from the schools of today. The required change will not occur if we continue to prepare teachers for school circumstances now prevailing.

Toward Understanding the Problems

Educational journals are replete with articles on teacher education: accounts of curricular revision, surveys of teachers' opinions of their preparation programs, effects of student teaching, and much more. Indeed, some journals are devoted solely to the publication of such topics. An even larger body of published material deals with matters less directly related to teacher education—mostly research on learning and teaching believed to constitute a knowledge base for teaching and therefore for teacher education. This body of literature suggests some of what is wrong with and some of what is needed for the teacher education enterprise.

The limitation, however, is that most such research, useful as it is, uses the individual as the unit of analysis. One must make rather large intellectual leaps to interpret what research on

individuals means for institutions. A handful of research-based
books written almost simultaneously late in the 1980s provide useful insights into both the institutional context of teacher education
and the conduct of programs.[55] They raise profound issues, most of
them deeply embedded in the history of the past 150 years and in the
troubling legacies that make real reform in teacher education (and
indeed in schools) so difficult.

Genesis of a Study

In the mid 1980s, a colleague and I wrapped up the loose
ends of a long-term program of seeking to understand and improve
schools in southern California—and, indeed, to study them in selected communities across the United States—and came to the University of Washington. The school reform debate was then in full
voice. Our own thoughts on education, however, were still directed
to the successes and failures we had experienced a decade earlier in
trying to bring the eighteen school settings constituting the League
of Cooperating Schools beyond the stage of collegial dialogue. It
had been necessary to create at each school site a process of renewal,
for which teachers and principals clearly were ill-prepared. Our
later comprehensive nationwide study of schools, which culminated
in the early 1980s in the publication of my book *A Place Called
School* (1984), confirmed that the orientation and behaviors that
teachers and principals bring to schools are ill-suited to challenging
and changing existing practices. Many of the practices in which
they become engaged are far removed from what educational research recommends and, ironically, from what many able, experienced teachers believe to be best.

Provoked by such thoughts, we joined with a new colleague
(who was then engaged in a study of factors in most and least
effective schools), created the Center for Educational Renewal, and
in 1985 launched three initiatives. First, we set out to learn a good
deal more than we knew then about the conditions and circumstances of educating educators for the schools. Second, we embarked
on an inquiry into the education of professionals in several fields to
learn whatever might be applied usefully to teacher education.[56]
Third, building on work begun in southern California, we became

strong advocates for our conviction that the necessary renewal of schools is most likely to be advanced when renewal efforts are linked closely to the teacher education and research activities of universities.[57] Indeed, we were convinced that such joining is both necessary and natural.

Had we not believed in this hypothesis as though it were a principle, we would not have proceeded as we did. "Unless [one] is armed with such a conviction, [one] will not proceed with the laborious testing of the deductions from the generalization."[58] We deliberately embarked on a kind of social experiment, in which we encouraged school districts and universities to join in partnerships for the simultaneous renewal of schools and the education of those who work in them. These we then attempted to connect through the National Network for Educational Renewal, now consisting of fourteen school-university partnerships in as many states. From the beginning, we engaged in formative evaluation and endeavored to keep the educational community informed of progress, problems, and emerging issues.[59] At the time of this writing, a comprehensive effort to evaluate the whole and to determine the status of similar efforts nationwide is under way.

This book deals primarily with the first of these initiatives— a comprehensive study of the education of teachers—and draws from the second—a study of the education of professionals in some other fields. I do not return to the third until the concluding chapter, where creation of a school-university partnership becomes a critical component in a model for the redesign of teacher education.

To inaugurate the first initiative, we began to conceptualize our inquiry into the education of educators: What should be expected of teachers? To what ideals and circumstances should the mission of preparing teachers be directed? What contextual conditions are necessary to the health of preparation programs? Who should be in charge? What insights might be gained from the history of teacher education in the United States? Unless we were able to produce thoughtful, informed answers to questions such as these, there was no point in turning to the usual research problems of selecting a sample of institutions, formulating questions for surveys and interviews, seeking out descriptive documents, and all the other steps that go into a study of the kind proposed. Chapter Two is

devoted primarily to the answers to these and other questions developed over the two years immediately preceding a year of gathering
data.

First, however, some background information. The more we
probed into the literature, and the more the educational reform
efforts of the second half of the 1980s turned to teacher education,
the more convinced we became that this neglected enterprise was at
a critical juncture that had been confronted decades earlier by other
professions. This juncture is where a craft either continues to take
its cues almost exclusively from practitioners of the craft or opens
itself up to the research and theory of those who inquire into it.

This is precisely where medicine and medical education were
at the turn of the century. We turned naturally to the study that
propelled medical schools away from the proprietary model operated by practicing doctors to the university-related model then
emerging in England and best represented in the United States at
Johns Hopkins University.

When the Carnegie Foundation was endowed near the beginning of this century, there was little unity of purpose or of standards
among institutions calling themselves colleges or universities. Yet
the trustees found themselves entrusted with resources to be expended for the benefit of college and university teachers in Canada
and the United States. They became interested in the relationships
between colleges and secondary schools and between the professional schools and the rest of the institution—relationships that
surely are of equal or greater importance in teacher education. In
only a small number of cases was the school of medicine an integral
part of the university and influenced by its standards. To the trustees, the looseness of the link between universities and medical
schools was dysfunctional, given both growth in the fundamental
sciences upon which medicine depends and the development of new
means for diagnosing and combating disease. They were aware, too,
that many doctors did not acquire the necessary basic knowledge in
secondary schools or in colleges (some of which were little more
than secondary schools) and did not encounter the new means of
diagnosing and combating disease during their apprenticeships to
practicing physicians. "Under these conditions and in the face of
advancing standards of the best medical schools it was clear that the

time had come when the relation of professional education in medicine to the general system of education should be clearly defined. The first step toward such a clear understanding was to ascertain the facts concerning medical education and the medical schools themselves at the present time."[60]

There have been many calls for a study of teacher education—a study both descriptive and prescriptive—comparable to that of Abraham Flexner on medical education, published by the Carnegie Foundation in 1910. We had neither the intent nor the resources to undertake a study of that magnitude. Our more modest interest in Flexner's work was twofold. First, there clearly were distinct parallels between the context and conduct of medical education in 1910 and the context and conduct of teacher education in 1985. Second, there were profound methodological implications in Flexner's institutional approach. The reform of teacher education is short-changed by its attention only to individuals: Get better ones, refine the behavior desired in them to proficiencies and competencies, rev up their productivity, entice them with carrots or drive them with sticks. Yet a horse cannot pull an unhitched wagon.

Flexner said only a little about the characteristics desired in doctors: They were to be well-educated citizens of the community who cared about their patients and who had benefited to considerable degree from educational programs encompassing the knowledge and skills required to care for the health and illness of these patients. This approach sounded eminently sensible to us, and so we sought to apply lessons derived from Flexner's work. Consequently, more than a passing reference to his report on medical education appears warranted.

Lessons from a Reform Model

In the early years of this century, medical education was shoddy. In his landmark study of medical schools in the United States and Canada, Abraham Flexner, a former high school teacher, painted a shocking picture.[61] Candidates seeking—and granted—admission displayed near-illiteracy. Medical teaching was almost exclusively in the didactic mode. Some students never got to see a cadaver. When twenty students in a class were fortunate enough to share one, their perspective must have been akin to that of the blind men groping to understand the whole elephant from a piece. Most of what they learned was through apprenticeship to a physician who had acquired knowledge and skills in similar fashion. Rarely did their period of induction include full care and treatment of a patient. Because of this poor training, there was little at the time to warrant the words *professionals* and *profession* in referring to physicians and their calling.

Flexner could have ignored what he saw in most of the so-called medical schools he visited and aligned himself comfortably with the conventional wisdom of the time. He could have proposed the simple, inexpensive, commonsense route: Persons wishing to become doctors should seek out and associate themselves with practicing physicians who would be their mentors. Had he done so, the for-profit, sorely inadequate, proprietary medical schools operated by physicians might have continued for many more years. But Flexner believed that the interests of both the public and medical education were best served when medical schools were attached to first-rate universities, where practice and theory would be entwined. The Johns Hopkins University Medical School and exemplary components of a few others provided him with models on which to build.

The academic and clinical components of medical education were to be fused, with the teaching hospitals under educational control of the faculty. Faculty members were to divide their daily schedules between teaching and inquiry conducted in the laboratory or clinic. Flexner even foresaw the disjuncture between a sound conception of clinical training and the availability of well-trained clinical teachers—a problem that has plagued medical education to this day.[62] Flexner was not to be put off by the arguments of critics pointing to those successful practitioners who had managed quite well without benefit of the demanding program he recommended. Nor did he accept the proposition that faculty and students were as well off without the "tools," as he called them—the clinic and the laboratory.

In Flexner's specifications, the future physician was first to be an educated person in the community. Two years of general education were to be followed by two years of medically related subject matter, such as anatomy, pathology, and pharmacology, and increasing amounts of practical work, and then by two years of both specialized subject matter and hospital-based practice.

Three characteristics, in particular, make the Flexner report both remarkable and compelling. First, although the writing is implicitly driven by the highest ideals of human welfare, it is strikingly devoid of the high-sounding, abstract goals so often found in educational reports and treatises. Second, instead of specifying educational objectives for students toward which weak schools of medicine might claim to be endlessly striving, he set down specific *conditions* to be met by all. Third, largely through use of the data gathered in visiting 155 "schools of all medical sects," Flexner not only described what must be tolerated no longer but also undercut most of the anticipated arguments against change. In effect, he nullified most of the "yes, but" objections before they could be voiced.

Of course, the report was immediately and subsequently criticized as well as lauded. Aware that meeting Flexner's recommendations would be costly, nearly half of the existing medical schools soon went out of business. In the remainder, reform was at first slow, but increasing financial support from the private sector accelerated change during the 1920s. Would change have come so quickly without the foundation money that became available? That is a matter often debated, but it seems reasonable to assume that the allocation of tax dollars to university budgets for the support of medical schools responded to the incentive of philanthropic funds. In any event, medical education successfully navigated the critical juncture.

There are clear parallels between medical education in 1910 and teacher education eighty years later. There is still little unity of purpose and standards among the 3,000 or so colleges and universities in the United States, some 1,300 of which prepare teachers. There are vast differences among the departments, schools, and colleges of education that prepare teachers in these 1,300 institutions. Among these differences are those pertaining to their acceptance and integration into the mission, purposes, and standards of the colleges and universities of which they are a part. There has been developing, particularly in the last quarter-century, a body of knowledge believed to have significant implications for teaching.

Further, there are now available new and tested means for diagnosing and remedying an array of learning ills. Much of this lore is scattered about in various units of the university and not even brought together in journals read commonly by those who have or should have an interest in it. Many of those persons now teaching or teaching teachers do not even know it exists. Finally, the relationship today between schools of education and practicing educators is as loose or looser than that between schools of medicine and practitioners in 1910.

These observations support the argument that teacher education today, like medical education at the beginning of the century, is at a critical juncture. Virtually every element common to a profession and necessary to that profession's impact on the common welfare is out of kilter. Nothing will suffice short of addressing in concert, and within an integrated vision of the whole, the omissions and shortcomings with respect to each element.

A Study of the Education of Educators

As was stated in the Preface, my colleagues and I set out to provide a kind of mural depicting as comprehensively as possible the conditions and circumstances characterizing the conduct of teacher education in a small but highly representative sample of college and university settings in the United States. There was much to be done before purchasing our first plane tickets. In addition to creating the mural, we would ultimately have to employ criteria for judging the adequacy of what it depicted—indeed, for determining the nature and seriousness of omissions. We decided to set forth our criteria—the conditions necessary for exemplary teacher education—early on, so that readers could judge the criteria themselves, as well as our assessment of the existing conditions.

We were in agreement virtually from the beginning that the criteria for judging the adequacy of teacher education programs arise out of conceptions of what education is, the nature of learning and teaching, and the role of schools in a democratic society; so we turned our attention to those difficult issues. We read a great deal and put incomplete thoughts on paper. These rough drafts then became the subject of much dialogue. Chapter Two seeks to distill the essence of this necessary part of the inquiry and particularly to provide readers with the criteria that guided us throughout.

With this work behind us, we were ready to think our way through the tasks of determining whether, how, and how well a representative sample of teacher-preparing institutions was meeting these expectations. We did not, however, set out to test a specific set of hypotheses derived from a theory in the manner of traditional behavioral science. Instead, we sought to find out what was going on in these colleges and universities, guided throughout by a conceptual map of the constituent elements we thought to be important if not essential. We set out to situate the study in the context of institutions, taking into account the rich diversity of these settings. We sought evidence to suggest the extent to which extant practices were consistent with the working assumptions guiding our inquiry.

This design permitted the discovery and inclusion of new ideas and the realignment of working assumptions while enabling us to probe deeply for those features we believed to be crucial for the effective education of educators. The various methods chosen for collecting information included survey questionnaires for faculty and students; interviews with students, faculty, administrators, and field-based educators; observations of education classes and classes taught by student teachers in the field; and an extensive review of documents secured in advance of and during our visits.[63]

We conducted comprehensive forays into life at twenty-nine sites during the 1987–88 academic year. We spent from 10 to 14 researcher-days at each site—about 300 days in all. During these days, the two teams, one with three members and the other with two, conducted more than 1,800 hours of individual and group interviews and class observations. In addition, nine historians, each visiting from two to five sites and studying relevant documents, provided us with brief case histories.[64] To this rich body of contextual information were added data from the surveys and programmatic documentation. Inquiry conducted in this fashion is much more consistent with the naturalistic methods of case study than with the traditional methods of experimental and correlational research.

We began our search for a representative sample of the variety of preparation programs by first developing a typology of

colleges and universities. Assisted by the classification scheme produced by the Carnegie Foundation for the Advancement of Teaching,[65] we came up with six broad categories. Then, from eight of the
nine census divisions of the United States, we picked eight states,
each among the top producers of teachers in its division. Because
the state legislature in 1987 required all institutions in Texas to
conform to eighteen credit hours of professional education (including student teaching), we followed good advice in choosing Oklahoma as the divisional alternate. The states finally chosen were
California, Colorado, Georgia, Illinois, Iowa, Massachusetts, Oklahoma, and Pennsylvania. These account for 30 percent of the population of the fifty states and the District of Columbia.

    With the typology and selection of states to guide us, we then
sought to pick the institutions. We attempted to approximate an
equal division between the public and private dimensions of the
typology, with two exceptions: a slight overrepresentation of regional public colleges and universities in view of their relatively
large numbers and their history as former teachers' colleges, and a
slight underrepresentation of the four-year liberal arts colleges, most
of which prepare only a few teachers (although the teacher total from
the combined group is substantial). Our collective professional experience helped in building diversity into the small sample. We deliberately included, without violating the overall sampling design, two
regional state colleges or universities with nearly all-black student
populations (the student mix having emerged either historically or
due to demographic shifts in the surrounding community); one institution that is still primarily in the business of preparing educators;
and four private colleges and universities explicitly affiliated with the
Roman Catholic, United Methodist, Lutheran, and Southern Baptist
religious denominations.

    The selection of sites, like the rest of our work, took place
within tight time constraints. Because of this, we were unable to
replace one of the five institutions that declined (mainly because of
the burden of accreditation and self-study activities already scheduled). Of the final twenty-nine, twenty were accredited by the National Council for Accreditation of Teacher Education, twenty-two
were members of the American Association of Colleges for Teacher

Education, and seven belonged to the Holmes Group. The smallest enrolled slightly over 900 students; the largest, more than 35,000.

In all of the initial telephone calls and correspondence, we promised institutional (and, of course, personal) confidentiality. Yet this matter rarely rose again subsequently. Indeed, by the time of our arrival on a campus, at least some people on the host faculty knew where we had come from and where we were going next. The host institutions welcomed us most hospitably, often using our visit as an occasion for a reception or other gathering. Although institutional confidentiality appears to be not much of a concern for participating institutions, fictitious names of colleges and universities are used in the typology below and in the narrative that follows. I often refer to the institutions descriptively—for example, a small liberal arts college in the Southwest. However, when this would be cumbersome, the fictitious name is employed. It is, then, a literary device. Although patterns in the condition of a given college or university emerge from time to time, the reader is urged not to attempt to connect the various references. This rarely will prove useful in seeking to understand the whole.

If readers, especially those connected with the institutions studied, identify a particular college or university, we hope that this knowledge will be used constructively. Our purpose is to promote improvement in the education of educators and not to indulge in the condemnation of a given institution or its administration, faculty, and students.

The Sample of Public Institutions. Major research universities, often referred to as "flagships," are usually named "the University of (State Name)." These contain many graduate programs, professional schools, and extramurally funded research projects. Almost invariably they have the highest entry standards for public undergraduate and graduate education in the state. We selected four such: Kenmore, Northwood, Sherwood, and Vulcan, widely separated geographically. All but one are located a considerable distance from the state's major urban centers.

Major comprehensive universities, which closely parallel each state's flagship university, generally have a somewhat lower extramurally funded research budget and are commonly named "(State Name) State University." Although not all five of those in our sample are so named, the fictitious names follow this pattern: Jewel State, Forest State, Underhill State, Telegraph State, and Legend State. The former normal schools (the original U.S. teacher-preparing institutions) in this group had come a long way from their beginnings. One had once been a private university. Research and research aspirations are strong in the ethos of all five. Two of the five bear addresses of major cities; two of the other three are within an hour's drive of rather large cities.

Regional universities and colleges are often named according to the region of the state represented (for example, "Eastern" or "Central") and so are designated "(Region plus State Name) University or College." These are dominantly undergraduate, with some graduate studies, several professional schools (such as education, business, and nursing), and a small number of extramurally funded research activities. Entry standards are almost always lower than for the above two groups of institutions. These institutions were often normal schools, then state teachers' colleges, then comprehensive state colleges before becoming regional state universities. As a group and usually individually, they prepare large numbers of teachers. We chose seven of these: Central Rutherford State, Northern Horizon State, Eastern Oliver State, Southern Inverness State, Southwestern Bistwick State, Northwestern Prairie State, and Western Willis State. Five of the universities in this group had moved to this status rather recently. Two are urban, one suburban, three distinctly rural, and the other relatively rural but located about an hour's drive from a major city.

The Sample of Private Institutions. *Major comprehensive universities and colleges* are a highly visible component of the higher education landscape. They offer both undergraduate and graduate programs, maintain professional schools (sometimes including medicine), and frequently rival comprehensive public universities in extramurally funded research programs. Their entry standards are usually relatively high. Rarely do they retain the designation "college" today, but a few still do—probably for purposes of identity and tradition. We chose five of these from across the nation: Revere, Quadra, Mainstream, Ivy, and Merrett. Two of these, both barely warranting "major" status, are characterized by rather small education faculties and teacher education enrollments, resembling in these respects relatively large liberal arts colleges. Indeed, both place high emphasis on their undergraduate core in the arts and sciences. Two have schools of education qualifying them for admission to the Holmes Group. In one, the school of education had once been one of the heaviest-enrolled units of the entire campus. All five have urban addresses.

Regional comprehensive universities and colleges usually have a substantial undergraduate tradition, with professional preparation programs at both undergraduate and graduate levels. They generally serve the teaching, business, nursing, welfare, and technical needs of the immediate community and region of the state. Most have lower entry standards than do the institutions in the category above. We included four of these in our sample: Broadmoor, Gerald, Pilgrim, and Alton. Teacher education had played a substantial role in the historical development of three and was viewed as a major service to the community in the fourth, a relatively new campus. One was very much an urban university; the other three were located in the suburbs.

Private liberal arts colleges are primarily undergraduate in nature. Many include within the baccalaureate the courses required for teacher certification. Indeed, many began with the mission of preparing teachers and ministers, and some added preparation in nursing, business, and other fields. Commonly, they began with and maintained a religious affiliation. Entry standards vary widely. Some of these colleges have national reputations and academic requirements that make them highly selective. We picked four: Dorsey, Ellsworth, Lakeview, and Sterling. Teacher education has been part of the mission of each traditionally, but all four see the arts and sciences and general, liberal education to be central to their present principal purpose. Three have a rural, small-town ambience; one is suburban but very close to the city center.

Dealing with the Data. By late summer 1988, we had in our hands an extraordinary body of information on the twenty-nine sites gathered from the following sources: (1) administrator, faculty,

and student *interviews;* (2) *observations* of teacher education classes
in schools, colleges, and departments of education, and of student
teachers at their field placements; (3) reviews of relevant *documents;*
(4) modest *historical analyses* of each site; (5) *student and faculty
surveys;* and (6) demographic and other institutional data gained
from *institutional surveys.* The task before us was to collate these
data in such way as to portray the conditions of and circumstances
surrounding the education of educators in these colleges and universities. We sought to produce information-based portraits of each
institution to be used in exploring trends in consistency and inconsistency across the sample.

   As I stated earlier, we were guided in all of this by the conceptual work that preceded data gathering. What proved to be even
more helpful than expected was the interactive process surrounding
our visits and the powerfully cumulative insight gained as we added
site after site: a week of visits by each team, followed by several days
of synthesis, followed by another week of visits and several days of
synthesis, throughout an entire academic year. As soon as possible
after each observation or interview, each member of the team prepared a written summary based on notes and quotes during the
session. Then, as soon as possible after visiting a given site, the
members of each team prepared an overall summary document.
Finally, after both teams had visited the same institution, a synthesis report was generated.

   But the above does not adequately describe the whole. On the
plane to each destination, we tuned up, so to speak, for a particular
college or university by reading "information books" gleaned from
available documents. We entered each setting with sensitivities already attuned to nuances in greetings, hallway conversations, bookstore activity, questions directed to us, informal faculty and student
interactions, and more. The cumulative insights gained in both
formal and informal data and impression gathering simply could
not have been obtained from surveys and documents (although
those added useful information, of course). Further, we would have
shortchanged the study had we simply relied on observers and interviewers trained by us rather than personally visiting the twenty-nine
sites.

   With the data gathering and synthesis described above behind us, the two teams spent additional days teasing out from the entire experience the major themes that seemed to us to pervade the teacher education enterprise. If the nineteen postulates (Chapter Two) guiding the data-gathering process are the warp, then these themes are the woof of the cloth on which the twenty-nine portraits provide a multicolored pattern. This is the cloth I try to describe in Chapters Four through Seven.

But getting to the subject matter of these later chapters required more than a year of additional work. It must be remembered that we had before us by the fall of 1988 "slices of life" from each of the colleges and universities of our sample. The task before us was to put these slices side by side and together, as best we could, so as to acquire a reasonably comprehensive understanding of the teacher education enterprise at each institution and collectively. We found that the themes arising most consistently out of our experiences at the sites served best to synthesize the large bodies of related but as yet physically separated data. These themes provided the subjects of nearly all the technical reports listed in Appendix A and the doctoral dissertations of several research assistants engaged in the study. This book reports the results of dealing with the whole corpus of rich material at our disposal.

A Nation Ready?

The conditions are ripe for far-reaching reform in the education of educators for our nation's schools. The need of the schools for excellent teachers who understand what their mission is and how to fulfill it has never been greater. Nor have the agenda for school reform and the importance of teachers to it ever been clearer. Presidents and their boards are beginning to realize that colleges and universities can no more ignore the ills of schooling than they can ignore air pollution and soil erosion. In settings far beyond academe and teachers' workplaces, citizens and public officials now recognize the urgent need to provide teachers with the knowledge and skills they require as well as the professional recognition and rewards they deserve.

What has been missing, however, is a reasonably detailed description of the teacher education landscape—a cultural portrait similar to the one that trustees of the Carnegie Foundation thought essential to the definition of medical education in 1910.[66] This present-day landscape, profiled in subsequent pages, is a kind of historical marker, a product of yesterday and a prelude to tomorrow. Chapter Two puts forward the expectations that reformers must strive to meet and the conditions necessary to success that must be put in place.

There must be no slowing down in the redesign of schools if the necessary renewal of the education of teachers is to occur. Both redesign and renewal must proceed simultaneously and in concert if our system of schooling is to be first-rate. Is our nation awake and ready? After an exhaustive review of the school reform reports and completion of an extensive itinerary of visits and interviews, William Chance was cautiously optimistic: "It has taken nearly 95 years, but at last the country may be starting to take seriously the principle of universal education."[67] There can be no universal education of our young people, however, unless the education of those who are to teach them is completely redesigned.

Chapter Two

Reasonable Expectations

❖ ❖ ❖

Blessed is the man who expects nothing,
for he shall never be disappointed.
                                              —*Alexander Pope*[1]

We have expected a great deal of our schools and our teachers and
have often been disappointed. The answer is not to lower our educational expectations, however, but to state them clearly so that the
conditions necessary to their attainment also become clear. That is
the intent of this chapter.

Reasonable Expectations

What might our nation reasonably expect of its teachers?
First and foremost, we might reasonably expect that they be men
and women to whom we would comfortably entrust our children.
That is, those who choose (and are chosen) to teach might minimally be expected to meet the moral criteria we apply in selecting
our baby-sitters: that they be models of deportment and character.
It is also reasonable to expect that teachers be among the best-
educated citizens of the community—that they bring to everyday

43

discourse and civic decisions a broad background of knowledge and understanding. That is, teachers should participate widely in the human conversation and, in doing so, provide models of good judgment and clear communication. If a teacher is not a strong intellectual and moral force in the community, to whom do we turn?

Further, we should expect in our teachers a driving purpose: to maximize the learning of those placed in their charge. And because even sincere educational purpose can be corrupted by misguided beliefs about learning potential, our educators in this nation of minorities must also believe in the ability of *all* to learn; and they must hold steadfastly to this belief in their work.

But even purpose and belief together are not enough. These attributes must be supported by pedagogical knowledge and skills not easily acquired. Deeply engrained principles of pedagogy help to enlighten the thousands of decisions made each day in unpredictable learning contexts. And a teacher's pedagogical knowledge must be tempered with humility; to try again and differently with a pupil is to admit humbly that one's earlier teaching efforts did not suffice.

It is reasonable, also, to expect teachers to be responsible stewards of the schools in which they teach. They and they alone are in a position to make sure that programs and structures do not atrophy—that they evolve over time as a result of reflection, dialogue, actions, and continuing evaluation of actions. Teachers are to schools as gardeners are to gardens—tenders not only of the plants but of the soil in which they grow.

The above is only part of what we can reasonably expect of our teachers. Yet for some readers, even these few expectations may appear to be unreasonable. Why? Are we so used to disappointment, having for years expected the schools to remedy ills that were only peripherally in their domain, that we are willing to settle for very little? Perhaps. But the *educational* expectations stated here are reasonable and feasible. Our nation *must* not settle for less.

What might our teachers reasonably expect of this nation? Above all, they should expect its respect, which is revealed in myriad ways. A fair share of the gross national product is one of these; that share is more than a symbol. Respect is closely tied to cultural vision as well. If we believe that the *ideas* as well as the rights of the

Constitution come to each of us with birth, then the role of schools and teachers is diminished. But if we believe, as we must, that the rights inherited at birth depend on careful cultivation of ideals and ideas in the community, then schools and teachers rise to positions of paramount importance. Clearly, our record of omissions and commissions falls far short of these ideals, and the respect given to teachers suffers accordingly.

Certain conditions and circumstances have effectively blocked attainment of reasonable expectations for teachers. Those of our best-educated citizens who choose teaching careers might reasonably expect—but still have not received—salaries commensurate with their skills; decision-making authority that comes with recognition as a professional; the assurance that professional certification and licensing will not be undercut by deals between states and school districts when fully qualified teachers are in short supply; and the cooperation of national, regional, and state accrediting agencies and of college and university presidents in eliminating or upgrading weak teacher education programs.

The above and more are reasonable expectations for teachers who, in turn, meet the reasonable expectations of this nation. Even loftier expectations are voiced again and again. Yet simply closing the gap between present practices and what is merely reasonable is a monumental challenge to America.

And what might this nation and its teachers reasonably expect of teacher education programs? Considering the importance of teachers and the nation's expectations for them, it is reasonable to expect that colleges and universities will take on the task of educating future teachers most seriously—or not at all. This seriousness will be revealed in, for example, a president's expressions of commitment in addresses to alumni and friends of the institution, the careful selection of applicants, the equitable allocation of resources, the institution's clear delegation of authority to those responsible for preparation programs, forthright specifications and provisions of curricula, the development of exemplary field sites, appropriate recognition of site coordinators and master teachers in the schools, and much more.

These expectations are hardly in the realm of idealism, any more than are parallel expectations in the education of doctors, lawyers, and dentists. People planning to spend their lives teaching in elementary and secondary schools have a right to expect quality in their professional education programs; and the United States of America can ill afford anything less.

Nonetheless, a significant shortfall continues year after year, like a bad debt. For example, the shocking reality is that many presidents of institutions now preparing teachers measure their institutions' "progress" by the degree to which they have distanced themselves from teacher education in evolving from normal school to teachers' college to state college to state university.[2] Instead of educating future teachers, many professors of education, especially in the most prestigious research universities, only conduct studies of them—if these professors are involved in teacher education at all.

The Dimensions of Teaching

Having considered the expectations that might reasonably be held by teachers and those they serve, we turned our attention to the task of public school teaching. Just what does that profession entail? After considerable discussion, we isolated four dimensions of teaching: facilitating enculturation, providing access to knowledge, building an effective teacher-student connection, and practicing good stewardship.

Perhaps a bit of background will clarify my subsequent discussion of the individual components. At the time my colleagues and I were dealing with these issues, strong currents favoring the reduction of *all* teaching into a few technocratic elements were sweeping through schools. Administrators, in particular, were mesmerized by the simplistic rationality of techniques that anyone could learn quickly in order to teach anything to anyone.[3] They hastened to allocate staff-development monies to short workshops designed to bring teachers quickly up to date in these generic models.

There is no doubt that beginning teachers, especially—many of whom were poorly prepared in pedagogy—benefited from what they experienced.[4] Forward-looking school leaders, including teachers, wisely incorporated what was useful into a broader program of instructional improvement and avoided being caught up in a fad. Some critics expressed concern, however, over the degree to which preoccupation with the mechanics of teaching might impede teachers' professional growth.[5]

Our reflections, meanwhile, were turning us toward a conception of teaching that encompassed much more than instructional method. We began to define teaching in the nation's public elementary and secondary schools as a special case. First, as a special case of *teaching*—one not completely paralleled in private schools. Private schools are not required to take all comers, for example; nor do they face the same requirements of accountability in regard to helping those that they do take. And teachers in private schools are not required to be licensed by the state.

Yet teaching in public schools is not only a special case of teaching but also a special case among occupations and professions. What makes teaching in public schools particularly unique is the extraordinary confluence of circumstances at what at first appears to be a rather simple point of interaction—namely, the ongoing relationship between teacher and student. The teacher's relationship with "clients," for example, is so different from the relationship of doctors, dentists, and lawyers with their clients that the word *clients* is rarely used in speaking of students. The student relationship with teachers in schools is sustained and, up to a given age, required. With doctors, dentists, and lawyers, no relationship is either sustained or required.

We came to see with increasing clarity the degree to which teaching in schools, public or private, carries with it moral imperatives—more in public schools, however, because they are not schools of choice in a system requiring compulsory schooling.[6] At first we viewed these moral imperatives as composing one leg of the chair on which rests teaching as a profession. Collectively, they pointed to a body of subject matter to be synthesized into part of the teacher education curriculum. We soon abandoned this view, however, in favor of one in which the moral imperatives in schoolteaching were seen to characterize *each* of the four legs—indeed, the entire chair.

If teaching in public schools is a special case of teaching, then preparing teachers for those schools is a special case of teacher education. One does not look, then, to other instances of teacher education or to other professions for ready-made models of what to do. One begins, rather, with the special circumstances of teaching in public schools. If public school education is already exemplary and contains all the elements necessary to continuing renewal, we need look no further; we can mold the teacher education enterprise in the shape of the school-based enterprise. But clearly this is not the case. Consequently, we must be guided not by what *is* with respect to schooling, but what *should* be. Teacher education has much to do, then, with normative matters pertaining to the nature of education and what one's conception of education means for the conduct of schooling in a democratic society.[7]

Facilitating Critical Enculturation. The school is the only institution in our nation specifically charged with enculturating the young into a political democracy. The education of teachers must, therefore, be specifically directed toward this end. Our students must understand not only the underlying ideas of the Constitution[8] but the quintessential expression of the American idea: "We hold these truths to be self-evident, that all men are created equal, that they are endowed by their Creator with certain unalienable Rights, that among these are Life, Liberty and the pursuit of Happiness. That to secure these rights, Governments are instituted among Men, deriving their just powers from the consent of the governed, That whenever any Form of Government becomes destructive of these ends, it is the Right of the People to alter or to abolish it, and to institute new Government." Schools, through their teachers, must introduce our young people to the ideas inherent in our political democracy and the ideals from which they are derived. To believe that saluting the flag and repeating the oath of allegiance are sufficient is to be egregiously naive.

There is more to a democracy, however, than a system of governance. The culture into which children are born is not perfect. And "children do not enter the world compassionate, caring, fair, loving, and tolerant."[9] We created schools primarily out of concern for the welfare of our culture, particularly in regard to the preservation of our religious and political values. We broadened their purposes over time until they included the whole process of developing effective citizens, parents, workers, and individuals; these are now the educational goals of our school districts as well as our nation.[10] Schools are major players in developing educated persons who acquire an understanding of truth, beauty, and justice against which to judge their own and our society's virtues and imperfections. Schools join with the home and other institutions in seeking to ensure that these individuals will be humane. This is a moral responsibility.

Providing Access to Knowledge. The school is the only institution in our society specifically charged with providing to the young a disciplined encounter with all the subject matters of the human conversation: the world as a physical and biological system; evaluative and belief systems; communication systems; the social, political, and economic systems that make up the global village; and the human species itself.[11] The educative processes advanced by schools must go far beyond the mere recapitulation of information so encouraged by many instructional practices.

Teaching how to structure one's experiences through these encounters is a major part of the task entrusted to schools. "It is morally fundamental; it is necessary for all in a just society; it is basic to every person's learning humankind's repertoire for structuring experience."[12] What one needs to learn is embedded in the subject fields of the school curriculum.

The first moral dimension of this teaching responsibility demands that the teacher possess what Donna Kerr calls "canons of assessment"[13] derived from humankind's sustained studies. (Moral responsibility here extends to those who set licensing and certifying standards; they must be sure that teachers are not permitted to teach under false pretenses.) The second is embedded in teachers' stewardship of their classrooms and school. They must be diligent in ensuring that no attitudes, beliefs, or practices bar students from access to the necessary knowledge.[14] From Chapter One, we know that the chasm between ideal and reality is broad. Programs for the education of educators carry some of the responsibility for closing it.

Building an Effective Teacher-Student Connection. The moral responsibility of educators takes on its most obvious significance where the lives of teachers and their students intersect. The complexity of this relationship is such that there is little likelihood that someone will simply acquire—through the gaining of common sense and the process of growing up—the skills, understanding, and sensitivities necessary to make this relationship work. A few people do, but not enough to staff our schools. This is why the careful educating of our schoolteachers is so essential.

It is unlikely that mere exposure to a few courses in education and a brief immersion as a student teacher will suffice. And the folly of trusting the quality of the teacher-student relationship to a few generic principles now becomes sharply apparent. Generic knowledge of teaching that might be applied in a whole host of teaching situations—by instructors in cosmetology and beauty schools, by teachers of diesel engine care, by dog trainers, by drill sergeants, by public school teachers—embraces only a very small part of what teachers of the nation's children and youths must know and be able to do. The very claims of a pedagogy so universally applicable to all teaching trivialize the wide variations in the significance and complexity of the forms of teaching listed. The trivialization is complete when those versed in such teaching promise to pass it along to others in a matter of hours or days (or however long a time the market will bear).

To seek to build a profession and professional status for public school teachers solely or primarily on such a pedagogy is to perpetuate the follies of the past—and to make of comparable significance and complexity the fixing of our machines, the care of our hair, the training of our pets, and the education of our children. Given our extensive fascination with such follies, it is small wonder that advances in the science of teaching have failed to advance significantly either the professional status or relative income of public school teachers. Indeed, the extent to which teachers' associations, teacher educators, and others have perpetuated hopes among teachers for easy steps to success in teaching constitutes a pedagogy of the oppressed.

The epistemology of teaching must encompass a pedagogy that goes far beyond the *mechanics* of teaching. It must combine generalizable principles of teaching, subject-specific instruction, sensitivity to the pervasive human qualities and potentials always involved, and full awareness of what it means to simultaneously "draw out" and enculturate. The necessary research has begun, but it is far from sufficient. [15] Nonetheless, as we shall see, teacher education programs lag dangerously far behind available research and are not adequately connected to ongoing inquiry. Little wonder, then, that teachers turn all too readily to the promise of panaceas.

Practicing Good Stewardship. Some of our most sobering discussions during the early stages of our project carried us back to the study of schools in which two of us had been engaged for several years (reported on briefly in Chapter One). Many of those we had visited were woefully neglected places, not just physically but in their total ecology. In *A Place Called School,* I referred frequently to two that were particularly shabby in every respect: condition of the buildings inside and out, behavior of the students, morale of the teachers, relationships between principal and teachers and teachers and students, and more. I recall my visit to the teachers' lounge of one: a bleak and untidy room filled with abused furniture, poorly groomed teachers, dispirited talk. The superintendent who was my host appeared not to see the gloom, however. He spoke proudly of the program in cosmetology and of the fact that the teachers were not unionized; indeed, they were on annual contracts and had security of employment for only a year at a time.

These were not inner-city schools overwhelmed by circumstances. Both were at the edge of big cities; the economic level of parents was above the average for our sample. These were schools left to deteriorate because of human neglect—on the inside and on the outside.

The best schools in the sample were schools that, in the words of some teachers in them, "took care of business." This, we discovered through research and experience in working with teachers and principals, is an ability learned on the job and learned only with difficulty. The learning is much easier than the doing, however. Settings designed to be like prisons are not readily turned into "places for learning, places for joy." [16]

The two strands of educational reform beginning to be joined by the end of the 1980s were coming together around a concept of schools as centers of change and principals and teachers as those empowered to renew them (see Chapter One). If this is an idea

whose time is come, much more will be required of teacher education programs than simply preparing teachers for the individual
classroom, as if the rest of the institution did not exist. And much
more will be required by way of support from the outside. If all our
institutions are the bones of our civilization, they must be well
nourished and carefully nurtured. If schools are part of this skeletal
structure, as we so often claim, they must not be neglected or they
will decay. Teachers are their primary stewards. Their preparation
programs must alert them to this responsibility and begin to prepare them to assume it.

In sum, then, our conception of schoolteaching embraces
four components, with moral imperatives embedded in each. The
first two emerge out of the functions specifically assigned to
schools: enculturation of the young into a democracy and inculcation of the disciplined modes of thought required for effective, satisfying participation in human affairs. The first of these requires
that teachers themselves possess a deep understanding of both the
governance structures and processes of this political democracy and
the requisites of humane citizenship. The second requires that
teachers learn the necessary subject matter twice—the first time in
order that it be part of their being, the second time in order to teach
it. Both sets of learning are best acquired simultaneously or in
juxtaposition.

The other two components are intended to ensure the first
two: a comprehensive grasp of pedagogy and of the values, knowledge, and skills to be brought to bear in the ongoing renewal of the
schools in which teachers will spend their professional careers. We
know that neither of these requirements is part of general education
in colleges and universities. Consequently, a special program of
professional studies is required, just as it is for all the other professions. These are the critical components of teaching in schools that
simplistic reform proposals so often seek to eschew.

Society's moral shortcomings lie primarily in grossly misun-
derstanding what our schools are for and underestimating what is
required of those who are their daily stewards. The school system's
moral delinquency is in structuring the enterprise in ways that deny
students access to the knowledge they need. *All* students are disadvantaged; some—largely those who are poor and from minority

groups—are disadvantaged more than others. The most compelling moral imperatives for teachers pertain to their necessary vigilance in ensuring that their school fulfills its designated functions well and equitably and to the nature of the unique relationship between the teacher and the taught.

Conditions Necessary for Effective Teacher Education

Having formulated a conception of teaching, our group now faced the task of determining the conditions necessary to teacher education programs driven by reasonable expectations. Clearly, there is no way to deduce these conditions from empirical studies. One does not, for example, deduce moral imperatives from what works. One deduces them from reasoned argument with respect to what is right and just.

It became necessary, therefore, to extend our discourse to presuppositions about teacher education programs supported, designed, and conducted so as to fulfill the above-formulated reasonable expectations for teachers and to address the four dimensions of teaching. The conditions postulated had to connect with these expectations and dimensions so closely that someone following our line of argument carefully would say, "Of *course*."

The critic might then say, "But I don't agree with the basic line of argument." Although we would prefer agreement, we are well aware that disagreement is to be expected. Our answer necessarily becomes, "Disagreement is your right and privilege. We ask only that you take the same care in carefully constructing an alternative line of argument and deducing from it the conditions of teacher education that emerge from it." Ours is the kind of society that thrives on alternatives. Because of the importance of teacher education to this society, however, alternative conditions deemed necessary to it must be carefully deduced. Reforms not carefully thought out, reforms passed along without careful analysis, have already gotten our educational system into much difficulty.

Throughout our formulation of these conditions, we sought to maintain a reasoned discourse that would result in conditions of teacher education that were both reasonable and necessary. We developed a working paper arguing the special case of teaching in

public schools discussed earlier in this chapter. It concluded with a list of conditions necessary to the preparation of teachers for such teaching: institutional commitment and support, a faculty group responsible and accountable for the whole, programmatic autonomy and protected resources, student candidates committed to meeting the requirements of teaching as we defined them, curricula providing for all four dimensions of teaching (and the moral imperatives accompanying them), laboratory facilities capable of accommodating all the students admitted, state deregulation of curriculum requirements, and more.

We postulated nineteen of these conditions, beginning with institutional commitment and concluding with the regulatory context. In our conceptual schema, these were not hypotheses to be tested. Rather, we regarded them as essential presuppositions—postulates—against which extant conditions might be judged and toward which redesign of teacher education might strive. The list follows.

Postulate One. Programs for the education of the nation's educators must be viewed by institutions offering them as a major responsibility to society and be adequately supported and promoted and vigorously advanced by the institution's top leadership.

Our children, their parents, and the nation are ill-served by colleges and universities and their presidents lukewarm to educating teachers. Failure to identify a normal-school past in promotional documents or to name the school of education in a presidential report on the university's professional schools conveys something much less than pride. It is outrageous that a president, academic vice-president, or provost, without any stated revision of policy, can cripple something as important as teacher education through neglect. Likewise, it is outrageous that institutional leaders often turn their backs when their schools or colleges of education operate shoddy—but profitable—off-campus programs for the preparation of school administrators. The message must go out and be backed by forceful action: Get on with it properly or be forthright in deciding not to participate any longer. There is no place on a college or university campus for an enterprise viewed as not worth a strongly supported, stable identity.

Postulate Two. Programs for the education of educators must enjoy parity with other campus programs as a legitimate college or university commitment and field of study and service, worthy of rewards for faculty geared to the nature of the field.

It is hypocritical for institutions to include teacher education in their offerings and then be lukewarm about rewarding the work that goes with it, and it is inexcusable for faculty members engaged in teacher education to maintain that the work they do does not lend itself to scholarly activity. Likewise, it is indefensible for institutions to increase research demands on faculty without creating the necessary supporting conditions. There is urgent need to clear up the present ambiguity regarding the not-quite relationship of teacher education to the rest of the higher education enterprise and the K–12 system of schooling. With functions and tasks clear, the criteria for rewards can and must be made explicit.

Postulate Three. Programs for the education of educators must be autonomous and secure in their borders, with clear organizational identity, constancy of budget and personnel, and decision-making authority similar to that enjoyed by the major professional schools.

In other words, boundaries and resources must be protected with the same vigor that characterizes academic departments and the education of doctors, lawyers, and dentists. We are dealing here with the education of those who will join parents in ensuring that our young people become humane individuals and responsible citizens. Do universities take on any matters of greater importance? Persons planning to become teachers must enter programs with assurance that the integrity and quality of those programs are not to be eroded by intrusions from within or without.

Postulate Four. There must exist a clearly identifiable group of academic and clinical faculty members for whom teacher education is the top priority; the group must be responsible and accountable for selecting students and monitoring their progress, planning and maintaining the full scope and sequence of the curriculum, continuously evaluating and improving programs, and facilitating the entry of graduates into teaching careers.

The existence of a department, school, or college of education is no guarantee of these conditions. Nor is the allocation of resources for teacher education to such a unit a guarantee. Clearly, some of the necessary faculty must come from the schools that provide student teaching and internship experiences, as well as from the arts and sciences departments. These faculty members perform different functions but enjoy equal status in planning and conducting the programs. Patching together a curriculum and a faculty on a year-to-year basis, however, is inadequate and inexcusable. Teacher education must have an integrity backed by security of programs and responsible persons.

These first four postulates outline reasonable expectations for a college or university that takes on as one of its functions the education of educators for the schools. To assume the function but not provide the implied resources on the grounds that limited budgets do not permit is to shortchange children and youths, teachers, and the public. The only responsible, moral thing to do under such circumstances is to admit inability to prepare teachers adequately and close down the programs. On the other hand, when colleges and universities meet these conditions, they set the proper moral tone for students and faculty.

Postulate Five. The responsible group of academic and clinical faculty members described above must have a comprehensive understanding of the aims of education and the role of schools in our society and be fully committed to selecting and preparing teachers to assume the full range of educational responsibilities required.

Clearly, faculty members who perceive the function of schools narrowly and teaching as a mechanistic series of steps provide the wrong role models. Professors who impatiently and reluctantly drag themselves away from their research and graduate seminars to teach required courses in the teacher education sequence probably do not think much about what teachers should do. Professors of mathematics who advise their best students not to become teachers defeat the implications of this postulate. And cooperating teachers in the schools who tell their student teachers that teaching is a miserable occupation should themselves be out of it. Future teachers deserve more encouraging messages.

Postulate Six. The responsible group of academic and clinical faculty members must seek out and select for a predetermined number of student places in the program those candidates who reveal an initial commitment to the moral, ethical, and enculturating responsibilities to be assumed.

Fulfilling this postulate requires the preparation of recruitment and admissions documents describing the entrance requirements. It calls for the presentation of supporting credentials from each candidate and an admissions interview. Other professional programs require these things. Why not teacher education programs? Students admitted want to know that they have met high standards, that they have been carefully chosen. Teaching our children is not a given right. It is an opportunity to be earned.

The omission of basic literacy as a requirement is not an oversight. I have more to say about this in the postulate below. Increasingly, both states and educational institutions are requiring the passing of tests in basic skills prior to admission to teacher education programs. I shall argue later for resources to assist candidates to secure any necessary remedial assistance. Academic shortcomings on the part of highly committed individuals are easier to overcome than a lack of commitment to teaching.

With the institution fully committed, an able faculty group clearly in charge and responsible, and students who perceive themselves as carefully selected, we are ready to consider the necessary programmatic conditions. These are laid out in the much longer list of postulates below.

Postulate Seven. Programs for the education of educators, whether elementary or secondary, must carry the responsibility to ensure that all candidates progressing through them possess or acquire the literacy and critical-thinking abilities associated with the concept of an educated person.

There are at least three sets of requirements here. First, there are entry minimums to be met through examinations. It is important, however, for the results to be built into a counseling process. Students who show an eagerness to correct deficiencies should be provided with the opportunity to do so. Universities spend millions of dollars keeping athletes eligible to play, some of whom can barely read and write. We do not want people teaching in schools who set a poor academic example, but we must provide opportunities for those seeking to meet acceptable standards to do so—over and beyond the prescribed curriculum, of course. Second, the required preteaching general-education curriculum must be adhered to by all—both traditional students entering undergraduate and nontraditional students entering graduate programs—with the opportunity to examine out in most areas. Third, candidates must demonstrate, as they progress through this curriculum, the intellectual traits associated with continued development as educated persons. Assessment here is difficult, but the responsible faculty group must take it on, must counsel students along the way, and must make tough decisions as deemed necessary. There are bright, intelligent people teaching in classrooms who have never confronted intellectual challenge. Perhaps this is why a common criticism of schools is that they do not emphasize development of the mind.

Postulate Eight. Programs for the education of educators must provide extensive opportunities for future teachers to move beyond being students of organized knowledge to become teachers who inquire into both knowledge and its teaching.

I argue here for coupling general education—especially the study of subjects ultimately to be taught in schools—with pedagogy. What is called for here is less an inquiry into generic methods—the psychology and sociology of individual and group learning, for example—than an inquiry into the means for teaching embedded in the domains of knowledge. For example, how do I as a teacher help students draw from the particulars of a time and a place principles of historical analysis that would help them in studies of other times and places? How do I connect the lives of students and these historical themes? Somewhere in the upper-division curriculum there should be a jointly taught seminar in which professors of pedagogy and of the specialized field explore questions such as these with future teachers. Not to effect the necessary transcendence while students are still involved in the general-education and specialized-subject curricula is to lose a most significant opportunity.

Postulate Nine. Programs for the education of educators must be characterized by a socialization process through which candidates transcend their self-oriented student preoccupations to become more other-oriented in identifying with a culture of teaching.

Socialization is a process of taking on certain cultural norms over time. The socialization that occurs, formally and informally, in a teacher education program tells us a great deal about the images of teaching and the expectations for teachers guiding that program as norms. Such norms are apparent in both the explicit and the implicit curriculum. How long and what it takes to absorb the moral and ethical norms of the teaching profession is not known; we have not tried to find out. We can be almost certain, however, that preparing to take some sort of examination on teaching will not suffice. Nor can such an exam tell us much about whether or not such socialization has occurred.

Postulate Ten. Programs for the education of educators must be characterized in all respects by the conditions for learning that future teachers are to establish in their own schools and classrooms.

The field of education has declared for itself prime competence in and jurisdiction over such subfields as curriculum planning, instruction, student counseling, evaluation, testing, group climate setting, and the like. Consequently, it is entirely reasonable to expect teacher education programs to be characterized by exemplary practices in all of these areas. Modeling is regarded as a powerful teaching device. For teacher education programs not to be models of educating is indefensible.

Postulate Eleven. Programs for the education of educators must be conducted in such a way that future teachers inquire into the nature of teaching and schooling and assume that they will do so as a natural aspect of their careers.

It is reasonable to assume that descriptions of teacher education programs will emphasize an inquiring approach instead of a series of hurdles to be cleared, that general traits of intellect will take precedence over narrow, specific competencies, and that "covering" course content and passing tests will be secondary to relating to children and youth and exciting them about learning.

   Postulate Twelve. Programs for the education of educators must involve future teachers in the issues and dilemmas that emerge out of the never-ending tension between the rights and interests of individual parents and special-interest groups, on one hand, and the role of schools in transcending parochialism, on the other.

   To allow students not to grapple with these issues is to leave them hopelessly ignorant and exposed to pressures from all sides— pressures so contradictory in the context they create that educating in any real sense is virtually defeated. Earlier, I addressed the general education required of all prospective teachers. This education is necessary, but insufficient. The goals and organization of schooling and the role of schoolteaching pose issues for which special, professional education is required. The discourse may well begin in a course on the philosophy of education, but the fundamental issues must become underlying themes throughout both the academic and clinical components of programs.

   Postulate Thirteen. Programs for the education of educators must be infused with understanding of and commitment to the moral obligation of teachers to ensure equitable access to and engagement in the best possible K–12 education for all children and youths.

   As a nation, we simply have not internalized either the realization that the right to education now embraces the secondary school or the devastating consequences that will result if large numbers of young people do not complete it. Belief in the incapability of many children and youths to learn abounds. Horrifyingly large numbers of teachers share this belief; indeed, they use it to excuse their own failures. Teachers must come out of a preparation program with the belief that they can and will teach all their pupils to the best of their ability and that they will share in both their successes and their failures. Preparation programs that steer their students only into field settings where family backgrounds and educational resources almost ensure success are programs that disadvantage future teachers and shortchange society.

Postulate Fourteen. Programs for the education of educators must involve future teachers not only in understanding schools as they are but in alternatives, the assumptions underlying alternatives, and how to effect needed changes in school organization, pupil grouping, curriculum, and more.

As we shall see, the education of educators is tightly coupled with the status quo. Few changes are needed if the purpose is to prepare teachers for the status quo, but if we think our schools need restructuring and renewal, then preparation programs must be involved with ideas for change and the spirit of change. And the relationship between universities and surrounding schools and school districts must be conducive to collaborative improvement, in part through the infusion of new teachers committed to and capable of effecting change.

Postulate Fifteen. Programs for the education of educators must assure for each candidate the availability of a wide array of laboratory settings for observation, hands-on experiences, and exemplary schools for internships and residencies; they must admit no more students to their programs than can be assured these quality experiences.

The range and stability of these resources are crucial. Additionally, observation in settings, good or bad, must be accompanied by critiques; practice and theory go together. Settings for internships and residencies must be examples of the best educational practices that schools and universities are able to develop together, and the internships obviously must be conducted collaboratively. These are "teaching schools," paralleling the teaching hospitals essential to medical education. It is the responsibility of universities to work with school districts in ensuring that these teaching schools are in economically disadvantaged as well as advantaged areas and that future teachers get teaching experience in both. The availability of such schools at any given time must govern the number of students admitted to a program. When forty future teachers are ready for intern placement, there must be forty places available. These forty candidates become junior colleagues in the elementary, middle, and high schools that serve as teaching schools. The number that can be accommodated by a participating school is an important detail to be worked out, as is the necessary overall funding and staffing arrangement.

Postulate Sixteen. Programs for the education of educators must engage future teachers in the problems and dilemmas arising out of the inevitable conflicts and incongruities between what works or is accepted in practice and the research and theory supporting other options.

Not only do such problems and dilemmas arise during observations of school and classroom practices, but the responsible faculty must see to it that they are brought to the forefront and discussed—with both practitioners and scholar-researchers engaged in the dialogue. It is not good enough to tell student teachers, caught in the middle of such conflicts, that they must not, while "guests" in the classroom, "rearrange the furniture in the minister's house." It is immoral for professors to tell their students, for the sake of keeping peace with the affiliated schools, to do what neither they nor their students believe to be right. Such inexcusable behavior arises out of the general failure of clinical and academic faculty to come together in a genuinely intellectual collaborative enterprise.

Postulate Seventeen. Programs for educating educators must establish linkages with graduates for purposes of both evaluating and revising these programs and easing the critical early years of transition into teaching.

It is generally known that virtually all practitioners are at first highly critical of their professional preparation programs, whatever the field. "You simply didn't prepare us for the real world out there," they accuse their professors. It is perhaps uncomfortable to hear the complaints, but consistencies in them can be woven into evaluative patterns that can be useful for program review and revision. Beginning teachers, for example, would find it exceedingly valuable to meet throughout at least the initial year with other neophytes in a seminar guided by someone more removed, such as a professor engaged in teacher education. Because teacher education and placement are generally so local in character, most beginning teachers would once more be with their initial mentors from their training days. For those who move elsewhere after graduation, reciprocal, interinstitutional arrangements are called for. Rarely, however, are the necessary funds available for follow-up, either locally or reciprocally. Given the loss of so many teachers during the first few years following graduation, the returns from such an investment would be substantial.

Postulate Eighteen. Programs for the education of educators, in order to be vital and renewing, must be free from curricular specifications by licensing agencies and restrained only by enlightened, professionally driven requirements for accreditation.

State authorities are responsible for setting licensing standards to protect the public. The long-standing practice has been to eschew graduation standards in favor of curricular requirements. In so doing, creativity and innovation in program planning within colleges and universities have been stifled. Now that states are turning to tests of basic literacy and knowledge about teaching as requirements for obtaining a teaching credential, they must get out of the business of prescribing the teacher education curriculum. This step would go a long way toward encouraging faculty members to initiate program renewal.

Postulate Nineteen. Programs for the education of educators must be protected from the vagaries of supply and demand by state policies that allow neither backdoor "emergency" programs nor temporary teaching licenses.

Over and over, morally driven efforts to mount first-rate teacher education programs have been defeated by this action or that designed to relieve teacher shortages or satisfy special-group interests. Many teacher educators who once participated in renewal efforts, often more than once, now swear never to be stirred to undertake still another. They are cynical and often bitter, waiting for the next shoe to fall and adjusting accordingly. There are many appropriate ways to bring able people into schools and classrooms who are not certified or who have not yet made up their minds to teach. Providing them with licenses of any kind is a disservice to them and certainly to the teaching profession. When temporary licenses *are* granted, we make a mockery of all the postulates listed above.

The nineteen postulates put forward here do not encompass the whole of the conditions to be met in order to ensure able, committed teachers for our schools. I have deliberately concentrated on those lying within and necessary to the control and fulfillment of the moral responsibilities taken on by colleges and universities when they select or are called upon to educate teachers and principals for our schools. Included in these conditions are working arrangements with nearby schools of a kind never before attempted but absolutely essential to exemplary teacher education programs. Included also (in Postulates Eighteen and Nineteen) is a necessary relationship with the state that has from time to time been recognized and even respected but that has been breached so often that many teacher educators believe that any efforts to mount quality programs will ultimately be defeated by state omission or commission.

Seventeen of the nineteen, then, concentrate on what lies primarily within the will of the nation's colleges and universities. There are clearly identifiable actors to whom these postulates are addressed. In Chapter Eight, I tie specific responsibilities to each group of actors.

But these institutions can be held accountable only for carrying out a mission agreed to in the larger society. If we want our schoolteachers to be only baby-sitters, we should leave parents to hire their own, using whatever selective criteria they consider relevant. If we want our schoolteachers to teach only the mechanics of reading, writing, and figuring, then we would be well advised to turn to the software and computer companies as the most expeditious means to this end, once again leaving parents to make whatever baby-sitting arrangements are necessary.

But do we want more? If I am even close to the mark in stating reasonable expectations for our schools and teachers and in laying down the conditions necessary to educating these teachers, the challenge ahead is formidable. If I am significantly above the mark, however—that is, if these expectations and conditions are too demanding—many of the stirring speeches, high-sounding documents, and perilous warnings of reform reports regarding the critical importance of our educational system must be tossed aside as grossly inflated puffery. I am confident that our founding leaders, were they still with us, would recognize and accept the challenge. I assume that our present leaders and large numbers of our citizens are similarly prepared to do so.

Clearly, then, the mission for teacher education presented in the foregoing pages (and deliberately restated in various ways) must become the mission for more than teacher educators and university administrators. There is much to do outside of higher education and the necessary collaboration with schools: the close joining of parents and other lay citizens with schoolteachers in educating the young, the creation of a community context of pride in teachers and teaching, the translation of this pride into recruitment of able future teachers, scholarships and fellowships for candidates from limited financial backgrounds, salaries and benefits sufficient to support the families of teachers in comfort and dignity, acceptance by teachers' unions of the necessity for differentiated salary schedules for differentiated levels of preparation and responsibility, and support from our elected officials commensurate with their and our rhetoric of commitment.

Another set of necessary conditions pertains to the conduct of our schools and the necessary linkages between them and higher education institutions—not just for the education of teachers but for the health of both. Universities have contributed significantly (though not always constructively) to the management side of the school system and to its bureaucratization. Surely universities have much more to contribute to the nature of a school's curricula and the instruction that goes on there—and much more to learn in the process.

Toward Agendas for the Redesign of Teacher Education

Our intent from the beginning of the project was to lay out the components of an agenda for the redesign of teacher education derived, on one hand, from a carefully executed study of existing conditions and, on the other, from a set of carefully argued alternative conditions. It was not our intent, however, to state this agenda in such specific terms that it would be a blueprint. The extant conditions we set out to describe would vary from institution to institution, we knew, regardless of the broad generalizations that might apply to all or most. Similarly, the conditions laid down in the postulates can be achieved in a variety of ways. The gap between what exists on a given campus and what should and can be is different for each setting. Thus there is the potential for many agendas.

In the preceding pages, I have endeavored to satisfy one criterion of a good agenda: a vision of conditions that would be superior to those prevailing. In Chapter One, I laid the groundwork for satisfying a second criterion: a picture of these existing conditions. It is the gap between existing conditions and apparently more desirable alternatives that motivates. I believe and will argue that this gap is large and serious, and that closing it will be difficult.

The first part of my argument rests on the assumption that the postulates advanced here are reasonable presuppositions of moral commitment. They prescribe necessary conditions for the responsible conduct of teacher education. The second part rests on the assumption that the sampling of teacher preparation programs described in subsequent chapters is indeed representative of a larger number of such educational settings. The findings reported are those that emerged consistently, hammering home the conclusion that there is a formidable gap to be closed in seeking to fulfill the reasonable expectations with which this chapter began.

Chapters Four through Seven present four chunks of data and the conclusions derived from them: the institutional and regulatory context, some demographics and views of faculty members on a wide range of educational topics, and students' characteristics and views, added to our own observations on the programs in our sample of teacher-preparing institutions. These are then fused into a composite description (Chapter Eight) organized around the postulates so as to portray the gap between the conditions described and the alternatives put forward in preceding pages. In addition, Chapter Eight puts forward some suggestions for closing these gaps and identifies the most relevant actors and their responsibilities. Chapter Nine develops an illustrative exemplary model.

In presenting the data, I attempt to be as dispassionate as possible—an effort that sometimes requires great restraint. Recorded in our field notes are countless incidents of indifference and neglect on the part of individuals who have it in their power to make a difference, and of thoughtlessness among individuals casually perpetuating tired practices of yesterday that should never have been resorted to in the first place. I cite a few.

- A university we were about to visit sent us an array of documents about its history and accomplishments. Not one contained any mention of the fact that this university had recently been a normal school.
- In a telephone conversation with a university president who extolled the emergence of new academic undertakings at his institution, I asked about the teacher education program. "Oh, yes, teacher education. . . ." I could almost hear his eyes glazing over.
- A dean of humanities angrily and sarcastically denounced education professors but remained adamantly unwilling to devote any humanities resources to the teacher education program. He did not believe the education professors to be qualified to teach methods courses in the disciplines of the humanities, but he had no intention of "lending" people in his division to do so.
- A young education professor looked at me in disbelief when I asked him about his involvements with schools: "The problems of the schools are no concern of mine," he said.
- A superintendent of schools, when asked his opinion about a well-researched approach to the teaching of reading, condemned it as impractical. His district, he said with pride, required all student teachers from the nearby university to conform to the traditional approach "we have always used."
- In one state, first-year teachers were required to conform to a state-imposed lesson-planning procedure in order to be certified—and professors in college and university preparation programs were repetitiously teaching it.

- Members of several campuswide committees responsible for policies regarding admissions and other standards for teacher candidates admitted that these requirements were being enforced only casually.
- Faculty members in a historically black college were struggling to ameliorate the academic deficiencies of students aspiring to teach, but the state had provided no resources for this purpose. In the meantime, reports on the desperate need for minority teachers pile up.

I have at my disposal enough deprecating anecdotes to fuel once more all the charges against schools and professors of education put forward by their critics since the beginning of the century. But even the small number of anecdotes presented here shows that the sorry history and state of teacher education are not solely the fault of shortcomings in our schools of education—serious though these are and have been. One more indictment of these schools and professors serves no constructive purpose.

In *A Place Called School,* I rejected the convenient "villain" theory. In the criticism of teacher education over the years, there have been more suspects than in a clutch of Agatha Christie mystery novels. Were I to add just a few more anecdotes representing the full array of problems and issues, it would become abundantly clear that, in teacher education as in schooling, we are *all* culpable.

When one considers in its length and breadth the history of selecting, educating, and rewarding our schoolteachers, anger stemming from anecdotes such as these is pushed aside by overwhelming sorrow. The legacies of neglect and mindlessness hang heavy over the necessary tasks of renewal. It is to some of these legacies that we now turn.

Chapter Three

Legacies

❖   ❖   ❖

All of these circumstances—the lack of authority and stability, of sensible working conditions and adequate compensation—add up to one major defect: the denial of truly professional consideration for teachers.

—Jurgen Herbst[1]

Barbra Streisand's lump-in-the-throat rendition of "Second Hand Rose" conveys just the right blend of pathos and self-pity for the theme music of a documentary film on the history of teacher education in the United States. Yet it would be necessary to intersperse this theme music with snatches of "Yankee Doodle Dandy" to accommodate contradictions in the status of teacher education and teacher educators during the 150 years or so since some training of teachers was first recognized as desirable.

These historical contradictions arise in large part out of this nation's ambivalent regard for its teachers. On one hand, we go to the outer reaches of oratorical excess in heaping praise on the Teacher of the Year, and a teacher was deliberately among the first nonastronauts chosen for flight to outer space. On the other hand, only parents of first-generation college students rather consistently view teaching as a proper career for their offspring. Many other people regard teaching as a noble calling—for somebody else.

Students of education have not quite been able to grasp and articulate this strange, elusive relationship between general approval and specific rejection. It is not a love-hate relationship. Nor is it one of master to servant. In its rhetoric, our society values teachers, but little is done to ensure that individuals attracted to teaching will find conditions conducive to staying.

Similar ambivalence has characterized teacher education. For a time, high expectations ran with the normal schools,[2] although these schools lost their clear purpose early on. Later, the schools and colleges of education in the research universities were heralded as saviors of teacher education; but they soon found more prestigious things to do than to prepare teachers. Affiliation with higher education might have been expected to bring higher status to teacher education, but it did not. The education of teachers was and remained a poor relative.

This poor-relative status of teacher education cannot be explained entirely by the ambivalent public perception of schoolteaching, although this certainly has been and still is a powerful contributing factor. An array of other circumstances must be examined as well.

A History of "Not Quite"

There has been over the years much talk among educators and within their professional organizations about the emergence of teaching as a profession. "Hasn't the damn thing emerged *yet?*" asked a colleague in exasperation. The answer is "not quite."

The conditions necessary to a profession simply have not been a part of either teacher education or the teaching enterprise: a reasonably coherent body of necessary knowledge and skills; a considerable measure of "professional" control over admissions to teacher education programs and of autonomy with respect to determining the relevant knowledge, skills, and norms; a degree of homogeneity in groups of program candidates with respect to expectations and curricula; and rather clear borders demarcating qualified candidates from the unqualified, legitimate programs of preparation from the shoddy and entrepreneurial, and fads from innovation grounded in theory and research.[3] With these conditions largely lacking, teacher education and the occupation of school-teaching have been at the mercy of supply and demand, pillages from without, and balkanization from within. Even today, teaching remains the not-quite profession.

Normal Schools. The call in the fourth and fifth decades of the nineteenth century to formalize teacher training was intended primarily to meet the demand for enough teachers to staff schools to be attended by all children—the common school. Little thought was given to the knowledge and skills these teachers might require. Consequently, teacher education lacked intellectual coherence from the outset.[4] The normal schools, those first centers of teacher education, announced a growing source of employment and a reasonably certain route to a job.[5] They also provided convenient, inexpensive schooling to persons *not* planning to teach. In general, then, the normal schools did not attract a cohesive student population, relatively homogeneous in its aspirations.

It is significant that normal schools were called "schools." At first, they were aligned with the lower, common schools—not with secondary, let alone higher, education. Their mission had much more to do with fostering character and morality in line with religious orthodoxy than with fostering intellectual curiosity and independence. The extant knowledge of pedagogy, such as it was, embraced little more than helpful hints on controlling and managing children, handling classroom routines, and the like. An elementary schoolteacher—envisioned as female—did not need a liberal education but was to be virtuous, hardworking, and obedient to superiors.[6] These traits are far afield from those associated with higher education and the professorship. There was room, then, within the ill-defined intellectual borders of teaching, for persons of widely varying educational backgrounds, provided that they appeared to be virtuous. Still today, there is little agreement on how academically well prepared elementary schoolteachers should be; and there is now, I fear, much less attention to and agreement on the moral requisites.

Later in the nineteenth century, the pedagogical component

of the normal-school curriculum was to be tied to the prospect of rather immediate, practical results. Ways of teaching were to be routinized (as is commonly the case still) into orderly, easily visualized steps—Pestalozzi's "object lesson," the Oswego Method or Herbartianism[7]—largely unaccompanied by their conceptual context. Even an approach as complex as John Dewey's method of inquiry, central later to progressive education, was reduced to a series of sequential steps. The search for *the* way, reduced to what can be conveyed economically to teachers, continues today, provoking to considerable degree the widespread contempt for methods courses.

Whereas New England normal schools usually consisted of training departments attached to public schools, midwestern and western normal schools represented adaptations or extensions of secondary education.[8] For many communities, they provided convenient access to secondary education, offering curricula not much different from academies and public high schools. By 1900, some resembled colleges.[9]

We begin to see, then, that teacher training enjoyed neither an intellectual nor a clear organizational identity. It was born out of intimacy with the public schools, for which teachers needed no clearly defined preparation. By offering secondary and later a form of higher education, normal schools served the educational needs not only of prospective teachers but also of young people having no aspirations to teach. Indeed, it was in the best interests of these latter students for normal schools to become increasingly diverse in their functions and curricula, because they were the most inexpensive and accessible sources of general and vocational education. These schools, then, not only had no clearly defined intellectual borders: they had no clearly defined borders between students seeking to teach and the rest. Normal schools cultivated, probably unwittingly and in good faith, the seeds of enrollment growth and diversity that would become more compelling institutionally than would the best interests of teacher education. The poor-relative syndrome took up the void not filled by increased identity and autonomy for teacher education within the dynamic, twentieth-century evolution of higher education.

Regional Public Universities: An Era of Transition. There emerged in higher education a rite of passage—from normal school to teachers' college to state college to regional state university. By 1940, the first and only century of the normal school was over; the term was becoming obsolete. Teachers' colleges experienced an even shorter life, evolving into state colleges and universities during the 1950s and 1960s. This transition was virtually complete by the early 1970s. Within these large and multipurpose state institutions was the teacher education enterprise that once had been dominant, now organized within schools and colleges of education.

This transition was accompanied by a severe loss of identity for teacher education. Several universities characterized by this rapid, recent transition were in the sample my colleagues and I visited. On none of these campuses was the education of educators (or, for that matter, the college of education) the crown jewel. The bundle of catalogues, recruitment documents, and the like forwarded prior to our arrival to one such campus, known by us to be one of the earliest and most respected normal schools, included no mention of this august past. At another university, the one-room schoolhouse recently transported to the campus appeared to be less a nostalgic symbol of worthy services rendered than a monument to an impoverished background thankfully left behind. Better, apparently, to be a not-yet-distinguished university than a first-rate manifestation of a former normal school.

One would have expected the identification of teacher education with the higher education system to have warranted, in time, a blast of "Yankee Doodle Dandy." Alas, it was "Second Hand Rose" all over again. Encompassment within schools or colleges of education brought no secure borders for teacher education. My colleagues and I found teacher education programs scattered geographically across the campuses of comprehensive universities, for example. Nothing comparable exists in law, medicine, architecture, or dentistry. Nor were there borders providing a clear identity for teacher education within the schools of education of these former normal schools. Deans of education interviewed commonly identified something other than teacher education as their top priority for the future—this at a time when public clamor for educational reform included teacher education as well as the schools.

Creation of the New York College for the Training of Teachers in 1887 carried with it great expectations for a new era.

Grafted onto Columbia University in 1892 and renamed Teachers College, this institution clearly brought the preparation of educational leaders and normal-school instructors into the university domain—within a distinguished university and at the graduate level to boot. "Yankee Doodle Dandy," indeed! But 120th Street in New York City—with Teachers College on one side and the rest of Columbia University on the other—has often been described as the widest street in the world. Furthermore, because Teachers College was for teachers of teachers and for educators planning to leave (or already out of) the classroom to become administrators, the notion of something much less being appropriate preparation for classroom teachers was exacerbated. The preparation of teachers in institutions going through the rite of passage just described remained the norm.

Beacon Schools of Education and the Rise of Research. Between 1900 and 1940, there emerged what Geraldine Clifford and James Guthrie refer to as the "beacon" schools of education[10] in major research universities that had never been normal schools or teachers' colleges.[11] Rather than metamorphosing from one type of institution to another, they grew outward and upward from a core commitment to scholarship that was increasingly being referred to as *research*. Schools of education (such as those at the University of California, Berkeley, and the University of Michigan), created from the outset as professional schools among several representing various professions, gained respect and recognition outside their settings, but little within. Rather than being regarded as poor cousins to be taken care of, they were (and usually still are) commonly looked down upon as unwanted sisters—siblings who, if they did not actually besmirch the family name, were nonetheless to be disavowed.

It is not clear how much of this early disaffection stemmed from the fact that these schools trained common-school teachers—a task perceived to lack an intellectual core. Certainly, however, this was (and remains) a factor. Also, scholars in the arts and sciences who taught without benefit of training perceived the emergence of pedagogical science as a kind of insult—a put-down of their self-acquired art. College and university teachers, if not born with the requisite skills, acquired them through rigorous inquiry into their disciplines. Their studies did not and needed not include pedagogy. Suggestions to the contrary were an affront.

Commonly, professors in the arts and sciences still perceive their colleagues in the education schools to have made out of teaching in the lower schools a kind of pedagogical mystique that they, in the higher levels, can get along very well without. Apparently, education professors get along without it very well, too—so the argument goes—or else college students would be flocking to their classes to partake of masterly teaching. Alas, a widespread complaint of teachers and future teachers is that teachers of teachers are less than experts in the teaching craft and often fail to practice what they preach.

In the research universities, claims of teaching expertise or interest in pedagogy among professors of education are only a little more common than are those of their academic colleagues. Indeed, much of what goes on in these schools of education has little to do with teaching or preparing teachers for the lower schools. Professors study educational phenomena in the same way that colleagues in other departments and schools study biological, geological, architectural, and chemical phenomena. Some hold joint appointments, especially in such departments as psychology, sociology, philosophy, and anthropology. Inculcating in others the ability to teach school subjects or doing research in that area holds no special interest for them. Their scholarly interests, taken as a whole, cut across a considerable spectrum of campus academic life. The education of teachers commonly ranks low, and it is often shunted off to adjunct, part-time, temporary, nontenured instructors. Teacher education is a neglected cousin once again, but at least it shares a corner of the same living quarters and is thus not easily put out of sight.

This is an irony that Clifford and Guthrie sought to sort out in their penetrating historical and contemporary analysis of schools of education in ten major universities.[12] Judge unearthed many of the same paradoxes and dilemmas in his earlier study of almost the same sample;[13] the British visitor, on asking the dean of education (a composite of several Judge interviewed) about the school's teacher education program, is told that the faculty does not *prepare* teachers; it studies them.

These schools and a handful more like them prepare the lion's share of doctoral graduates, who become top candidates not only to replace their own professors but also to replenish the education faculties of the regional universities and private colleges preparing the bulk of the nation's teachers. Yet teacher education would be identified by few, if any, of these beacon schools as their top priority. Nor do professors in these schools customarily exhort their own graduate students to seek careers in teacher education.

Most of the top-ranked five in Cartter's 1977 ranking of leading schools of education prepared no teachers or just a few.[14] The production of each in the top dozen was small when compared with that of almost any regional (formerly normal school) university chosen at random. Transition from much to little attention to teacher education appears to be a rite of passage for all schools of education seeking national recognition—a transition comparable to that of normal schools that became regional universities. Through this transition, they hope to join the ranks of the beacon schools, flashing the signal that dumping at least some of the freight of teacher education hastens the passage.

We have in the above, then, the extreme irony. At the head of the class are not schools of education with exemplary records of preparing teachers but rather schools of the *study* of education—not much of it having to do with pedagogy or teacher education.

Before voicing too much surprise or outrage over this phenomenon, however, we should consider a trend in this direction by schools of medicine. In his 1910 report on medical education, Flexner expressed concern over securing medical school professors capable of guiding the hands-on clinical component of medical education.[15] His fears were well founded. Eighty years later, university rewards for research are such that professors of medicine are increasingly writing so much of their time into the budgets of their research grants that little is left over for teaching or the other demands of preparing doctors. The parallel in leading schools of education cannot be understood and judged apart from evolution of the scholarly ethic and ethos in higher education generally.[16]

This nation can well afford a dozen or so major educational

research institutes within the context of comprehensive universities, even if they do not prepare teachers. And because educational phenomena are what they largely study, even non-teacher-preparing institutions are, in fact, schools of education. The issue of interest here (and which I address again later) is whether such research-oriented institutions should dictate the future of teacher education. And if not, who should?

In our top universities, securing grants and conducting research are the queen and king. The role of these institutions in producing knowledge has come to overwhelm their role in teaching that knowledge directly to students. This is a matter of growing concern both inside and outside of universities. Yet putting the two in balance is as difficult as putting intercollegiate athletics into an academic perspective.

For successful professors, research grants and accompanying scholarly production bring visibility, geographical mobility, and free trips (with honoraria) to faraway places. Fame as a teacher, on the other hand, rarely travels beyond the local campus. A university competing for research talent often spends into the millions to attract a sought-after scholar in the natural sciences, offering a package that may include laboratory facilities, graduate assistants, secretarial help, a very light teaching load, and more. The grants such scholars attract bring recognition to them and their universities and incentives to attract other bright young scholars. This is heady stuff—a far cry from yesterday's image of prosaic academe.

What many people, including those who seek reform in teacher education, do not understand is that the above scenario applies, admittedly to a somewhat lesser degree, to professors in the behavioral sciences, including professors of education. The National Academy of Education comprises several dozen scholars whose reputations derive primarily from studying educational phenomena, including practice. The list of members is a kind of educational *Who's Who*. Although some are housed in university departments such as psychology and sociology, a substantial number are card-carrying professors of education. Some have taught future teachers at some time in their careers; few do now. Most, perhaps all, are known and respected by colleagues outside schools of education on and often beyond their own campuses.

It is clear that education as a field of study has quietly come of age, but that news is bad as well as good. First, education has come of age within the norms of the arts and sciences departments, not the professional schools. Second, it has come of age without bringing with it prestige and recognition for teacher education. Indeed, one could say rather safely that this maturation has been at the *expense* of teacher education—not just because, in the most prestigious schools of education, teacher education is so often turned over to temporary faculty members, but because a norm other than teacher education is established for lesser institutions on the rise. If the teacher education flag is missing or flies below the other flags on the flagpole of the top universities, a powerful message regarding teacher education goes out: Leave it alone or handle with care.

Third—and of great importance—a new kind of school of education has emerged, staffed in large part by professors whose interests and backgrounds are far afield from teacher education and (quite frequently) even schools. Yet they make up the voting faculty in the vital business of setting priorities and firming them up with those who are recruited to carry them out. Many of the persons actually conducting the teacher preparation programs in these universities—in other words, the temporary faculty who do the bulk of the teacher preparation—are, by university statute, mute in this process. Even when the faculty solemnly agrees that the next faculty position approved must be filled by a person who will shore up the erosion of tenure-track faculty members in the teacher education program, this criterion usually loses ground to others during the selection process.[17]

Is it right and proper for teacher education courses to be taught by adjunct, temporary instructors while the school of education selects still another scholar to enhance its reputation in something other than teacher education? Of course not. But the problem extends across the campus. There are professors and departments in the university that have as much stake as the education department—sometimes more—in who teaches the required education courses taken by prospective teachers of English, history, mathematics, biology, and so on. The education department often "borrows" faculty from these other disciplines, yet the lending disciplines rarely hire new faculty on the basis of their interest in or qualifications for teaching methods classes.

Many of the necessary conditions postulated in Chapter Two for creating and developing a strong, professional teacher education unit and program are either missing or shaky in such institutions. Who speaks for teacher education on the campuses of our major research universities? Who should? By what norms should they be guided?

Clearly, these questions are not easily answered. Above all, however, the answers must not advance the scholarly role of the university by compromising the conduct of teacher education. If universities teach teachers only out of a sense of noblesse oblige, teacher education will be better served by moving elsewhere.

Liberal Arts Colleges. Regional and national public and private universities are not the only institutions engaged in the education of educators for our schools. Private liberal arts colleges, with a core educational purpose and some additional functions around the edges, currently prepare a substantial portion of the nation's teachers.[18] These institutions—more often than not created by a religious denomination—proliferated during the second half of the nineteenth century. Commonly, their founding charters stated the purpose of preparing ministers and teachers for the schools. Given this mission, the widespread offering of teacher education programs in so many of these colleges, and the sheer numbers of teachers they have turned out, their general neglect by historians of teacher education is surprising.[19]

Whereas the normal schools had the avowed purpose of attracting and preparing future teachers, increasingly expanding their curricula to satisfy other students, the liberal arts colleges saw preparation to teach as something added to a general, liberal education. The women's colleges, for example, did not view their role as preparing young women for careers outside the home. Rather, they provided education designed to enrich and buttress home and family. As a long-term president of Agnes Scott College in Decatur, Georgia, once said to me, "Educate a woman, and you educate an entire family."

During the nineteenth and well into the twentieth centuries, it was not uncommon for more than half of the students in such colleges to enroll in a teacher-preparing curriculum—partly as a kind of employment insurance, apparently, because a smaller proportion actually entered teaching. Students could take teacher education classes—especially for a secondary certificate—without seriously jeopardizing general studies. It simply required careful planning that allowed few electives. The early popularity of normal schools and teachers' colleges pushed the liberal arts colleges into promoting the claim that they offered something more—adherence to the liberal arts disciplines, an intellectual core of required subjects, and a scholarly faculty, many of its members recruited from the best universities. By the 1950s, prospective teachers were a minority group in the student body of most, although an upsurge of teacher education enrollees began in the late 1980s.

There has been in the liberal arts colleges no rite of passage resulting in the evisceration of teacher education programs. Rather, the norms of general education have simply overshadowed those of vocational education, particularly as public higher education has expanded and the more expensive, small, private schools have had to find a distinctive niche. These norms cast some aspersions on departments of education and the people in them.

It is interesting, however, that the propinquity of faculty members in a small college, often located in a small town, draws colleagues together. One tends to find the general-specific ambivalence of attitude reversed—that is, faculty members tend to see teacher education as a low-level intellectual enterprise but feel fortunate in having such able colleagues. It was fascinating to encounter this phenomenon in conversations with many administrators and arts and sciences faculty members on the campuses we visited. It gave me a new slant on the secondhand status of teacher education. The prevailing attitude suggested that although colleagues in the education department stray dangerously close to academic sin, they do so as if members of the Salvation Army.

There are factors in the small liberal arts colleges that appear favorable to the education of teachers. First, there is a strong, shared ethos regarding the priority of general education and the liberal arts. "Where is there an intellectual environment more suited to assuring a solid education for teachers?" I heard again and again.

Second, these colleges generally lack the luxury of being able to provide many electives or, for that matter, alternative courses in required fields. Consequently, considerable thought has usually gone into determining the best general education for all, including future teachers. Third, attention to religious orthodoxy has largely disappeared over the years in church-related colleges, but there remain many concerns for moral and character development that translate well into expectations for teachers.

Fourth, although liberal arts colleges have not been passed by in the emergence of research as king, small individual research projects dominate, the stated purpose often being to augment one's understanding and teaching of a subject. There are not, customarily, large, deadline-driven research contracts to be managed. This characteristic appears more to support than to endanger a very important fifth asset, which is the centrality of teaching. In these environments, consistent neglect of teaching is quickly known. There is a considerable degree of student and peer pressure to teach well. This does not eliminate, of course, the neglect of teaching for research among some faculty members, particularly those who have the "big-time" gleam in their eyes and who see their present positions merely as stepping stones.

Sixth, limited graduate programs and budgets result almost automatically in substantial undergraduate and even lower-division teaching loads. If there are "stars," they are likely to be teaching freshman classes side-by-side with colleagues. When there are large introductory classes, they are likely to be taught by professors and not teaching assistants—although this may be less true than in the past.

Seventh, classes in the subjects a future teacher plans to teach and in education are taken simultaneously in what has traditionally been a four-year program. Thus teacher education students have at least the opportunity to take advantage of this juxtaposition in thinking about the teaching of the subject. Unfortunately, this is a possibility largely left to chance. Nonetheless, the potential is there, whereas it can be created only with great difficulty in postbaccalaureate programs—something that advocates of the latter have not adequately considered.

Before enthusiasts wax too eloquent over these liberal arts

colleges as ideal settings for teacher education, however, they need
to examine some troubling conditions as well. The faculty in education is almost invariably small, for example—a range of from three
to five being quite common. In part because of enrollment uncertainties and their impact on small institutions, not all of these
teachers hold funded positions in the tenure track, and staffing for
each coming year is often uncertain. Yet the department, usually
through a tenured, overworked department chair, must relate to
accrediting and licensing agencies as well as ensure the continuation of stable programs. A course required for certification cannot
be dropped because there is no instructor. Yet rarely does a college
provide adequately for education departments with respect to teaching loads, secretarial support, and the like. Whatever nonpressured
image one may have of the professor's life at a small college, it is far
from the life actually lived by chairpersons and full-time faculty in
education. A scholarly career with time for research is hard to come
by given the daily workload. Consequently, able faculty members,
even though dedicated to the small-college ambience, are easily
tempted by the promise of scholarly opportunities elsewhere, especially if these come early enough in their careers.

　　As we shall see later, socialization into the life of the college
as a whole is far more powerful for students than socialization into
teaching; and this, of course, is better than socialization into
neither. Working against socialization into teaching is the perception, common among both students and arts and sciences faculty
members, that education courses are required for certification rather
than because they are intellectually appealing in their own right.
Some of the students in these classes have no strong drive to teach.
As a result, the homogeneity of purpose and commitment necessary
to strong professional preparation programs is difficult to create
and maintain. Although it takes a little more probing in a liberal
arts college than on former normal-school campuses to ferret out
prejudice against education departments and professors ("Some of
my best friends are . . ."), it ultimately emerges. (Academe is not
without its share of people so skillful with the verbal stiletto that
the victim is scarcely aware of having been cut until the blood
spurts.)

　　In the small liberal arts college, teacher education has a room at the inn but still sits at the bottom of the academic table. Preparing to teach is often lauded as a fine thing to do in such a college, but schoolteaching remains, nonetheless, the not-quite profession.

Regional Private Universities. In addition to the regional public universities, liberal arts colleges, and major public and private universities, there are regional private universities, many in urban settings, that have prepared teachers since their founding. Some with national reputations are listed in the second category of doctoral-granting or comprehensive universities because of a level of research funding below that of the first grouping.[20] They produce most of the teachers not accounted for in the types of institutions already discussed.

A handful of these regional private universities were single-purpose teacher-preparing institutions that resisted erosion of this centrality of function into the 1960s and 1970s, when an abundant supply of teachers threatened their enrollments. Among those relatively well known to educators, such as George Peabody College for Teachers, National College of Education, Bank Street College of Education, and Wheelock College, only the last two are still listed as teachers' colleges in the most recent edition of the Carnegie *Classification of Institutions of Higher Education*. George Peabody is now the college of education of Vanderbilt University, and National College has been reclassified as comprehensive because of its expansion outward into additional professional and paraprofessional fields. Bank Street has diversified its teacher education–related activities, but they remain the focus; and Wheelock apparently remains committed to its long-standing specialization in early childhood education.

It is interesting that these single-purpose institutions probably came closest over the years to being colleges for the training of teachers, in the sense that medicine and law schools train future doctors and lawyers. Few students went to these colleges because they were convenient and inexpensive; nearly all went specifically to prepare to teach. Although each institution drew primarily from the local and regional area, all attracted some students from across the nation. Indeed, Peabody drew substantially from the entire South and, to some degree, from other parts of the country. The significance of this emerges when we come to realize that all but a few institutions of higher education draw the bulk of their students from close by, and initial teacher preparation is almost exclusively a local affair.

Although regional private universities did not promote and experience the rite of passage of many of their public counterparts, the music and lyrics of the teacher education story tend heavily toward the somber. There was evidence in the documents sent to us prior to our visits of an early, happier day for teacher education—in commitment and in numbers. On many campuses, it appears, the school, college, or department of education (SCDE) was at one time the largest and the dominant unit—often larger and more visible than the college of arts and sciences, for example. The primary reason for attending these institutions, as I have noted, was to prepare to teach. Early on, many of these colleges and universities prepared administrators as well, staffing the top positions in surrounding school districts. Usually the deans of education were well known in state capitals, where they worked closely with department of education officials in writing the teacher certification requirements and curricula.

It should not be assumed that education deans in the flagship universities were backward in these state-related activities. They were simply outnumbered by their counterparts in the regional universities. It is fair to say that education deans in the private, tuition-driven regionals found it necessary to be more entrepreneurial. Over the long haul, these external connections and alliances with state officials enhanced the coffers of not only the school or college of education but of the campus as a whole. Successfully fueling the political, entrepreneurial process brought power to colleges of education, if not love and respect.

Nonetheless, these private regionals increasingly perceived themselves to be comprehensive universities, with the liberal arts at the core of their reputations—so announced on the colorful burgees figuratively flown on their mastheads. The school or college of education was not what they wanted foremost in the public eye. Professors of education, during the heyday of steadily rising enrollments and powerful connections beyond their campuses, were not always sensitive to this intellectual self-perception. Indeed, they were sometimes perceived by their arts and sciences colleagues to be arrogant. Moreover, they did not establish the internal connections that might have served them well when the halcyon days came to an end.[21]

The fall was long and hard. Although these private campuses suffered as a whole from the downward spiral in the need for teachers during the 1970s, their schools and colleges of education suffered more—not only in the loss of resources but in the sometimes ill-concealed glee of some academic colleagues. Several top-level administrators were candid in telling me that budget cuts were disproportionately severe for the college of education. On one campus, they were so obviously inequitable, I was told, that members of other faculty units rallied around the college of education, embarrassed over the lack of parity. I was told on another campus that the depth of the cuts in the college of education was motivated not entirely out of need but involved both long-standing prejudice and punishment for not keeping the good times rolling.

Enrollments—and with them hope—were picking up a bit at the time of our visits. Clearly, however, events on many regional public and private university campuses have been devastating to the morale of education faculties. The wounds were still bleeding; bitterness and cynicism were widespread, particularly among older professors. Although most of the administrators who had carried the unenviable burden of balancing budgets were gone, some of the distrust that went with the process had spilled over onto their replacements.

It would be rather surprising to find, on the campuses briefly described above, carefully thought-out responses to the increasing calls for reform in teacher education. As later chapters will make abundantly clear, we found scarcely any. Teacher education is inescapably tied up with the fate of the larger institution of which it is a part. The regionals we visited, both public and private, appeared to be in a period of bumpy, uncertain transition—much less certain about where they are going than about leaving behind where they have been.

An Unclear Mission

It would be a serious mistake, however, to attribute the degree of faculty uncertainty we found on the campuses of both the public and private regionals in our sample solely to this period of attrition. (In what follows, I lump the two types of regionals together.) Entire university faculties were adjusting, with considerable pain in many instances, to rapid evolution in higher education. For some colleges and universities, such as those with historically black enrollments or serving relatively low economic groups, the transition period was and is especially wrenching.

At the time of our visits, a long dry spell in faculty hiring was just coming to an end, largely because of the need to replace aging professors. There was lingering bitterness over the earlier dismissal of some tenured faculty members and the strain of negotiating sometimes-unwanted early retirements. There still remained many persons who, though well along in their careers, were a decade or more from retirement. Among some of these, the worst of all doubts ran deep: the self-doubt that comes with the realization that the times are changing but the personal capacity for change is running out.

Changing expectations on the campuses of both major and regional universities also contributed to the strain we perceived. Large numbers of faculty members now in their fifties or older joined their college or university with the understanding that teaching and service were the uppermost expectations. In the intervening years, however, research and scholarship have come to hold the position of honor, especially in the major universities. How did this shift in expectations come about?

When hard times struck, most of the major universities, both private and public, were carving out a commitment to research. Their success in securing federal funds, accelerating from the late 1950s into the 1960s—particularly in the physical, biological, health, and engineering sciences—had placed them more and more in a competitive position that clearly demarcated the haves from the have-nots in the pecking order of American universities. Substantial extramural funds provided the flexibility needed to buffer declines in enrollment in the humanities and some social sciences and accompanying losses in income. A few schools of education at these major universities, accurately reading the changing climate, were able to adjust (with varying degrees of success) by developing beaconlike candlepower through prowess in securing grants and contracts.

The regionals enjoyed none of this maneuverability, however. Most public regionals hunkered down, effecting cuts and waiting for conditions to improve. The private ones, more accustomed to entrepreneurship, diversified. Their results with diversification were a mixed bag, more success usually coming with expansion into the field of business than into nursing, for example. Consistently, however, teacher education declined in emphasis and importance.

When these institutions began to recover some lost ground in the 1980s, the landscape of higher education had changed significantly. The clear research role of the flagship universities had brought them into the forefront. The rapid expansion of advanced graduate work supported by external funding had produced in some fields an oversupply of aspiring doctoral students looking for faculty posts. Many found them in the ranks of regionals, where retirement and some enrollment growth had created positions. They brought with them the research norms of their former professors.

Although some of the presidents of the regional universities either did not come out of academic careers heavily oriented to research or had left them behind, they were adequately sensitive to the changes taking place to assure that the appropriate signals would go out to the faculty. Most saw to it, as best they could, that the position of provost or academic vice-president was filled with someone whose own career or previous academic ties or both conveyed the impression of strong commitment to scholarship. The word went out quickly, creating a measure of dissonance that we often encountered within hours after arriving on these campuses. It is interesting that the conception of desirable scholarly work expressed in later conversations with these administrative appointees usually conveyed something much broader and more eclectic than was articulated by faculty members in both education and the arts and sciences. Nonetheless, publication in refereed journals almost always emerged, among both administrators and faculty members, as the *sine qua non* of exemplary scholarship.

Impact of the research expectation, accelerating from the 1950s, on many midcareer professors in major universities was severe, especially in professional schools with a commitment to training and human services. Many faculty members were torn by the juxtaposition of two cultures: one dedicated primarily to research, usually made up of the younger professors, who (at best intolerant of the old) were contemptuous of the lack of research expertise among their elders; the other, made up of the more senior professors, increasingly bitter over the relentless vicissitudes of change and critical of the "less caring" younger colleagues. But, as was previously stated, the situation was ameliorated somewhat in the major universities by the greater flexibility of resources.

Not so in the regionals. The message coming down from on high, however distorted in passage, almost invariably preceded the conditions perceived to be necessary to serious scholarship: time, a modicum of secretarial and research help, computers (or, in some instances, even typewriters), and the like. Further, although most full professors had published a few papers over the years, few even knew where to begin in seeking grants or writing the kind of papers sought by the major journals. To learn that these would be necessary for future salary raises was both frustrating and humiliating. Deans sometimes spoke to us proudly of the support from the provost in bringing to the campus persons of considerable scholarly renown. Many faculty members, on the other hand, expressed outrage over rumors of the higher salaries, better offices and secretarial support, and other perquisites given to "stars" recently recruited. Some felt pushed aside. Said a professor of mathematics education with twenty-five years of service, "The reward structure changed from primarily teaching in 1975. I wanted to teach. The young folks don't know anything else [other than the current reward structure]. A person like me [a slight shrug of the shoulders]—I'm tolerated."

The reader must not assume that what has just been summarized from interviews with administrators and faculty members covers only schools and colleges of education. On the contrary, the dissonance was pervasive. In spite of the many obvious differences among members and units of the academic community, these are more of degree than of kind.

On virtually every campus we visited, there had been recent increases—sometimes modest, sometimes considerable—in teacher education enrollments, whether of "traditional" undergraduates or "nontraditional," older individuals at the postbaccalaureate level. These increased enrollments were having a positive impact on morale, assuring endangered faculty that their services would probably be needed after all, and creating the need for a modest amount of new hiring. Because growth, on one hand, and retirements, on the other, constitute the major opportunities for change and redirection, I engaged education faculty members in discussions of the criteria that were being used (and that should be used) in choosing new colleagues.

To my dismay, the promise of renewal inherent in faculty growth rarely had been seriously addressed by the faculty as a whole. For the most part, any job description being circulated described the position as it *had* been; the work of the retiring faculty member was to be replicated and improved upon. There were in front of the faculty no careful plans for the future, no estimates of possible or probable retirements, and no recruitment strategies resulting from deliberation and hard choices. This is not to say that there were no soaring statements of philosophy and reflections on the present and future state of the world. These—and they were plentiful—simply had not been brought down to the level of providing guidance during a period of opportunity for change.

Although it appeared that there had been little previous dialogue regarding criteria for selecting new colleagues, faculty groups participated with gusto in the one I initiated. On every campus, I presented for discussion the following scenario: There are two finalists for a position requiring a substantial commitment to the teacher education program. Both earned their doctorates at major research universities. One, the younger of the two, is fresh out of a three-year postdoctoral fellowship with her major professor and has a substantial bibliography of papers published in refereed journals. She has not taught in elementary or secondary schools and is not particularly interested in teacher education, although she is well qualified academically for the course she would teach in the preparation program, and she is anxious to get on with her research career. The other has taught a subject (I varied the selection) in a secondary school (local circumstances sometimes caused me to choose elementary school teaching) for several years and taught for three years in the teacher education program during her doctoral studies, but she has a much shorter list of publications (focused primarily on teaching and teacher education). She wants the job in teacher education, is well prepared to teach the specified courses, and hopes to get some time and support for scholarly work.

After several discussions about which of the two the participants would choose, I was able to predict their course with considerable precision. There was little initial hesitation among faculty members in the research-oriented, beacon schools of education: The first of the two was the clear choice. Usually, however, we were not long into the exchange before someone said that there should be—or must be—room for the second kind of candidate or the institution might as well forget any serious interest in teacher education. There was generally some agreement with this point, although the first candidate remained first choice. Invariably, the discussion then turned to the future and to the role of the heavily research-oriented school of education. Usually, faculty members agreed that participation in the teacher education program was good training for doctoral candidates, many of whom would teach in preparation programs, at least for a while. But most of these professors felt that working in teacher education programs was not for *their* graduate students.

In those regional universities that had enjoyed university status for some time, the course of discussion varied in almost direct proportion to the faculty perception of a research *geist* emerging on the campus. In those where the dean of education and a core of faculty (some brought in recently to strengthen the research thrust) had already aligned themselves with a general institutional research commitment of several years' duration, the course of the discussion paralleled rather closely that of the group described above. However, many faculty members in these regionals rose to argue the necessity for even greater attention to research than in the past. Some were themselves experiencing the heady business of going to conferences where they rubbed shoulders with peers and role models, and of being in demand on the speakers' circuit. Some of their colleagues were apprehensive about the changes taking place, however, admitting to the probability that the first of the two candidates would be chosen, but raising questions about whether she *should* be.

In the regionals that had just become universities, however, there was little hesitation in choosing the second candidate. Some participants expressed a strong desire to have someone like the first on the faculty, but such a person would require relief from the standard teaching load and would need resources that the institution was as yet unwilling or unable to provide. Even then, they said, the first of the two, if chosen, would soon leave. Indeed, in almost every discussion in these faculty groups, some faculty members said that they would use the interview process to discourage the first candidate. Some said that they would discourage the second one, too, because it would be dishonest to offer even limited time and support for scholarly work.

The rhetoric over research expectations varied much less than the differences in choice of candidates might imply. The message that has been picked up by institutions calling themselves universities, our data suggest, is that scholarly work is now the name of the higher education game. A clear definition of just what this means is as conspicuous by its absence as the rhetoric is by its presence. The definition we heard ranged from "evidence of a mind at work" to the publication of at least four papers a year in journals requiring juried approval. One faculty group was seriously and somewhat contentiously involved in refining the award system: from four points for an article in a refereed journal down to only one for an internally published committee report—with each point cut in half for a coauthored piece!

The panic and pathos evidenced most in the just-become universities are muted in the major research universities and in the liberal arts colleges we studied. Those in the major research universities know rather clearly who they are and where they are heading. They know that teaching is in some danger and most have created awards for excellence in teaching; they know that there is concern in the external world about slippage in the place of teaching and that more must be done to ensure a better balance. Some thoughtful administrators are worried, too, about the appropriate future role of their human services professional schools, and—even as their schools of education enhance their scholarly reputations—they worry about the campus role in teacher education.[22]

The liberal arts colleges, virtually from their beginnings, have placed high value on both teaching and faculty scholarship. Although we found no severe shock waves running through the faculty because of rhetorical intensification of the importance of research, it is clear that the scholarly reputations of their faculty members are close to the surface of what really matters.

One's expectations would need to be low indeed before one could conclude that teacher education on any of these campuses is healthy, let alone exemplary. For the regional universities, in particular, a certain schizophrenia with respect to institutional mission compounds the problem of deriving clear directions for the school or college of education and the teacher education enterprise. To put the matter mildly, faculty members in just-become universities—endeavoring to cope with a teaching load twice that of faculty members in the major research-oriented schools of education, lacking secretarial help (and sometimes even typewriters) for such basic needs as preparing course syllabi, enjoying little hope of grant money, and being aware that much of what they do is little appreciated—have difficulty taking seriously the ambitions of newly arrived administrators who appear bent on having their institution become another Berkeley or Harvard. Indeed, the heads of these two institutions and others like them would view such ambitions to be more than a little strange—and, I would hope, quite inappropriate.

Nonetheless, the growth of research and its impact on all aspects of faculty and campus life are significant elements of today's higher education enterprise. An associate professor of counseling in a liberal arts college summed it up as follows: "The reward structure is the same as everywhere, it seems. A lot of publishing is now expected, a change in the last five years. We've lost a lot of good people who came in here to teach and didn't get tenure. The administration wants to go *national*, believe it or not. They're already regional, they think, and are positioning themselves for bigger and better things."

A major strength of American higher education is the diversity of its 3,389 colleges and universities[23] in mission, program, and student body. They should not and need not seek a uniform mold, nor should the schools, colleges, and departments of education housed in some 1,300 of them. But whether all of these SCDEs should seek to prepare teachers and whether the education of educators for the nation's schools should be left to the exigencies of their institutional contexts are quite different questions. Of course, teacher education has not been left to the autonomous care of higher education. One of the characteristics of its evolution has been its vulnerability to state and other intervention, a situation contributing significantly to its not-quite-professional status. Similarly, the nature and degree of the relationship of preservice teacher education to the public school system and its accoutrements has been a powerfully shaping force. However interesting and initially compelling comparisons with the emergence of professional education in other fields may be,[24] they do not carry us far in seeking to understand teacher education—this peculiarly troubled, resilient orphan that seems unable to get things straight and yet survives anyway.

Keepers of the Gates

No higher education specialty approaches teacher education in the degree of influence exerted by outside agencies, particularly state agencies controlling entry into public school teaching.[25] It takes myopia or a lack of concern among those in education—both of which seem to have tranquilized normal sensitivity—not to question the degree to which curricular autonomy, in particular, has been eroded.

Recent interest in tightening up graduation standards for elementary and secondary schools has spread to an intense parallel interest in upgrading requirements for teachers. Today very few people would argue against the proposition that teachers should be among our best-educated citizens. This requires, in the eyes of most people, simply a four-year college education. Many, however, would argue that teachers should come from the top half, academically, of their college class, while former U.S. Commissioner of Education McMurrin proposed that only the top 10 percent be chosen.[26] In addition, many persons call for more than academic requirements. Few, if any, would argue that teaching school is a right open to all.

Historically, however, our gates to teaching have been ajar or at least easily opened. The problem, worse sometimes than at others, has been the sheer need for bodies. The abysmal incompetence of Massachusetts teachers and the urgent need for more and better ones led in the 1830s to pleas for state provisions of preparation.[27]

An idea that has reemerged more than once surfaced then: Appeal to intelligent citizens to give up their normal pursuits for a time in order to render noble service as seasonal teachers. When that idea failed to win support, the legislature established four state normal schools, three of which were exclusively for women. Like most U.S. institutions that would recruit and prepare educators, these were founded because of the need for teachers, not because of the emergence of a scholarly domain relevant to teaching.

Principal Pierce of the normal school that opened in Lexington in 1839 found the academic knowledge and skills of the handful of women who came to be abominable. For years to come, normal schools devoted themselves primarily to remedying the deficient common-school education of their students. With the need for teaching grammar, spelling, composition, arithmetic, and the like to those who came to the normal schools, and without a commonly recognized need for the ill-defined pedagogical sciences, the length of the required *academic* program increased. In addition, as was stated earlier, the normal schools offered one of the few opportunities for advanced public education; this factor contributed to their gradual transformation from pedagogical to academic institutions.[28] Ultimately, belief in the necessity of a four-year college education for teachers became the conventional wisdom. Because the "What else might be needed?" question was not powerfully and convincingly put forward by the SCDEs of these four-year institutions, the pedagogical component became vulnerable to special interests from the outside. It also provided a convenient outlet for releasing some of the pressures exerted by those interests on state policies and procedures.

The states had found themselves with a set of internally conflicting demands: Improve quality, but guarantee a body in every public school classroom. Periodic severe shortages of teachers are much more obvious and compelling than the need for higher quality, however—especially during such shortages. Thus the states have found it necessary to keep the gates unlatched. Temporary and emergency certificates ease the shortage in times of undersupply; while in times of oversupply, a glut of teachers removes any rising interest in providing incentives for the improvement of quality. The call for higher salaries is muted when many of those teaching have done little to be temporarily certified, just as it is muted when there are dozens of applicants for each vacancy.

The call for improved qualifications is easily muted as well. High-level preparation may improve one's credentials, but if the school district must pay more because of them, that preparation may become a handicap. If getting high-level credentials costs more in time and money but does not assure a higher return, why get them? Therefore, why mount a larger, more demanding teacher education program when the one next door provides the same bottom line for less? Quoting my colleague Roger Soder, "When rewards and outcomes remain constant, competition drives quality down."

The internal inconsistency involved in endeavoring to provide simultaneously some measure of quality assurance to the public and a body in every classroom shows up particularly in the state's confusion over certifying and licensing. For a host of reasons embedded primarily in the early history of American public schooling—no special requirements for teachers even decades after specialized preparation was offered—states moved slowly to anything resembling a license for teachers. Virtues such as piety and hard work were easily attested to in the community, after all. Consequently, certification, when it came, was tied to a few common denominators in the preparation curriculum, not to indicators of skills and knowledge possessed. These curricular domains enlarged and diversified over time, making it increasingly difficult for state officials to determine the range of acceptable options. Channels of communication designed to clarify the fit between certification requirements and teacher education curricula emerged naturally out of necessity.[29]

In a chapter on keeping the gates in *The Education of American Teachers*, James B. Conant writes about his effort in the early 1960s to test the often-stated charge of a conspiracy between the state apparatus of teacher certification and professors of education, the result of which (or so the charge alleges) was considerable protection of education courses in the curriculum of higher education. His initial skepticism regarding this "devil theory" was strengthened by his inquiry into it,[30] although he found education deans and professors to be much more influential players in state capitals

than they are today. What we found recently was that heads of
teacher education commonly square their curricula with the most
recent list of state requirements, more or less resigned to circumstances beyond their control.

Although Conant rejected the notion of a conspiracy, a close
communication between heads of teacher education and of those
controlling certification existed and worked rather well up to the
relatively recent past. Both participated in state and regional meetings, which often included academic deans and vice-presidents as
well as representatives of schools and parent groups—a coalition
that was beginning to unravel at the time Conant conducted his
study.[31] There was in these joint meetings, considerable sensitivity
to changes occurring in supply and demand, the interests of persons
close to schools, and the entry and potential impact of emerging
fields such as guidance and counseling—and sensitivity to what
these changes boded for teacher education programs. There were
few surprises, in part because the collaborative process lacked some
of the urgency provided by today's sometimes near-hysterical
Chicken Little warnings of educational collapse.

Such meetings go on today, usually with less broad representation. An official with statewide education responsibility captured
in one sentence the significant change that has occurred: "While we
talk, the state legislature is passing bills that will render impossible
what we're proposing." The movement of the responsibility for the
lion's share of funding to the states, along with an array of other
factors, has pushed each state's political apparatus into the driver's
seat of the educational van. Unfortunately, an understandable desire
to get the van into high gear tends to push aside the deliberative
process of choosing the best road. The history of past ventures along
a number of roads—the history that would enlighten the present—is
largely ignored.

In moving with increasing speed toward attesting to teacher
quality through some kind of test for a license, the states show little
inclination to abandon the now-bureaucratized process of specifying the content of programs for certificates—a responsibility once
shared by a state agency and teacher-preparing colleges and universities. The state has every right—indeed, great responsibility—to
protect public interests through a licensing process. It does so in

exercising control over who will drive an automobile, for example. But the state does not prescribe the curriculum for drivers' training or require a certificate of completion prior to taking the licensing test. Nor is it interested in supply. Consequently, it is not caught in the inconsistency of seeking to ensure good drivers but easing up on the licensing requirements to guarantee a steady supply. States should assiduously avoid getting into this box in the area of teacher education, and all those now in it should get out as quickly as possible.

The only hope for balancing educational quality, on one hand, and supply and demand, on the other, lies in a system of checks and balances within which component parts function with considerable autonomy but in unison. No occupation or profession has achieved the ideal balance, but most of the professions are clear on the component parts, some of the autonomy each needs, and how they must function together. Most of their admitted deficiencies arise out of the usual human frailties—particularly the tendency to place individual interest above the common good. These same deficiencies will corrupt and disrupt the checks and balances required in regard to teaching and the teaching occupation, but they are insufficient reasons for not moving ahead.

The first step is to sort out the differences among *licensing, certifying,* and *accrediting.* All citizens have a stake in all three, but we have varying degrees of authority and responsibility over each. The state and the general public have the paramount interest in licensing. At best, however, licenses denote only minimum competency, and they are unable to predict human behavior. John Doe gets a perfect score on both the knowledge and performance sections of the driver's test, for example—only because he was wise enough to take it on one of the rare days when he was sober. And when he pile-drives his automobile into another, the police, the insurance company, and the state do not waste time looking for his tutor or driving school.

The more complex the knowledge, skills, and even attitudes to be accounted for in providing a measure of protection to the public, the more complex and expensive the licensing process. The state then finds itself in the position of having to hire an array of experts not only to prepare paper-and-pencil tests but to observe the candidates in performance settings beyond those simulated in the examination. The credentials of the "experts" now come into question.

Further, increased complexity of the licensing process causes potential candidates to turn to preparation programs, which blossom as need intensifies. More and more, the state then turns to the teachers and graduates of these programs to find its experts. Why not just turn the licensing process over to those providing the training programs? By so doing, the growing burden of costs, as well as accountability for the quality of available programs, could be shifted elsewhere. The state then could demonstrate its concern for quality control by joining in the public clamor over deficiencies in these programs. Further, it could specify what should be in them and withhold approval until the prescriptions are in place. In addition, the state could choose to waive the prescriptions when the supply of needed personnel is low. (This is the position of many states now in regard to teacher education, but they got there in a manner different from that described above.)

This solution sounds good on the surface, but it is not the answer. The state simply may not get rid of its responsibility in this way; protecting the public requires that *it* perform the licensing role. By taking on the role of program specification as well—a role that it is *not* obligated to perform—the state rises to its level of incompetence. This is where the concept of balancing a shared responsibility—each domain with considerable autonomy—comes into play.

The field of law provides a useful example of successful shared responsibility. The state exercises control over both quality and, to some degree, supply through the bar exam. The exam is sufficiently complex to require expert input, the necessary expertise coming from both law professors and experienced lawyers in the community. Two quite different domains collaborate, but final decision-making authority and responsibility rest with the state. Nobody involved takes seriously the notion that the bar exam predicts the behavior of lawyers in the courtroom or with their clients (although, largely through public prompting, it includes questions on ethical behavior). The license, once obtained, simply announces that the holder possesses certain legal knowledge. Neither the exam nor the state licensing agency prescribes a preparatory curriculum. This is left to the law schools, which in turn are required to meet accreditation standards set by the profession.

Nor do most law schools "teach to the bar exam." The university-based law schools share in the institution's search for knowledge and understanding of the entire corpus of beliefs, knowledge, and codes surrounding humankind's efforts to forge and live by protective, humane agreements. The law that results from this corpus is not static; it evolves. To prepare students for just the bar exam is to assume the law to be static. Law professors are attentive to the exam and participate in modifying it—and the dean and faculty members turn their attention to the school's curriculum when a rather large proportion of their graduates perform poorly in any exam area—but the curriculum responds primarily to other drumbeats. Graduates receive the ceremonial stamp of approval of both the university and its law school whether or not they pass the bar exam. Some fail the exam more than once and then resort to a law course proclaiming to prepare students for it; but it is the certificate of alma mater that appears on the office wall and testifies to completion of a program.

As I have noted, the law school is not free simply to follow its scholarly nose. The law profession, through procedures developed and revised over the years, sets standards and conditions to be met internally and defended uniformly. These are intended to ensure quality programs, on one hand, and the barring of alternative, back-door routes to practicing the law, on the other.

This professional accreditation process is addressed to programs, faculty qualifications, and support from the larger university context, while both certification and licensing are addressed to the education and performance of individuals. Although a few individuals not certificated and not products of accredited programs sit for the bar exam each year, this route is almost closed. Very soon, all candidates will be certificated graduates of accredited programs.

As I stated earlier, the system described for law (and common among the major professions) does not work perfectly. The battles at professional meetings over curricula and standards among practicing lawyers and professors and between the two groups are legendary. One wonders how the law student who has just failed the exam got through the system. Yet no human-made system is fail-safe.

As in the three-part executive, legislative, and judiciary system put together for this nation's governance, the faults appear to be more in human character than in structure. A comparable approach to licensing, certifying, and accrediting in schoolteaching and teacher education is badly needed. Ironically, some parts of the needed structure appear to be in place, but without the whole, they function like crippled animals.

One fallout of the troubled system is worth noting—the stultifying impact of curricular requirements on program renewal. My colleagues and I were startled not only by the lack of long-term plans regarding faculty replacements and additions, as noted—in the regional universities in particular—but also by the dearth of sustained discussion regarding programs. Yet on pushing a bit, we found that individual faculty members were neither short on ideas nor reluctant to express them. The mechanisms for bringing these ideas together in forums out of which might emerge fundamental programmatic changes appeared not to be in place—either because of disuse or omission.

We were sufficiently curious about this phenomenon to pursue it vigorously and in depth. Relatively early on in our travels, we discovered such variations in institutional adjustments to state regulations that we were prepared to downplay the restraining influence of these regulations. What we increasingly unearthed, however, was something much more disquieting: The changing and often abrupt state intrusions into the curriculum of teacher education have effectively stifled the creative process. Why bother to go through demanding, time-consuming efforts of program renewal when one must ultimately simply adopt or adjust to state-imposed requirements? Some faculty groups were waiting not for the second but for the tenth shoe to drop. One of the best arguments for a free-enterprise system emerges out of the consequences of stifling enterprise in the education of educators. The prescient recommendations of the California Commission on the Teaching Profession that no state requirements on the teacher education curricula of colleges and universities be imposed cry out for implementation.[32]

Unrequited Courtships

We have seen in the foregoing some of the close linkages that existed between schools and the programs and people in colleges and universities seeking to prepare personnel for them. I use the past tense because these linkages are much weaker today. The idea of renewing partnerships and collaborations of various kinds has emerged recently as part of the fabric of proposed reconstruction.

The historical connections have always been more interpersonal than interinstitutional:[33] future teachers enrolling in classes of normal-school, college, and university instructors; aspiring principals and superintendents flocking to summer sessions at major universities; university professors addressing teachers' and administrators' conferences; and the like. Rapidly expanding school populations have stimulated school districts to request surveys by professors of school administration, curriculum, and finance, while urgent need for new school buildings during the 1950s and 1960s created a heavy demand for enrollment-projection studies by university experts.

The need for teachers following World War II taxed the ability of higher education institutions, then swelling with enrollments, to provide the undergraduate academic and pedagogical preparation increasingly required for the baccalaureate degree and a teaching certificate. The glut of teachers seeking to upgrade themselves likewise taxed the ability of schools of education to provide the evening and summer-session classes required—a glut fueled by salary schedules geared to additional course credits and advanced degrees.

Several factors combined to substantially close down this production factory by the 1970s. The triggering factor, of course, was the decline of population growth and accompanying rapid diminution in the need for teachers. Those without a bachelor's degree who had been granted temporary certificates in the 1950s were now fully certified, and many had a master's degree. With jobs uncertain, candidates for preparation programs precipitously declined in numbers. Increasingly, and to a considerable degree unnoticed or ignored by schools of education, school districts were granting credits on the salary schedule for attendance at workshops and institutes conducted internally. In spite of predictions, appearing as early as the late 1960s, of pending severe declines in the need for teachers, most schools and colleges of education were caught unprepared. I have already described the devastating impact of subsequent severe cuts in their budgets and professorial ranks.

A prescient nation committed unwaveringly to its schools might have taken advantage of an opportunity to first assess the consequences of the extraordinary expansion that had taken place over two decades and then project plans for shoring up omissions, errors in commission, and the like. The earlier need to take care of huge enrollments, especially in the cities, had combined with increased use of so-called modern management techniques to bureaucratize the system. Departments of school administration in colleges of education had played a role in all of this, but there had been little parallel scholarly attention to classroom practices. For a time in the 1960s, federal and some foundation funds attracted clusters of academicians out of their normal pursuits to engage in designing new school curricula.[34] But this activity, too, faded almost into obscurity by the 1970s, when the nation itself went into a period of declining economic leadership and self-assurance. Had the opportunity to transfer the attention of thousands of university teachers and researchers to school improvement been envisioned, funding for its fulfillment probably would not have been forthcoming anyway.

Assuming that both interest and financial support had been available, could such a bold move toward school improvement have produced significant results? Perhaps not. Higher education has never been disposed to working collaboratively with the lower schools. The inclusion of secondary schools at one time and laboratory schools even yet within the purview of universities has been primarily to serve self-interests. Virtually the only claims that higher education can make regarding its interest in schools pertain to the quality of students coming from them and the production of teachers for them. The ironic backlash is the degree to which university professors complain about both the products of the schools coming to their classes and the poor quality of those who taught them.

The schools, on the other hand, would have had little reason to celebrate the appearance on their doorstep of a sometimes-discordant army of crusaders from the universities intent on a pilgrimage. Teachers, like practitioners in other fields, are chary in their praise of preparation programs, lauding some professors but highly critical of others for the abstract irrelevance of their teaching. They have no reason to be pleased about the degree to which university professors have participated in the creation of "teacher-proof" curricula designed to circumvent instructional shortcomings in the schools' teaching force.

I have already discussed the impact of the rise of research on those universities preparing the bulk of the nation's teachers. But I have not described the rather subtle way in which the scholarly paradigms that became popular in many major schools of education helped to cool prospects of promising courtships between schools and universities. The scientific and technical viewpoints commonly adopted by researchers fit not only the ethos of the twentieth century but also the value commonly placed on highly scientific knowledge by the university community.[35]

By rigorously advancing scientific inquiry, professors of education might have expected to bring both the field of education and schools of education into the mainstream of academic life, provide at long last the needed knowledge base for teacher education programs, and make of teaching a profession. Alas, several decades after the first clear stirrings of this movement,[36] one can argue rather convincingly that the outcomes have been quite different.

I engaged dozens of academic vice-presidents, deans, and department chairs in discussions regarding the emergence of education as a field of study. Their views ranged from "beginning to come of age" to "absolutely useless." The sum total of their reactions placed the quality and value of educational research at or near the bottom of the academic totem pole. Often discussion then moved to the question of why professors of education appear to be so little involved in studies likely to improve the quality of teaching, not only in schools but also in colleges and universities.

Johnson points out that "as education professors attempted to establish academic credentials and forge academic careers, their research became more and more methodologically sophisticated and thereby less and less accessible to practitioners."[37] Further, for reasons already stated or implied, only a little of this research was directed to teacher training. By contrast, the research universities led an intellectual revolution in professional training in law and medicine early in this century. The Flexner report, for example, equated in importance clinical expertise and scientific evidence. Scientific evidence, to a considerable degree, took "its meaning in the light of the current clinical situation and past clinical experience."[38] Such a view takes for granted the importance of clinical knowledge.

Education as a field of study emerged out of a different context. Johnson points not only to the low prestige attached early on to teaching as a female occupation, but also to the nineteenth-century conventions of female reticence—regarding, among other things, claims to knowledge.[39] Alongside these circumstances was the general view that elementary teachers, in particular, did not need to know much that one teacher could not pass easily to another. Even today, student teachers quickly shed their university learnings in favor of those practices favored by their school mentors.[40]

In education, clinical experience provides a check on the validity of a novice's methods but not a check on the validity of educational research. Indeed, educational researchers have found it necessary to mount massive arguments to convince themselves and (they hope) others that their work is relevant to practice.[41] It appears, however, that such relevance has not been the beckoning star for most professors of education. The words of John Dewey on this matter have been more quoted than observed: "Actual activities in *educating* test the worth of scientific results. They may be scientific in some other field, but not in education until they serve educational purposes, and whether they serve or not can be found out only in practice."[42]

The low regard for clinical knowledge in schools of education, coupled with the low status of teaching, turned the beacon schools toward the academic rather than the professional orientation. After all, the arts and sciences have always been the core of academe. Robert M. Hutchins saw the university as endangered by the intrusion of vocationalism and proposed the relegation of professional schools to institutes at the periphery of his ideal university.[43] For him, education warranted at best only a closet in the inn. But, in largely eschewing teacher education and instead embracing scientific research, the aspiring field of education saw itself eventually with its own table in the arts and sciences section of the Faculty Club.

At the beginning of the century, Dewey advised otherwise. He urged the newly emerging schools and colleges of education to seek lessons from "the matured experience" of other professional callings.[44] After studying ten of the major schools of education, Clifford and Guthrie agree.[45] But in his critique of their positions, Burton Clark foresees schools of education continuing to "muddle along" with an ambiguous and conflicting mission.[46]

Perhaps they will. A clearer, less ambiguous mission will not come easily. And perhaps universities and the nation can afford the muddling along. Meanwhile, however, powerful external forces are shaping the education of educators. Professors and schools of education are minor players. Most universities, not necessarily those with beacon schools of education, soon must make decisions as to the role they wish to play.

There are no compelling models. The relationships built by universities with the elementary and secondary schools fall far short of a romance. Similarly, efforts of their schools of education to carry on a courtship with the arts and sciences go unrequited. The circumstances appear to call for bold innovation.

Reform and Reformers

The scope of schooling and the sheer magnitude of the effort to staff schools have attracted an enormous range of reformers and reform proposals. Because no authorized expertise has been called for, critics and advocates have included the wisest of men and women, angels, fools, and zealots. There has been little cumulative impact, however, even over relatively long periods of time. Something not adequately tried and tested in one era shows up with new clothes in another. "Universities did not lead an intellectual revolution which transformed the training of teachers. The experience in education is better described as a series of local uprisings each decade or so which have had little enduring impact except, perhaps, to clutter the curricular landscape with dead or wounded programs and theories."[47]

One recommendation frequently put forward would put an end to reform in teacher education: Kill it. But as Fenstermacher has pointed out, "Flush it down the drain and it comes crawling back up again."[48] Three proposals have surfaced regularly (only to be met by the "kill it" squad) over the years: a solid general education, few or no education courses, and apprenticeship with a mentor.

In Chapter One, I described the general failure to unite the reform of teacher education and of schools during eras of intense interest in educational reform. In addition, however, I described not only the recent emergence of reform reports to some degree linking both but also a growing awareness on the part of policymakers of the need to expand the lens focused on schooling to include the education of those who work in them. The reports of the Holmes Group[49] and of the Carnegie Forum on Education and the Economy[50] were among those linking teacher education to the task of school reform; and they attracted the attention of significant numbers of these policymakers.

The relationships of the colleges and universities we visited to this nationwide interest of policymakers and others in the reform of teacher education are rather consistent with the norms to which these institutions respond. Administrators and faculty members in the arts and sciences at top-level institutions were generally aware of and interested in the work of the Holmes Group—in part, no doubt, because initial invitations to join had gone out to provosts and deans of selected universities. At the regional universities, these administrators and arts and sciences faculty members appeared to be more aware and interested than were their colleagues in the college of education; they agreed with the strong general-education thrust of the group's report.

It is surprising, however, that both groups were less interested in the report of the Carnegie Forum. Yet the National Board for Professional Teaching Standards, created in response to this report, and its proposed examinations for teachers promise to affect significantly the higher education role in teacher education. College and university administrators shrugged off its importance on learning, however, that the initial selection of board members, in their judgment, seriously underrepresented the academic community. Once more, we saw demonstrated the prevailing view that developments of profound significance to the schools (and ultimately to schools and colleges of education) are somewhat remote to the central concerns of universities. Educational administrators and faculty members—especially those in schools of education—were far more ready to recognize the potential impact of developments in the state's licensing and certification of teachers.

Concluding Comments

Four factors in the contemporary scene become strikingly apparent as one contemplates the direction of and logistics for obviously necessary reform in the education of educators. First, the legacies of the 150-year history of teacher education present an extraordinarily complex and cluttered landscape. Second, judging from the repetitious nature of recommendations to date, and their general ineffectiveness, reformers have been unaware of this complexity. (Or perhaps, aware of and overwhelmed by the complexity, would-be reformers have thrown hand grenades in the hope of hitting whatever unseen logjam was blocking forward movement.) Third, even when particular pieces of the landscape are seen with some clarity, they are still *only* pieces, detached from the whole. Consequently, reform efforts tend to be piecemeal rather than systemic. Fourth, and of great importance, reform efforts in schooling and in the education of those who work in schools are rarely joined. It is in part because of the necessity of making this connection, and past failure to do so, that teacher education has been described, as I noted earlier, as an "unstudied problem."[51]

Chapter Four

The Institutional
and Regulatory Context

❖　❖　❖

> An excellent and self-confident university . . . can
> proudly have within its midst an ebullient and pro-
> ductive faculty group seeking in appropriate ways to
> confront the serious problems of education in
> America.
>
> —*Ira Michael Heyman*[1]

It is remarkable that so enduring an institution as the university has
emerged out of the wanderings and settlings of a few itinerant,
largely self-appointed and self-anointed scholar-teachers. It is
equally remarkable that there emerged from such humble beginnings both the mind-boggling array of colleges and universities that

Note: This chapter draws on one of our technical reports: M. C. Reed, "Leadership, Commitment, and Mission in American Teacher Education: The
Need for Culturally Attuned Organizational Change," Technical Report no.
9 (Seattle: Center for Educational Renewal, College of Education, University
of Washington, 1989); one of our occasional papers: D. L. Ernst, "The Contexts of Policy and Policy Making in Teacher Education," Occasional Paper
no. 11 (Seattle: Center for Educational Renewal, College of Education, University of Washington, 1989); and chapters in two companion books: J. I.
Goodlad, R. Soder, and K. A. Sirotnik (eds.), *The Moral Dimensions of*

characterize the higher education system of the United States and the college teaching profession, once simple but now complex. Even more remarkable, perhaps, is the sharp contrast between the rather simplistic perception of universities and university life held by a large part of the general public and the subtleties and intricacies of the sentiments, understandings, norms, hierarchical arrangements, and languages of the culture on the inside—with some of the most significant elements unrecorded. The best glimpses of life on the inside available to people on the outside have come from the pens of novelists.

Academe and the Public Interest

Most people on the outside see considerable differences among the institutional types in our sample—between, for example, the private liberal arts college and the major public university. A visit to Ellsworth College, one of the liberal arts colleges we surveyed, would confirm for them a common stereotype: rather quiet, unhustled academic life, in and around halls of ivy. And they could not wander far over the grounds and through the buildings of Sherwood University without concluding that this must be what is called a world-class university. But what kind of institution is Central Rutherford State, with its buildings packed into small space, its shoulder-to-shoulder bustle of hurrying students, and (when my colleagues and I were there) its carnival-like ambience? This regional state institution is very unlike another in the same classification, Southwestern Bistwick State, which is, in turn, very similar in ethos to Ellsworth College.

In spite of the apparent differences among institutions of higher learning, these are more of degree than kind. Faculty rank—assistant, associate, and full professor—and progression up the ladder are extremely important in them all. The criteria for promotion

---

Teaching and *Places Where Teachers Are Taught* (San Francisco: Jossey-Bass, 1990). See in particular, in the latter, chap. 7 by L. Eisenmann, "The Influence of Bureaucracy and Markets: Teacher Education in Pennsylvania" and chap. 8 by K. Cruikshank, "Centralization, Competition, and Racism: Teacher Education in Georgia."

are much the same, but the balance among those criteria differs markedly by institutional type (and even between institutions of the same type). There are enormous differences in governance patterns, with faculty members usually close to and very much aware of the more paternal (only recently maternal, even in many former women's colleges) governance role of presidents in the small, especially private, colleges.

With the increased size characteristic of universities, faculty members often feel remote from centers of administrative power. Some university professors have never seen the president; a few have difficulty recalling his or her name. Many feel detached from their employing universities and even campus colleagues, deriving feelings of worth and professional satisfaction from discipline-oriented national and international associations. With research grants coming to them as individuals, they feel free to take them with them to a new setting ("Have grant, will travel")—to which they may feel no greater attachment than the university they just left.

Yet to leave the impression that the above description is of the whole cloth is unfair and misleading. Faculty members at all types of colleges and universities spend an enormous amount of time on institutional governance—from work on campuswide budget and faculty review committees to participation in a seemingly endless array of departmental task forces and other committees. The fact that there is so little reward for this component of the job helps to explain why the work is often unevenly distributed—avoided by some faculty members and assumed by others out of a sense of service or commitment to the institution or because they actually enjoy it. The history of every college and university is marked by the selfless labors of administrators and faculty members, sufficient to ensure a considerable degree of stability and continuity. (Universities are among the oldest and most stable of our institutions.)

We set out to study the education of educators, not the *whole* of higher education or, for that matter, the whole of each college and university in our sample. Nonetheless, the processes of conceptualizing the inquiry and gathering data brought us more and more into the institutional context and to the realization that teacher education cannot be well understood apart from it, any more than it can be well understood apart from the elementary and secondary school context. Our work would have been aided enormously by a previous study of a place called college (or university) comparable to our earlier study of a place called school. Nonetheless, we learned a great deal about the larger setting in each instance as we proceeded, especially from our visits and from the institutional case histories written by our colleagues.[2] These sources serve as a backdrop and are woven into subsequent chapters.

We would have been aided, too, by a more extensive contemporary literature that provided a broad, comprehensive perspective on colleges and universities, the external and internal factors likely to affect higher education profoundly in coming years, and the academic profession. There is, of course, an enormous body of research and writing on the *pieces*. But the task of examining all of these pieces in order to arrive at a synthesis useful to our purposes was beyond the time and resources available to us. We found Ernest Boyer's *College* very useful in our attempts to understand the range of institutions offering undergraduate education and the issues connected with it.[3] And we would probably have looked in vain for a richer account of the academic profession than is provided in Burton Clark's *The Academic Life*.[4] Both books are enlightening, whether one stands outside of academe or spends much of one's life within. As we pursued various themes and perspectives in considerable detail, we were also well served by the many dozens of volumes in the Carnegie series on higher education edited by Clark Kerr.[5] In seeking to understand the ambiguous place of teacher education in schools of education located in major universities—an inquiry begun in this chapter and further developed later—we found useful the long-overdue analysis now available in *Ed School*, by Geraldine Clifford and James Guthrie.[6]

At the time of this writing, there is rapidly growing curiosity outside of universities—especially outside those supported in large part by tax dollars—regarding what goes on inside of them. For governors, legislators, other policymakers, and segments of the business community, the interest goes beyond curiosity into questions of mission, leadership, efficiency, costs, returns, and more. Immunity from scrutiny beyond that of boards of trustees is fast crumbling.

As long as town and gown were largely separated, the pursuit of knowledge viewed generally to be somewhat disconnected from practical affairs, the costs low and largely hidden from public scrutiny, and professors close to the clergy in impoverishment, colleges and universities were left to conduct their little-understood business without attracting much attention. But all of these conditions are of the past. The changes that have occurred, together with the dissipation of the mystique surrounding higher education, have profound implications for tomorrow's universities and all those who work in them. Unfortunately, the rapid growth in public interest is not yet accompanied by equally rapid growth in public understanding.

In his introduction to *The Academic Life,* Clark states the following: "If individuals cannot get anywhere without some book learning, then the occupations richest in intellectual content move to the center of the stage. It follows that those who seek to understand modern society can hardly know too much about the academic profession; yet inquiry and insight have lagged.[7]

In coming years, intrusions into academe from the outside will far exceed public enlightenment about the role that colleges and universities have played in our society and should play in the future. There are no clear models of institutional organization and conduct in the surrounding society that apply neatly to higher education, largely because there are no other institutions charged with the same mission. Yet there are principles and concepts of organization, administration, and leadership that apply to most institutions and that may be expected to apply fairly to universities. Unfortunately, it will often be to the application of these principles and concepts in other institutions—rather than to the concepts and principles themselves—that critics will turn. We saw much of this in the school reform initiatives of the 1980s. Thus colleges and universities could be in for bumpy times well before the twenty-first century is ushered in.

Difficult though the coming years will probably be for higher education, I am cautiously optimistic about the possibly positive fallout for teacher education. First, the present status and neglect of teaching appear to be attracting on many campuses the attention of both administrators and faculty members. As a result, there is likely to be a fresh focus on teaching inside the university.[8] That this focus will affect the mission and emphases of regional universities more than of the major research-oriented universities is probably a safe bet. Nonetheless, the latter group is likely to send a powerful message regarding renewed commitment to the oldest university function. Such a development, if it occurs, will carry with it the possibility of benefiting the function of preparing teachers for the nation's schools, given the natural connections between teaching and preparing people to teach.

Second, no matter how grandiose is the stated mission of a university seeking to be known as world-class, teacher education is a homegrown, homefed, local enterprise that connects with nearby communities, homes, and families—in other words, with the citizens whose views can make or break the political careers of their representatives in the statehouse. Canny boards of trustees and their appointed presidents will surely come to appreciate the significance of this fact and use it to the advantage of their institutions. Universities will continue to reach for the prestige and (usually) financial returns that come with the successful recruitment of outstanding researchers from competing institutions. But increasingly, public universities will find it expedient to foster and draw attention to programs and activities more visibly responsive to local needs. Many already have made productive use of their schools of agriculture, fishery, forestry, mining, and business in their public relations endeavors and in their budget appeals to state legislatures. The connection between the activities of these schools and the economic health of the state and local community is not difficult to explain. Likewise, it may not be difficult to explain the relationship between producing a supply of good teachers and the educational health of the state and community. I predict that, in coming years, universities will find it not only expedient to be seen as concerned about the welfare of the lower schools but shameful to be viewed as uncaring and uninvolved.

Competition for resources is fierce and becoming fiercer— with public universities competing with private universities in financial sectors once left to the latter. In seeking their basic operating budgets, however, the former will continue to rely on public funding, and they will be pushed harder and harder to justify their requests. In this context, making dominant and visible the better selection and education of schoolteachers—a function of great public importance that is easy for legislators to understand and support—may be precisely what is required to gain related support for those many other enterprises much valued by universities but little understood by the general public. Given the neglect and shoestring budgets of teacher education in the past, the commitment, leadership, and dollars required for it to go first class may be perceived on all sides as gratifyingly modest.

The evolving context of higher education implied above provides no guarantee that the teacher education enterprise in colleges and universities will prosper, however. Chapter Three developed the thesis that its position and status have been precarious since the opening of the first normal schools a century and a half ago. Subsequent chapters support the thesis that the enterprise remains weak today. Given skepticism regarding its efficacy among many people on the outside, including legislators and even teachers, and its marginal status within many universities, teacher education could be lopped off as part of the selective pruning effected as these institutions seek to become leaner and better. The number of individuals and groups proposing and trying alternatives—from mentoring arrangements that bypass college- and university-based programs to examinations that replace all of the licensing, certifying, and accrediting procedures traditionally required for passing through the gates—has never been larger or more visible. Will the scales of teacher education tip toward the entrepreneurial, proprietary medical model of the early years of this century so vigorously attacked by Abraham Flexner or toward the university model now chosen by all the major professions? The balance is a delicate one.

My unwavering position has been stated both implicitly and explicitly in the preceding chapters: The proper initial and continuing education of a schoolteacher takes place in a scholarly setting, in a program vastly different from those generally prevailing today—one that ensures the blending of the theoretical and the practical through a unique joining of school and university cultures. Now that the data of the study reported here are in and my colleagues and I have studied them carefully, I am convinced and shall argue that neither those who call themselves teacher educators nor schools, colleges, and departments of education (SCDEs) alone can bring off what is required. Others (both within and outside the academic community) must join in creating the necessary conditions. I am equally convinced, however, that if teacher educators—especially their designated leaders—are not courageously, energetically, and creatively proactive and perceived to be close to the public interest, these others will not rise adequately to the tasks and the conditions will fall short of what is necessary.

Life may be for most of us, as Irwin Edman once wrote, "what someone described music to be for the uninitiated, 'a drowsy reverie interrupted by nervous thrills.'"[9] Many—probably most—teacher educators came into teaching for the very best of reasons (see Chapter Six). They have experienced the neglect, frustration, and status deprivation of the occupation. In effect, they have been initiated, and thus they have no excuse for lapsing into the drowsy reverie of the uninitiated. They must bring to the essentially moral challenge of renewing teacher education their own commitment and vigor as well as all those individuals and agencies necessary to success. The necessary but not sufficient conditions are clarity of mission, breadth and depth of commitment, and tough-minded, skillful leadership. Important to the maximization of these are enlightened regulatory circumstances.

Institutional Factors That Affect Teacher Education

A major purpose of this chapter is to provide some insight into the mission, leadership, and commitment of the colleges and universities in our sample and the impact of these factors on the health and well-being of their programs of educating educators for the schools. Are their missions clear? Do their respective cultures appear to be well positioned for goal attainment? To what degree are cultural missions and meanings shared on the inside, and to what degree are these compatible with expectations on the outside? What appears to be the nature and depth of institutional and leadership commitment to teacher education? What is the fit between institutional culture as a whole and the SCDE? What is the fit between both of these together and programs for the education of educators?

The primary data are drawn from documents sent to us or collected on-site and from interviews with presidents, provosts, deans, and some faculty members. Because these fall far short of telling the full story of what interests us here, however, we only begin the story. It is revisited in subsequent chapters, primarily from the perspective of students and faculty members in teacher education. Similarly, the hypotheses advanced here reappear later. Ultimately, conclusions and generalizations emerge as a result of the degree to which all of the data examined converge to produce the repetitive patterns of a patchwork quilt.

The voluminous body of material we collected—hundreds of documents and thousands of pages of field notes—cannot be reduced to the limited confines of these pages. I cannot both spare the reader the tedium of working through the whole and preserve his or her opportunity to render independent judgment. The reader desiring to reserve some measure of independence in coming to conclusions is urged to examine the documents listed at the beginning of this chapter and in Appendix A. But even this effort will fall short, because most of this part of the story is best revealed in the data gathered from interviews—from being there on the campuses of the colleges and universities in our sample. I suggest, then, that the reader suspend judgment and proceed hypothetically, as I endeavor to do. In later chapters, I add data more readily put before the reader—faculty and student responses to the many survey questions. These generally support the hypotheses formulated here.

Clarity of Mission. Webster's *Third New International* Dictionary begins its definition of *mission* in religious and humanitarian terms—terms very appropriate to the beginnings and subsequent development of colleges and universities and virtually essential to the education of teachers for our schools. Statements of mission define the central function of an institution and frame the responsibilities of those persons encompassed by it. They guide and drive the work of those entrusted with the institution's stewardship, providing criteria for including some activities and excluding others. Clarity of mission helps those on the outside to understand what the institution seeks to do and is doing and to come to some conclusions about omissions and commissions. A compelling mission might be expected to attract supporters and, in the case of universities, professors and students. Vague, hollow, or nonexistent statements of mission leave people on both the inside and the outside to make up whatever they wish about the institution's functions and worth. Broad slogans such as "We educate" or "We are committed to excellence" appeal to the faith in education of only a very small audience.

Various omissions and commissions in the mission documents we read and in the statements of those interviewed suggest two hypotheses. First, there is among those who speak for institutions of higher learning a strong belief either that there is little need to articulate their mission clearly or that their activities bespeak the mission. Perhaps these leaders assume that education is widely regarded as good and that their college or university shares in the resulting dividends. Second, there is little in these omissions and commissions to suggest that the education of educators for the schools is a top priority. Indeed, this aspect of mission appears to be well back from center stage in most of the institutions in our sample.

Mission statements in the documents of seven institutions were sufficiently clear, we concluded, to provide both a good deal of understanding to those on the outside (suggested earlier as desirable) and considerable guidance to those at work on the inside. Those from another six appeared sufficient to provide some of this understanding and guidance but fell short of the precision and clarity necessary to usefulness in making clear distinctions between appropriate and inappropriate activities. Statements from fifteen might as well have gone unwritten. Indeed, the one remaining institution sidestepped the exercise, skipping the matter of a written mission and even the brief history almost invariably provided, and went straight to a listing of its administrative officers, faculty, and services.

At the low end of quality were statements that had nothing to do with mission regardless of the heading: references to famous alumni, public figures who had appeared on campus for various reasons, distinguished faculty members, outstanding facilities, advantageous locations, and more. A step up were statements regarding the discovery and transmittal of knowledge, as well as the role of wisdom and values in the survival of present and future generations. Missing at both these levels, however, were affirmations of what the university actually stood for and strived to attain. Further up on a scale of quality were the documents of several colleges and universities that spoke to programmatic and instructional commitments in phrases such as "comprehensive curriculum made up of a broad range of degree programs based upon the needs of students and social demands" and "improvement of instructional quality via modifications of teaching strategies." Yet either of these—and the sort of statements mentioned earlier in the paragraph—could have been written for *any* institution in our sample and probably for all other U.S. colleges and universities.

Although we found interesting and sometimes even compelling most of the short histories submitted, the sections headed "mission" were commonly vague, abstract, dull, or all of these. Sometimes, however, we were agreeably surprised by succinct statements conveying a great deal: "The mission of Sterling College is to serve humanity by inspiring and educating students regardless of their economic status. Sterling emphasizes a comprehensive educational program committed to high academic standards, Christian values, and practical work experience in a distinctive environment of natural beauty." Needless to say, one of the first questions I asked of an administrative officer was whether Sterling College admitted any non-Christian students and employed any non-Christian faculty members. Given the following statement in the same document, we sought to find out whether teaching enjoyed the attention implied: "Consequently, while research, publication, and other evidence of scholarship are valued, our faculty and staff dedicate themselves primarily to teaching effectively." We probed deeply into the degree to which the following statement was a reasonably accurate description of reality: "The individual permeates our principles."

We found these statements and others submitted by Sterling extremely useful as we talked with administrators, faculty members, and students about their responsibilities and activities: the place of Christian values in policies and practices, the place of teaching in the reward structure, and the individual attention perceived by students. Unfortunately, a rather small minority of the institutions in our sample sent us this sort of mission statement, and our visits to others failed to turn up what was missing in documents sent in advance of our coming.

We rated mission statements of the twenty-nine colleges and universities in our sample with respect to the clarity and substance of their articulation of the following: what education is, the particular educational contribution of the institution, and the qualities sought in candidates and to be developed in students. In judging quality, we gave additional credit when historical accounts or descriptions of general studies added to our understanding of institutional purpose and belief. After completing the review of documents for each, we rated its mission statement or statements from 0 to 3, a process that resulted in the following breakdown: one with none (an overall rating of 0), fifteen that provided little or no understanding to persons on the outside or potential for guiding those within (1), six that provided a measure of understanding and guidance (2), and seven that reflected a serious effort to define what the institution is about (3). We then reassembled all twenty-nine into the six classifications of the sample and attached to each college or university the rating already assigned. The results appear in Table 2.

Overall, the private group fared best with respect to our view of their mission statements—particularly the liberal arts colleges, all four of which appear in the top category. We disagreed over whether Dorsey should be rated 2 or 3 and finally agreed on 3. None

Table 2. Ratings of Mission Statements for Colleges and Universities Grouped by Types.

Flagship Public	Major Public	Regional Public
3 Sherwood	0 Jewel	1 Central Rutherford
1 Vulcan	1 Forest	2 Northern Horizon
1 Kenmore	1 Underhill	1 Eastern Oliver
1 Northwood	1 Telegraph	1 Southern Inverness
	1 Legend	2 Southwestern Bistwick
		2 Northwestern Prairie
		2 Western Willis

Major Private	Regional Private	Liberal Arts Private
3 Revere	2 Broadmoor	3 Dorsey
1 Quadra	1 Gerald	3 Ellsworth
2 Mainstream	1 Pilgrim	3 Lakeview
1 Ivy	1 Alton	3 Sterling
3 Merrett		

of the major public universities was rated 3; indeed, one rated 0 and the others only 1. Revere, which barely warrants classification as a major private university, clearly deserved a rating of 3. We were in some disagreement over Merrett and Sherwood Universities, a major private and a flagship university, respectively, but finally agreed on 3. All seven of those rated 3 employed a good deal of the "boilerplate" language of general, liberal education. In other words, they wrote what any of the twenty-nine might have written, had these thought a statement of mission to be important or necessary. But they also added something growing out of the unique history of the institution (for example, the importance of religious values) or pertaining to a perceived necessity (such as good teaching or deep concern for individual students).

The consistency among the liberal arts colleges is a result, no doubt, of these institutions' not expanding much beyond their long-term functions of educating undergraduates in a single college. There is *the* dean presiding over this one function, not a dozen deans presiding over as many functions (including a dean of arts and sciences presiding over both the general education and preprofessional functions that characterize the multipurpose university). In Chapter Six, we see that students in these colleges, more than those in universities, identified strongly with the institution—above their identification with the teacher education program in which all polled were enrolled.

The low to moderate ratings of the regional public universities probably reflect the uncertainty of mission that has come with their transition from normal schools or, in the case of several that were never normal schools, their passage from a heavy emphasis on teacher education to more diverse pursuits. In my judgment, the low ratings of the regional private universities reflect the entrepreneurial role they have played in recent years for purposes of maintaining enrollments. The low ratings of the major and flagship public universities (with one exception) may be the result of their diversification and division into professional schools, each with its own mission. Or perhaps it is simply that the responsible people in each believe that the status and academic standing of their university is such that little explanation or articulation of mission is called for—it is generally assumed. The speculations above are strengthened by the addition of data and impressions reported below and in subsequent chapters.

It is interesting to note that Merrett University advanced only recently to its classification as a major university after a rather long history as a strong regional university—one that took pride primarily in its undergraduate curriculum and teaching and had only a few professional schools and divisions. Even today its publications announce the liberal arts college to be the core of the whole, and the language of its mission corresponds closely to that of the four liberal arts colleges. With a physical education program focused on the health and fitness of individuals and interinstitutional athletics confined to such sports as wrestling, swimming, and golf, Merrett University follows in the tradition of the University of Chicago.[10]

Although the sections of the documents emphasizing mission focused primarily on each institution's overall educational emphases—and these are what we looked for—there were often references to fields, programs, or even schools of perceived strength. None of these references was to the school, college, or department of education, however, although two of our sample institutions—both regional state universities—referred to their tradition of and continuing obligation to teacher education. Neither the mission statement nor the history of one of the earliest normal schools in the country— one that remained so for many decades and earned a considerable reputation as one of the best—mentioned this beginning and tradition. Indeed, it rather conspicuously announced its founding as a public institution of higher education, although it did admit in another section to graduates holding positions in education. Presumably, there are regional state universities that still proudly announce their normal-school beginnings, but for those in our sample the rite of passage referred to in Chapter Three appears to have been successfully accomplished—their normal-school beginnings have been left far behind.

The data and impressions we gained in interviews with presidents, provosts, and academic deans follow rather closely the patterns introduced above, except that the place of teacher education in the liberal arts colleges came out much stronger than implied by omissions in their documents. All four liberal arts presidents—two women and two men—spoke with enthusiasm about the centrality of teaching, the commitment of faculty to teaching and students, the steadily improving quality of the student body, and more. The two women spoke of great women who had preceded them at some time in the college's history and of their own efforts to sustain traditions established early on. All four were obviously accustomed to speaking about their colleges to varied groups and to extolling the virtues of the institutions over which they presided.

All four unequivocally supported a teacher education mission, viewing it as necessarily linked and compatible with their emphasis on quality teaching and the undergraduate general-education mission. All four were critical of teacher education as conducted elsewhere and of education as a field of study but gave high marks to their own faculty members in education, some of whom taught courses accepted as general-education electives. Although there was some skepticism among faculty members in teacher education regarding the amount of trust to be placed in these statements, they regarded the institutional context as generally favorable to their endeavors. The liberal arts colleges are the only institutions in our sample for which this generalization regarding context can be made rather confidently for an entire group.

Other generalizations can be made about the universities, however. Had I chosen to linger for very long on philosophical or educational issues pertaining to the mission of higher education in general or the overarching mission of a particular university, my interviews with most of the central administrators in the universities would have been much shorter than they turned out to be. In all fairness, most had been reasonably well briefed prior to the interviews regarding the nature of our study, and all had crowded schedules and wanted to get quickly to what they believed to be my particular interests; so most of our time was devoted to questions pertaining to their SCDE and their teacher education program. Nonetheless, the singularity of mission and the centrality of a very few functions that presidents, provosts, and/or academic deans of the liberal arts colleges revealed in discussions of their institutions were almost entirely missing in discussions with university administrators.

The parallel administrators in the several types of universities responded quite quickly and comfortably to questions of balance among research, teaching, and service and to queries regarding fields of strength, emphasis, and anticipated growth. Although the presidents and provosts in the regional private universities viewed their institutions as having increased the research emphasis in recent years and being likely to increase it more in coming years, they were virtually unanimous in proclaiming the importance of teaching now and in the future. Those in the regional public universities, on the other hand, more often viewed research as needing to be expanded soon and rapidly—but not at the expense of teaching. There were exceptions, however. The president at Southwestern Bistwick—known for his long and deep commitment to teacher education—viewed the narrow focus of much current research as detrimental to the teaching and teacher education functions.

In several instances, the academic vice-president or provost appeared to be the prime messenger regarding the growing importance of research and scholarly work on the university campus. Commonly, too, he or she appeared to be in a position of a good deal of authority in defining the meaning of this emphasis, regardless of the degree of faculty involvement. The ground rules for fulfilling this emphasis were not usually spelled out, although the provost was in a position to determine if and how they would be (and to determine the criteria used in judging conformity to the ground rules). Not surprisingly, the institutional dissonance on the regional campuses regarding the absolute and relative place of the several faculty functions—research, teaching, and service—was considerable, varying only in degree.

The word *dissonance* fails to describe this important part of the ethos of the major private, public, and flagship universities. The problem surrounding the dominance of scholarly work appeared to be more one of faculty adjustment than of ambiguity; research reigns supreme. Nonetheless, some presidents, provosts, and deans did express worry over decline in attention to teaching—particularly over the degree to which professors with grants were "buying out" part of their teaching load. But most, though expecting scholarly work of all faculty members, reported recent steps to reemphasize the importance of teaching.

Additionally, they reported that the problems of adjusting to rapidly increasing research demands over the past decade or so were declining with the retirement of the faculty members most affected. Whereas in most of the regionals there was no clear alignment of expectations and specifications of appropriate, rewarded work, this alignment was not much at issue in the majors. (We revisit this matter later, particularly as it appears to affect faculty members, students, and programs in teacher education.)

My queries to key university administrative officers regarding peaks of excellence and commitment, usually coming early in the interviews, proved to be extraordinarily revealing and useful. (I passed quickly over these in the liberal arts colleges, except with respect to the place of teacher education, because the responses invariably singled out a component of the general education mission—a distinguished department in the arts and sciences or, the quality of collegewide programs in the arts.) For the sample as a whole, the person interviewed ran out of his or her list of strengths without mentioning either the SCDE or teacher education in all but a few instances.

Not surprisingly, the presidents and academic vice-presidents of the major universities hesitated to identify any one field or professional school. More often, they referred to the overall strengths of departments in the academic disciplines and then singled out a group: the physical sciences or the humanities or the health sciences. Sometimes they included an interdisciplinary institute, almost always in the physical sciences, that enjoyed substantial federal funding. Almost always some school—law, engineering, business—was at the forefront of a current funding drive. Medicine was not included, perhaps because it had figured significantly in an earlier period of development or because the continued need for funds to ensure stability was taken as a given.

In the regional public and private universities, recent and pending development efforts were almost invariably focused on much narrower targets—and on business education more than any other area. During the 1970s in particular, when regional institutions of higher learning were struggling to maintain enrollments and budgets—some suffering from significant declines in enrollees in teacher education programs—most of those in our sample became entrepreneurial, reaching out into other locations with new programs in the paraprofessions and with extensions of campus programs in fields such as law and business and even the arts and sciences. These moves met with mixed success. But expansion in business coincided with and probably helped stimulate the growing attractiveness for employment in this area that marked the late 1970s and the 1980s. As a result, the status of the business school on campus rose markedly. At one regional public university we visited, the business school building under construction would exceed in size and height the education building that had dominated since the 1950s.

It was clear from most of our interviews that whatever had been going up in university mission over the past two decades had been balanced by the SCDE and teacher education going down. (We probe a little more deeply into some nuances of this decline in the succeeding section.) Clearly, too, the recent gradual turnaround in teacher education enrollments on virtually every campus was beginning to have a positive impact on its place in the future of the institution. It is sobering to contemplate the degree to which institutions of higher learning are market-driven.

There were no indications, however (despite teacher education enrollment increases), that current thinking and planning will soon redirect institutional mission toward an SCDE and teacher education star that is about to emerge from behind scurrying clouds—with one notable exception. The president of an essentially regional public university recently classified as major (primarily because of substantial federal funding for research and development in just a few fields) viewed some recent developments in his state as presenting a unique opportunity.[11] He hoped to return teacher education to the center, where it had once been. "I would rather this university be known for the outstanding quality of its education programs for schoolteachers and administrators," he told me, "than be just one more undistinguished midrange university."

The foregoing discussion has focused on institutional mission and the place of teacher education in it, omitting the context provided by the mission of the school, college, or department of education. This omission is deliberate. Data regarding faculty members (Chapter Five), students (Chapter Six), and programs in teacher education (Chapter Seven) help considerably to illuminate the impact of the SCDE context. Consequently, I leave most of this part of the story to unfold in these later chapters. The succeeding section of this chapter deals with elusive indicators of administrative leadership and commitment that appear to bear on the fulfillment of mission. Some data on the tenure of deans of education, together with impressions gained in interviews, illuminate the degree to which the SCDEs in our sample appear to provide a context hospitable to teacher education.

The picture beginning to emerge is that the missions of departments of education and teacher education in the liberal arts colleges are virtually one and the same; while in the major private and public flagship universities, the mission of teacher education in the schools of education more often than not takes a back seat to other functions and activities. In the regionals, the uncertainty characterizing the place of teacher education reflects the considerable ambiguity in mission of both the institutions as total entities and the schools and colleges of education within them.

Administrative Stability. As I have noted, the documents made available to us were sufficiently provocative in their omissions and commissions to suggest questions for further probing through interviews. They told us very little, however, about the commitment of designated leaders and the degree to which their exercise of leadership might be substituting for the absence of clear mission statements. The interviews held promise for getting the necessary information. Some repetitions soon suggested patterns worth exploring through questions in addition to those planned initially.

One of the patterns that appeared early on to be emerging was instability in the tenure of key administrators: the president, academic vice-president or provost, dean of arts and sciences, and dean of education. Because instability is such a relative concept, it is difficult to attach comparative meaning—to determine whether it is dangerous instability, of no great significance, or whatever. Checking the data available to us, we concluded that 11 of these positions out of a total of 116 (4 per institution times 29) were occupied by someone in "acting" status during the year of our visit (1987–88). Is this significant? It is of interest that we had to go back in the records to the 1980–81 academic year to find a higher figure. The frequency with which one of these four positions was occupied by an acting official for the intervening years ranged from only 2 to a high of 6, with 4 the mode. In the year after our visit, 1988–89, 6 positions were filled in an acting capacity and 3 were vacant. It appears that 1987–88 was an unusual year, with 1988–89 not far behind.

In our reading of the short histories usually contained in the documents, and our pursuit on campus of the question of leadership stability, a pattern of earlier stability followed by recent instability emerged. We checked back over a twenty-four-year period—1965–66 to 1988–89—and then examined these years in clusters of six sequential years. We discovered that 18 of the positions were either vacant (5) or occupied by someone in acting status (13) during the six-year period from 1965–66 through 1970–71. There was an increase to 24—5 vacant and 19 acting—for the next six-year period. Only twice during these twelve years did this total reach 6 for a single year.

The picture changed markedly for the six-year period beginning in 1977–78 and concluding in 1982–83: 45 acting and 4 vacant for a total of 49. This total, which exceeds the total of 42 for the preceding twelve-year period, declined to 36—32 acting and 4 vacant—for the six-year period of 1983–84 to 1988–89. In summary, the total number of positions vacant or filled by someone in an acting capacity for the most recent twelve-year period was double the total for the previous twelve.

I will return shortly to a breakdown of the four positions of president, provost (or academic vice-president), dean of arts and sciences, and dean of education. First, however, I note a revolving-door syndrome of a different sort for the year of our visit—a syndrome that could not be reliably checked out over a long period of time. As we moved from campus to campus, we became more and more aware of the number of administrators in the above categories who had recently arrived or were about to leave. In several instances, an individual was reported by faculty members to be in some difficulty and "on the way out." If some of these presumptions turned out to be correct predictions, the picture of turnover is worse than is depicted in the breakdown below. Our data and interviews revealed an extraordinary picture of movement with respect to the top leadership position in education and teacher education. The president of Northwood had arrived only recently, the president of Jewel State

was just back from an extended leave, and the president of Mainstream was still enjoying a year of leave. The president of Legend
State had just resigned, and the presidents of Southwestern Bistwick, Gerald, and Central Rutherford were in their last year.

For a variety of reasons, the deans of education at Sherwood,
Vulcan, Telegraph State, and Mainstream were in their last year,
and the plans of two others for the coming year were far from clear.
In their first year were the deans of education at Northern Horizon,
Southern Inverness, Western Willis, Ivy, and Ellsworth. It was not
clear whether the dean at Jewel State was an interim appointment
or a likely prospect for the announced vacancy. In two instances, a
dean and chairperson (reporting directly to the provost) had just
switched positions with the former dean and chair under the rules of
a campus rotating policy.

In progressing through our schedule of visits, I became increasingly aware of the frequency with which the provost or academic vice-president apologized for his or her potential inability to
respond to my questions because of newness to the job. Similarly,
faculty members (particularly those in the regionals) often referred
to their "new" provost and to problems in figuring out his or her
expectations and intentions. The majority of these new leaders had
been recruited from the outside, although it was more common for
the academic vice-president or provost to be recruited from the inside in the major universities than in the regionals. Several of the
longer-term incumbents were in their last year.

As our hard data reveal, the job of provost or academic vice-
president not only had the highest turnover rate among the four
positions for 1987–88 but also, on the average, for the preceding
quarter-century—24 percent and 21 percent, respectively. In other
words, about one in four of the provosts holding office in 1987–88
was no longer there the following year. Looked at from another
perspective, the average length of tenure in this position over
twenty-five years was 4.7 years—the shortest of the four posts.

In our sample, the position of president proved to be the
most stable. The average tenure over the past twenty-five years has
been almost 8 years. Further, this position was filled most rapidly
when vacated—and rarely with someone of acting status. The average tenure of education deans over this period was 6.6 years, but this

was the position most frequently filled on an acting basis or left vacant. (Unfortunately, we did not secure data to tell us whether this situation is unique to the deanship in education or characteristic of the professional school deanship generally.) Deans of arts and sciences averaged 5.3 years in the job, and the post ranked just behind that of dean of education in being filled on an acting basis. However, the job ranked next to that of the presidency in being filled promptly.

Whereas the data presented earlier on vacant and temporarily filled positions reveal a marked increase over the past dozen years (as compared with the preceding dozen years), no such differences can be noted for length of tenure and turnover rate. For the twenty-four-year period, the average turnover rate of nearly 11 percent for presidents, 21 percent for provosts, nearly 18 percent for deans of arts and sciences, and almost 16 percent for deans of education also turns out to be the mode.[12] The change over the quarter-century, then, pertains only to the growing tendency to take longer to make a permanent appointment—a generalization that does not hold for the presidency. It is conceivable that the cumbersome process of seeking candidates nationwide for even a relatively low-level administrative post, advertising the position over a period of months, and then interviewing a range of candidates—all part of affirmative action—accounts for most of the differences in today's and yesterday's statistics regarding unfilled or temporarily filled positions.

Much more significant than the data for any one office, however, is the degree to which a given president, provost, and dean of education experience concurrent tenure. The early histories of several institutions in our sample are replete with chronicles of a normal-school or university president who picked someone to head the teacher education program (and perhaps a demonstration school as well) and of their joint accomplishments over many years. There are similar accounts of long-term stability of leadership during the first few decades of the twentieth century. World War II and subsequent growth in higher education and in mobility generally changed all that. Presidents moved from regional to major universities; provosts were the natural candidates for the presidencies thus left open or in the new universities being created. Deans of education moved from less to more prestigious institutions.

A dean with an average tenure of fewer than 7 years, reporting to a provost with an average tenure of fewer than 5 years, reporting to a president with an average of fewer than 8 years, creates a chain whose links are likely to be broken with greater frequency than these statistics by themselves suggest. This became sharply apparent as we moved from institution to institution. A president in office for the past 8 years, deeply immersed in annual budget negotiations with the legislature, had just turned over internal academic responsibilities to the new provost, who had before him the promotion recommendations of the dean of education, who had just announced his resignation. Elsewhere (to illustrate virtually *all* the links broken), the academic vice-president, then serving as acting president, was continuing with previous efforts to shape up the school of education, in tandem with the acting academic vice-president who was temporarily replacing him—but the dean of education had had enough and was about to abandon ship.

The data on percentage of turnover, length of tenure, and unfilled and temporarily filled positions create for me some unease regarding the stability of leadership in colleges and universities— particularly when coupled with the general lack of clarity of mission. But there is no way of comparing all of this, no norms against which stability and instability might be judged and from which conclusions might be drawn. Far more revealing is the way these circumstances occur and play themselves out, defying all possible interpretation of the numbers, in individual institutions and groups of institutions. For example, although the data show recent tenure of 8, 7, 4, and 4 years, respectively, for the current president, provost, dean of arts and sciences, and dean of education in a major university, they tell us nothing about the devastating consequences of there having been as many deans of education as years over a long preceding period—and the position of academic vice-president had been only slightly more stable. In another university in our sample, five of the seven major administrative positions from president to dean of education were vacant or occupied by an individual in his or her first or last year, or filled with acting personnel at the time of our visit, and the academic vice-president (the senior official in a nonacting capacity) was in his second year. I have to wonder about that institution's prospects for decisive action, particularly in areas of controversy.

Among our six categories of institution, the private liberal arts colleges come out ahead with respect to stability in administrative leadership, judged from the several perspectives presented so far. Over the last quarter-century, the average length of tenure for the four positions is 7.5 years. The figures decline as follows for the other five groups: 7.2 for the private regionals, 6.5 for the private majors, 5.9 for the public majors, 5.7 for the public regionals, and 5.6 for the public flagships. The differences become more marked from the perspective of vacant or temporarily filled leadership positions over this period of time: only ten for the liberal arts colleges, but the numbers climb from fifteen for the public flagships, to eighteen for the public majors, twenty for the private regionals, thirty for the private majors, and forty for the public regionals.

At the extremes, our data support the picture of stability in mission and leadership among the liberal arts colleges and instability among the public regionals, the latter condition presumably part and parcel of rapid transition from principally teacher-preparing to multipurpose institutions. In a small sample of this kind, there is little point in probing much further into quantitative indices, because individual cases—such as long tenures of 26 years for a dean and chair of education, respectively, in a private regional university and a private liberal arts college—distort the averages of the still-smaller groupings of institutions. But perhaps two observations are worth pulling out: first, the consistently below-average tenure for the deans of education in the regional public universities (a short time in the saddle seems to have accompanied the rather rough ride of these universities from normal-school to university status), and second, the relatively short tenure across all types, noted earlier, of academic vice-presidents or provosts.

This second condition presents a problem for education deans whose visions and plans depend for their implementation on the approval of the provost. In view of the markedly longer tenure of presidents—both overall and for all types of institutions—and the greater rapidity with which presidential vacancies are filled, it is the canny dean who keeps the president fully informed as to visions and plans and who greets his or her successor early and warmly. It is the wise and prescient dean who builds the mission of the programs for which he or she is responsible into the fabric of the institution.

Administrative Coordination. What we found out frequently, mostly during interviews, is that only a few deans or chairpersons were canny, let alone wise and prescient, in this important arena of leadership. The president and dean at Underhill University, closely linked in commitment to a strongly research-oriented school of education for the future, were among the wise. Together they had done what was necessary to bring in a nationally recognized scholar who was now well funded from both institutional and extramural resources. Administrators and faculty members in the school were busily responding to requests for proposals from an array of funding agencies. Faculty members marveled at the unprecedented support from central administration and the excellent communication between the president and the dean. Yet good communication does not ensure good programming. Some faculty members worried about the long-standing traditional orientation to teaching and teacher education in the increasingly research-driven context. A predicted massive shortage of teachers in the surrounding urban school district for the 1990s caused others to wonder if the current thrust was in the institution's best interests.

Although Underhill provided our best example of a president and dean of education working in tandem, the presidents of several other universities appeared to be quite well informed by and supportive of their deans or chairs: Legend State, Central Rutherford, Southwestern Bistwick, Northwestern Prairie, Merrett, Gerald, and Pilgrim. However, both knowledge and support on the part of the president appeared to become fuzzy once our interview got into plans, issues, or problems of the school or college of education as an entity. Indeed, contradictions with respect to mission and priorities often appeared when we compared the responses of president and dean. The rather favorable picture of communication and understanding conveyed by the presidents of the liberal arts colleges reflected the department and program of education and teacher education as a whole (rather than focusing on the chairperson). These presidents viewed teacher education as intimately woven into the fabric of the arts and sciences and evaluated it and the chairperson according to the degree of fit with this image.

We encountered some striking instances of dissonance. Because identification of institutions and individuals serves no good purpose here, not even the fictitious names need to be used. At a major state university, the president and dean of education never spoke to one another unless circumstances forced interaction. The dean made derisive comments about the president at least a half-dozen times in the course of an hour. At a regional state university, the dean made clear to me that he never tries to tell the president anything, because the president does not listen; the president calls the shots solo. I had several opportunities, including an hour-long interview, to observe this president, and what I saw supported what the dean had told me.

In a public flagship university, the president (then in his second year) had asked the deans of all schools for a short statement of plans for the future—nothing elaborate, but enough to help him identify the needs, problems, and aspirations of each unit. A year later the dean of education was the only dean who had not responded. This same dean told me that the president had no interest in the school of education. "Why do you say that?" I asked. "Because in a year and a half, he has not come to visit me," he replied! Please, dean, when the new president or provost arrives, get on his or her calendar quickly—and often. And do not just present your laundry list of needs. Tell him or her what your unit is trying to do, what is good about it, and what you are doing to make it better—and suggest how he or she can help in the near future.

I have in my notes and my head dozens of similarly revealing anecdotes. Instead of recounting more, I conclude this section with a few general observations emerging from the whole.

First, most of the SCDEs in our sample, particularly in the regional universities, had come through bumpy times in the 1970s and into the 1980s—bumpier times, for the most part, than were experienced by the institution as a whole. Second, in the aftermath of these hard times, many of these SCDEs displayed an almost crippling bitterness that often created faculty distrust of the administration and a tendency on the part of education deans to remain somewhat isolated and aloof from the president and provost—usually

successors to the administrators who effected the earlier cuts (and
sometimes attacks). Third, there appeared to be a general lack of
awareness—with notable exceptions, of course—among SCDE administrators of the degree to which their presidents and provosts
were both aware of agitations for reform in schooling and teacher
education and unclear about what (if anything) their institutions
should do in these areas. These overall administrators generally
appeared to be obtaining no sense of direction from their education
dean. Fourth, there was considerable puzzlement among central administrators—and academic deans and faculty members, for that
matter—as to what their schools and colleges of education do and
should do. The degree of such puzzlement appeared to be quite
directly proportional to the size and research orientation of the university. These people were particularly puzzled about the many
things these units do that are not clearly connected to preparing
teachers and administrators, and they wondered why the faculty in
education is not more demonstrably involved in ensuring that the
lower schools teach children to read, write, and spell (by staffing
them with good teachers).

There was an extraordinary mismatch between the above observations and the current behavior of many of the SCDEs in our
sample. First, there appeared to be a paucity of comprehensive planning in most of the SCDEs regarding growing enrollments, the
reality or prospect of new positions, and pending retirements in an
aging faculty—despite the eagerness of presidents and provosts to
receive such plans. Many of the SCDEs were recruiting, but almost
invariably to fill a position to be vacated or a position added to cope
with increasing enrollment in a given area; they were not recruiting
out of a plan geared to changing circumstances in the external
world or to visions of tomorrow. The combination of new positions
and pending vacancies, in some settings representing a 30 to 40
percent turnover of faculty during the next few years, is an extraordinary opportunity for rethinking and change—one that usually
occurs only once in even a very long career as a dean, if he or she is
lucky. Yet in our formal and informal conversations, only two or
three deans even got close to suggesting that they were aware of the
opportunity, knew who these potential retirees were likely to be,
and had already planned or were busily planning with faculty

members the shape of the future and how new appointees might assist in attaining a vision. We must consider, of course, the degree to which the revolving-door syndrome described earlier inhibits such planning. Nonetheless, planning for the long-term allocation of resources in relation to clear priorities was generally missing, even in settings where the position of dean had been stable for some years.

Second, in all but a few instances, the personal hopes and aspirations of education deans for their schools or colleges were in those non-educator-preparation areas least understood by central administrators and by colleagues in the arts and sciences. These aspirations included a doctorate in comparative education, a leap forward in educational technology (stated by four or five deans), expansion of a collaborative research-and-development program abroad, and a more aggressive stance in seeking research funds; rarely did they include a fundamental rethinking of teacher education or, for example, the establishment of strong links with surrounding school districts to establish professional development or "teaching" schools.

Third, in most of the multipurpose schools and colleges of education, the dean delegated responsibility for teacher education to a director, who often carried the title of associate or assistant dean. The size and complexity of the various programs appeared to deny some deans broad understanding of the issues; their attention tended to be diverted to other matters, particularly in institutions moving toward increased attention to research. Because responsibility for teacher education was often located in a department or area of study such as curriculum and instruction, with the organizational structure granting considerable autonomy to this and other subdivisions and authority to their heads, and because the associate dean usually lacked authority over these heads, the prospects for doing much more than staffing and maintaining existing programs appeared dim.

Fourth, there appeared to be two kinds of disjuncture with respect to the determination and communication of mission within multipurpose universities, especially the public and private regionals and those major public and private universities that recently made the transition from regional status. The first disjuncture was between the office of the education dean and the faculty. I had trouble lining up statements of mission and goals made by the dean so as to see their congruence with those of faculty members expressed to me or my colleagues. The relationship between the two was often remote or even nonexistent. Although both parties expressed directions that they would like to pursue, rarely did we see scheduled provisions for dialogue and decision making that might move these ideas to action.

The second disjuncture was between the office of the education dean and the central administration. Long-established connections between the two served only for making decisions on budgets and on faculty promotions. We found little evidence of new connections, however. Rarely did deans successfully line up support of the president and provost for the joint pursuit of a major new thrust or for the resolution of one or more of the persistent problems we so frequently heard about. In a school of education where every faculty member appeared to be teaching at or nearly at the maximum load specified, for example, a strong central administration message for increased emphasis on research had not been accompanied by such incentives as added resources or reduced teaching loads. This was a faculty group that impressed all of us with its conscientious attention to students and teaching as well as program revision. Administrative attention to research criteria in the most recent review of faculty members had created anxiety and tension, and there was no sign of a helpful light at the end of a dark tunnel. We could not find mechanisms connecting faculty members, the dean, and the academic vice-president by means of which the growing strain might be relieved. A formerly healthy situation—in spite of the workload—was in serious danger of deteriorating to a level of crisis. Business was still being transacted as usual, but leadership appeared not to be transforming a potentially troublesome set of circumstances.

None of the above observations is intended to point blame. There is plenty to spread around among the various responsible parties. The legacies described in Chapter Three are a contributing factor, as is the apparent brevity of tenure among key administrators (especially when we go beyond the statistics to examine the unique situations of particular institutions). My purpose here is simply to lay bare a set of circumstances regarding the college and university context for teacher education—circumstances requiring unusual commitment and leadership for their improvement.

An anecdote is both revealing and suggestive of directions for change. I had an opportunity during the 1987–88 year to talk somewhat informally and at length with the president of one of our great universities—one that has had trouble over the years in developing a school of education to match the institution's sense of mission and excellence. First we talked about my growing realization that most of the midrange regional universities in our sample were taking as their model universities like his own. Startled, he questioned the need for and the cost of hundreds of universities heavily committed (as his was) to research and to the solicitation of contracts and grants required to support it. He then suggested that he and others in like positions should help create alternative expectations so that the regionals might avoid the dangers of emulation—might prosper according to their own terms instead of vainly seeking to keep up with the fast-moving flagship universities.

Our conversation then turned to the school of education in his university. I asked whether it was doing what he had hoped for five years earlier when he had taken a strong hand in shaping its future. "It's been moving in the right direction," he said. "But are you satisfied?" I persisted. "Well," he responded, "I wish that faculty members were messing around more in the schools." I reminded him that such activity would not get them promoted.

This led us into a discussion of promotion criteria in other professional schools on campus. The law school, for example, provided its own definition of scholarly work and service to the campuswide review committees—a definition that such committees respected. "The school of education, on the other hand," said the president, "has never provided such information. Committees are left to determine for themselves what is appropriate work for professors of education. I don't understand why schools of education sit back and let others, particularly their arts and sciences colleagues on these committees, determine the criteria to be applied." Neither do I.

Transforming Leadership. The loose couplings discussed in the foregoing section provide a challenging agenda for proactive leaders. Our interviews and informal conversations on the campuses suggested, however, that several elements of universities (to a much lesser degree liberal arts colleges) inhibit or at least fail to support such leadership. Our reviews of the literature and collective experience with universities beyond our sample suggest, further, that the circumstances we found are not at all unusual; in fact, they may be the norm.

The rise of higher education in the United States paralleled the growth of industrialism, an acceleration in the secular rationalization of Western hierarchical bureaucracy, and the increased use and refinement of the *transactional* mode of management.[13] In the bureaucratic framework, the transactional leader is a pragmatic power broker who seeks to convince workers that their needs will be met if and when the organization's needs are met.

We find in the chronicles of higher education evidence of such transactional leadership, but for the most part a more benevolent, avuncular mode has prevailed. Many of the early institutions were church-connected and family-oriented. The faculty was itself a kind of extended family, presided over by the president; its members were to take care of the institution and it was to take care of them. This close relationship between the individual and the institution may account in part for the much slower rise of unions in colleges and universities than in industry.

There is evidence in the chronicles, too, of a considerable measure of charisma in early university leaders. They were able to mobilize energy in support of their visions via what students of leadership sometimes call *synergy*. (Ancient theological doctrine combines divine grace with human activity in synergism: The total effect is greater than the sum of the parts.) These leaders usually did not line up the pieces necessary to the whole, however—and probably could not have, even if inclined to do so. They focused on the bigger picture. There were missions to fulfill and tasks to accomplish in exemplary fashion—not products to complete on an assembly line.

Not all college and university presidents were charismatic, and some who were charismatic were also despotic. Others were pragmatic power brokers in the transactional, bureaucratic mode. It is necessary to remember the degree to which higher education was being shaped as our democratic society and form of government were being shaped. The connection between educational and political leadership was often close, the history of the University of Virginia providing a good example. Not surprisingly, then, governance and leadership in universities constituted in themselves an experiment in democracy. A *transformational* kind of leadership—a leadership that attempted to draw out and improve on the best in its followers and, in the process, to transform the institution—best fit both the theological and religious traditions of the university and the emerging need for it to be a model of democracy. Required was the leader who sought "a relationship of mutual stimulation and education that convert[ed] followers into leaders and [might] convert leaders into moral agents."[14] The ideal result was steady, cumulative transformation of the university into a community of purposeful, mission-oriented, mutually attentive, democratic moral agents. The individual and the institution would benefit accordingly.

So long as the growth of higher education was relatively slow and steady, successive institutional leaders appeared in general to effect a gradual but steady transition from the avuncular mode of leadership to a transformational style. That steady growth was interrupted by more rapid increases in enrollment, however, and not all institutions responded with equal success. The clearer its mission and singularity of purpose, the easier it was for the college or university to weather the traumas of war and depression that so discombobulated institutions generally. It should not surprise us, then, that the liberal arts colleges in our sample appear to have fared best at creating an organizational culture that reduces ambiguity, resolves confusion, increases predictability, and provides direction through shared symbols and metaphors.[15] At these colleges, individual faculty members, programs requiring collaborative endeavor, and the institution as a whole appear to have benefited mutually and accordingly.

What appears to have emerged in many of the universities in our sample, by contrast, is an ethos that is neither hierarchically bureaucratic nor transformationally democratic. It is to a considerable degree iconoclastic, but within an institutional context—an environment requiring that certain principles of governance, leadership, management, and participation be understood and prevail. Unfortunately, exigencies of growth, attrition, and growth again, and the traumas brought about by wars and economic upheavals on the outside, have combined with changing rules on the inside to create ambiguity and uncertainty. Rapid transition has been accompanied by an attrition in shared symbols and metaphors, and the role and nature of leadership in creating new ones is not at all clear.

What *is* clear in the flagship and major research universities, however, is that an alternative drummer has largely replaced the president, provost, or dean, whatever his or her leadership style. This drummer is research. Its preeminent symbol is a grant; and its metaphors are couched in the language of personal recognition, power, and independence from the institution and even colleagues (because the drumbeat is more compelling than colleagueship). It speaks scarcely at all to service and program development. The dean, meanwhile, cheers the dance on, massages the dancers, and blocks out the dissonance of other drumbeats.

With the recently increased tempo and clarity of the drumbeat came decreased clarity in the role of administrative leadership. Clearly, the transactional leader—one seeking to convince faculty members that their needs will be met when the organization's needs are met—is now out of step. The few presidents sufficiently tough and entrepreneurial to have had longevity in this mode are living legends. Similarly, the transforming leader—"the value shaper, the exemplar, the maker of meanings . . . the artist, the true pathfinder"[16]—is an endangered species, virtually an anachronism, although a few extraordinarily charismatic transforming leaders have survived. The shortness of tenure among the four positions reported earlier—especially provost and academic vice-president—is probably testimonial to the absence of light on the leadership path during the very recent history of our flagship universities.

In the regional universities, all of the traditional academic drummers are still being heard, but together they create a dissonance. These institutions would probably find their way to an appropriate mission more easily and quickly if their designated leaders were not dazzled by the bright lights of the major research universities. Instability in leadership appears to be less the consequence of overindulgence in transactional or transformational leadership than in the absence of sustained, effective exercise of either sort. Conventional wisdom says that bold leadership is dangerous for those who risk it. However, given the ambiguities and uncertainties in the mission of our regional universities and the role of leadership in them, the exercise of bold leadership appears no more risky than the exercise of little or none. Indeed, the fluid context appears to be more hospitable and inviting to the bold.

The future of teacher education in universities is intimately tied up with the future ethos of higher education. If an increasingly iconoclastic ethos is to prevail, then teacher education will suffer grievously—perhaps so grievously that society will find alternative settings for it. Or is it to be that the institution's and the workers' needs will be met if and when society's needs are met? To the degree that such an ethos comes to characterize higher education, teacher education will prosper—and increasingly so as colleges and universities move closer to its realization.

I am convinced that the opening up of universities to public scrutiny, tumultuous though this may be for them, will be constructive in the long run. The time is fast approaching when large numbers of people will see that these institutions and those who work in them have responsibilities far beyond only what is good for one or the other or both. Moral agency must extend to the larger community. The needs of the university and its professors will be met if and when the needs of the community are met—that is, when both are seen to be demonstrably concerned with and constructively affecting the educational health of the community. The exemplary education of teachers for and in exemplary schools will increasingly be seen as proof of this concern.

Two major factors could contribute significantly to such a development. First, groups competing for public money may find that their chances will improve to the degree that their goals are sensitive to public rights and needs. Second, world events and sentiments could push the business and corporate world toward a more sensitive and humane conception of capitalism: Intense competition in the private sector reduces profit margins, makes a wide range of goods available at affordable prices, and thereby enhances the economic life of the community. (I hear the cynic muttering "And cows might fly, too.") Views and developments such as these are compatible with the ideals of education and teaching. Teaching and teacher education would grow in status were an ethos of concern for the common welfare to characterize the rhetoric and reality of business.

A third factor is embedded in data presented in Chapter Five. It appears from our sample that professors of education in all types of institutions are more deeply committed in spirit to teaching, teacher education, and service in the cause of improving schools than the message of the beacon schools of education would lead one to believe. The promise embedded in these data depends for its realization on unusually charismatic, transforming leaders capable of sensing the nature of the moral imperatives stemming from responsibilities outside of the university and reducing ambiguity, increasing predictability, and providing direction on the inside. It will help if these leaders are seen as being able to walk on water.

Regulatory Factors That Affect Teacher Education

One of the legacies discussed in Chapter Three is the degree to which the state has prescribed the curriculum of teacher education, on one hand, and has compromised or ignored its own curricular prescriptions—most conspicuously during times of shortages in the supply of teachers—on the other. The control exercised, combined with confusion regarding differences among and appropriate authority for licensing, certifying, and accrediting, has contributed to the previously mentioned not-quite status of teaching as a profession.[17]

During the year of our visits to campuses, most of the states were more actively engaged than usual in revising old standards or implementing new ones—often because of active interest on the part of the governor or legislature or both. Also, as was stated in the preceding chapter, the reports of the Carnegie Forum on Education and the Economy and the Holmes Group (both of which have significant implications for the regulatory context) had been circulating for more than a year, stirring up considerable attention nationally. We were interested in assessing how people connected with teacher education perceived the potential impact of the two on their programs. Another restraint that emerged over and over in our travels was the degree to which school district requirements impinged on the conduct of preparation programs, the full impact occurring during the student-teacher phase.

We had endeavored to select colleges and universities that were midway in the cycle of accreditation by the National Council for Accreditation of Teacher Education (NCATE) so that they would not be carrying the double burden of visits by us and a review team. Nonetheless, NCATE and its impact emerged over and over as topics of discussion.

State Regulations. It is clear that the several colleges and universities in any given state respond varyingly to the same state regulations governing teacher education. In spite of their regulating influence, then, the states have not succeeded in attaining consistency in programs. For the most part, the liberal arts colleges we visited had made adaptations or negotiated modifications that left them with tightly packed curricula but reasonably comfortable with their degree of autonomy and independence. In most of the major universities, there was tension regarding state regulations and considerable resentment of intrusions into institutional autonomy—but the degree of tolerance seemed higher than would be expected if these intrusions were into law, medicine, and the arts and sciences. In the public and private regional universities, on the other hand, the responses to requirements and changes in requirements appeared to be more mechanistically compulsive and conforming than in the other types of institutions. Ironically then, intrusions from the outside most strongly affected programs in those colleges and universities that most needed to gain self-confidence from a mission determined within—a mission based on careful analysis of needs in the surrounding society and on commitments that would supplement rather than merely follow the trail of the major research universities. Sadly, more than a few faculty members, again primarily in the regionals, viewed these outside directives and restraints as providing both a sense of direction and protection for teacher education that they saw unlikely of attainment through internal processes of attempted renewal.

In individual and group interviews—including those with campuswide policy and regulatory committees—I tried to elicit the

views of faculty members and administrators with respect to autonomy in the area of teacher education. Invariably, state intervention
loomed large. As I stated earlier, there were differences between and
within institutional types regarding the degree to which state requirements were viewed to be crippling.

Three patterns of interest emerged from these interviews.
First, there was widespread agreement among education deans and
faculty members that state credentialing requirements interfered unduly with the freedom of the college or university to design the best
possible programs through faculty planning in a context of autonomy and freedom. Almost invariably, the president and provost also
disliked the state's intervention, but their distaste was more on principle than on the basis of knowledge of specific restraints. They
were generally ill-informed about the degree to which their institution bent to meet requirements. The campuswide councils and committees on teacher education, on the other hand, spent a good deal
of their time on new and changing state regulations, and most
members objected to their dominance on the agenda.

Second, although many of those interviewed objected to the
intrusion over the years of very specific requirements (for example,
requirements specifying units on drug and alcohol abuse and required hours of student teaching), complaints were focused less on
specifics than on the general existence of regulations and on the
tendency of regulations to change for no apparently sound reasons.
Commonly, faculty members perceived the unrelenting intrusion of
the state into the curriculum and the frequency of state-mandated
change as foreclosing the prospect of faculty-driven change. Why
make the effort, many asked, when the ultimate determinant will be
the state?

The third pattern—one opposing those above—was quantitatively smaller, but the lower frequency of the response was made
up for by the intensity of its expression. It came in two quite different colors. Some faculty members referred somewhat bitterly to the
lack of established mechanisms within their institution for planning, change, and renewal and said that, without state specification,
the curriculum in teacher education would be chaotic. They feared
that it would come to reflect the interests of the strongest departments and the biases of the most powerful faculty members. They

felt much better served by what the state prescribed. The other color in the pattern blended: If the state did not prescribe the curriculum, the arts and sciences would take it over completely. This view was often expressed in words and body language that revealed a deep, ongoing animosity between education professors and professors in the arts and sciences (even though politeness usually prevailed).

Commonly, those interviewed were apprehensive about the future. In the colleges and universities of two states in our sample, faculty members were particularly uneasy about the close working relationship between the governor and the state superintendent of schools—and about the new framework for teacher education likely to emerge. Some worried that this relationship was politicizing education more than had been the case in the past and that both teacher educators and universities were becoming increasingly impotent as a result.

In one regional public university in the state just mentioned, the dean of education thought his days as dean might be numbered because of the extent to which he had been vocal in seeking to temper the changes being effected—especially given that the president, who had been a rather strong ally in the process, was about to retire. In a major private university, the faculty was looking to the new dean, regarded as strong and as having the support of the president, as their champion in eliminating regulatory efforts viewed as dysfunctional. In general, however, the colleges and universities appeared to be more observers than participants in what was increasingly being viewed by faculty members as a political coalition in which they were not represented.

In one state, a recently enacted lesson-planning requirement affecting all first-year teachers was viewed almost unanimously by education deans and faculty members as a most unwelcome intrusion into their curricular arena as well as damaging to teacher education and to the development of teaching as a profession. During the year of our visit—the first year of the requirement's implementation—each beginning teacher was being visited three times and evaluated according to demonstrated ability to develop and execute a lesson plan geared to criteria established by the state department of education. The evaluators had been trained in what to look for in the demonstration, but not by teacher educators in colleges and

universities; nor were these teacher evaluators among the evaluators. With over 6,000 new teachers in the state that year, some 20,000
visits and evaluations would be conducted.

The reactions of the teacher educators interviewed ranged
from amusement to disgust to anger. Their programs devoted some
attention to the new requirement; to varying degrees, students were
being taught how to meet it. In several, students complained about
the extent to which their methods courses repetitiously taught them
how to plan and teach a unit according to state specifications. We
did not visit one institution identified frequently by other deans and
professors as weak, but we heard from them and from students that
it was the place to get "quick and dirty" certification because the
major program component was repetitious training in the new state
requirement. It would be interesting to find out how graduates from
that institution ultimately fared in the ratings. On the basis of this
and other experiences with curricular conformity to state standards,
Roger Soder formulated the principle presented earlier: When rewards and outcomes remain constant, competition drives quality
down. The principle is strengthened when these outcomes are
simplistic.

For the overwhelming majority of persons in our sample, the
state context was seen to be the prime regulatory force, now and in
the future. Although there was some awareness on all campuses—
far more on some than on others—of the Holmes Group and the
Carnegie Forum on Education and the Economy, there was little
knowledge. This generally low level of knowledge and understanding came as a surprise. For most faculty members, if they knew
anything about the reports of either group, the implications were
vague. Even the Carnegie proposal of an examination for national
board certification, when presented to them, aroused little interest.
In general, this initiative was seen as remote from both the local
character of teacher education and state licensing prerogatives.

Clearly, most of those we spoke with—particularly deans and
faculty members—felt more comfortable with the state as a known
quantity than with remote developments on the national scene; and
they identified with state intitiatives, even though many aspects of
recent developments worried them. The impression conveyed to us

was that "these are not the best of times, perhaps, but these things too shall pass."

National Accreditation. Twenty of the institutions in our sample were accredited by NCATE. We probably would have heard a good deal more about the requirements had we not endeavored to select institutions with the process of renewed accreditation behind them or well ahead. Presidents and provosts in the major universities were generally skeptical of the value of NCATE, questioned the costs, and regarded the process as cumbersome. The view in the regional universities was more positive, largely because NCATE accreditation provides validation that is important in the community and for students. Presidents and provosts in the major universities and liberal arts colleges made little or no mention of these positive attributes.

It is clear that institutions seeking initial accreditation or renewal prepare for a visiting team seriously. The process is so costly and so demanding of time that it pushes aside other kinds of long-term planning and renewal in teacher education. Consequently, the value of NCATE accreditation must be weighed in large part on the scale of impetus for reform. My conclusion, based on the several different kinds of data available to us, is that the NCATE review process is better at detecting serious deficiencies (such as those in institutional support) than at stimulating processes of renewal. Perhaps the apparent failure of NCATE reviews to promote programmatic renewals is both the cause and the result of institutions' tendency to regard the process as a necessary chore and to relieve a small group of other responsibilities (at considerable cost in their salaries) to take care of it with minimal interruption of ongoing activities. The costs could be justified if they were accompanied by renewal of programs. Attention to the process and recognition of its importance appear to vary in rather direct proportion to the security and status of the institution and the place of teacher education within it. For Sherwood University, securely at the forefront, NCATE accreditation is of little note. For Western Willis State, with several of its programs recently disaccredited or placed on probation, it is devastating—and not just for teacher education but for the well-being of the institution as a whole. Because teacher education constitutes a significant part of Western Willis's total enrollment, serving a surrounding region not otherwise so served, the impact of disapproval by NCATE is as likely to lead to budget cuts by the state as it is to budgeting allocations designed to correct deficiencies.

As subsequent chapters unfold, it will become increasingly clear that many of the necessary conditions set forth in the postulates of Chapter Two were missing or scarcely present in the colleges and universities of our sample. In some instances, these are conditions required for NCATE accreditation.[18] NCATE requires follow-up of graduates during their initial year of teaching, for example. Yet this condition was almost completely absent in the institutions of our sample—including most of the twenty accredited by NCATE! Oklahoma provided a notable exception. Several deans of education there had taken the initiative to get a bill approved and funded in the legislature that brought faculty members into the classrooms of their former students. In Georgia, faculty members lamented the unavailability for this purpose of the considerable amount of money being expended instead on evaluating beginning teachers during their entry year.

We were sufficiently puzzled by the disparity between what we found and what NCATE visiting teams found with respect to several conditions necessary for accreditation (including the above-mentioned follow-up) that the second of our teams again pursued our initial inquiries about follow-up. Many deans and faculty members were frank in telling us that, although they would like to find out how their graduates were doing and to get feedback with respect to their programs, there were simply no resources for that. Others reported that their institutions gathered routine data (often through a mailed-in questionnaire)—perhaps to satisfy an NCATE visiting team.

A plausible hypothesis to explain the above-described discrepancy is that a visit such as ours carries no liability beyond the time of the host group. An NCATE visit and subsequent report, on the other hand, carry with them a bottom line of considerable import. The problem is that the enormous amount of time, energy, and money expended on the accreditation process appears to stimulate the remediation of serious deficiencies but does not promote and massage processes of continuing improvement. Indeed, to the degree that resources are expended in this essentially evaluative process, they may be lost to that of renewal.

School District Regulations. This study of the conditions and circumstances of teacher education was motivated in part by the proposition that teachers teach the way they teach as a result of what they observed and learned about teaching over their many years as students in the classroom. Their preparation programs are simply not powerful or long enough to dissuade them from what has already been absorbed from role models. In fact, as we discovered, these programs do not necessarily *try* to dissuade them. Data to be presented in subsequent pages reveal that the part of their preparation programs that has the most impact *reinforces* these earlier lessons. I leave the details to later chapters and focus here only on the regulatory control of school districts frequently imposed on student teachers.

It would be comforting to believe that all university-based teacher education programs have built up over the years a stable of first-rate cooperating teachers who regularly induct neophytes into exemplary teaching practices. A few have done so, but they are exceptions. For the most part, colleges and universities are hard-pressed to find enough cooperating teachers—let alone unusually able ones—to take care of the numbers of student teachers. To expect these cooperating teachers, for a token payment that is virtually an insult, to immerse themselves in the practices being taught in the university and monitor their use by student teachers is to expect the ridiculous.

The convention is for future teachers to be immersed in and judged on whatever the teachers to whom they are assigned actually do in their classrooms. This situation is complicated by the fact that, in some school districts, the cooperating teachers are following prescribed practices that may conflict with what they would prefer to do.[19] Where there is a discrepancy between, let us say, the approach to the teaching of reading taught on campus by a specialist in this field and the approach officially approved by the school district, the latter prevails—even if the cooperating teacher would prefer the former! The controlling hand of the practice context is heavy.

This intrusion of the conventions of practice into the presumed professional education of teachers may be the most pernicious component of the regulatory context. These conventions of practice are highly vulnerable to the capricious exercise of power on the part of school district administrators. In addition, the intrusion can be and often is covert, because the practices to which student teachers are required to conform are not sanctioned by a licensing or accrediting agency or any other body open to public scrutiny. The only recourse for a college or university, it seems, is to send student teachers elsewhere, but this is often difficult or impossible.

To make matters worse, school districts sometimes employ a kind of extortion by hiring only teachers who have experienced in their training program practices endorsed by the employing district. For example, we learned of one school district that had adopted a highly touted approach to teaching—but one with flimsy claims to a research base—and expected applicants for teaching positions to be competent in this approach. Needless to say, this expectation was deeply resented by the teacher education faculty of the nearby university. And whereas states tend to be *generally* prescriptive, districts often are very specific. For example, a state readily prescribes a course in the teaching of reading for elementary school teachers but stops short of specifying phonetic approaches and accompanying textbooks—details stipulated by some school districts.

Our data are disappointingly replete with examples of faculty members who told students encountering discrepancies between what they were being taught and what the district required of them simply to conform—to do what they believed right only when ultimately in charge of their own classrooms. This is akin to telling intern physicians to do what the hospital administrators tell them to do until being licensed to practice—and only thereafter to do it *right*. Until we can have confidence that the settings for internships in teaching are exemplary, we have no assurance that teachers are being professionally prepared. Such exemplary settings will require collaborations between universities and school districts going far beyond those effected to date and a comfortable merging of the best that has been learned by competent practitioners and able researchers.

Conditions for Renewal

Perhaps it is becoming increasingly clear to the reader, as it became depressingly clear to my colleagues and me, that institutional mission, leadership, organization, and commitment with respect to teacher education fall short of the necessary conditions postulated in Chapter Two—from far short to somewhat too short in the colleges and universities of our sample. And the data presented in succeeding chapters support and strengthen this conclusion.

Given these institutional shortcomings and the regulatory context within which teacher education is conducted, can circumstances be sufficiently changed to ensure the conditions laid down in the earlier postulates? My answer is a qualified yes. Although I do not believe that any one person or group of persons can effect the necessary reconstruction, the solutions will emerge out of correctly diagnosing what is missing, dysfunctional, or out of shape.

In my judgment, a large part of the diagnosis as well as the remedy lies in the concept of *syzygy*—the straight-line configuration of relevant, separate, but interrelated parts both inside and outside of colleges and universities. These parts are not well lined up now; and as a result, the efforts of people with leverage on one part (however inspired and energized they are) do not and cannot affect the whole—only a part, and even that only for a short time and under the most fortuitous circumstances. There is a double negative here. The first part is the condition of nonlinearity, the absence of syzygy. The second is the benumbing frustration that accompanies recognition of this absence—a frustration ultimately replaced by benign neglect and ennui. Many bright and able people in our sample had come to recognize their benumbed state; some had bestirred themselves from previous periods of ennui to join in the visions of a charismatic leader who soon moved on. They were not in a mood to bestir themselves again. Nonetheless, I believe that there are out there in our colleges and universities enough believers in the importance of teachers, teaching, and teacher education—

some new to the theater and some burned but willing to try again—
to bring off the necessary evolution.

The problem is that work must proceed not only on the
disconnected major pieces but also on the connections necessary to
bring them together into a coherent whole. First, there is the matter
of mission. A college or university unwilling to put the flag of
teacher education high on its masthead should go out or be put out
of this part of its present business. The same fate should befall any
institution unwilling to provide or seek the resources and relations
with schools necessary to quality programs—resources substantially
beyond those now committed to the general education of undergraduates in the academic departments.

And these resources must be made secure for the purposes
intended. That is, they must be earmarked for and assigned to a unit
with clear borders, a specified number of students with a common
purpose, and a roster of largely full-time faculty requisite to the
formal and informal socialization of these students into teaching.
Put negatively, these resources must not go to the larger, multipurpose unit of which teacher education is a part; there they run the
danger of being impounded by entrepreneurial program heads and
faculty members.

The head and the diverse academic and clinical faculty
members comprising this unit must enjoy the authority and bear
the full responsibility for the conduct and welfare of this teacher
education unit. Teacher education must be the top priority of those
devoting full-time or nearly full-time attention to it; for those participating on a part-time basis, teacher education must be a high
priority, and their participation must include the planning and
evaluation necessary to a first-rate enterprise. In other words, the
common practice of using a scholar-researcher from some other
specialization in the school of education to teach a required foundations course in the teacher education program must come to an end.
The message in that practice is clear: Your work in educational
psychology is primary; your service to teacher education is secondary. Programs staffed by persons whose interests in them are secondary are almost always second-rate. The faculty responsible and
accountable for a teacher education entity must decide on the components of its program and the qualifications of those who will

teach them and conduct its own recruitment accordingly—using its own resources. Otherwise, teacher education will remain an orphan, dependent on charity and goodwill.

But even when all the component parts are functioning well and together, the potential for excellence is diminished by state intrusions. The intrusion of state licensing requirements into the curricular specifications of teacher education is precisely the static that interferes with a productive configuration of mission, commitment, organization, and program. As was noted in Chapter Three, states generally forego licensing in favor of certification, prescribing for colleges and universities what the curricula for prospective teachers shall be. The state has the right and the responsibility to set and enforce standards for those who would teach—standards designed to protect students in schools, their parents, and the general public. To the degree that setting the standards for licensing—and also for certifying and accrediting—involves lay and professional collaboration, so much the better. But when licensing becomes confused with certifying completion of a state-prescribed program and a state-mandated curriculum results, deterioration sets in. State specification of programs invites entrepreneurial efforts to provide them quickly and cheaply; quality is driven down. Faculty groups must be challenged by virtue of the absence of such specification to find the best routes through creative inquiry and careful, deliberate experimentation. When the routes are already laid out and required, creativity will wither and lie dormant or be directed toward other endeavors. Such has been and is a large part of the sad story of teacher education.

In all probability, states will continue to regulate teacher education, if only because politicians must respond to the various demands of their constituencies. Current procedures drive down quality. Are policymakers ready and willing to boost quality by insisting that all teacher-preparing institutions put the necessary conditions in place and by ensuring the necessary resources? That would take remarkable moral courage.

Chapter Five

Teachers of Teachers

❖ ❖ ❖

Faculty are defined by the institution that hires them.
A doctor is a doctor wherever he may be, but a professor is a professor only if employed by a college or
university. This close connection with one type of institution means that the structure of the institutions
and the nature of academic work always have inter-
acted with each other.

—Donald Light, Jr.[1]

Professors in colleges and universities who engage seriously in preparing educators for the nation's schools straddle two cultures: that
of higher education and that of the K–12 educational system. A
quarter-century ago—a period of time transcended by the career

Note: This chapter draws heavily from four technical reports by Roger
Soder: "Faculty Work in the Institutional Context," Technical Report
no. 3; "Status Matters: Observations on Issues of Status in Schools, Colleges, and Departments of Education," Technical Report no. 4; "Faculty
Views of Schooling, Schools, Teaching, and Preparing Teachers," Technical Report no. 5; and "Students and Faculty in Teacher Education: Views
and Observations," Technical Report no. 8 (Seattle: Center for Educational
Renewal, College of Education, University of Washington, 1989).

span of many teacher educators still teaching—the culture of the school entered significantly into their mission. They not only taught the campus curriculum for prospective teachers but followed their students into the schools to supervise the student-teaching experience. Publication was expected on some university campuses, but on many others it was an appreciated extra.

Today the culture of the college or university, far more than the culture of the schools, is the compelling context for teacher educators. This is true of all of the institutions in our sample, to varying degrees. Higher education has evolved substantially within the career span of many professors, profoundly changing the expectations and circumstances under which they work. The impact of this evolution on those who prepare teachers and, indeed, on teacher education programs has been substantial.

The data base for this chapter is made up of the responses of 1,217 faculty members to our extensive questionnaire; the interviews enriched these source materials.[2] On subsequent pages, I briefly describe the sample and then probe the perceptions of this faculty group regarding their work and its status, schools and schooling, their teacher education programs, and more.

There are some constants in the ways that the institutions in our diverse sample prepare teachers. And there are some constants in the ethos of the teacher-preparing institutions. But there are also differences—differences in degree that cannot be encompassed by a single description or a set of recommendations that is equally valid and compelling for all colleges and universities. Nonetheless, the pervasive common themes cannot be ignored.

The Sample

Whereas 80 percent of the future teachers we studied were female, the percentage of females teaching them was precisely half this figure. Although the male-female ratio of faculty members in higher education is changing, men still constitute a substantial majority. As with the student sample, minorities were grossly underrepresented, constituting just 6.7 percent: 4.4 percent blacks, 0.9 percent Asians/Pacific Islanders, 0.7 percent Hispanics, and 0.7 percent Native Americans. (It is important to remember that the removal of just two institutions from our sample would drop the percentage of black teacher educators to the level of the other minorities represented.)

We were getting the views of experienced individuals, an overwhelming 60 percent of whom had been employed at their *current* college or university for at least eleven years. Forty-two percent had been there for sixteen years or more. Not surprisingly, then, almost 65 percent held the rank of associate or full professor. Age levels corresponded: 45 percent were fifty or older; all but 17 percent had celebrated their fortieth birthday; more than 12 percent were over sixty. Seventy percent of the faculty members in our sample were born between 1928 and 1948—and had no doubt been deeply affected by living through one of our most devastating economic depressions and one of the world's most destructive wars.

The students in our sample may have been correct in their criticism that too many of the faculty had not taught in schools recently, but they were wrong in saying that *many* never had. Only 27 percent had not taught at the elementary level, and only 18 percent had not taught in a secondary school. Approximately 54 percent and 38 percent, respectively, held a valid secondary or elementary teaching certificate at the time of our inquiry.

It was impossible for us to connect these kinds of data precisely to the major academic activities of faculty members in our sample. It must be remembered, however, that although over 83 percent were affiliated with an SCDE, many (especially in the flagship public universities) were involved not at all or only marginally in their institution's teacher education program. Consequently, the statistics regarding school experiences on the part of those actually working with prospective teachers may be rosier than the preceding data suggest. Nearly 8 percent of our respondents were affiliated primarily with a department within the liberal arts and over 5 percent with another professional school. Thus faculty members of the SCDEs in our sample clearly carried responsibility for most of the sequence in the so-called professional teacher education curriculum.

We looked at the question of who participates from another perspective as well—that of individual faculty involvement in teacher education. Overall, 69 percent of our sample reported that they had taught one or more courses or supervised student teachers in their institution's teacher education program. Predictably, considering information provided in preceding chapters, the percentage of such involvement climbed from a low of 58 percent in major public universities to 73 percent in regional public universities to 91 percent in liberal arts colleges. The percentage of female faculty members involved in teacher education was consistently higher than the percentage of male faculty members so involved. (Virtually every set of statistics cited in this book in some way reflects a greater female than male connection with the occupation of schoolteaching, particularly at the elementary level.)

All members of our two traveling research teams found the long daily schedule of interviewing to be both grueling and extraordinarily productive. Presidents, provosts, deans, professors in all fields, part-time and adjunct personnel, superintendents of schools, principals, cooperating teachers, and others gave of their time generously. Most of those who were reticent initially became increasingly absorbed in the questions asked, frequently becoming quite loquacious. A few—but only a handful—remained reserved and even taciturn. On the whole, the conversations were lively; respondents were open and candid. The team following up the first encountered very positive feedback regarding the group discussions and individual interviews conducted two or more weeks earlier by the first team. All of us were impressed with the ideas for program and other changes brought forward but depressed over the frequent references to the lack of a structure for change and the degree to which faculty members perceived long-term improvement efforts to be futile. It was the certainty of certification and accreditation restraints, more than the fact of present specific requirements, that was widely perceived as most debilitating. Many also spoke of school conditions that would quickly nullify their efforts and stultify the creativity of their most promising graduates.

I am convinced that considerable experience with the kinds of phenomena we sought to study was a necessary prerequisite for the research staff—especially given that we intended to go beyond summaries and conclusions to recommendations. Thus members of the traveling teams were experienced in higher education or schooling or both. They were treated as peers by interviewees, as were the educational historians who visited the sites later. The respect and cooperation we received stemmed in large measure from general recognition of the seriousness of our mission, the care that had gone into preparing for it, and the fact that the whole was carried out by an experienced, relatively senior research staff.

The Work and Its Status

Higher education is sometimes referred to as America's substitute for a royal family. We are left to read into this observation whatever we wish. There is privilege, certainly—the privilege of tenure, for example, which frequently stirs debate among those outside the institution. And the cap, the gown, and the academic procession tie us to tradition at a time when tradition is hard to come by. The work is clean, there are no sales quotas to meet, and the regularities of life are relatively well established and understood, at least by the professors who come and go each day. Former Governor Jerry Brown of California once said that professors should be willing to give up a good part of their salaries for the privilege of having such good work.

There are subtleties to the regularities and mores of campus life not easily discerned by the uninitiated, however, as we saw in Chapter Four. At first blush, the ladder of promotion from assistant to full professor, the criteria of scholarly work, teaching, and service, and the peer review process appear to be reasonably straightforward. But there are layers of complexity: the methodology and the place of publishing research, whether students' ratings of teaching are valid and fair, the focus and trajectory of one's scholarly activity, the status of the field of study, and more. On most campuses, the so-called hard sciences prevail: physics, chemistry, and mathematics. Biological and neural research basic to medicine have also come up in the academic pecking order in recent years. The humanities may have become a little threadbare, but their poverty is genteel. The social sciences, on the other hand, are the somewhat brash newcomers on academy row, with sociology often suspect. Education generally claims status as a social science, providing the latecomer, sociology, with the opportunity to look down at a lower rung on the academic ladder. In addition to these distinctions, there are status differences among branches of each discipline—for example, between experimental and clinical psychology.

Many academicians place all professional schools at the periphery of the institution[3]—but not together. They would put a good deal of space between medicine and law, at one end, and journalism and social work, at the other. Those who compare the professions readily separate the strong from the weak. Regrettably, education is usually ranked among the weakest of the weak.[4]

It is a serious mistake to assume that the subtleties of academic status are merely quaint, or of moderate importance at most. The college or university campus is a kind of city-state into which are compressed values and symbols paralleling those of the nearby town or the surrounding city. But instead of there being many roads to success and recognition, there is really only one: a composite of the norms of academe. Individuals and clusters of individuals are spread out along this single road, separated by status differences. The old saw, "The reason that academic politics is so vicious is that the stakes are so small," still brings wry chuckles, even among academicians. The politics can be vicious, to be sure, but the stakes are not at all small. They are similar to those driving junior executives to get multiwindowed corner offices, preferably close to where the chief executive officer presides.

What illuminates life behind the ivy (or darkens it by absence) is the sense of personal worth that faculty members derive from estimating the value of what they do against the ambiguous and indeterminate yardstick of academic work generally. Clear cues are hard to come by. One edits a special issue of a prestigious journal but hears not a word of praise from colleagues down the hall. One slips away from the campus for a few days to be honored by peers elsewhere—perhaps abroad—and returns unnoticed to find a mail slot filled with announcements of others' newly published books. David Machell, himself a professor, refers to factors inherent in a professor's job and in the academic environment that contribute to a crisis of low self-esteem, concluding from his research that the proportion of faculty members exhibiting symptoms of "professional melancholia" is as high as 20 percent.[5]

Because university contexts differ, there are differences from setting to setting in the severity of the problem. But there is something unique to academic life (or, if not unique, shared only with certain other intellectual lines of work) that brings with it ambiguity with respect to success. Alexandre Kojève's observations are worth quoting at some length:

> Men do a particular thing in order to *succeed* or "to win success" (and not to fail). Now, the success of an undertaking based on action may be measured by its objective "good results" (a bridge that does not collapse, a business that makes money, a war won, a state that is strong and prosperous, etc.), independent of the opinion that others have of it, while the success of a book or of an intellectual discourse is nothing but the recognition of its value by others. The intellectual depends then very much more than the man of action (the tyrant included) on the admiration of others, and he is more sensitive than the latter to the absence of this admiration. Without it, it is absolutely impossible for him to admire himself with any valid reason, while the man of action can admire himself on account of his objective—even solitary—"successes." And this is why, as a general rule, the intellectual who does nothing but talk and write is more vain than the man who, in the full sense of the word, acts.[6]

Our data suggest that self-perceived ambiguity with respect to personal worth is exacerbated by a general condition of self-perceived prestige deprivation with respect to the values placed on one's work by others. Professors of education have found it necessary to grapple with at least three interlocking sets of conditions that seriously influence their perceptions of personal worth. The first is the rite of institutional passage that eviscerated many institutions' once-substantial involvement in teacher education; this passage (discussed in Chapters Three and Four) is most obvious in the transition of regional universities from normal schools to teachers' colleges to their present status as universities. The decline in the status of teacher education in these mostly regional universities was paralleled in other institutions by the general failure of SCDEs to shake off the low status of teacher education during the rapid growth of higher education following World War II. The second set of debilitating conditions emerged out of the rising importance of research during a time of declining enrollments and faculty mobility. Colleges and universities have been and to a considerable degree still are market-driven, with benefits accruing to growing fields. The third set of conditions hovers in that low-hanging cloud of prejudice toward schoolteaching, teacher education, and both the field and professors of education.

There was substantial convergence in two different sets of data we collected on status: interviews with campus administrators and with faculty members in the arts and sciences, and both interview and questionnaire data from the sample of education and teacher education faculty described earlier. Although the interinstitutional range was substantial, the education unit and teacher education (and faculty members connected with one or the other or both) were viewed by those outside of both to be of lower status than the arts and sciences, most other campus units, and the professors connected with them. The responses ranged from thoughtful reflections on the unfortunate prejudicial legacy to angry denunciations of "those people over there in the ed school." Sometimes it took a great deal of probing to reach admissions of prejudice and low regard; at other times the interviewees appeared to relish the opportunity to lash out. References were frequently made to a pervasive condition of low status, and sometimes to its unfairness. But some deans, department chairs, and faculty members—particularly young ones—were very open in expressing their personal reservations and even hostility.

Certain patterns appeared to be embedded in the nature and history of institutional types. On all of the liberal arts college campuses, for example, the incumbent education faculty fared better than their courses. Indeed, all four presidents and other administrators and faculty members spoke with some pride of "being lucky" to have such a good group. On three, I was told that some education courses were good enough to be included in the general-education undergraduate offerings—an observation that other data confirmed. On two, I learned that education faculty members were among the most productive scholars and best teachers—again confirmed by other data. Yet almost simultaneously, there were admissions that education just did not meet high academic standards as a field. Commendations of faculty had more to do with individuals and their commitment to teacher education than with the scholarly nature of the work and field.

Some of the most vicious attacks erupted at former normal schools and at other regional universities with a different past but a long-term, substantial involvement in preparing teachers. I found on these campuses many people outside of the SCDE who viewed the earlier dominance of teacher education as a cancer that was only now coming under control. Negative perceptions were often directed not only to education courses but also to education professors on that particular campus. The desire to disassociate from both sometimes carried over into off-campus social life. "There are some faculty get-togethers to which we're never invited," I was told during a conversation with several long-term members of the education faculty at a regional private university.

On this group of campuses, there was also a greater brouhaha over methods courses, but the nature of the hubbub varied. On some, they were simply condemned as weak, too plentiful, repetitive, and so on. On two, in particular, the complaint was that the education professors allegedly lacked the content knowledge for teaching them—but the chairs of the relevant content departments wanted no part of such courses. On several, the quarrel was over the respective authority and jurisdiction of the education and arts and sciences departments. It is important to note that many academic deans and professors who viewed methods courses to be squeezing out general-education requirements were egregiously ill-informed regarding the general-education requirements prevailing for teachers on their own campuses. And when the fact that fields such as business and journalism cut as deeply or sometimes more deeply into such requirements was pointed out to them, it prompted no equivalent angry or prejudicial statements.

In general, the criticism of teacher education at the major public and private universities was of a somewhat different timbre. First of all, I should note that ignorance among faculty members in the arts and sciences regarding what was going on in their institution's school and college of education was widespread. It came as a shock to some deans and arts and sciences professors to learn (from me) that large numbers of professors of education on their campus were neither involved nor interested in teacher education. And some who already knew that were angry about it. I recall vividly a professor of philosophy who spoke passionately about the importance of preparing teachers and of learning a great deal about teaching—"to help us all," he said. "What are those people over there doing?"

Many of the arts and sciences administrators and faculty members of major universities perceived inquiry into education to be a field of growing legitimacy—though not quite worthy of full academic status, perhaps. Clearly, there were some faculty members of repute delving productively into it. Commonly, however, those in the arts and sciences viewed research in education as poorly conducted. First, many professors of education were second-rate scholars, they said. Second, education professors frequently addressed insignificant problems or problems better handled by scholars in other fields. Third, they frequently made their work inaccessible to practitioners by the use of unnecessarily complicated and often inappropriate research methods.

The most interesting criticism, from my perspective, was the perception that education professors had strayed too far from the central, traditional role of preparing teachers and from research closely connected to this enterprise. Some were harsh: "Our young people cannot read, write, or think, and teachers seem unable to improve matters. What's the ed school doing about this?" In general, they shrugged off my observation that preparing teachers is very labor-intensive, not conducive to securing grants, and likely to interfere with research demands. Surely, many said, schools of education ought to be able to make a legitimate case for successful university careers closely associated with educating teachers and improving schools.

Beyond the above tilt to our discussions with noneducation personnel at the major universities, there was much of the usual criticism of nonintellectual education courses, the intrusion of methods courses into the undergraduate curriculum, and the general low caliber of work and professors in education. This group of interviewees also exhibited ignorance regarding the actual work going on in the school or college of education (as I noted earlier) and the teacher education requirements of their own institution.

There was a considerable degree of correspondence between the above views and the response of our sample of education and teacher education faculty to parallel kinds of questions on our questionnaire. Although only 9 percent of the liberal arts teacher education faculty in our sample said that their colleagues in the arts and sciences would give their teacher education faculty an A, a whopping 65 percent said that they would give it a B. By contrast, these percentages for flagship public universities were 2 and 18 percent, respectively, and for major public universities only 1 and 14 percent. Whereas only 7 percent in the liberal arts colleges said that their colleagues would give the teacher education program a D (and none would give it a failing grade), these percentages were 22 and 2, respectively, for the flagship university sample, and 27 and 5, respectively, for those in our major public university sample. Across the board, the private college and university sample of education professors perceived their teacher education programs to be rated higher by their arts and sciences colleagues than did those in the public university sample.

This pattern of institutional differences was to a considerable degree paralleled by the views of education and teacher education faculty on the quality of the liberal arts education provided in their institutions. Those in the private institutions gave generally higher ratings than did those in the public universities: A startlingly high 42 percent of those in the liberal arts colleges awarded an A to the education being provided by their arts and sciences colleagues. As was suggested by other data, there appeared to be a more generally positive attitude in the small liberal arts colleges to one another and to the institution as a whole.

The education faculty showed no reluctance to pat themselves on the back. Their views of their own programs were uniformly high, but self-congratulation was more dominant in the private group. Asked to give a grade to their own teacher education program, over 90 percent of the liberal arts college group assigned an A or B, as did 87 percent of the respondents in major private universities and 80 percent of the regional private group. The corresponding percentages for the public institutions were lower: 72,

67, and 77 for flagship public, major public, and regional public universities, respectively.

Faculty members in the major universities, both private and public, believed their teacher education programs to be held in low regard on campus. The percentages in this group responding that teacher education ranked generally lower than other programs ranged from 66 to 73 to nearly 98 for major public, major private, and flagship public universities, respectively. Whereas only about 25 percent of faculty members in this group perceived their teacher education programs as having about the same status as others, 66 percent of those in the liberal arts colleges gave this response. It becomes increasingly clear that teacher education faculty members in the liberal arts colleges in our sample suffered less than those in the other types of institutions from both actual and perceived status deprivation.

The responses of teacher education faculty members in both public and private regional universities to certain of our questions were thought-provoking. First, they led the other groups in perceiving their programs to have higher status than others on campus: 15 percent and 31 percent, respectively. The highest percentage for any other group (major public) was only 5 percent. Although both types perceived that rather large percentages of noneducation faculty members on their campuses would rate teacher education courses as less rigorous than their own—48 and 67 percent, respectively, for regional private and public universities—these figures were 86 and 81 percent for major private and flagship public universities! The spread of differences in small samples becomes significant only when it is marked, and the above differences are substantial indeed.

I note that for SCDEs in private liberal arts colleges and regional public and private universities, preparation of educators for the schools is the major game in town—and has been since their earliest beginnings. Further, although research is being increasingly emphasized, it is still not primary. Certainly, research is by no means as compelling there as on the campuses of major universities—as we shall soon see, as far as our sample is concerned.

A hypothesis begins to emerge: The more exclusively an SCDE embraces teacher education (and perhaps the education of other K-12 practitioners) as its prime or sole function, the stronger the vital signs of the enterprise. Put differently, teacher education is increasingly endangered to the degree that the unit traditionally charged with its conduct—namely, the SCDE—proliferates in functions. As this proliferation expands, institutions may find it increasingly important to differentiate sharply between the school or college of education as a whole and the teacher education enterprise—to help ensure clear and discrete missions, distinct faculty and student bodies, unambiguous programmatic boundaries, and undisputed resources.

In our Technical Report no. 4, Roger Soder provides a quote from William Pfaff that is clearly applicable to the conditions necessary to the identity of teacher education: "The gross political disruptions dominating the twentieth century have actually resulted from defective or unsatisfied nationalism—from the struggles of societies to become nations, to acquire the maturity and 'national security' that comes from a confident political identity, a cultural autonomy, a homogeneity of population, and, finally, clear and secure borders."[7] These are the conditions generally enjoyed by the strongest and most prestigious departments and professional schools on university campuses. Surely an enterprise of such magnitude and importance as teacher education deserves no less.

Institutional Mission and the SCDE

Chapter Four presented data illustrating that SCDEs and teacher education rank low in the mission of most of the institutions in our sample. Additional data led to the conclusion that schools and colleges of education in developing universities increasingly downplayed their teacher education function as other functions emerged and expanded. This low status was not only institutionally assigned, however: Few of the deans of education in our sample identified teacher education in their *personal* plans for their school or college.

Chapter Six will reveal that students in teacher education programs are aware and resentful of this low status, but they shrug it off, at least partially, as indicative of misplaced priorities in society and higher education. Prestige deprivation characterizes the teacher education enterprise generally, affecting its clarity of mission, faculty, students, and coherence of program.

It would be a mistake, however, to suggest that prestige deprivation is the sole cause of deficiencies. Rather, my claim is that it has exacerbated for teacher education the strain of rapid and universal change in higher education experienced by colleges and universities, their academic units, and persons connected with them. The past quarter-century or so has been tumultuous for the whole of our society—and indeed the world. Universities have not been spared the tumult.

Exponential growth in information and knowledge has profoundly influenced all sectors of society, but because universities are so close to the center of knowledge production, they were caught up in the rapid cultural evolution. In careers spanning twenty-five years or so, many professors have watched their institutions pass them by. Some have successfully jumped from setting to setting, sometimes interacting successfully and productively with their new academic cultures, sometimes not. Others have been fortunate enough to change and adjust to the culture in which they remained.

I noted earlier that adequate supplies of teachers contributed severely to enrollment declines in schools and colleges of education during the 1970s. I also noted that cuts in resources within campuses were, for these units, sometimes more severe than actual circumstances warranted. We were informed during our visits of some concomitants, including somewhat older and somewhat more embittered faculty members in education than on the campus generally.

Adapting to Research Priorities. Data from all of our sources converged on the conclusion that the importance of scholarly work had increased on all campuses during recent years, not only adding to expectations for faculty members but shifting the order of their priorities. Colleges and universities differed in their definition of such work and in the intensity with which they stressed it. There was little ambiguity in the flagship public universities and their private counterparts: An assistant professor would advance neither fast nor far in the absence of research and publication. Overall, and for all types of institutions, respondents to our questionnaire predicted that the importance of research in the institutional mission would remain high—would in fact increase in institutions that now assigned it only moderate importance. Overall, research was seen as twice as likely as teaching to increase in centrality and importance.

Yet respondents placed high value on teaching in the college or university mission (whether teaching was stressed in the mission statement or not). Given a choice among four ratings for teaching, an overwhelming majority chose the highest, "centrally important." The range was from 76 percent in the flagship public universities to nearly 94 percent in the private liberal arts colleges.

We gathered a large body of information on faculty perceptions, preferences, and predictions regarding the importance of teaching, research, development, school improvement, teacher education, and other factors in institutional mission. My prime interest here is in analyzing collations of such data to determine congruence and dissonance between faculty members' orientations to their work and the institutional emphasis now and in the predicted future—in other words, the nature of the connection between our sample of education faculty members and their college or university cultural context. It is reasonable to argue that faculty members are likely to be more productive when what they prefer to do fits nicely into their institution's mission. A college or university involved but not much interested in preparing teachers is not a congenial environment for a teacher educator.

Within the sample of liberal arts colleges, dissonance between perceived institutional mission and preferences of faculty appeared to be relatively low. Education faculty members perceived teaching to be centrally important in the eyes of their institution (83 percent) and expected it to remain so (83 percent) or to increase in importance (nearly 9 percent). Nearly 96 percent of them approved of this status for the present; over 50 percent preferred teaching to hold steady in the future, while nearly 47 percent wanted the importance of teaching to increase. They perceived preparing teachers to be centrally important to their institution today (78 percent) and predicted continuing centrality (78 percent) or even some increase (20 percent). There was considerable congruence between their perceptions of institutional mission and their preferences: 89 percent wanted this function to be central, and nearly 97 percent wanted it to remain stable or increase in importance.

In our interviews with faculty members on liberal arts campuses, we found the greatest dissonance over mission at the college most recently emerging from very local to more regional status. Here we immediately encountered statistics on the national distribution of the student body and the national reputations of the faculty, although we also encountered faculty members who spoke nostalgically of the days when the institution was lauded locally (and even from a distance) for its unique educational role with the young people of the surrounding community. In all four, we learned that scholarly work had been elevated during recent years but that it had always been recognized as important—next to teaching. Teaching was still more important than research in the liberal arts colleges, we learned, and it was essential that faculty applicants for positions there be good teachers; but those who might want to move on to a major university had better publish.

These favorable data on compatability of personal and institutional mission take on added significance when viewed in the larger institutional context of the liberal arts colleges already described: considerably less prestige deprivation for teacher education and comparatively higher acceptance of education faculty, high regard for the general-education program by education faculty, and acceptance by campus administrators of a teacher education past and present. It must be remembered, too, that the education faculty in our sample of the liberal arts colleges regarded their students as being of relatively high academic quality and that the students identified closely with the college as a whole and regarded their teacher education programs quite favorably. In looking toward the improvement of teacher education on these campuses, it would appear that incompatibility between faculty members conducting it and institutional context is not a critical entry point. To the degree that improvements are needed, the areas for change lie elsewhere.

Compatibility between preferences for and perceptions of institutional mission on the part of respondents in the major private universities appeared to be relatively high as well. Most (nearly 72 percent) perceived teaching to be centrally important to their institution now; nearly 99 percent predicted that it would remain that way or increase in importance. The majority perceived research to be of moderate (31 percent) or central (nearly 53 percent) importance now. Nearly 47 percent predicted that this mission would remain the same, and another 52 percent believed that it would increase in importance.

Faculty preferences were not far removed from the above perceptions. Nearly 95 percent wanted teaching to be centrally important now and to remain that way (40 percent) or increase in institutional importance (nearly 59 percent). Clearly, they wanted it to be even more important to institutional mission than they perceived it to be now, and they predicted that teaching would be of increased future importance. Similarly, they wanted research to be of more importance than it was (nearly 63 percent preferred that it be centrally important), and 58 percent wanted it to increase in importance (compared with the 52 percent who believed that it would).

There is comparable compatibility with respect to perceptions and preferences regarding the importance of preparing teachers. The percentage perceiving this function to be centrally important in institutional mission (nearly 72) was lower than that wanting it to be (nearly 83). But nearly 32 percent of our sample in the major private universities predicted that preparing teachers would become more important, as compared with 49 percent who wanted this function to be more important in the future; nearly 62 percent predicted that it would remain the same in importance.

A rather large percentage of education faculty members in our sample of major private universities perceived their institutions to be evolving along lines that were quite compatible with their own desires. This group gave high marks (a grade of A or B by over 83 percent) to the liberal arts education being provided by their universities and to the quality of their own teacher education programs (a grade of A or B by over 87 percent). The downside is that a whopping 86 percent estimated that the faculty outside of their school or college of education would judge their courses to be less rigorous than their own. Although this was the highest estimate in this category of any faculty group, it is a view shared by education colleagues in the flagship public universities (over 81 percent) and to considerable degree by the others. Even in the liberal arts colleges, over 64 percent of the respondents believed that their colleagues in the other departments would grade the teacher education courses as less rigorous than their own. Invariably, it seems, we come back to the cloud of low status that hangs over education departments— commonly for the courses, somewhat less generally for teacher education programs, and perhaps more selectively than inclusively for education professors.

The overall dissonance between faculty preferences and the reality of institutional mission was slightly greater in the flagship public universities. There has been growing concern both within these institutions and without regarding adequate attention to teaching. Yet so long as these institutions continue to derive their comparative status on the basis of research grants and contracts, to emphasize the dominance of research in the faculty reward structure, and to enroll large numbers of undergraduates, this tension will continue. And as long as these universities continue to prepare teachers, certain dissonances between faculty preferences and perceptions regarding institutional mission will be particularly exacerbated for those education faculty members whose academic lives revolve around the teacher education enterprise.

Whereas only 29 percent of our respondents in flagship public universities perceived teaching to be centrally important to institutional mission today, over 81 percent perceived research to be centrally important. Only 18 percent saw teaching as likely to increase in importance; 41 percent predicted that research would increase from its already high level of importance. These perceptions were considerably out of sync with their preferences: Over 76 percent wanted teaching to be centrally important, and over 60 percent wanted a future increase in importance for teaching. Nearly 61 percent wanted research to be centrally important, but only 24 percent wanted an increase.

There was also considerable incongruence between their preferences and perceptions regarding the mission of preparing teachers. Whereas less than 39 percent perceived preparing teachers to be centrally important today, less than 22 percent predicted an increase in the importance of this mission in the future. But nearly 67 percent wanted teacher education to be centrally important now, and an increase in the importance of this mission in the future was desired by over 52 percent.

There is a somewhat parallel pattern in our data for the

major public universities. However, whereas 49 percent of the respondents perceived teaching to be centrally important now, a
whopping 80 percent wanted it to be of central importance now;
and nearly 55 percent wanted it to increase in importance in the
future—but only 18 percent predicted that it would. Nearly 44 percent of this group perceived research to be centrally important now,
and nearly 53 percent predicted that it would increase in importance. These percentages are reasonably close to the percentages
wanting research to be centrally important now (nearly 53 percent)
and in the future (nearly 50 percent).

The discrepancies between what was perceived and desired
with respect to the importance of preparing students for teaching
careers were quite marked. Nearly 60 percent perceived this mission
as centrally important, but nearly 76 percent wished that it were.
Over 55 percent wanted it to increase in importance, but less than 30
percent predicted that it would.

The data from our respondents in both the major public and
private universities and the flagship public universities clearly reflect a preference for a greater emphasis on teaching and teacher
education now and in the future, along with the prediction in all
three that research will increase in importance. When we lay these
data alongside education faculty members' perceptions of the low
status of their courses and teacher education programs as perceived
by colleagues in other departments and campus units, it is difficult
to be sanguine about the future of the teacher education enterprise
in these types of institutions. Unless a marked shift occurs in university mission—and this appears unlikely—faculty members must
invent ingenious ways of meeting research expectations while simultaneously devoting themselves seriously to the preparation of
teachers.

One solution widely used by schools of education is to secure
research grants that provide full-time faculty some release-time
from teaching and free up money to hire adjunct faculty members—
who then become the prime factors in teacher education. The probable greater use in the future of this solution does not bode well for
teacher education. Moving teacher education to the graduate level
(where, presumably, teaching can be better related to faculty
members' research activity) as proposed initially by the Holmes

Group, is a step that has already been taken by some universities, predominantly those in the flagship public and major private categories. But such a step discourages all those students described in Chapter Six who eagerly look forward to teaching careers even before going to college. Further, the needs of teacher education are once again subjugated to the research function.

Another alternative—one already taken up primarily by major private universities—is to go out of (or almost out of) the teacher education business while retaining a school of education as part research institute and part graduate center of study for experienced teachers and school administrators. Because this sends an unfortunate message regarding the scholarly importance and status of preparing teachers, however, such a move may become increasingly unpopular (and therefore untenable for public universities).

The regional public universities exceed all other types in their production of teachers, and the output in the regional privates is also substantial. The centrality of the teaching mission in these regionals will be affected considerably in the future by the fate of teacher education in the several types of major universities. The patterns of faculty preferences and perceptions with respect to mission were somewhat parallel in the regionals and majors, with research clearly at a lower level of intensity in the former. Teaching was perceived to be centrally important now (76 and nearly 74 percent for private and public regionals, respectively) but was predicted by only 17 and 25 percent of respondents in private and public types, respectively, to increase in importance. Research was perceived by only 25 percent of respondents in the public regionals to be important now, but over 50 percent predicted increased importance in the future. These two sets of figures for the private regionals were nearly 33 and over 52 percent.

By contrast, nearly 92 percent of respondents in the public regionals and over 93 percent in the private regionals wanted teaching to be centrally important now, and nearly 59 and 47 percent, respectively, wanted this mission to increase in importance. Only 32 and 41 percent in public and private regionals, respectively, wanted research to be centrally important now. These percentages increased to 36 and over 44, respectively, in regard to desired future importance.

These data lead to the conclusion that there is more concern among faculty members in both types of universities regarding the present and future centrality of teaching than there is over the present and future centrality of research. Put another way, many faculty members appear to be more resigned to the prospect of increasing centrality of research than to an accompanying lessening in the centrality of teaching in the institutional mission.

We get a little more insight into present (and possibly future) congruence between faculty work preferences and campus culture when data on the importance of preparing teachers are added to the above. Respondents in both public and private regional universities perceived the importance of teacher education as an institutional mission to be quite high; over 78 and over 72 percent, respectively, saw it as centrally important. Nearly all predicted that it would remain so and perhaps even increase in importance. But they preferred that the preparation of teachers be even more central now— with over 86 and over 83 percent, respectively, selecting this preference; and over 57 percent in the public regionals and nearly 50 percent in the private regionals wanted an increase in importance. Forty percent of the former group and over 33 percent of the latter predicted that teacher education would increase in importance in their institutions.

It is important to remember that most of the regional public universities evolved from normal schools and teachers' colleges and that teacher education loomed large in the history of most of the private regionals. Faculty members being interviewed frequently spoke of coming to these colleges or universities specifically to teach teachers and referred to this mission as important and labor-intensive. Many perceived the increasing rhetoric regarding research as threatening what they had come to do. Some were bitter in their expressions of betrayal. As was noted in Chapter Four, provosts on several of these campuses were selected and appointed for the specific purpose of increasing research productivity. Rarely, however, was the rhetoric accompanied by reduced teaching loads or the support services seen by faculty members as necessary. They still had to teach as much as before; but teaching, they observed, no longer counted much in the reward system. They perceived the downplaying of teaching as reflecting negatively on the importance of teacher education, because the teaching load of a relatively large percentage of the faculty in these regionals was primarily in teacher education classes. Many of these faculty members said that they simply could not give the attention to their students that they once did and simultaneously find time for research and writing.

Our field notes prepared during and after interviews reveal that most faculty members across the range of institutions in our sample were attuned to expectations—especially changing expectations—on their campuses and were very much aware of what these meant for their own behavior. In the flagship public universities, there was little ambiguity: Getting grants and publishing in high-quality refereed journals was the name of the game. The change in focus from teaching to research, which evolved over the past fifteen to twenty years, was secure and accepted. Dissonance regarding preferred and perceived emphases was greatest for the older faculty members who had come when teaching and service were much more highly valued. Many viewed themselves as not much respected by the younger "hot shots," who were well prepared in research techniques; and the latter frequently observed that Professor So-and-so would not make tenure if evaluated today. Given a choice between an applicant for an assistant professorship with no school experience and little or no interest in teacher education but a substantial list of published research articles, and another with a short publication list but experience in schools and interest in teacher education, the former invariably got the nod of approval in these flagships. There were, however, frequent expressions of regret over the necessity of this choice: "It's only fair to let the one not chosen know what the game is here [usually from older faculty members] and advise him to apply elsewhere."

A marked shift from the centrality of teaching to the centrality of research has occurred in the major private universities, too, as was noted earlier; but our interviews suggested somewhat greater ambiguity among faculty members with respect to its implications. Clearly, research and publication were viewed as the sure road to tenure. But teaching was still viewed as important as well—more so than in the public flagships. There also appeared to be somewhat more varied routes to advancement in the private majors, particularly if one had already achieved tenure. We got the impression that the promotion process was somewhat more individual and personalized, with some professors being rewarded for visibility in the university and the community that resulted from good teaching and an active service role. Central administrators hedged somewhat with respect to a definition of *scholarship,* seeing it as varying for different fields of study. (It must be remembered that the major private universities in our sample are not as visible nationally as are, for example, Harvard, Chicago, and Stanford, where scholarly work has long loomed as central.)

The impression we gained from interviews on the campuses of major public universities was that, as on their private counterparts, research was of central importance—and its importance had created considerable dissonance among faculty. There was an implicit pressure to catch up to the best (which translated to the best *researchers*), accompanied by a realization that the necessary reductions in faculty load and increases in support services had occurred for some but not all faculty. Yet research and publishing were expected of all. Many faculty members remembered early signals of the change, usually coming on strong in the early 1980s. For example, when a dean of education sent up eleven names for tenure decisions by the central administration and only one was approved, he received three important signals: There were new rules for advancement, a campuswide peer review system had been established, and the dean had lost some important prerogatives. Faculty members spoke of some perceived concomitants: decline in the importance of teacher education, decline in collegiality accompanied by increased importance of individuality, and an absence of rewards for program planning and development.

Faculty members in the major public and private universities joined those in the flagship universities in their clear expectation that the young researcher would win out handily over the former schoolteacher with a more modest publication record in a competition for an assistant professorship. However, they were somewhat more likely than their colleagues in the flagships to express regrets over the need to make such a choice. Here, though, we did encounter more intense sentiments among some younger faculty members about the necessity of making the kinds of appointments that would ensure fast progress in the institutional catch-up race.

As a group, the regional public and private universities in our sample were the most ambiguous in their mission and the most varied with respect to their present stage of development. They were less clear than others on where they are and where they are going; they had no common star to guide them. Consequently, the appointment of a strong president or a determined provost could make a great deal of difference. Unfortunately, because successions of administrators often create successions of emphases, not always congruent, it has been (and may remain) difficult for faculty members to know what is expected of them.

There is no doubt, however, that a greater emphasis on research now and in the future permeated the culture of these regionals. To a considerable degree, emphasis on this mission leaped forward for many public universities with each transition in classification—from normal school, to teachers' college, to regional college, to regional university. And each such leap intensified ambiguity and uncertainty for long-term faculty members called upon to interpret and internalize changing expectations. For many, the transitions have been painful and the expected adaptations difficult or even impossible. Some—usually among the youngest and themselves graduates of major research universities—welcome the changes.

In interviews, faculty members were generally candid and reflective in their perspective on changing expectations in the regional universities. Sometimes they were wryly humorous in describing the exhortations of a president, academic vice-president, or dean who clearly wanted the institution to be molded in the image of Harvard or the University of California, Berkeley. Others saw such a mission as more dysfunctional than comical, wreaking havoc in its negative impact on teaching, service, and program development. Still others were bitter over having to do so much that would not be rewarded and being provided with little or no support for what would be rewarded: The rewards for research and publication are infinite, while the rewards for teaching and everything else are finite, we were told.

The dissonance and accompanying dissatisfaction that we encountered in these interviews were much more over the downgrading of the old, established functions than over the intrusion of the new, and somewhat more severe in the public regionals than in the private regionals. Although rhetorical support for teaching remained high on both types of campuses, the gap between the rhetoric and the reality (as denoted by rewards) was noticeably smaller in the private universities in our sample. This could well be a realistic response to private institutions' need to compete for students at a much higher level of cost; these universities may attempt to justify the tuition by their attention to teaching.

When faculty groups in the regionals were asked which of our two hypothetical candidates they would hire for their assistant professorship, responses were quite varied. In general, faculty support was with the second candidate—the one who had taught and who wanted to work with future teachers. In the few instances where rather senior scholars with grant-getting reputations had already been brought on board and been given reduced teaching loads and more space, there was considerable resentment over the special privileges granted; among these resentful faculty members, the second candidate was the clear winner. But there was also support for the first, on the grounds that there was need for broader representation of such individuals on a faculty engaged primarily in teaching and not well versed in research methods. Some went on to say that it was not fair to bring young researchers on board, because the conditions in which they would find themselves were not conducive to scholarly activity.

Forging a Link with the Schools. During the past decade, in particular, there has been a strong push from many different individuals and groups for the higher education community to participate more actively in school improvement. Theodore Sizer set a high moral tone for such involvement: "Teacher educators can thus only save their souls by joining with their colleague professionals in the schools in an effort to redesign the ways that students and teachers spend their time in order that effective teaching and thus learning can take place."[8] Toward this end, some states have enacted bills recommending or stipulating that those college and university personnel who teach methods courses be required to seek periodic experience in schools. In addition, there have been specific proposals for the close coupling of schools and universities for purposes of renewing schools and the preparation programs of those who work in them,[9] and some of these have been at least partially implemented.[10] Many of the most visible educational reform reports of the 1980s also referred, at least generally, to the necessity for stronger school-university linkages.[11]

In a spirited state-of-the-school message to faculty and students of the Harvard Graduate School of Education, Dean Patricia Graham reflected in 1983 on the possibility that schools and colleges of education not closely connected with the schools would be regarded by 1990 as irrelevant.[12] With the decade of the 1980s now behind us, is it reasonable to anticipate by the year 2000 what Dean Graham had in mind?

Two sets of our data suggest the need for some revision in the mission of colleges and universities if we are to take seriously the forging of close linkages between colleges of education and the schools. In the present institutional mission, teaching and scholarly activity are the most commonly defined categories of faculty work and reward. Behind these is the variously defined category of service, which is sometimes subdivided into professional, community, college or university, and more. Just as it is variously defined, it is variously rewarded; but usually it stands well behind research and teaching in recognized importance.

We probed into several of these service subcategories. The two most relevant for this discussion are ad hoc services (such as a faculty member's response to a school's request to review the research on student grouping patterns) and effecting change in schools—both of which are relevant for schools and colleges of education. The discrepancy between their perceived and their desirable importance in the eyes of the faculty members in our sample was substantial. Neither was perceived by large numbers of faculty members as centrally important to institutional mission. The percentages perceiving ad hoc services to be centrally important ranged from a low of 7 in flagship public universities to a high of 22 in regional private universities. The range for effecting change in schools was from 12 percent (flagship public universities) to nearly 37 percent (regional private universities). The vast bulk of the respondents perceived both to be either marginally or moderately important to their institution. The percentages in both categories increased when faculty members were asked to predict future importance: a range of from over 18 percent in flagship universities to 41 percent in public regionals for ad hoc services, and a range of from 29 percent in liberal arts colleges to 47 percent in public regionals for effecting change in schools. Even though effecting change in schools was seen by few faculty members in flagship public universities as centrally important, nearly 37 percent predicted an increase in its importance.

The percentages desiring central importance for these two sets of activities, now and in the future, were markedly higher for nearly all types of institutions. The range for desiring central importance for ad hoc services now was from a low of 9 percent for liberal arts colleges to a high of nearly 38 percent for public regionals. The percentages hoping for increases in future importance ranged from 38 (major private universities) to 54 (regional public universities). The percentages wanting central importance for the function of effecting change in schools ranged from 38 (liberal arts colleges) to nearly 62 (major private universities). The range for percentages wanting a future increase in the importance of the function was from 53 (liberal arts colleges) to 68 (regional public universities).

Although support for increasing the importance of ad hoc services was not overwhelming, substantially more faculty members wanted an increase in the future than saw it as likely. And although there was relatively strong support for increasing the importance of effecting change in schools, the percentage predicting this increase was likewise much lower.

One might have thought that faculty members in the public universities would overshadow their colleagues in the private ones in their desire to effect school change and provide ad hoc services to schools. But the differences between the two types are relatively small. Regarding help to schools, it is interesting and somewhat puzzling that only 9 percent of the faculty in the liberal arts colleges wanted increased centrality for ad hoc services now, yet 40 percent wanted the importance of these to increase in the future. Perhaps the problem now is busy schedules: Given some relief in the future, these faculty members would like to provide such services.

Teachers often reproach education faculty members with what they perceive as lack of interest in their problems and in those of schools generally; they complain that faculty members either do not want to assist or are incapable of doing so. There probably is some truth to the allegations, as there is truth in similar complaints about the university by practitioners in other professions. But the allegations oversimplify by placing blame without offering solutions. A more productive approach would be for both groups—teachers and education faculty members (including teacher educators)—to determine jointly which of their self-interests overlap and might be satisfied through collaboration.[13] Then both groups might pressure the state for more functional allocations of funds and pressure colleges and universities for revisions in their reward structure. With this approach, collaboration might move beyond the discussion stage.[14]

Collaborative arrangements must ultimately extend beyond schools and colleges of education to involve the greater university in the educational health of schools and communities. Campus inventories taken today would reveal for school and university people alike a rather astonishing array of collaborative arrangements, many worked out by entrepreneurial individuals and never written into any record book. But *successful* collaborations? The number of long-term partnerships between and among groups of university and school personnel, funded so as to make an impact on both cultures, is small. The few that begin often die without the autopsy that might help prevent similar deaths in the future.

The need for higher educational involvement in the schools is great. If we are to have good schools and good teachers for them, the simultaneous effort to improve both must proceed under conditions that make it possible for such a venture to succeed. Recognizing the work as fundamental, intellectual, and entirely appropriate for serious faculty engagement is the first step that our institutions of higher education must take. Until they do, the status of teaching and teacher education will continue to be that of Second Hand Rose and our schools will continue to maladjust to the profound changes taking place in our communities and beyond.

Institutional Mission and Tenure. No matter how much faculty members might wish to change the ordering of priorities in the missions of their college or university, requirements for acquiring tenure push them toward the behavior known to be most rewarded. It is reasonable to assume that faculty morale is significantly affected by discrepancies between the mission they prefer and the mission they perceive as most closely related to criteria for tenure. To the degree that this assumption is correct—and our data support it strongly—the information presented in Table 3 is cause for alarm.

Examine, for example, the discrepancy between faculty members' preference that the importance of teaching be recognized and their perceptions of the attention given to teaching as a criterion for tenure. Those in the public flagship and major public and private universities, in particular, would prefer that substantial attention be paid to teaching but perceive teaching as ranking very low among the requirements for tenure. Across all types of institutions, those surveyed perceive that the research mission dominates the tenure-granting process to a much greater extent than they would prefer. They would prefer that preparation of teachers be substantially more highly valued than they perceive it to be now.

These data raise troublesome questions about the present and future direction of higher education and of teacher education—questions that can be raised but not answered by the research on which this book is based. If the activities required of teacher educators who fulfill their function well are not rewarded at the critical career stage—gaining tenure—teacher education will suffer grievously.

Faculty Perceptions of Schools, Teaching, and Teacher Education

Certain faculty perceptions are likely to affect teacher education programs and the student socialization processes connected with them. Faculty members' views on what schools are for, the nature of teaching, and such matters as the content and conduct of teacher education, especially on their own campuses, are particularly important. (A few of their perceptions regarding these issues are compared in Chapter Six with students' views on the same matters.)

Schools. As we will see in Chapter Six, students in our sample viewed as paramount their role in helping their students

Table 3. Perceived and Desired Importance of Institutional Missions as Essential for Tenure by Institutional Type.

Mission	% Flagship Public	% Major Public	% Regional Public	% Major Private	% Regional Private	% Liberal Arts Private
Teaching:						
Perceived	17.0	40.4	60.0	25.4	74.7	69.2
Preferred	77.6	80.1	89.7	84.0	81.2	93.2
Research:						
Perceived	92.8	72.6	52.2	91.5	58.6	74.7
Preferred	58.6	58.6	29.7	56.6	40.6	23.3
Development:						
Perceived	6.9	7.1	11.1	10.9	9.1	12.5
Preferred	21.6	17.4	23.8	22.9	23.5	11.6
Ad hoc services:						
Perceived	2.7	8.8	10.3	4.5	11.4	0.0
Preferred	10.4	23.3	21.6	17.6	20.0	9.1
Effecting change:						
Perceived	2.9	2.2	4.5	4.7	7.9	0.0
Preferred	25.9	27.2	25.3	27.6	25.0	9.1
Preparing teachers:						
Perceived	7.4	14.8	32.8	11.9	39.2	26.3
Preferred	45.8	46.0	58.7	43.2	60.8	67.4

develop interests and abilities. In interviews, it proved difficult to get them to talk about other possible functions of schools and teachers. They came to teacher training with this view, by and large, and strengthened it as they progressed.

Data from the teacher education faculty members reveal that they reinforced this view in the formal socialization process of their teacher education programs. Across all institutional types, faculty members rated highest two of four choices regarding the overall functions of K–12 schooling: focusing on individuals to develop their full potential, and developing an awareness of existing social conditions and helping the young participate in improving them. Of these two, the first was perceived as more characteristic of what their teacher education programs were actually doing. Although their third-highest rating went to the function of helping the young challenge unjust conditions and transform society, they saw their programs as paying less attention to this area. They perceived their programs as stressing much more the function of helping students adjust to society and take their place in it. Faculty members' desires for and their perceptions of the functions of schooling stressed in their teacher education programs were quite congruent, then, in regard to developing individual potential. On the other hand, there was considerable incongruence in regard to the function of adjusting to society; the perceived programmatic emphasis was far greater than most wanted. In the areas of improving and transforming society, however, faculty members perceived much less programmatic attention than they wanted.

A close look at faculty preferences for school goals (with eleven to rate) reinforces an irony developed further in Chapter Six: Basic skills rank high in both personal preferences and perceived program emphasis, yet the need to improve basic skills of children and youths is always central to public criticism of schools and proposals for reform. If prospective teachers and their teachers see this goal not only to be very high in importance but also among those most stressed in their teacher education programs, why does it continue to top the list for needed improvement?

Most of the scholarly critics of schools are more likely to see schools as deficient in the development of students' critical-thinking skills. Faculty respondents placed critical thinking high in their value systems—at the same level as basic skills in relative importance. But their perceptions of what their teacher education programs were doing in this area were much lower. Aspiring teachers also placed high value on this goal—but higher toward the end than at the beginning of their programs, suggesting an impact on their thinking by the faculty. However, our total body of data pertaining to this area leads to the conclusion, to be developed further in Chapter Seven, that the heavy dominance of lecturing by teacher education faculty (and the resulting passivity on the part of the students) allows little opportunity for critical, independent thinking to flourish among teachers in training. Not surprisingly, there is a considerable parallel between rote learning and passivity in teacher education classes and the same ethos in the elementary and secondary school classes observed in our earlier work.

On one hand, then, we should be encouraged over the fact that the teacher education faculty members in our sample placed relatively high value on schools' teaching basic skills and cultivating critical, independent thinking. But our teams were less than satisfied with the degree to which teacher education programs actually prepared graduates to advance these twin goals in the schools in which they would teach.

Teaching. During periods of intensive attention to educational reform, such as the one extending from the early 1980s into the 1990s, many ideas surface. Some drift around unnoticed and then disappear until another round of reform, some manage a brief hearing, some get quite thoroughly chewed, and a few make it into an implementation stage. Rarely, however, is the process of idea legitimation accompanied by a carefully designed strategy that includes analysis of the likely acceptance or rejection of the idea by those who will ultimately be called upon for implementation.

We listed twenty-two proposals for enhancing teaching as a profession that have been put forward during recent years and asked the education faculty in our sample to express their level of agreement as to the potential of each. Those proposals are listed in Table 4 in the order assigned them by their mean ranking (across all institutional types) on our seven-point scale.

As Table 4 documents, there was rather broad agreement

**Table 4. Extent of Agreement with Selected Strategies Proposed
to Enhance Teaching as a Profession.**

Item	Strategy	Mean	N
A.	Higher teacher salaries	6.3	1122
C.	Altered working conditions	5.8	1095
P.	Teacher leadership	5.7	1071
Q.	More participatory management	5.5	1053
O.	Differentiated staffing	5.4	1054
E.	Higher entry-level standards	5.2	1102
B.	Scientific basis of teaching	5.1	1087
N.	Teaching perceived as art, science, and craft	5.0	1066
R.	Moral basis of teaching stressed	4.9	1090
U.	Elimination of emergency certification	4.9	1036
G.	Better arguments for teaching as profession	4.7	1073
S.	National program accreditation	4.7	1080
H.	Master's degree	4.5	1098
J.	Five-year program	4.4	1085
T.	Training programs modeled after medicine, law	4.2	1047
D.	National exit exam	3.8	1074
F.	National certification board	3.7	1056
V.	High-level preparation for 20 percent, lower level for others	3.2	1007
K.	Six-year program	3.1	1065
L.	No undergraduate education majors	3.0	1074
I.	Doctoral degree	2.6	1081
M.	No undergraduate education courses	2.2	1077

Note: Table entries are mean scores on a 7-point scale of increasing
agreement.

among those in our sample regarding how best to enhance teaching
as a profession. The most promising route, teacher educators said, is
to make teaching more attractive along rather standard lines of
appeal in our society: higher salaries and increased power for
teachers in the decision-making structure. These ways emerged over
and over in our interviews with faculty members, just as they
emerged clearly from the questionnaires. The prospect of low financial returns and limited power does not attract the best and the
brightest.

The second route they favored places responsibility directly on teacher educators: higher standards for entry into programs, provision of a solid knowledge base, programmatic blending of theory and practice, and stress on the moral imperatives of teaching and being a teacher. Better conditions for teachers must be accompanied by better programs equipping them to do the work well, said our respondents.

Rearranging the basic institutional structure of the enterprise—a route frequently suggested in reform proposals—was seen by most of our respondents as having little promise. Perhaps this is why so many teacher educators see policymakers and reformers as having the wrong agenda. Prescribing more years before there is clear delineation of what teachers should do and what they need to know puts the cart before the horse. Until such delineation takes place, how do we know that a master's degree is the necessary requirement? And moving much-criticized undergraduate education courses to the graduate level does not change them. More fundamental efforts to design coherent programs are necessary.

The Holmes Group, during at least the first year of its existence, pushed for teacher education to become a graduate enterprise, leaving the clear impression that they also favored the elimination of undergraduate education majors (and, some interpreters assumed, the elimination of undergraduate education courses)—all included in our list of twenty-two proposals to enhance teaching as a profession. I would have expected our respondents in the flagship public universities and the major public and private universities to have responded quite positively to these suggested reforms, given that the Holmes Group membership is drawn almost exclusively from such institutions. I was wrong. The low ratings shown for these proposals in the list above were almost uniformly distributed across respondents in the six different types of institutions. Indeed, uniform distribution characterized responses to all the proposals, although agreement was particularly pronounced for the top-ranked and bottom-ranked items. There was almost uniform agreement across types of the five proposals having the greatest potential and the four having the least potential for enhancing teaching as a profession. Similarly, there was almost uniform agreement on the modest power seen in master's degrees, five-year programs,[15] and a national certification board.

These data help us to understand why the Holmes Group, after a most auspicious beginning and then a substantial expansion in membership, began to have difficulty agreeing on the specifics of an agenda for their internal restructuring of teacher education. It was politically easier to get agreement on conducting an inquiry into the design of professional development schools. These data help us understand, too, why the members of the Board of Directors of the American Association of Colleges for Teacher Education, at a meeting in 1989, were able to secure quick agreement on rejecting as unacceptable certain provisions announced by the National Board for Professional Teaching Standards in its report published several months earlier.[16]

Overall, then, these faculty views are encouraging. They suggest a strong desire on the part of teacher educators to see teaching rise above the legacies that prompted Jurgen Herbst to entitle his historical account of normal schools, *And Sadly Teach*.[17] Given their considerable desire to elevate "effecting change in school" in the university reward structure (discussed earlier in the chapter), presumably many are interested in helping to improve teachers' conditions of work. When these conditions *are* improved, the campus image of teacher education may shed its poor-relative status. But this will not occur unless teacher educators rigorously renew their part of the enterprise—something they probably cannot do by themselves. Fortunately, the data suggest that they are wise enough not to buy quickly into all those proposals for restructuring that skirt the necessity for a collegewide or universitywide examination of commitment to and programs for the education of educators. Nothing less will suffice.

Teacher Education. Our data point consistently to the local nature of teacher education. This, in turn, suggests that improvement is likely to be locally inspired and driven. Our most intensive data gathering occurred more than a year after the release of two well-publicized reports addressed to the reform of teacher education—that of the Holmes Group (just cited in connection with our discussion of the teaching profession) and that of the Carnegie Forum on Education and the Economy. The former had aroused interest in and debate about teacher education on the campuses we visited.

Neither report appeared to be fueling a drive for change on the campuses visited. The shape of things to come would be determined, we learned, primarily by the commitment of the institution to teacher education, the degree to which working with prospective teachers entered into the faculty reward structure, and the role of the state in setting requirements for programs and teachers. This latter factor was perceived by most of the people we interviewed who were active in teacher education as having the greatest impact. (New state initiatives were being anticipated on most of the campuses we visited.)

Given our data, any optimism regarding major change must be cautious and muted at best. Although recommendations for giving colleges and universities much more autonomy with respect to their programs have surfaced in some states, there has been no stampede in this direction. Our sample of respondents provided us with no encouraging news of a state context supportive of fundamental internal change. Nor do we get from our data much encouragement regarding the prospects for self-renewal. However, plans for increased use of state-mandated tests to determine *entry* of candidates into teacher education programs and then teaching suggest the possibility of a marked decline in state specification of *program* requirements.

Only respondents in the liberal arts colleges gave reasonably high ratings (on a 7-point scale) to their institution's provision of essential resources: 5.0 for material resources, 4.7 for human resources, 4.5 for public relations pertaining to teacher education, and 4.4 for development (for example, fund raising). For the flagship public universities, these ratings were 3.5, 3.4, 3.2, and 3.2, respectively. Corresponding figures for the major public and private universities were only a shade higher. In the flagship public universities, faculty views of institutional support to teacher education as compared with other professional programs were even lower, the ratings for all four areas being 3.0, 3.0, 2.8, and 2.9. Faculty respondents in the liberal arts colleges gave the highest ratings: 4.4, 4.4, 4.0, and 4.1, respectively.

In the eyes of our respondents, teacher education was better supported by the SCDE in which it was housed than by the institution as a whole, but even here the data were less than gratifying. Not surprisingly, the liberal arts college faculty members perceived substantial education department support for the teacher education program. The ratings were 6.2 for material resources, 6.0 for human resources, 5.5 for public relations, and 5.7 for development. (Of course, teacher education was the primary activity in all the education departments of liberal arts colleges in our sample.) In the ratings of SCDE support by faculty in flagship public universities, the means dropped: 4.3, 4.3, 4.0, and 4.1 for the four categories of support, respectively. Changing the *institutional* support picture will not be easy. But surely it is possible to create a campus unit regarded by its own faculty members as giving wholehearted support to teacher education as its central mission. The ratings for all four areas of necessary support surely should be in the range of 6.8 to 7.0.

It is also reasonable to expect that faculty members in this unit would perceive that the needs of their students were being well met—especially given that (as was noted earlier) they perceived the major role of K–12 schools to be helping individual students achieve maximum potential. The extent to which faculty members perceived their teacher education programs to be meeting student needs is more encouraging than the picture of support above; but it falls far short, I believe, of what is reasonable. Our questionnaire probed into four types of institutional support for students, and faculty rated their perceptions of these on a 7-point scale. Means for "students made part of community of people" ranged from 3.8 in the major public universities to 5.6 in the major privates. For "quality of attention to individual learning needs," the means ranged from a low of 3.8 in the public majors to 6.0 in the private liberal arts colleges. There was little variation among institutional types for "amount of help students can expect in finding teaching positions": from 4.4 in the public majors to 5.4 in the private regionals. Lowest overall ratings were given for "amount of assistance for improvement after securing position"—means ranging from a low of 3.5 in the flagship public and major private universities to 4.2 in the liberal arts colleges.

Overall, the data regarding support for teacher education and for students preparing to be teachers is discouraging, whether one looks at them from the perspective of institutional or SCDE commitment. Surely those who will teach our children in the nation's schools deserve more.

Our questionnaires and subsequent interviews sought to get at factors from which to make judgments about current prospects for the renewal of teacher education programs. The most encouraging data came from respondents in the liberal arts colleges. Somewhat more than those from the other types of institutions, they perceived themselves to be engaged in continual change, to be proactive rather than reactive, and to be engaged in collaborative decision making. Not surprisingly, then, they were less inclined than their colleagues in the other types of institutions to perceive a need for major restructuring. The perceptions of faculty members in the major private universities were quite similar. Respondents in the flagship and major public universities, on the other hand, were more likely to perceive the change process as static, sporadic, piecemeal, and effected by administrative decree. With overall mean ratings (again on a 7-point scale) ranging from 3.1 to 5.2 (the mode being about 4.1 for all but the liberal arts colleges), we have to conclude that a dynamic process of proactive change is *not* the ongoing condition in the colleges and universities constituting our sample.

We gained the impression from interviews that, in most instances, a clear structure for effecting change was not in place. In any case, the effort involved in renewal was not worth the results, we were told, because teacher education programs were initially determined and then frequently changed by state fiat. Most faculty members volunteered interesting ideas for change, however, and an overwhelming percentage in all types of institutions expressed (on the questionnaires) the desire to be involved if any major restructuring were to take place. Similarly, large percentages said that they had a responsibility to be involved.

In Chapter Seven, I raise the question of whether self-renewal is feasible, given the low prestige of the teacher education enterprise, the low levels of institutional support perceived by many faculty members, the self-image of prestige deprivation, and the degree to which tentacles of external control of program requirements reach inside colleges and universities. But self-renewal by

SCDEs is not the only available alternative. If colleges and universities are to continue to prepare teachers, they must make the necessary commitment and provide the moral support and resources necessary to comprehensive renewal of the education of educators, simultaneously taking the initiative in involving nearby schools in a collaborative enterprise.

Summary and Discussion

One need not travel far across the landscape of higher education in the United States to conclude that the institutions conducting it vary enormously. Yet there are commonalities, and these commonalities ease for the visitor the task of sustaining discourse around the same set of issues as one moves from campus to campus. And even the differences, though great, are differences of degree rather than kind (as I noted earlier). They tend to cluster by types of institutions, and those of a given type vary widely so as to overlap considerably with those of other types.

In the last quarter-century, there has been a profound shift in the balance of the various institutional missions. Scholarly work, particularly of the kind supported by direct grants to professors from governmental and private philanthropic agencies, has risen to preeminence at the expense of teaching and service. Although the argument that research and teaching go hand in hand holds some water, the reality is that the box of academic work is finite: Give more time and attention to scholarly activity, and some must be taken from teaching and service.

The preeminence of scholarly work and the faculty perquisites that go with it are pronounced on the campuses of the major public and private universities. It does not take long even for the previously uninitiated to pick up some of the subtleties of prestige differentiating fields of study, kinds of publications, awards, and the like. And it does not take much probing to find that gaining campuswide recognition as a scholar is exceedingly difficult if one is connected with a school, college, or department of education. Although attention to educational matters by economists, political scientists, and psychologists is tolerated by colleagues (especially if the lapse from more orthodox domains of inquiry is brief), for physicists, mathematicians, and the like to venture seriously into curriculum development for students in elementary and secondary schools is to endanger their careers.

For many faculty members in all fields, weathering the shift in the balance of missions has been painful. Not only have they not adequately adjusted to the new expectations or gained the coveted perquisites, but many have failed to enjoy the admiration of the young colleagues thriving—sometimes rather arrogantly—in the race that left these older men and women behind. The older men and women left behind in teacher education also witnessed a decline in the status of the work they believed they could do well—and a frequent eschewing of this work by young colleagues advancing up the promotional ladder.

Although this shift in mission has been most profound and pervasive in the regional universities, every college and university we visited was having to come to terms with it. The dislocations being caused by increased emphasis on scholarly activity were now part of the recent history of the flagship public and major private universities. There was little ambiguity with respect to expectations; new faculty members were almost always well informed before coming regarding work requirements. Likewise, the dislocations in the liberal arts colleges appeared to be relatively mild. In these, we were told, scholarship and teaching—particularly scholarship to support teaching—have always gone hand in hand. Such institutions cannot announce that research has moved above teaching in importance and still survive. Nonetheless, faculty members with no publications over the last two or three years were looking ahead with some apprehension to their next promotion review.

The dislocations we noted were most severe in the private and especially the public regional universities. A whole array of the issues constituting the themes of this book come together there like a pileup of vehicles on a foggy freeway. Appropriately or not, the regionals model themselves after the major universities, apparently unable to define a distinctive mission for themselves. Thus they perceive progress to be leaving behind what they were in order to become what they probably cannot and should not become. The fate of teacher education in these institutions, which prepare such large percentages of our teachers, is inextricably linked to the vision of the trustees and administrators responsible for them. It has been said many times that education is too important to be left to the educators. I am forced to conclude that the future of regional universities and the education of educators in them is too important to be left to the institutions' leaders. But if not to them, whom?

In Chapter Four, I discussed the productive power of an enterprise in which workers at all levels are driven by a clear, internalized mission and participate in collaborative decision making. Syzygy occurs. Yet our data suggest that the necessary alignment of institutional mission and individual goals is missing for teacher education and may be missing for other components of the higher education enterprise as well. Studies into these other components— studies similar to this one of the education of educators—will be required in order to determine whether what the workers perceive to be good and satisfying work is out of sync with evolving institutional mission, and whether this mission is grounded in fundamental educational principles. I am not alone in observing that principles of the economic marketplace, more than principles drawn from the marketplace of educational ideas, now govern the behavior of universities, their administrators, and (increasingly) professors.

Earlier, we saw the considerable discrepancies between what faculty members perceived to be required for tenure and their preferences. It is difficult to imagine an enterprise being conducted well when the balance of work activity perceived to be required for rewards is so divergent from the balance of work activity desired by the workers. Under such circumstances, it is difficult to imagine that the workers enjoy high morale and derive high satisfaction from their work.

Field notes from our one-on-one interviews reveal a considerable amount of bitterness, often growing out of feelings of betrayal. Some faculty members we spoke with felt trapped. Though they saw themselves as having given the work their best shot, it had not resulted in publications; thus there was now little likelihood that they could go elsewhere. But in their present settings, they found the road until retirement (perhaps ten or more years away) no longer appealing.

In spite of this (and other) evidence of low morale, it appeared that most faculty members continued to derive satisfaction from the courses they taught and the students they supervised. They seemed tied to and inspired by immediate work demands, not some ongoing collegial effort to make the environment better. They could talk about what *might* be, but mounting the necessary effort to effect wholesale change appeared unlikely and even unreasonable in many settings.

In light of our data, a reform effort geared more to the immediate and short-term than to some unclear future makes sense. Indeed, it is probably the only healthy approach, given the circumstances. In addition, in order for energies to be galvanized for purposes of change and renewal, faculty members need to be convinced that the direction of change will be toward their preferences for good work. They are not convinced of that now: Where these faculty members see their institutions to be and to be going is often quite out of line with the desires of most. Why get in line to hurry the pace toward an unappealing destination?

If faculty members' time and energies are to be mobilized for renewal, they must hear an alternative drumbeat and subsequently see progress toward the promises of the drumbeat: an elevation of teacher education to a central place in institutional mission, resources allocated via a formula that recognizes the high time and energy demands of a first-rate teacher education program, an equitable share of scholarship funds and support services, additional funds for creating "teaching" schools in collaborating school districts, and faculty rewards geared to the nature of the required work. Unless it is clear that the work of planning and renewal are to be rewarded, there is little likelihood that it will begin.

And much more than *self*-renewal is required for the culture of teacher education to become healthy—for the structure of the institutions and the nature of academic work to interact productively. Our data suggest, however, that teacher educators *want* to become involved, once they hear a truly encouraging drumbeat. Where will it come from? Charismatic, transformational leadership from the inside? A dissatisfied polity on the outside? Ideally, there should be a joint effort, with leadership from inside and outside of the higher education establishment driven by a shared vision of what could be and the moral commitment to attain it.

Chapter Six

Becoming a Teacher

❖   ❖   ❖

Teaching begins where the subject matter ceases to be
subject matter and changes into inner power.
                                —*Franz Rosenzweig*[1]

Education is usually thought of as the deliberate cultivation of desirable traits and sensitivities, while socialization is commonly defined as training for a particular culture or segment of culture.
Education plays an important role in the development of critical
capacities to be applied, in part, to improving one's cultural circumstances, whereas socialization is more an adaptive process. The
two combined presumably produce individuals capable of and disposed toward cultural adaptation while continually seeking the
very best cultural conditions.

Note: Most of the data on which this chapter depends are presented in detail
in R. Soder, "Students and Faculty in Teacher Education: Views and Observations," Technical Report no. 8 (Seattle: Center for Educational Renewal,
College of Education, University of Washington, 1989); and Z. Su, "Exploring the Moral Socialization of Teachers: Factors Related to the Development of Beliefs, Attitudes, and Values in Teacher Candidates," Technical
Report no. 7 (Seattle: Center for Educational Renewal, College of Education, University of Washington, 1989).

Both education and socialization are viewed by the major professions as powerful contributors to the enculturation of their members. Flexner, for example, saw the four-year medical education curriculum he proposed as performing two functions. It would provide a professional academic minimum via the formal curriculum in chemistry, physics, biology, and the like; and it would also provide more subtle elements—elements he saw as difficult to come by: "One must rely for the requisite insight and sympathy on a varied and enlarging cultural experience."[2] The precise nature of these elements (and of their cultivation) remains elusive throughout Flexner's report, but the perceptive and appreciative "apparatus"[3] he saw as critical was to be provided in large measure by the close association of students with their peers and professors through an extended period in the university environment.

Nearly eighty years later, the National Board for Professional Teaching Standards echoed Flexner's recognition of these two elements in professional preparation but was much more explicit regarding cultivation of the second: "The combination of a rigorous assessment, an extended course of professional study, and a well-supervised practicum provides the strongest warrant of competence. Such a requirement assures not only that certain studies have been completed, but that certificate holders have been socialized in college and university settings where there is extended time for interaction and reflection with peers and faculty on matters of professional practice, ethics and tradition. Similarly, engagement in professional training on a full-time basis enhances the character of study, the quality of inquiry and the commitment to scholarship of the entering novice."[4]

The *apparatus,* to use Flexner's word, is both formal and informal in professional education. There is a program of studies, with prerequisites, sequences, and choices (if any) specified. In addition, there are daily interactions and both planned and spontaneous social activities, sometimes involving both students and faculty. The formal and informal components of this apparatus create opportunities for person-to-person communication among students and faculty members not directly attainable through either alone. Professional schools of law, medicine, and dentistry generally encourage an intensification of the educating and socializing apparatus by determining a clear point of entry and completion for students, who progress together in unified "cohort groups." Being a member of the class of 1942 or 1988 or 1995 identifies students and graduates with peers who now share or once shared the common hardships, pleasures, and expectations associated with becoming a professional. Being of the same graduating class creates lifetime bonds, often of deep friendship.

There is, then, in professional education, both a formal and an informal process of learning, and both an explicit and an implicit curriculum of values and beliefs. What is left out of that curriculum may be as important as what is included; it often conveys powerful, if subtle, messages. A planned, integrated process of socialization has the advantage of creating a varied array of opportunities for bringing sometimes-controversial subjects to visibility and discussion. Novices can thus receive valuable feedback in sensitive, critical areas that may be avoided in the formal setting of classes. When these areas remain covert, the beginner is left to work out his or her position on the job, where peer competition often works against open discussion and resolution.

Before we look into the formal and informal processes and curricula of becoming a teacher in the settings we studied, let us take a quick look at the student body. What are some characteristics of a sample of men and women in today's teacher education programs?

Teachers-to-Be

Some popular beliefs about the characteristics of people preparing to teach were confirmed by our data, while others were denied. The following account is based on just under 3,000 usable survey questionnaires returned by students nearing program completion (64 percent of all those in this category) and over 650 interviews, almost half with individual students. It is enriched at times by information gleaned from faculty members, documents, observations, and the data gathered by the historians who visited each campus.

Seventy percent of the survey respondents were scheduled to complete simultaneously both the baccalaureate and requirements for a teaching certificate. Approximately one in five was enrolled at the postbaccalaureate level, completing either requirements for certification or combining completion of such requirements with a master's degree. The bulk of the productivity in these colleges and universities was, then, of the so-called traditional students; but the nontraditional group, most of whom came from other lines of work, constituted a substantial source of teachers.

Our data confirm the stereotype of teaching as an occupation that attracts women and white candidates—80 and 92 percent, respectively. By removing just two institutions from our sample, the percentage of black candidates (4.6) would be cut virtually in half. The combined percentage of Asians/Pacific Islanders, Hispanics, and Native Americans totaled only 2 percent. Almost uniformly, the percentage of minority students in the teacher education programs we studied was significantly below the percentage enrolled in each institution as a whole, and nowhere did we pick up any encouraging data regarding recruitment efforts likely to change this situation in the near future. Yet as we know from the experience of the College of Education at the University of Arizona (not in our sample), deliberate, focused recruitment efforts that stress criteria likely to attract certain minority candidates pay off: Minority enrollment there increased from 12 percent in the fall of 1988 to 29 percent a year later, following the widespread announcement of interest in students with particular cultural experiences and languages in addition to English.

It would probably be a mistake to assume that today's teachers come predominantly from a narrow income or academic range. Nearly 85 percent of our sample had enjoyed a middle or higher range of income during their K–12 years. Their financial situation now was quite different, however: Nearly 40 percent were being supported by someone else, and 30 percent were being supported by a combination of self and others. Just over 50 percent claimed incomes that placed them below the middle range. About half viewed teaching as being capable of supporting an individual, but only 10 percent saw teaching as capable of providing the sole or even main support of a family. Just over 40 percent anticipated that teaching would be combined with another source of income in providing family support. Clearly, teaching was not regarded by most of the candidates in our sample as the kind of occupation that can stand on its own in providing the income required to raise a family. There are no surprises in this conclusion.

Nearly all of the colleges and universities in our sample had raised academic requirements for admission to their teacher education program for the year of our study or the year or two previously. Perhaps this accounts for an academic showing among candidates that ran somewhat counter to conventional wisdom. While some clearly lacked basic literacy skills, as evidenced by their failure to pass tests and their enrollment in remedial programs, those in our sample spread across a wide range, with all but a small percentage meeting the commonly required undergraduate grade point average of 2.5 on a 4-point scale. Over 70 percent had undergraduate grade point averages of 3.0 or higher.

Overall, education faculty members viewed students in their teacher education programs as of average scholastic ability compared with students on the campus generally. Interestingly, however, those in the private colleges and universities perceived their students in a more favorable light: About 22 percent of the faculty in both regional private universities and liberal arts colleges viewed their teacher education students as above average, with only 15 percent and 12 percent, respectively, viewing them as below average. By contrast, only 10 percent of the faculty in the flagship public university sample rated the teacher education students as above average, whereas 35 percent rated them below average. (These latter are the institutions with schools of education devoted heavily to research and graduate education.)

Some of the perceived low academic status of future teachers and their programs appears to stem in part from the extent to which some students of low academic competence get into and complete programs.[5] The fact that many very able students enter is commonly overlooked. Many of those we interviewed were bright and articulate, falling short only on responses to questions in areas pertaining to larger social and educational issues—a widespread shortcoming in our society, according to those critics who perceive average Americans, including college graduates, to be uninterested in and incapable of discourse going beyond the activities of immediate daily life.

In talking to faculty members not associated with teacher

education programs (and sometimes even faculty members connected with them), we sensed considerable contempt for the scholastic ability of teacher education students. These students were well aware of the negative perceptions but were not daunted by them. Most had experienced strong negative pressure regarding their career choice from parents, peers, former teachers, current professors, and even current supervisors of student teaching—sometimes from all of these.

I recall vividly an interview with a young woman enrolled in a postbaccalaureate program who spoke of her father (a physician), who refused to support her in college unless she gave up plans to teach. Now, after a disappointing year in business, she had to support herself while in the program because her father still refused to help. My question in group settings regarding the attitude of others always brought an outburst of giggles and a boisterous exchange of anecdotes. All participating had experienced reactions ranging from surprise to outright derision. Yet their peers, in particular, ultimately came around to supportive, sometimes admiring views: "What you plan to do is needed and important," they said. "Someone must do it."

The drive to teach was strong among both the traditional young undergraduates and the older postbaccalaureate students. For 85 percent, teaching had been and was the first career choice, even though 27 percent in our sample had previously engaged in some other line of work. Although business continues to be a strong career choice of college students, 31 percent of those coming from other work had left employment in business. Interviews brought out a strong desire to begin teaching just as soon as possible. Students often expressed impatience with certain requirements, including required courses in general education that appeared to them only to delay their entry.

The pool of people coming to teaching from the military, business, and other walks of life does indeed represent a valuable source of teaching talent. But it became clear to us that any steps to reduce or eliminate the traditional undergraduate routes to teaching could have dire consequences, not only in reducing the supply of teachers but also in cutting out many exceedingly enthusiastic young people for whom teaching is a strongly preferred career choice. The idea of delaying preparation to teach until the graduate level proved to be very unappealing to many students. They simply could not envision four years of general and specialized academic study prior to involvement in their career choice.

We also discovered that the teaching occupation has not lost the local, family character commonly attached to its past. One candidate in five and one in ten reported a mother or father, respectively, who had or still taught. Almost all candidates came from nearby communities. They rarely selected a preparation program because they knew and liked its known philosophy, or because of its high entry standards, or because they were actively recruited. The main reason for choosing a major public, regional public, or regional private university was its nearby location. In fact, location ranked high for all institutional types except major private universities and, to a lesser degree, private liberal arts colleges. Economy was an important factor at all the public colleges and universities (though less important at flagship state universities) but was of relatively little importance at the private types.

The preference for a local institution was due in large part to the belief that it gave students their best shot at a local teaching position. In our interviews, we learned that large numbers of students wanted to get a job locally; they were not interested in leaving the state or even the region of the state for job opportunities elsewhere. I recall, for example, the group of undergraduates completing their student teaching at Southwestern Bistwick State. They had grown up in the immediate region, were student teaching in schools familiar to them, were dating and planning to marry young men or women from nearby, and were fearful that local jobs would not be available. Major universities may advertise themselves as world-class, but most students in their teacher education programs come from the immediate region. Few major state universities attract teacher education students from beyond state lines. Those private colleges and universities that attract more widely do so because of their institutional, not their teacher education, reputation.

In Chapter Four, I suggested that there may be an important lesson here for public colleges and universities in these days of careful budgetary scrutiny by state policymakers. Legislators are likely to be more impressed by what the institution does for the state than by statistics on the cosmopolitan nature of the student body or faculty. A strong commitment to the education of teachers may not bring prestige of the kind many top administrators and faculty seek, given the place of research grants in the pecking order of universities, but it may go far in ensuring support at upcoming sessions of the legislature.

The Formal Curriculum

A detailed discussion of programs for teachers in our sample of colleges and universities is the subject of Chapter Seven. The following section is thus restricted to a short discussion—one sufficient to provide background for subsequent conclusions and observations on student experiences.

On the surface, James Conant's 1963 description of teacher education programs still stands: They have a "democratic social component," a component dealing with the way behavior develops in groups of children, knowledge of the growth of children, and principles of teaching.[6] These various components were provided for, he found, in some kind of social foundations course (educational history, philosophy, or issues), an educational psychology course, a course on child or adolescent development, general and/or "special" methods courses, and student teaching—commonly in that order.

The major change we saw from that earlier description was in the social foundations component. Whereas in the early 1960s one could virtually count on students' taking a fairly solid course in the history and philosophy of education (or an introduction to American education from a historical and philosophical perspective), this was the minority pattern in our sample. There was invariably an introductory education course, but it was almost impossible to predict the content of that course. Occasionally, the course proved to contain rather straightforward educational history or philosophy, but more often it was devoted to an overview of program requirements, demands and expectations of teaching, and lectures (more than discussions) on selected, rather contemporary topics: AIDS instruction, how to pass a minimum competency test, how to manage a class, and multicultural education, for example—often with one class period devoted to each topic.

Educational psychology in some form proved still to be a consistent, predictable program requirement, as did methods courses. Even the old debate over the relative value of general methods or "special" methods (in subject fields) proved to be alive and well. A tug-of-war between the education and arts and sciences faculties over allocation of responsibility for special methods courses was under way to some degree on most campuses and was waged rather bitterly on several. The problem of squeezing into the curriculum methods courses in as many as eight subjects for prospective elementary teachers was almost universal—and almost universally controversial. Likewise, the issue of general versus special subject courses for prospective secondary school teachers, with its long history, was a lively presence still.

Student teaching was still a regular component as well—but by no means an uncontroversial one. Visiting interviewers did not talk long with a faculty group about student teaching without stimulating discussion of the old issues: How much student teaching is desirable? Should it be broken into two or more short sessions or span an entire quarter or semester? Should it be offered with or without an accompanying integrative seminar? How are future secondary teachers to get a concentrated block of time without the disruption of returning to campus for the remaining required courses in a major? How do we include all of the requirements, including those for the baccalaureate, in just four years—especially when the total program is already 12 semester hours or more over the standard 120 credit hours? These are what a former colleague of mine referred to as "gray cat problems": They never go away; even if they appear to have gone, they always crawl back.

The above coursework describes that commonly taken by students in the general elementary or secondary education preparatory programs. There are variations, to be sure—greater emphasis on child growth and development in the early childhood education curricula, and special programs for students majoring in the arts, home economics, physical education, and industrial arts—but the general configuration is clearly identifiable for virtually all programs.

Far less consistent is the progression of students through it. There was not a clear point at which the class of 1992, say, came together and began its journey. We found no evidence of appreciation for or deliberate use of groups proceeding together in a common process of socialization. In the private regional universities, nearly 27 percent of the teacher education students had taken five or more teacher education courses before being formally admitted to a program! The percentage having taken three or more ranged from 54 in the private regionals to 17 in the major private institutions. Even in the liberal arts colleges, where one would expect close monitoring in a rather intimate campus setting, 35 percent had taken three or more teacher education courses before seeking formal admission. Only the major private universities in our sample managed to tie admission reasonably closely to the beginning of coursework. Perhaps high tuition at these institutions pushed students toward careful planning and selection.

We did not have these data before us at the time of our visits. Nonetheless, the existence, if not the magnitude, of this problem soon became apparent. Faculty reactions ranged from "We should be doing a better job of controlling admission and monitoring progress" to "This is the best way for students to find out if they want to teach before making a decision."

Accessibility of education courses to students not yet accepted to programs perpetuates the legacy of teaching as the not-quite profession. Even students who come to a campus planning to teach generally have no need to so declare. They can sit through several courses without any fear of being cut because of their low potential. Feedback from faculty is likely to pertain to success with the course rather than suitability for teaching. By piling up satisfactory grades in several courses, they almost ensure acceptance to the teacher education program. After they have come so far, it is, in the words of Eliza Doolittle in *My Fair Lady*, "not bloody likely" that they will be turned down for student teaching (generally the last point of entry to the program). Faculty members we spoke with, some serving on campus committees charged with keeping the gates, often admitted that mistakes had been made in letting students proceed through several courses without formal admission, but they felt that it was now too late to deny them entry.

It is difficult to think up any reasonable argument to support this haphazard approach to admission—an approach taken by many of the campuses we visited. The argument that dabbling in education courses provides opportunities to decide on teaching as a career simply does not wash. By general student and frequent faculty admission, many of the courses in which one might enroll pertain little to teaching anyway. The tragedy is that this kind of sloppiness only perpetuates the cloud of low status under which teacher education, teacher educators, and candidates for teaching labor and suffer. It is important that prospective teachers perceive themselves as meeting high standards for entry and high standards of performance throughout the entire preparatory curriculum. For programs not to meet this expectation is to do a disservice to students, to teaching as a profession, and to our children.

The Informal Curriculum

Teacher candidates, unlike trainees in other professions, have had the unusual opportunity to observe their own teachers at work for from twelve to sixteen years. Throughout this process of "apprentice-by-observation,"[7] they internalize to some degree the values, beliefs, and practices of former teachers.[8] As prospective teachers, they still frequently refer to the continuing influence of earlier mentors. As we shall see in Chapter Seven, the first courses that these prospective teachers take are "about" education; they do not confront students with situations that bring values to the surface—especially not conflicting or contradictory values. By contrast, the immediate pressures and ethos of the medical school situation, lacking much connection to students' previous experience, constitute the beginning of a powerful socialization process.[9]

Future teachers come into a teacher education setting of indeterminate boundaries. The lines between general studies and studies directed to becoming a teacher are smudged. In our interviews, we found that teacher education candidates in liberal arts colleges identified more strongly with the institution as a whole than with the department of education. Only during student teaching did the values of becoming a teacher take over—and at this stage these values were primarily in the hands of cooperating teachers in the schools.

In the large research-oriented schools of education, teacher candidates perceived themselves as on the fringes. They knew which education faculty members had national reputations, but they had little or no association with these well-known figures. Further, they knew that the school of education ranked rather far down on the scale of professional school prestige. Thus they found themselves in a second-class enterprise in a second-class unit of the campus.

Against this background of a poorly defined teacher education enterprise and its low status, it is important to juxtapose the strong teaching commitment of many of the candidates. When asked what they expected in a beginning annual salary, most gave a figure somewhat below existing pay scales in the state, and yet they were determined to teach, nonetheless. In a sense, the low financial returns anticipated by candidates appeared to be viewed by some as ennobling, like vows of chastity. Our field notes are filled with quotes from those interviewed: "Teaching is the only profession where you get an opportunity to enhance society by helping children"; "I've always wanted to teach since I was little"; "I could make twice as much money [in electrical engineering] as in teaching, but I feel that engineering is limiting"; "As a child, I had a lot of good teachers, and they inspired me to get into teaching." Regardless of the data reported earlier on the discouraging influence of friends and even teachers, large numbers of future teachers spoke of the positive influence on their decision exerted by previous teachers.

The tragedy is that this built-in readiness for preparing to teach was rarely capitalized on by the institutions in our sample. One would have expected to find on each campus an organized, welcoming group of students and faculty members and a series of extracurricular events designed to bring students and faculty together informally. The norm, however, was that students scarcely knew each other when they came together for the first time in a foundations course and were introduced to program requirements. The group assembled was not homogeneous with respect to the goal of teaching, and in no way was it a cohort group, aware of being together in the class of 1992. Commonly, the first and only recognition of a student as an aspiring teacher was tied to the formal curriculum.

There were exceptions, of course. The young mathematics major at Mainstream (unswerving in his intention to become a teacher in spite of the alternative opportunities blandished by professors of mathematics) spoke of visiting five campuses before selecting this major private institution, where he was warmly welcomed by both the university and the school of education. Unlike most of the institutions in our sample, this school enrolls prospective teachers as freshmen (as well as later). Even here, however, students identified as much or more with the university as a whole than with the school of education, in part because there were few efforts to bring the teacher education enrollees together as a common-purpose group.

Both Dorsey College (with its children's school) and Broadmoor University (with its own house for faculty offices and meetings) took advantage of their facilities in providing informal opportunities for students and faculty members to come together. Unfortunately, many of the institutions had large and somewhat formidable education buildings, apparently designed for students to pass through rather than settle into; these contrasted markedly with, for example, the education building at the University of British Columbia (not in our sample), deliberately designed around a large commons to encourage student-faculty discourse.

The lack of a group focus in the teacher education programs we sampled should come as no surprise, perhaps, given the solitary nature of teaching itself. Dan Lortie, in his *Schoolteacher,* painted a vivid portrait of the physical and particularly the intellectual isolation of teachers.[10] Kenneth Tye documented the individual orientation of teachers' in-service education: Teachers are taken out of their school settings and herded together with a cross-section of colleagues in workshops oriented to refining their individual skills.[11] The whole school ethos—for teacher and student alike—is one of individual, competitive effort.[12] As Albert Shanker of the AFT described it: "Working together in the office is regarded as cooperation. In school, the same thing is cheating." The teacher education enterprise, as we saw it conducted, is well designed to perpetuate these conditions of schooling and teaching.

One would expect students enrolled with others in a teacher education program spreading across two to four years of college to develop strong interpersonal associations. It seems surprising, then, that over 30 percent of those we surveyed (from 25 percent in the elementary programs to 40 percent in the secondary) had made only some casual acquaintances by the near-end of their training. We had expected the small size of an institution to make a considerable favorable difference, but the direction of the correlation was in the opposite direction: 21 percent in the flagship public universities as contrasted with 34 percent in the private liberal arts colleges had made only casual acquaintances; 42 percent as contrasted with 32 percent, respectively, in these two types of institutions had many friends and acquaintances or knew most of their fellow students.

What is going on here? Do private liberal arts colleges create a strong social press that somewhat excludes teacher education students (who in turn are not strongly socialized as future teachers)? Do faculty members in teacher education simply assume that the closeness many claim to share with colleagues campuswide in these relatively small settings is experienced also by students? Are the large public universities so impersonal that identification with a specific preparation program provides a source of friendship ties? Our sample of institutions is too small and the kinds of data gathered not appropriate for answering such questions. But our overall impression was that students in teacher education programs lack a sense of cohesiveness that would encourage close bonds of friendship.

This impression is strengthened by data on associations outside of regular classes. About 42 percent of the students had attended no orientation meetings with fellow students at the beginning of their programs, for example. We found evidence of efforts to create "buddy systems"—systems in which a first-year student associates with one further along—to support the beginners during their first year, and efforts on some campuses to put together cohort groups and/or clusters of student teachers. But these and similar efforts were usually initiated by individual faculty members and did not last long. Certainly, the prevailing pattern for student teachers, a group that could benefit from the sharing of experiences, was to be very much on their own. Had our sample included the University of Northern Arizona, we might have found what I observed there several years ago: When engaged in student teaching, a group of prospective elementary teachers and a couple of faculty members shared a temporary prefabricated building on the campus of the public school—a refuge for discussion of the students' teaching experiences and for providing support. All reported with enthusiasm the value of being able to talk with peers about their teaching experiences. Similarly, the College of Education at Michigan State University (not in our sample) is currently encouraged by recent efforts to organize teaching candidates into cohort groups, socialized into teaching as units.

Our data add up to the conclusion that both interest in and influence of a peer culture is relatively weak in teacher-training programs. When in need of advice, most students would go, they said, to professors or schoolteachers. Yet informal contact with these mentors was limited on most campuses, suggesting that students had little opportunity to seek counsel outside of the formal course structure. (One exception was Dorsey College, where the simultaneous joining of certain coursework and student teaching appeared to create both a stronger peer culture and considerable faculty-student interaction.) Not surprisingly, then, faculty members perceived themselves as only mildly influenced in their own beliefs by students.

Our data consistently point to a stronger informal support system among elementary school than among secondary school candidates. An obvious reason for this is that the students we spoke with from the former group did more work in common; the secondary candidates were scattered across university departments, coming together for a few education courses only to be separated again during student teaching. In addition, as many as two-thirds of the teacher candidates on most campuses we visited held part-time or full-time jobs. At urban universities such as Underhill and Central Rutherford, many rushed from jobs to take a class, then rushed back to work.

Overall, about 70 percent of the students commuted. There were substantial variations across institutions: While 52 percent of students in private liberal arts colleges and 44 percent in major private universities lived in dormitories on campuses or in residences close by, the figures for regional private and major public universities were 9 and 15 percent, respectively. Yet these differences were not paralleled by comparable or even nearly comparable inter-institutional differences in the strength of the peer culture.

Over 90 percent of the nontraditional postbaccalaureate students returning to complete teacher education requirements commuted. Most institutions did somewhat more for this group than for the traditional students by way of providing informal socializing experiences. Nonetheless, the friendship bonds established by this group were few and weak. The students were presumably too intent on preparing themselves for jobs and too involved with families and friendships already established to seek additional associations.

The emphasis of Western culture on individualism—in schooling as in other matters—had already shaped the behavior of most students we spoke with. In interviews, students were far from agreed on the value of group association. Some saw their individualism as setting them not only apart from but above peers. Others, however, saw the lack of strong peer association as a great loss. And at Dorsey College, with its deliberate effort to create a sharing experience, the organization of students into a group was almost—but not quite—uniformly appreciated.

In concluding her analysis of our data on the peer culture of teacher candidates, Zhixin Su writes the following: "The organization of the training program, especially the structure of the student teaching experience, also tends to encourage the development of teacher individualism. Data from the surveys and interviews indicate that students in the programs studied did not have many collegial interactions, either on a formal basis or an informal basis, among themselves. The image of student teachers projected in the present study is an aggregate of persons learning to teach on their individual motivation and initiatives. The student teachers confront a 'sink-or-swim' situation in physical isolation. The way most beginners are inducted into teaching therefore leaves them doubly alone."[13]

Internalization of Values and Beliefs

In both survey questionnaires and interviews, we asked students many questions pertaining to the function of schools, the role of teachers, their perceptions of program goals and emphases, their views on educational issues, and more. In the interviews, we were able to push beyond predetermined questions in order to gain impressions about what was going on in the minds of students as they transcended their student status in identifying with the demands and expectations of teaching. During their teacher education programs, students are not mere recipients of influences from others but are firming up many of the values that will guide them as teachers.[14] Thus we sought to discover what patterns of values, beliefs, and educational principles appeared to be emerging to guide them as teachers. We also wanted to know *how* these values, beliefs, and principles evolved.

Ideally, one would want to study over time this interactive process of value shaping. Although we did not have the luxury of time, we were nonetheless able to draw some conclusions. Because the findings reported on in the previous section (combined with other research[15]) led us to the conclusion that the student peer culture, both before and during student teaching, was neither well formed nor powerfully shaping, we concluded that the formation of educational values in fledgling teachers—to the extent that it occurred—depended heavily on the programs themselves. Before looking at what the programs appeared to be teaching, and how powerfully,[16] let us reexamine the values that students brought with them.

They were specifically and practically oriented to becoming teachers, and most came from close by. Students in all types of institutions rated "having a satisfying job" as their top reason for entering teaching (from 6.3 to 6.5 on a 7-point scale by institutional type). Liking and wanting to help children were reasons rated almost equally high. Such reasons as having a backup job or not knowing what else to do were rarely cited. The strong drive to become teachers was particularly obvious in nontraditional students leaving other lines of work. They and their younger counterparts were well aware of the low status of teaching in the surrounding society before entering their programs, and they soon became aware of the low status of teacher education in their institution. It is interesting that their frustration appeared to attach more to failure of others to recognize the importance of teaching than to their own disappointment. In shrugging off derision, many appeared to gain added conviction from the implicit virtues inherent in choosing an occupation devoid of power and status.

Although some students spoke of their interest in a subject as a reason for entering teaching—more, of course, among secondary than among elementary teacher candidates—we rarely got the impression that becoming an educated person was a powerful, driving goal. Indeed, many students were as impatient with their arts and sciences requirements as they were with their courses in educational foundations. Their interest in and satisfaction with the program increased in direct proportion to increased field experiences and then student teaching. Methods courses ranked on a scale of usefulness between foundations and actual classroom experiences.

Negative public and academic perceptions of education courses have been shaped in large measure by the degree to which those experiencing them downgrade their usefulness. These perceptions must be juxtaposed against the general background of teacher-training students' very practical orientation—an orientation that leads them to judge all education courses by utilitarian, instrumental criteria. Courses in the arts and sciences, on the other hand, are simply not expected to meet these criteria. Prospective teachers want to learn how to teach; they are not aspiring to be educational historians, philosophers, psychologists, or sociologists. Many of the professors of education they encounter early on, however, are precisely such specialists. Many professors, as we shall see in Chapter Seven, are as uninterested in turning their courses into such instrumentalities as students are interested in finding practical implications in them. Clearly, there is a misfit. In probing during interviews, we usually found that foundations courses in education were perceived by students to be neither more nor less intellectually challenging than their courses in general studies. What bothered them was that these courses appeared not to be sufficiently pointed toward teaching.

One wonders how much the negative image of foundations courses—more or less undifferentiated one from another—has resulted in their erosion as required courses, on one hand, and contributed to their garbage-can status (all kinds of state-imposed requirements end up being dumped in them), on the other. The "practical" methods courses tend to fill whatever space in the curriculum is vacated as foundations courses erode. Ironically, although students in the elementary teacher education program commonly complained of repetition and "busywork" in methods courses, large numbers wanted more. "You can never get enough," they said.

There is a still greater irony in the fact that two primary criticisms of education courses are in opposition. These courses are described as both impractical, largely by students (a common complaint in nearly all professional preparation programs, incidentally), and "Mickey Mouse," largely by faculty in the arts and sciences. Any push away from the impractical foundations courses—those cut from the cloth of education as a field of study—toward courses seen as more immediately useful exacerbates the Mickey Mouse status of education courses generally, while serious efforts to push away from the how-to approach and toward basic principles exacerbates the student charge of impracticality. Students and the education faculty alike, on survey questions pertaining to the theory-practice dilemma, wanted a blending of the two. Clearly, the field of pedagogy and the effective melding of pedagogy in a coherent preparation program for teachers are begging for inquiry and constructive action.[17]

Considering all this, the two major conclusions that emerged from our analyses should not surprise anyone. First, the transition from being a student to being a teacher appeared, for most students, to be more an occupational than an intellectual transcendence. That is, they shifted from being students in a college or university to teachers in a school, rather than from students of the contents of their own curriculum to inquirers into teaching, learning, and enculturation.

Second, internalization of what it means to be a teacher generally involved absorbing "what works" with a classroom of children or youths. Being "able to do it"—as, for example, one's mentor in student teaching did it—became more important to these students than questions of why a certain way was successful or an exploration of alternative possibilities.

Neither of these orientations could be considered intellectual. The first is an orientation to a job and a setting that students perceive as potentially satisfying. The second is somewhat tradelike: What is the state of the art as practiced by those who appear to be doing it satisfactorily? Because of these practical orientations, students stored up in the more protected environment of training as many practical ways as possible. The socialization process appeared to nurture the ability to acquire teaching skills through experience rather than the ability to think through unpredictable circumstances. Perhaps this explains, in part, why teachers, largely cut off from one another, appear relatively eager to attend practically oriented, short workshops but are reluctant to participate in in-service opportunities that emphasize principles and theories.

Nearly half of the students interviewed maintained that the basic educational beliefs and values they had held at the beginning remained unchanged throughout the length of their programs. Others saw themselves as coming with idealistic views of schooling and teaching and then becoming more realistic and practical. Most faculty members believed that students' values and beliefs changed. Probing revealed, however, that many interpreted "values and beliefs" somewhat narrowly. What faculty members perceived was a change from students' initial simple views of teaching to more complex views. Both groups saw the student-teaching experience as having a strong impact. Teacher education faculty members saw themselves as a source of strong influence as well, although students placed them significantly and consistently below cooperating teachers in their impact on educational values and beliefs. Those who went out from the university to supervise their student-teaching placements were ranked for influence below faculty members who teach campus classes.

In interviews with students—nearly all in or about to enter student teaching—we found that most had great difficulty recalling the substance of their foundations courses. With considerable probing, we were able to stimulate some recollections of a little history, some philosophical schools of thought, and issues pertaining to access to schools. Except in three or four institutions where there had obviously been powerful professors doing the teaching, we did not get very far. Very little of what was discussed in an introductory course reappeared later for these students. They made no connections, it appeared, between the early discussion—or, to be more accurate, lectures—and their own teaching. Most recognized that there is something more to teaching than technical knowledge and practices, but concepts of moral imperatives and ethical considerations to be taken into account slipped away from them. They had no context or vocabulary for moral discourse.

Again, we should not be surprised, given the practical orientation of teachers-to-be. Yet are education students different from students in other disciplines—philosophy excluded, perhaps—in their unwillingness and inability to engage in serious, informed discussion of major social issues related to their occupation? Would students in other professional schools be able to go beyond the vague and superficial? Have we any reason to believe that Richard Hofstadter would present a more uplifting picture today than he did in his book *Anti-Intellectualism in American Life,* published in 1963?[18] As I raise these questions, data increasingly suggest that the situation grows worse. After several years of horror stories about our general ignorance in mathematics and sciences, new reports now deplore our limited knowledge of history and literature as well. To remedy the ills of undergraduate education, the chair of the National Endowment for the Humanities proposed a strict core curriculum taught by colleges' most distinguished professors. At the center are six survey courses on cultures and civilizations that include history, literature, philosophy, and art.[19] Thus it appears that our conclusions regarding future teachers would apply to students generally. Nonetheless, the consequences of shortchanging prospective teachers in their general education are far more serious, because teachers perpetuate both what they know and how they learn.

In looking back to their entry into the teacher education program, students perceived themselves as valuing highly the teaching of basic skills as the prime goal for schools, rating this option 6.3 on a 7-point scale. This position did not change: Overall, their present rating of the importance of basic skills was 6.4 (the same level of importance given by faculty members). According to student perceptions, all eleven goals for schools listed on our survey questionnaire had climbed slightly in importance in the intervening months, although the relative position of each remained virtually constant. "Citizenship" and "enculturation," for example, were rated 5.0 and 5.1 in importance initially (that is, in retrospect) and increased to 5.5 and 5.7, respectively, but they remained at the bottom of the list.

It is interesting to note that "creativity," seen as near the bottom at the time of entry (rated 5.3), had climbed to 6.3 near the end of the program. This was the only goal that changed its relative position significantly; it moved from eighth on the list to fourth, close behind "basic skills," "interpersonal understanding," and "self-realization" (all three having held their initial high ratings). Faculty members, meanwhile, placed "critical thinking" along with "basic skills" at the top of their list of goals for schools. "Creativity" and "enculturation" were next to the bottom—just above "career preparation"—in the faculty ratings of goals.

The rather small top-to-bottom variation in ratings from means of 5.5 to 6.4 and 5.3 to 6.4 for students nearing the end of their preparation programs and faculty, respectively, reflects the broad set of public expectations for school goals.[20] Although school districts announce commitment to these expectations, in practice there is a lopsided emphasis on basic skills, to the neglect of other important areas. In view of this emphasis, we should not be surprised at the overwhelming dominance commonly found in studies of classroom teaching of teaching for relatively low-level intellectual skills—a condition that appears to have worsened in recent years.[21]

The study of 1,016 classrooms conducted by my colleagues and me in the early 1980s[22] led us to the conclusion that part of the problem can be traced back to teacher preparation. This hypothesis is supported by data from the work reported here. Both students and faculty members perceived their programs as placing most emphasis on the basic skills function of schools. (It is interesting that both groups ranked their programs' emphasis on *all* goals consistently lower than their own perceived importance of all goals, however. In other words, the conduct of programs did not quite live up to their expectations.) As we shall see in Chapter Seven, both students and faculty members viewed field experiences and student teaching— when students are immersed in the basic skills orientation common to schools—to be the most effective and useful components of their preparation programs.

There are, once again, ironies and paradoxes here. Evidence consistently points to the dominance of teaching for basic skill development in schools. Despite this emphasis, however, educational reforms have been directed mostly to basic skills, with remedial programs extending all the way into colleges and universities. In other words, although basic skills are the primary emphasis in the public school classroom, they are apparently not being taught successfully: Basic skills levels are still disturbingly low. As was just noted, our data also point to the dominance of basic skills rhetoric and programmatic emphasis in most of the teacher education programs studied. Yet both students and particularly faculty members often spoke to us eloquently and even passionately of the need for teacher education programs to prepare students much more broadly.

The more we probed during interviews with individuals and groups, the more it became apparent that domains pertaining to values, character development, and moral understanding have an ambiguous place in both schooling and teacher education. Neither students nor faculty members were reluctant to tell us that teachers play a highly significant role in the lives of children and youths, particularly given the decline in family and religious influences; and both students and faculty members valued highly what might be best described as a child-centered orientation to education—one embracing the full range of human potential. In addition, future teachers and their teachers perceived themselves as important role models for their respective groups of students, although we were usually hard-pressed to carry our discussions much beyond elements of deportment—dress, speech, personal habits, and the like—in seeking to attach meaning to this teaching function.

Every campuswide teacher education council I interviewed was skittish about discussing its role in selecting and monitoring candidates for teaching on criteria beyond the academic. Their concerns with broadened criteria centered on potential legal problems and fear of litigation. Two groups had recently considered broadening their selection criteria to include character traits, but they had reluctantly backed off. Others simply shrugged off the question as leading into a morass. Generally, too, these councils were reluctant to put forward an array of criteria against which to judge the progress of candidates toward some vision of teaching. Not only was there rarely agreement on a vision, but there was a hesitancy to impose a vision on individual faculty members—even if they were offered the opportunity to help determine it. A logistical complication was frequently noted: the difficulty of articulating the pieces of a program conducted by different groups of actors that were often not in very close communication.

The perception of teaching that candidates near completion were developing called for them simply to fit into existing circumstances. Thus, as I have noted, the transition was not a deeply intellectual one—from reflective student to reflective practitioner, so to speak.[23] Rather, students saw themselves as observing what teaching requires and then taking on the mantle of teachers observed. If, in student teaching, their reflective position on best procedures clashed with district ways of doing things or the cooperating teacher's practices, they yielded to the status quo. There were exceptions, of course; some students spoke enthusiastically of opportunities to innovate offered by their cooperating teachers. Not surprisingly, our system of cross-checking usually revealed that these cooperating teachers were highly regarded by campus supervisors.

The problem here is complex. It is expecting a lot to ask prospective teachers, most of whom were relatively passive in their *student* roles, to become both reflective students and reflective practitioners in the course of a relatively short teacher education program. And if the final socialization process is largely in the hands of practitioners in regulated, relatively conservative school districts, we can hardly expect novices to challenge the conventional wisdom from alternative, contradictory perspectives.

What we see running all through our data is a considerable readiness—more on the part of the faculty than the students—to talk about what could and should be the teacher preparation program geared to a comprehensive vision of teaching approaching that described in Chapter Two. We also encountered in our interviews with many faculty members, hesitation and even doubt regarding the ability of undergraduates to grapple productively with issues pertaining to the role of schools and teachers in our democratic society. Many of the students we interviewed perceived teaching to involve more than providing instruction in the basics, but they appeared to lack both a clear grasp of the larger context and their responsibilities to it. They clearly lacked the experience and the vocabulary essential to informed discourse.

Older students leaving other work to gain certification were more aware and more ready to go beyond the classroom in envisioning their role; but, for the most part, they also quickly found themselves in unfamiliar intellectual terrain. Somewhat more than the traditional students, they recognized inequities in the ways schools deal with different groups of children and youths and were somewhat more passionate in wanting to do something about such conditions.

The overwhelmingly dominant student view of the teaching role pertained to helping individual pupils and dealing with variability among them. The care and attention generally perceived by prospective teachers to have been their good fortune as students was something they wished to carry into their own classrooms. Likewise, they wished to provide for their pupils the models in dress, appearance, and deportment that their mentors had provided for them. But the future teachers we interviewed both individually and in groups usually became vague and incoherent when they tried to talk about their moral responsibilities to the community and those persons they would teach. Teaching was viewed by most as primarily a job—a desirable job, with good colleagues and needful young people in their care. For most, however, the concept of being an intellectual role model in the classroom and the community appeared not to be a powerfully influencing factor.

Summary and Discussion

Few of the students in our sample were enrolled in a particular teacher education program because of the powerfully beckoning influence of the institution.[24] Only the major private universities and, to lesser degree, the private liberal arts colleges provided for some an attraction that transcended state and local boundaries. Even then, however, the pull was the *institution*'s reputation, not the reputation of specific faculty members or the teacher education program. Students who saw a strong institutional reputation as an advantage in getting a job weighed that factor heavily in selecting a college or university.

But this kind of deliberate selectivity was overshadowed by propinquity. As was stressed earlier, teacher education is highly local in character. The overwhelming majority of both undergraduate and postbaccalaureate prospective teachers in our sample came from close by and commuted daily. Most held part-time (and some, full-time) jobs, at least until they engaged in student teaching. They were predominantly white and middle class, and they represented a wide economic spectrum, although most came from families with incomes a little above the national mean. The two historically black institutions in our sample—one rural and one urban—enrolled a majority of first-generation college students coming from low-income families. Only a very small percentage of these perceived themselves or schools as performing a role in transforming society.

Most of the students in our sample were strongly committed to teaching as a first career choice. Most had been and were criticized by friends, family members, and even teachers and professors for making this choice. Some were bitter over what they perceived to be public hypocrisy—extolling the importance of education and schools, on one hand, and denigrating teaching (by maintaining low status and low financial returns), on the other. They were well aware of and disappointed in the low status of teacher education in the college or university they attended but rationalized this situation to be the unfortunate consequence of others' misplaced values.

It appears to me that, in seeking to attract able people into teaching, we have looked above and beyond these important local circumstances. We do not need glossy brochures designed to attract young men and women from far away into teaching, and we certainly do not need to mail them out across the country. The prospective candidates, even for so-called world-class universities, are a few miles from the entry gates, ready and eager for a little encouragement—better still, a genuine, generous welcome, perhaps at a reception hosted by the president, when they arrive. Small incentive scholarships, perhaps carrying such well-known names as Kodak, Sears, Boeing, Xerox, Safeway, and Coca-Cola, would provide badly needed financial help and, more important, help to assure future teachers that the corporations doing business in the community care about our schools. We have heard the criticism of business for years. If the business world wants to help, here is a simple, direct way that would have a strong impact. Additional scholarships might be funded by the state and by private foundations as a means to convey prestige to both the students and teaching.

Campus recruiters often forget about the undecided undergraduates on their own campuses. We did at UCLA (when I was dean of education) until our head of teacher education came up with the idea of working with all the department heads in the arts and sciences. Suddenly, we had more good candidates than we could accommodate—a delightful situation in teacher education.

Some institutions we visited were talking about the need for more minorities in teaching, but many minority students already in the pipeline—prospective teachers still in high school, for example—would be faced with a year or two of remedial work in the skills of basic literacy. It is unlikely that they would be able to afford the added years of study in order to graduate from college and become teachers. Here is an obvious gridlock best loosened by direct financial assistance to such students. What better way for a corporate or other philanthropic foundation to do good and enjoy gratifying returns? The results would be immediate, highly visible, and very much in the public interest. But the private sector should serve primarily to raise public awareness of what is basically a public matter.

The argument we heard for allowing students to take several education courses before seeking admission to a teacher education program are weak and far outweighed by the negative consequences. First, this common practice denies students the opportunity to begin a collegial journey of professional education and socialization as a member of a cohort group. Second, because a course in educational philosophy or psychology is not an introduction to *teaching*, it falls far short of helping students to make up their minds about teaching as a career. The personality of the professor is likely to be the determining factor—and to weigh just as heavily in a negative as in an affirmative decision. Third, the indeterminate point of entry conveys the impression—too often a correct one—that there are no clear boundaries to the teacher education program. Students just take some prescribed courses and seek to get admitted in time to be placed in schools for student teaching. Fourth, because course requirements are almost exclusively academic, the criteria for advancing toward a teaching career also become almost exclusively academic. Criteria pertaining to character, ability to articulate, sensitivity to young people, ethics, and the like fade into obscurity.

With no clearly stated required entry point (and some students were admitted as late as the student-teaching stage), many institutions in our sample were defeating well-intentioned efforts to improve on the selection and admission process. What might have been a comprehensive admission review at the outset drifted piecemeal over a rather long period of time. Ultimately, students simply presented a record of courses taken. Given satisfactory grades in these and a favorable evaluation in some modest additional review, they were "in" the teacher education program. Many were so far along in their required coursework at that point that no responsible person felt comfortable blowing the whistle even when he or she had misgivings about them.

Helping prospective candidates decide whether or not they want to teach and to reflect on whether they are likely to be good at it is exceedingly important. But this can be done best through a series of planned experiences in schools prior to the official point of admission to a program or during the early stages of that program, as is done in law, medicine, nursing, and other professions. The solutions—and they are not complex—lie in the hands of the teacher education faculty and certain university officials (the registrar, for example), who need to recognize that credit must be given for an array of educational experiences other than and in addition to conventional courses. Some enrichment of the teacher education budget, particularly for conducting informal socialization processes, is also necessary.

The data reported on previous pages present a picture of students who began and progressed individually, only casually and for short periods of time sharing common programmatic experiences. This progression was capped by individual placements as student teachers. The individual rather than group orientation was further reinforced by the logistics of working and commuting. Formal courses emerged as almost the sole structure for shaping attitudes and beliefs about teaching. However, because most programs we reviewed lacked a clearly articulated mission and the infusion of its constituent elements into the curricular sequence, most of this potential appeared to dissipate. Consequently, the requirements and beliefs of individual instructors became the elements to be internalized or ignored. Students simply adjusted.

With courses increasingly behind them, student teaching looming or present, and actual teaching in their own classrooms not far beyond, the teachers-to-be increasingly relied on the regularities of teaching and of teachers already in classrooms. "How it's done" towered over research findings and principles espoused by leading figures in the field, past and present. These future teachers squirreled away their store of methodological nutrients to be brought forth in times of later need. To the degree that theory had taken some hold in their minds, prospective teachers appeared to view it less as impractical than as not *immediately* useful. They anticipated that it might well be dusted off and tested after they became more adept at classroom management.

It is important to point out that several of the postbaccalaureate programs in our sample were more coherent than the traditional programs described above. They, too, lost much of the potential of informal socialization processes, however, because nearly all of the candidates commuted and many carried family responsibilities. The main criticism of students and faculty members alike in these postbaccalaureate programs was that an academic year (or even an academic year plus a summer) is not sufficient time "to pack it all in."

As we shall see in Chapter Seven, the totality of a future teacher's education is in the hands of several different faculties. Communication and coordination among them is limited; sometimes there is scarcely any. Again, the problems are relatively clear. This time, however, they are not at all simple and easily resolved. The solutions get us into deep-seated faculty beliefs and attitudes, university reward systems, turf to be shared, complex relationships with schools, and more. I leave these issues until Chapter Seven, where the terrain is more fully described. But at least three of the major issues to be addressed arise out of the subject matter of this chapter and are therefore taken up here.

The first involves the apparent disjuncture between the highly practical goals and expectations of prospective teachers and the more generalized intellectual orientation of preparation programs in the college or university context. Most of the students are strongly motivated to teach; they judge the quality of everything encountered on grounds of perceived practicality. They are drawn powerfully to the discrete and utilitarian—things unencumbered by whatever intellectual roots once nourished them. Faculty members teaching the courses, on the other hand, particularly in the so-called foundations, lean toward the study of education: Several practical alternatives may grow naturally from common intellectual roots. The push of students toward what appears to work, backed by public perception of teaching as a natural activity based on common sense, had forced programs toward the technocratic rather than the theoretical. The consequences appear to be reinforcement of the conventional wisdom regarding the low intellectual content of teacher education, on one hand, and of an operational rather than intellectual socialization of students into teaching, on the other. Overcoming the disjuncture noted will require a transformation of teacher education going far beyond all the popular recommendations for reform proffered to date.

The second issue emerges directly from the first. Prospective teachers oriented to filling a large handbag with discrete bits and pieces of know-how may be destined to become pedagogical bag ladies and bag men, forever seeking more and more attractively packaged items to stash away. This image is far removed from that of the reflective practitioner, forever inquiring into relevant theories and principles and their implications for practice. Evidence suggests that the former rather than the latter image shapes much of what goes on in the staff-development or in-service activities experienced teachers seek out and participate in. To what degree do we value the second image over the first? Do we value it sufficiently to hold to it steadfastly in the face of the difficulties and costs involved in seeking to make it a widespread reality? These are questions we must face up to in any serious commitment to significantly raising the quality of our schools.

The third issue is closely related to the first two. It arises out of the conclusion that prospective teachers increasingly take their cues from the field as they draw toward the close of their preparation programs and teaching in their own classrooms. Because current practice is both appealing and has an impact, why not wipe out all else and simply apprentice novices to experienced teachers? The economics thus effected are in themselves appealing.

I sought to answer this question in Chapter One, in part

using Abraham Flexner's contribution to medical education as a model. As was noted, he was highly critical of the medical mentoring employed in the early years of this century and of the experience-based didactics accompanying it. Although his view of the doctor does not fit my view of the teacher, I share his fear about simply cloning practitoners in seeking to educate professionals. He saw the need to raise the quality not only of preservice medical education but of ongoing practice. He viewed the apprenticeship system as dangerously perpetuating outmoded procedures and treatments. He envisioned, instead, programs embedded in the scholarly context of the university, on one hand, and in the very best hospitals, on the other—these, in turn, under control of the university-based schools of medicine.

Given intense national concern over the quality of our present schools, why would we want to risk perpetuating their practices by socializing prospective teachers into them? And why would we want neophytes, lacking opportunities to learn and experience the best, to be trained in school practices mandated by administrative fiat? The arguments that Flexner employed so successfully in the case of medical education appear exceedingly well suited to teacher education as well—and ultimately, to justifying teaching as a profession.

The problems today are essentially those Flexner encountered and anticipated. Teacher education in the 1990s, like medical education in 1910, is something not yet seriously attempted. The fact that it is not commonly being *well* done in the universities is not a convincing argument for taking it away from them, however. Rather, we should study what is wrong and lay out what should be—and then do for teacher education what has already been done with notable success for medical education, always remembering, however, the fundamental differences between the medical and the educating professional. Not to do so will be to perpetuate teaching as, at best, the not-quite profession and to ensure continuation of the school practices that political, business, and educational leaders believe to be turning us into a second-rate nation.

Chapter Seven

Programs for Teachers

❖ ❖ ❖

It is not enough to teach a man a specialty. Through it he may become a kind of useful machine, but not a harmoniously developed personality. It is essential that the student acquire an understanding of and a lively feel for values. He must acquire a vivid sense of the beautiful and of the morally good. Otherwise, he—with his specialized knowledge—more closely resembles a trained dog than a harmoniously developed person. He must learn to understand the motives of human beings, their illusions, and their sufferings in order to acquire a proper relationship to individual fellowmen and the community.

—Albert Einstein[1]

Over a decade ago, President Derek C. Bok of Harvard challenged the university's prestigious Graduate School of Business to address more effectively in its core curriculum the proper governance of

Note: This chapter addresses the education of teachers only, although there are implications here for programs preparing special educators and principals. People interested in delving more deeply into the supporting data

corporations.[2] Presumably, he believed, as Bernard Gifford later noted, ". . . that, as a direct result of the introduction of more and better ethics courses and more and better courses on the mutual relationship between the public and private sector, the ethical practices of business leaders would improve."[3] The *New York Times* had made the same assumption in its earlier support of President Bok's challenge. Gifford, while dean of the school of education at another prestigious university, the University of California, Berkeley, raised troubling questions about schools of education: Would President Bok (or any other university president, for that matter) have made the same assumption about the curriculum of the university's school of education? And would the *New York Times* have agreed? Gifford rejected both scenarios.[4] He argued that low esteem would be equated with impotence in the field of education and that one could not count on a commonsense assumption regarding a close connection between the quality of educating in elementary and secondary classrooms and practices in schools of education.

Gifford concluded that "schools of education, especially schools of education located on the campuses of the nation's elite universities, suffer from congenital prestige deprivation."[5] This condition, as I argued in Chapter Three, is the legacy of all types of schools, colleges, and departments of education, with the ramifications varying rather widely from institution to institution. The critical question is whether these SCDEs can and do go about their business of educating teachers productively and satisfyingly regardless of the legacy they bear. Gifford is apparently not optimistic; he contends that "schools of education cannot heal themselves. They cannot arrest the pathologies that are produced by congenital prestige deprivation. Self-renewal in the face of constant devaluation is impossible."[6]

Transcending Prestige Deprivation

My interest in this volume is not in schools, colleges, and departments of education, as such, but in the education of teachers.

drawn upon are urged to read P. J. Edmundson, "The Curriculum in Teacher Education," Technical Report no. 6 (Seattle: Center for Educational Renewal, College of Education, University of Washington, 1989).

However, SCDEs and teacher education are closely linked. As we have seen in preceding chapters, teacher education appears to suffer prestige devaluation in the very unit created to support and nurture it. Indeed, as we saw in Chapter Six, some of the prestige deprivation suffered by future teachers in the university environment stems more from their enrollment in education courses than from their career aspirations.

Let us lay aside for the present the hypothesis that extreme prestige deprivation cripples the renewal process and apply the commonsense assumption of President Bok to the education of teachers rather than business leaders: The university program for elementary and secondary schoolteachers connects with their future behavior as teachers. What prima facie evidence can we garner to support this assumption?

Convincing indeed would be the deeply held belief of those conducting the teacher education program that their efforts make a difference. But does that belief exist? The data and analysis of Chapter Five present us with a mixed bag in this regard. On one hand, many faculty members in all types of institutions perceived themselves to be involved in important work that contributed to better teachers and better schools, simultaneously perceiving their efforts not to be adequately appreciated within their own institutions. On the other hand, many perceived their students to be too immature to grapple with the complex issues of education and schooling and saw themselves as settling for something far less than ideal preparation. If forced to rank on a 7-point scale the overall intensity of faculty members' belief that their teacher education programs produce outstanding teachers, I would circle the figure 4. (This estimate is derived from the impressions my colleagues and I formed while interviewing faculty members, combined with data on faculty perceptions of their programs.)

A second powerful indicator of the impact of programs would be students' perceptions. Are they strongly positive? Here, according to Chapter Six, the picture is even more complicated. In general, the students we spoke with appeared more confident of their own individual ability to serve school children and youths well than of the overall usefulness of the program. Yet most, once they were beyond foundations courses, saw the rest as helpful. Many were extraordinarily resilient in the face of knowledge that teacher education did not rank high among campus priorities and were able to shrug off the discouraging comments of peers, relatives, and even teachers regarding the unattractiveness of teaching as an occupation. My general impression is that large numbers of future teachers on all types of campuses are ready to rise to challenges and expectations beyond those prevailing. On a 7-point scale measuring students' perceptions that their programs make a significant difference, my rating would be 5. I would go to 6, however, in rating aspiring teachers' perceptions of their ability to perform well with their own students.

Given this apparent readiness for challenge and the appeal of an important "calling" on the part of students, it would appear that an enormous payoff lies in addressing the reservations of faculty members. My colleague Roger Soder urges educators to take notice of and address the apparent discrepancy between what education faculty members say they see as institutional mission and what they say they would prefer. He notes, in particular, the resentment that mid-career faculty members hired to conduct teacher education programs feel on learning of the desire of their president and academic vice-president to turn their former teachers' college into an internationally known research institution. "If we are able to speak seriously and beyond bland generalities about effecting major philosophical and structural changes in both schools and teacher education programs, then resentment is clearly a significant, perhaps overriding, variable to be accounted for and included in design and implementation plans."[7]

The implication for change in these observations lies in the fact that belief in the importance of what one does rarely thrives in a social vacuum. Awareness that significant others feel similarly is extraordinarily important. Thus any college or university assuming responsibility for teacher education must recognize the education of educators as institutionally important and reward faculty members for doing it well.[8] The degree to which institutional commitment must be reiterated and rewards made apparent and real emerges when we consider the prima facie evidence necessary to a program's assumed power and relevance. The distance to be traveled by teacher education faculties is such that they will never make it if they doubt that their belief in the importance of what they do is widely shared.

Let us imagine that a quarter of the 1,300 or so colleges and universities now preparing teachers rededicated themselves to the task, added to the resources already committed, and redesigned the faculty reward structure so as to evenly balance teaching, scholarly activity, and participation in the renewal of schools. Establishment of these necessary conditions—a process that would take three to five years—would not in itself ensure effective programs, of course. But given these conditions, it would be reasonable to expect the teacher education faculty to provide, within a few years, common-sense evidence sufficient to persuade a large segment of the public that there is indeed a connection between the education of educators and the later behavior of the graduates.[9]

The question now before us is this: How far from the necessary conditions are teacher preparation programs? To answer this broad question, we must address a host of subquestions: To what degree do the programs in our sample have goals of such clarity, focus, and compelling power that they give direction to major curricular and instructional decisions and activities? To what degree do the programs ensure immersion of future teachers in general, liberal studies likely to prepare them for intellectual leadership in the community and provide the necessary knowledge base for teaching? To what degree are the various components connected so as to ensure programmatic integrity and coherence? To what degree do the various parts of the programs have relevance for the situations likely to be commonly confronted by elementary and secondary school teachers? To what degree are future teachers being prepared to serve as moral stewards of schools, sensitive to the values of a democratic society and capable of joining with others in renewing schools in the face of changing conditions and circumstances? To what degree do programs and the faculty model exemplary practices, both implicitly and explicitly, that appear to be internalized by those enrolled as they progress toward teaching careers? To what degree are there processes of formative evaluation that help to drive renewal and recommitment to goals derived from the role of education, schools, and teachers in a free society? Other important questions arise and are addressed as we proceed.[10]

We can seek to answer these questions only for the twenty-nine settings we studied. Any potential for generalizing arises out of the consistency of our findings. There are settings in the United States to which only a few of our findings pertain; there are others to which most pertain. To the degree that responsible people in a setting perceive that these findings do pertain to it, they have before them the possibility of a compelling agenda.

Articulating and Meeting Goals

We saw in Chapter Four that most of the colleges and universities in our sample apparently perceived clear articulation of their mission to be unnecessary. Similarly, most of the SCDEs dealt lightly or not at all with their purpose; they got quickly to descriptions of programs and what they required of students by way of course specifications. Such omissions, as was noted, are not acceptable.

It should come as no surprise to find no clear, all-encompassing goals for the education of educators in institutions that have no clearly stated educational mission. The lack of goals is nonetheless a grave mistake. In the absence of goals, who determines the standards students are to meet and faculty members foster—and how? Among almost unlimited possibilities, what curricular experiences should be selected in preference to others? These are the kinds of questions that textbooks and courses in departments of curriculum and instruction in schools of education commonly address. They appear not to be the questions commonly asked and answered by *teacher education* faculties, however.

Very few of the programs we studied made clear in descriptive documents the qualities desired in students—those to be required as prerequisite to admission and those to be developed afterward. The only requirements common to all pertained to academic credentials: at least a specified grade point average (GPA) and usually a stated score on the Scholastic Aptitude Test (SAT) or on substitute tests, such as those of the College Board. Frequently, the SCDE reiterated requirements of the institution as a whole or stipulated slightly higher ones for admission to teacher education programs. We visited at a time of considerable national interest in the academic qualifications of teachers and future teachers. It is not surprising, then, that the GPA requirement in many programs had gone up a bit that year or the year before—from C to C+ or B to B+, for example. Curiously, in several instances, efforts to increase academic requirements above those of the campus as a whole had met with administrative resistance on the grounds that, once admitted, students had access to any baccalaureate program. Teacher education programs had no clear gates and no firm boundaries.

It is fair to say that teacher educators currently take *academic* qualifications of aspiring teachers as seriously as most campus admissions officers take them. As was noted in Chapter Six, they frequently require tests of basic skills, especially when they regard the campuswide requirements as low. Desperately needed, however, are the resources necessary to remediate the poor performance of many first-generation college students from low socioeconomic backgrounds who view teaching as an extraordinary opportunity to better their lot. To trumpet the need without providing the resources is a waste of time. Of course, the problem goes back into the elementary and secondary schools and the vicious cycle kept in motion by those teachers who are poorly educated.

Various types of data already presented led us to the following conclusions: that the expectations of teacher education programs are not clearly articulated to persons likely to be interested in them, that selection of programs by students is heavily influenced by geographical and financial accessibility, that selection criteria are narrowly defined and that adherence to them in some institutions is casual, that many faculty members and students believe that more care should be exercised in keeping the gates and monitoring the progress of those admitted, and that many qualities thought by faculty and students to be important requirements for teaching are ignored in the selection and guidance processes, in large part because of their rather sensitive nature. Although interinstitutional differences in general favored the small colleges, it is necessary to point out that the greater satisfaction of faculty and students with the selection process related in large part to admissions procedures and requirements of the campus as a whole.

Both a pervasive awareness of the sheer magnitude of the task of staffing our schools and a mistaken sense that people have a *right* to teach serve to favor opening the gates when doubt exists. We could view these circumstances somewhat magnanimously, perhaps, if we could be sure that programs were tied to clear ends and designed to have a cumulative impact. Perhaps the clarity of mission not articulated to the world on the outside prevails and is internalized by both the faculty and students on the inside—but our data suggest otherwise. The commonsense argument is that powerful, coherent programs can reach, motivate, and bring to essential levels of competence a wide range of candidates. In exploring this issue, the implicit curriculum may be more revealing than the explicit.

The clear conclusion from the student data gathered together in Chapter Six is that the dominant programmatic ambience was one of fitting in, rather than challenging; of dealing with students' needs in the classroom, not the redesign of schools; of how to do it, rather than why to teach in a given way—the "technification" of teacher education.[11]

Large numbers of faculty members favored a programmatic orientation that concentrated on helping future teachers develop the interests and abilities of children and youths, yet they perceived the existing dominant emphasis to be that of preparing teachers to help the young take their place in the existing society. Although faculty members in all types of institutions saw preparation for order and stability as dominant in their programs, they preferred something else. For example, although nearly 43 percent of faculty members in flagship public universities who responded to our questionnaire preferred an emphasis on educating young people to improve our society, only 14 percent perceived this to be the dominant program emphasis.

My colleagues and I puzzled again and again over the marked discrepancies—pronounced in the major and regional private universities—between faculty members' perceptions of the most important functions of schools and the ones they perceived to be most provided for in their teacher education program. It became increasingly clear to us that most of the teacher education programs we studied took their shape and substance from sources other than careful faculty deliberation. Our method of study provided a wealth

of data to support this observation—an observation that emerged
with increasing clarity during our visits.

One of the most revealing aspects of curriculum development
is the method or approach to determining its scope and sequence.
Two patterns emerged. The first pertains to the impact of state
requirements—not just what they specify but how they are internalized by a given institution. At Quadra University, for example, the
director of teacher education regarded them as "givens." She simply
worked each requirement into a course already offered or created a
new course, which then became part of the teacher education curriculum. Changes in requirements frequently necessitated additional
new courses. There was no ongoing faculty discussion of a mission
and how best to achieve it. Indeed, we were told, such discussion
would have been a waste of time (even though interviews with faculty members revealed that they were not without ideas for improvement): The conclusions arrived at would have had to conform to
state requirements in any case. Thus, completing the series of course
requirements automatically became the goal for students.

At Ellsworth, a liberal arts college in the same state, although
meeting state requirements was a major consideration, members of
the small teacher education faculty appeared to be making acceptable adaptations based on their beliefs about a good teacher education program. The department had neither a plethora of course
offerings to manipulate nor the willingness to bend unduly to ap
parent rigidity. There was clear evidence of compromises negotiated
with state officials.

The second pattern is a kind of overlay on the first and characterized most the multipurpose schools of education. It was common for a person teaching a required teacher education course not
to participate in determining its intended contribution to future
teachers. The course was plucked out of another educational curriculum (for example, that of educational psychology) and injected
into the teacher education sequence. Indeed, the teacher of one such
course told me that he had neither an interest in nor an obligation
to teacher education. He simply taught a course in educational
psychology that happened to be required for teachers.

Four of the elementary and secondary preparation programs
we studied appeared to have a coherent core of purpose and belief.

All were small—two in liberal arts colleges, one in a major public research university, and one in a regional private university. The two liberal arts college programs clearly involved much faculty discourse and participation in execution. At Lakeview, the problem-solving approach had been developed by the long-term chair, who insisted on adherence to it while working with colleagues toward improvement on it. At Dorsey, where reflective practice was a major theme, there was a long history of cooperative program development and continued faculty dialogue. The research-oriented university had a small, relatively well staffed postbaccalaureate program embracing only twenty students, organized around developmental theory. Program coherence in the regional private university pertained primarily to the so-called methods part of the curriculum; but it is still worth noting, because efforts were under way to extend the coherence to the student-teaching portion.

Small size does not guarantee program coherence, of course. Indeed, in one of the smallest programs we studied, students expressed the necessity of remembering whose class they were in so as to adapt to the views of a particular professor. However, as schools and colleges of education expand in size and function, teacher education increasingly loses much of the identity and singleness of attention enjoyed in liberal arts colleges. Schools and colleges of education in our sample were divided into areas or departments (or both), such as curriculum and instruction, educational psychology, foundations, and so on, with responsibility for teacher education housed in one of these—usually curriculum and instruction. This department then became either a beggar, seeking needed courses from other departments, or a despot, demanding this or that course (and sometimes using the leverage of licensing and accrediting requirements). Sometimes this department created courses for the teacher education program that somewhat paralleled courses already offered in other departments.

This is an indefensible curriculum-planning process. It appears to create a host of problems and to virtually defeat the prospect of having a committed faculty group that is free from all such departments and their turf problems—a group charged with setting goals and determining both scope and sequence of a coherent, focused program of teacher education. No program in our sample was guided by a comprehensive mission of the kind proposed in Chapter One (requiring the conditions laid down in Chapter Two).

Providing Ample General, Liberal Studies

Twenty-four of the twenty-nine settings we visited conducted undergraduate programs in teacher education designed to be completed in four years. The remaining five offered fifth-year programs leading to a certificate. Some of the twenty-four also offered a post-baccalaureate certification program. In several instances, completion of additional work qualified candidates for a master's degree.

Although the general-education requirements for future teachers in these colleges and universities were and are of interest to us, we lacked the resources for digging deeply into them. This has been done and is being done by others.[12] Currently, there is rather widespread interest in the substance and ethos of the undergraduate curriculum and in the quality of undergraduate teaching—an interest that seems to wax and wane over time.

Ironically, although strong undergraduate education has been at the forefront of recommendations for improving teacher education,[13] there has been enormous complacency in regard to ensuring it. Some vague, quantitative measure is often invoked: two years of general studies followed by concentration in a subject-matter major for prospective secondary school teachers; fewer methods courses and more academic courses for elementary school teachers. These were the recommendations we heard over and over in interviews with chairs and faculty members in the arts and sciences. These people usually proposed a minimum requirement of four semesters of general studies in the arts and sciences—a minimum that they generally perceived as exceeding existing requirements. Yet this very requirement for prospective teachers was stated in one way or another by all of the institutions in our sample.[14] (It appears that many faculty members in the arts and sciences are ill-informed about teacher education requirements on their own campuses.)

Uniformly, prospective elementary school teachers were able to meet this and their other program requirements only by careful scheduling at the outset. In at least two instances, it appeared that the two-year general-studies requirement was eroded at least a little because of other curricular demands in the four-year schedule. Generally, however, students completed more than the 120 semester hours conventionally thought to be the undergraduate specification. Sixteen rather than fifteen hours of credit per semester were typical, frequently increasing to eighteen or nineteen hours as students got more and more into their field experiences.

Some institutional documents openly stated a baccalaureate requirement of up to 132 hours for most students, regardless of field. Even in 120-hour institutions, however, it was not uncommon to find teacher education students enrolled in their ninth semester, and a few were in their tenth. Some students said that this situation was their own fault—they had not planned early and carefully enough— but others complained of inadequate program descriptions and guidance. Many insisted on the necessity for "truth in advertising": The added time was probably necessary, they agreed, but should be openly and widely specified. Some were bitter over the additional expense in time and in earnings lost as a teacher. Those about to graduate at midyear worried about their employment opportunities.

What I am describing here is not unique to teacher education or to the colleges and universities visited. There appears to be less threat to a two-year general-studies requirement for all students than to the four-year baccalaureate program. Special interests of all kinds are placing demands that cannot be met in the final two years. These come not just from undergraduate professional and preprofessional programs but from the demands that professors in the arts and sciences place on majors in their respective fields and the frequent failure to delineate clearly what part of the whole is required of future teachers. Like the high school, the undergraduate college becomes a shopping mall.

All of this causes one to wonder about the often-heated arguments over whether there should be a four- or a five-year preparation program for teachers. The former is fast-disappearing even where the latter has not been announced and legitimated. The liberal arts colleges in our sample appeared to be holding closest to the four-year pattern, but even in these, the elementary school preparation program was bulging at the seams.

Colleges of arts and sciences and professional schools within multipurpose universities commonly list prerequisites for entering professional schools through, for example, preengineering and pre-medical curricula. On the assumption, apparently, that candidates for these schools either make career decisions prior to coming to college or are willing to take additional time to meet prerequisites later, quite specific course requirements are stated. For teacher education, this kind of curriculum control would be a luxury.

The colleges and universities in our sample left to students in teacher education either the choice of arts and sciences courses within the general-education specifications of the institution or the choice of courses within broadly defined domains such as the humanities, social sciences, mathematics, and the natural sciences. Where students were directed with greater specificity, it was generally because of state certification requirements. Is one course about as good as another for teachers as long as it is designated as an option satisfying the institution's general-education requirements, as this free-choice approach suggests? I think not. Nor do I think students possess the information they need to make informed, intelligent choices.

Teachers are the only specialists in our society called upon to inculcate, not merely apply, the rules of their expertise.[15] For teachers—whether at elementary, secondary, or tertiary levels—a very large part of these rules constitutes the substance and structure of human experience incorporated over time into the arts and sciences disciplines. The education to be provided by schools (no other institutions assume it) is critical enculturation into the ways of knowing embedded in these subject matters and the problems and issues they seek to enlighten. Such enculturation "is morally fundamental; it is necessary for all in a just society; it is basic to every person learning humankind's repertoire for structuring experience."[16] How are teachers to succeed with children and youths in this enculturating task if their own enculturation is in question? And question it we must, considering the extraordinary range of general quality in baccalaureate programs, the clear tendency of most academic departments to give more curricular attention to requirements in their field than to those of general education, and the common omission of carefully thought-out preteaching general-education requirements for future teachers.

Necessary though spelling out this preteaching general-studies curriculum is, much more is needed. It is essential, too, that those responsible for tending the gates to teaching stiffen their spines. Data reported earlier reveal that once a student is admitted according to the narrow range of criteria usually used and sometimes casually applied, the later monitoring process is even more casual. Further, people deciding to enter a teacher education program may do so in most institutions at any number of entry points[17] and present for acceptance an extraordinarily wide array of previous studies, provided the GPA and SAT (or substitute) scores are high enough. (Much of what is described above pertains at the postbaccalaureate level as well.)

There is a substantial gap between the rhetoric and the reality of teachers' needing to be among the best-educated citizens of the community. There are many reasons for the gap. By and large, the academic community has managed to stay above the unseemly charge that the general-education curriculum does not receive the serious, continual attention it deserves. Yet that charge is warranted. And future teachers are no better prepared than other students to make intelligent choices from the range confronting them. We know that the time of a class and the appeal of scheduling several classes on just two or three days of the week loom large as criteria in choosing. It is serious enough for college students generally to make ill-informed choices; but we cannot afford for our teachers to have poorly balanced general-education programs. Such varied institutions as the Universities of Chicago, Michigan, and Western Washington have attracted attention over the years for their establishment of undergraduate colleges and faculties committed to curriculum development and teaching. Because such efforts are enormously demanding of professorial time and are often out of step with the research *geist* of the university as a whole, they are commonly short-lived. A less demanding but promising approach is that of the University of Washington, where a committee representing several of the arts and sciences departments has built a suggested general-studies program out of both existing and newly designed courses to guide students in their selection.[18] The suggested sequences include most of what I proposed for teachers in Chapter Two.

Another reason for the shortfall between reality and what is desirable in the general education of teachers is the degree to which the charge that education courses "clutter up the liberal studies curriculum" has served as a highly visible whipping boy. Whipping it vigorously during eras of intense concern over the quality of teachers obfuscates all else. Even in California, where high school teachers have been required since early in the century to complete the general-education requirements of the university, an academic major, and a fifth year of study, many academicians use "those methods courses" to explain their low views of teachers and the products of secondary schools. Regardless of whether or not the criticism is valid, it is dysfunctional, leading only to simple solutions to complex problems.

Building Program Coherence

The most common complaint among educators at all levels is that there is never enough time. In one sense, this is encouraging: It implies a desire to make a difference. One way for a program to make a difference is for all the component parts to be related—for there not only to be agreed-upon beliefs and goals but deliberate bridges at the points of desired connection likely to disconnect. There must be a group of worriers, reasonably comfortable with one another, who work together and continually toward improving the program's scope and sequence. The group must not be exclusive of any of the people on whom the quality of the program depends. These conditions were only partially met in the best of the programs we studied and scarcely at all in the rest.

General and professional studies are generally handled separately in teacher education, yet this is a misleading distinction. Because teachers initiate others into their expertise in and with knowledge (as was stated earlier), the knowledge they gain must be internalized as part of their professional repertoire. Mathematics for the teacher of mathematics is *professional* knowledge—insufficient, but an essential part of the teacher repertoire, nonetheless. Likewise, ethical and moral norms dealing with individuals and their right to learn are part of the essential repertoire, whether acquired in a school of theology, of arts and sciences, or of education. It is the task of teacher educators and the curriculum over which they preside to see that both the mathematics and the moral norms are learned and made functional for future teachers.

The problem is that the necessary pieces and connections are walled off by institutional organizational arrangements. Moving highways from here to there and digging tunnels under cities are child's play compared to breaking down those walls and creating new, functional arrangements.

Please understand: I am not calling here for one curriculum in mathematics (and other subjects) for teachers and another for everyone else. I am simply raising the question of how much of what kind of mathematics (or whatever) is necessary to its basic understanding—the criterion of "basic understanding" being whether or not it is sufficient for one person (not necessarily an aspiring schoolteacher) to teach it to another or to use it in some life situation requiring for its understanding some kind of mathematical analysis. Again and again, prospective secondary school teachers told me that they were unable to make connections between their undergraduate subject-matter education and the high school curriculum they were required to teach. This is not a "methods" problem; it is a problem of understanding what curriculum reformers of the 1960s referred to as "the structure of the disciplines."[19] The probability that few *teachers* graduate from college with the necessary understanding merely illustrates the probability that few college graduates of any persuasion do.

There was not on most of the campuses we studied either the ethos or the mechanisms essential to ensuring a curriculum for prospective teachers that balanced the major domains of knowledge and depth of understanding in the subjects they planned to teach. Faculty members in education referred frequently to the arts and sciences faculty "down there," "over there," and "across the street." My colleagues and I enjoyed some animated conversations with groups and individuals from both education and the arts and sciences (separately) about the importance of teacher education and how it could be improved on that particular campus—but such discussions were rare, we were led to understand.

We were told in some instances that dialogue, planning, and program articulation were the responsibility of a campuswide council or committee on teacher education. I met with these wherever possible. In all but two or three instances, routine committee business was devoted primarily to approval of courses and student programs. Most met infrequently; some had not met in months. It was common for members to have to introduce themselves to one another. Sometimes even the chair was hard-pressed to remember what had been discussed at the most recent meeting—usually held months before.

People we interviewed in liberal arts colleges perceived less need for this sort of coordinating body in teacher education. Faculty members knew one another and conducted business matters rather informally. The fact that some education courses met general-education requirements at Dorsey and Lakeview attested to the acceptance of education on those campuses. But there were no more signs there than elsewhere that the needs of teacher education had an impact on the general-studies curriculum. As was noted earlier, however, most liberal arts colleges lack the luxury of providing many electives and alternatives, so they usually have a well-thought-out general core of studies.

Ivy University had recently been through a comprehensive reconstruction of its undergraduate curriculum, and the results were encouraging with respect to providing a balanced program for future teachers. There were similarly encouraging signs at Pilgrim University: It was clear that a preservice teacher education council met regularly, took its business seriously, and paid careful attention to student selection and guidance and the curricular requirements of all programs. Recently, this council had discussed implications of the Holmes Group recommendations. Members viewed state regulatory bodies as inhibiting their work and impinging negatively on the quality of programs.

In general, however, the dominant campus perspective, language, and curricular reality reflected separate, loosely connected parts, each presided over by different faculties, with very little communication among and even within groups. There existed on virtually all campuses we studied an administrative arrangement whereby arts and sciences requirements for future teachers were specified. Similarly, in the larger SCDEs, the various departments provided the so-called professional courses specified. Some other person in an administrative capacity saw to it that students were assigned to student-teaching placements.

There was, however, no group with authority and responsibility over the whole; that is, there was no group able to determine and ensure a cohesive program of general education, special and general methods courses, foundations courses, field experiences, student teaching, and follow-up of graduates—all tied to a teacher education mission determined by its members. Indeed, in some instances, the near-absence of any continuity left students to contend with a series of disconnected, discrete segments.

If we were to examine just the campus portion of the professional sequence, we would see that several programs ensured considerable coherence for their students. But none exercised much control over either the general education required or student teaching. To a considerable degree, teacher educators go as beggars, cup in hand, for whatever concessions they can get. In many schools and colleges of education, they fill in critical portions of the curriculum by begging from their colleagues in the various departments of the unit. The result is a teacher education curriculum in disarray.

Over the years, responsibility for providing methods courses in secondary school fields has bounced back and forth between departments of education and of the arts and sciences, largely to the dissatisfaction of both.[20] The retirement of a math professor who has taught the course in the teaching of mathematics, for example, commonly provokes a crisis. Because of the low status of such activity (as viewed by colleagues), there is no rush of volunteers to pick up the work of retirees. Usually, the description of the vacancy in the arts and sciences department omits any reference to teaching a methods course. Yet that department is often reluctant to turn it over to the education department and may be highly critical of the conduct of whatever methods courses are already being taught there.

Although the question of jurisdiction over and responsibility for teaching these methods courses came up at some point during nearly all of our visits, the question of what the courses were for seldom did. At Central Rutherford State, where the turf problem had escalated to the level of an internecine battle between the school of education and several academic departments, there was widespread interest in the outcome of deliberation on the matter by a campuswide committee. Although the problem was almost universal, nowhere did we find a satisfying resolution or a carefully deliberated plan of action. The problem remains unresolved.

Our most dismaying set of findings in the area of program integrity pertained to student teaching. In the "professional" component of teacher education programs, there are often three sets of actors: those who teach the more academic courses (such as the history, philosophy, and psychology of education), as well as those in curriculum and instruction who teach methods courses; those who represent the college or university in supervising student teachers (in some cases, these are members of the previous category); and cooperating teachers in elementary and secondary schools who serve essentially as models and mentors but may also serve in a kind of clinical capacity, bringing the outside world of schooling into the campus class. Almost always, the first group of actors is on the tenure track of the college or university; in the larger schools and colleges of education, participation in the teacher education program may be a minor part of their work. This is sometimes the case with the teacher educators who go out to the schools as well, but it is more common for those individuals not to be on the tenure track, not to hold secure positions, and not to have much say in the mission and conduct of the teacher education enterprise. Cooperating teachers, employed by the schools, usually have little or nothing to say about the program. Where all three groups exist, there is a clear distinction with respect to their status in the college or university: The closer one gets to working with future teachers in the field and school classroom, the less prestige and security one has within the institution of higher education. In addition, this decline in status appears to be almost proportional to a decrease in influence over the teacher education program.

Typically, the colleges and universities in our sample exerted influence but did not control student-teaching placements. The final decision was commonly made by the schools—perhaps by a principal or by the district office on the recommendations of the school principal. The choices were often based on convenience rather than on what would provide the best experience for student teachers. In two settings, we found students busily seeking out their own placements; in one, several were still looking even though the scheduled period for student teaching had already begun. In virtually all, the placement process depended heavily on the goodwill and cooperation of school districts and specific persons in them—goodwill that most colleges and universities were careful not to disturb.

What the above findings boil down to is this: There is not for teacher education a faculty with influence sufficient to ensure a reasonably connected and integrated program of (1) general and professional studies, (2) observations of practice, and (3) supervised teaching experience—all driven by a clear mission and agreed-upon goals. At the upper end of the scale of variation are the several small programs and one relatively large program referred to earlier, in which the foundations and methods courses (and, to a lesser degree, observations in the field) cohere around a conception of what schoolteaching requires. Some of these and a few of the others have worked out quite satisfactory collaborations with a corps of cooperating teachers, although these teachers are more recipients of student teachers than colleagues in program planning. At the lower end are those where a director of teacher education patches courses together and places student teachers wherever he or she can find teachers willing, for whatever reason, to take them on—with all of this administrative entrepreneurship driven by state program and credentialing requirements. Not infrequently, the budget available to hire temporary adjunct faculty for supervisory functions is limited and remains uncertain even as the fall quarter or semester looms near.

The top end of the distribution is not satisfactory; the bottom end is outrageous. The concept of having the control and influence necessary to comprehensive program integrity is so far beyond the hope of realization for most teacher education faculty groups that it is difficult for them to discuss it seriously. Getting greater coherence in the portion under their control presents sufficient challenge, in their eyes, and is regarded as within reason.[21]

Ensuring Program Impact and Relevance

The most common lament of students in schools and colleges focuses on the irrelevance of much of what they study to what they perceive to be the real world. The lament is common in professional schools and programs as well. The closer to practice that program requirements appear to be, the greater the students' satisfaction with them. Yet in some fields, the more students absorb what practice models, the more their professors despair over the futility of their own teaching.

All of the above is particularly descriptive of teacher education. In interviewing prospective teachers as part of James Conant's research team in the early 1960s, I noted the degree to which they denounced courses such as the philosophy and history of education. In my probing, however, they admitted that the courses were as good academically as courses in the arts and sciences; it is just that students did not perceive them as useful for teaching. Once students start out to prepare for an occupation, they judge the curriculum marked off as preparatory on very practical grounds of perceived relevance.

Our data corroborated other findings in this area. On a 7-point scale of the perceived contribution of program segments to one's future success as a teacher, student ratings climbed steadily from a low mean of 3.8 for social foundations courses: 4.9 for educational psychology, 5.2 for general methods courses, 5.7 for special methods courses, 6.0 for field experiences, and 6.7 for student teaching. The pattern was almost identical for faculty members, but within a somewhat narrower range: 4.1 for social foundations to 6.6 for student teaching. It is interesting that interview data also revealed considerable impatience with general-education requirements on the part of some young people with a strong ambition to teach, particularly among first-generation college students. Many viewed completion of secondary school to be quite sufficient; all else, they thought, should be directed toward preparation for the classroom. Esteem for their program increased among aspiring elementary and secondary teachers as they moved toward completion— with appreciation increasing significantly at the stage of student teaching. More than at the outset, they believed completion of a program to be necessary to later good teaching—a view held more strongly by prospective elementary than by prospective secondary teachers.

Just as students perceived the "practice" part of the curriculum to be most useful, they also saw it as most influencing their values and beliefs. They rated student teaching, cooperating teachers, and pupils in the schools first, second, and third in influence (rating these 5.8, 5.5, and 5.3, respectively, on a 7-point scale). Those teaching the education courses were ranked fifth (at 4.8 on the scale), following family, relatives, and friends. Supervisors from the teacher education program ranked ninth out of ten groups (with a rating of 4.2). Student ratings of their preparation to carry out specific teaching tasks were almost uniformly quite high, the mean rating being 5.5. The area of perceived deficiency for both elementary and secondary candidates was preparation to work with handicapped children; 43 percent of both groups viewed themselves as insufficiently prepared.

Interview data were, in general, congruent with the above. Elementary prospects for teaching expressed general satisfaction with their programs, ranking foundations courses lowest and student teaching highest. More than secondary candidates—who were generally somewhat less satisfied overall—they spoke of being extraordinarily busy in an overly crowded program. They volunteered, too, that some of this was busywork—not intellectually challenging and somewhat repetitious—but that it was useful, nonetheless. They would not eliminate any of it, but they thought that some useful consolidation in the methods courses should be effected. They felt deficient in class management and wondered why no comprehensive course was offered in that area, instead of the bits and pieces of good counsel they received in methods classes. The major complaint of secondary groups pertained to student teaching: not enough, too interrupted by the need to return to campus for classes (usually in their majors), and too focused on the classes they taught (to the neglect of other areas of teacher responsibility).

A complaint of both groups—though more with the secondary teachers than elementary—was a lack of field experiences closely related to campus classes. Two far more satisfied groups in this respect were those in early childhood education and special education—the two groups most satisfied overall with the usefulness and relevance of their programs. All spoke, however, of the need for more contact with the field, particularly in conjunction with classwork (so that what they talked about in class would be observed immediately before or after). When I met with a cross-section of students, rather than just elementary or secondary candidates, for example, those aspiring to be high school teachers listened in virtual awe as the others described their field experiences and recommended improvements. They confessed to not knowing why the other students had any complaints; they would settle, by contrast, with field experiences of *any* kind, and confessed a hunger for them.

Earlier in this chapter, I discussed the jurisdictional problem with respect to methods courses, particularly at the secondary level. (Methods courses are almost uniformly within the province of SCDEs at the elementary level.) There is a serious substantive problem with these courses as well. There has been interest for a long time among students of pedagogy in the degree to which subject matters can be milked productively for guidelines to teaching them. Three decades ago, the psychologist Jerome Bruner was listened to attentively by curriculum reformers for his views on marrying intuition and the structure of the disciplines in seeking to teach them. He gave credibility to the idea that "any subject can be taught in some intellectually honest form to any child at any stage of development."[22] In recent years, psychologist Lee Shulman has raised to considerable visibility the potential of research into subject-specific pedagogy arising out of the unique nature and intellectual demands of a discipline.[23]

Little has been done in recent years, however, to probe deeply into the fascinating theses proposed by Bruner, Shulman, and others. It is regrettable that our data show that the organizational arrangements likely to promote such inquiry are virtually nonexistent. Only at one institution did we find a faculty staffing plan, partially implemented, directed toward creating what might be called "a pedogogy of the academic disciplines." On a few other campuses, interest was expressed, but for the most part this proved to be something less than a hot topic of conversation. Methods courses for prospective teachers of mathematics, history, English, and the like ranged from studies of secondary school content to reviews of relatively generic methods of teaching (such as small-group work, problem solving, use of technology, and so on)—commonly presented in lecture format.

On a couple of campuses, experimental programs directed toward curriculum development in mathematics and the natural sciences at the middle school level, supported by the National

Science Foundation, offered some hope that inquiry would lead to explorations of the Bruner-Shulman theses. In these programs, individual methods courses (or blocks of methods courses) at the elementary level both reviewed content and covered several of the relatively well known approaches to teaching. Eight programs organized the methods courses—typically on teaching reading, mathematics, science, social studies, and language arts—into blocks of time. Sometimes the arts also were built in. Health and physical education were usually taken care of in separate methods courses.

What became apparent in both the block and separate course patterns is the degree to which four or five different methods of teaching reappeared in each subject-specific block segment or course. Students complained not so much of the repetition, however, as of the failure to dig more deeply during each successive reappearance of an approach. For example, cooperative learning, now growing more popular, appeared in each course or block segment but at about the same level of development, whether in the methods course in social studies, science, or language arts. What appears to be needed is faculty agreement on the range of methods to be addressed, some allocation of responsibility for one or more to each subject course or segment, careful arrangement of accompanying hands-on experience with each method in selected school classrooms, and both formative and summative evaluation to ensure mastery of each. If each method were linked, in turn, with the subject for which it appeared to be particularly relevant and useful, greater depth and less repetition at a superficial level might result. Research-minded professors might probe productively into the elusive pedagogy of the disciplines.

Educating for Moral Stewardship

In Chapter Six, I concluded from our data that formal and informal socialization processes, as well as the intellectual orientation of preparation programs, came together to influence the operational role of teachers in the classroom. Most students remembered only vaguely the discussions of major issues in education and schooling that had been presented in a social foundations course near the beginning of their program, and they remembered the study of historical themes even more vaguely. One program deliberately delayed these larger issues until after student teaching, when, said members of the faculty, students would be more mature and have an experiential base to draw on. At both Mainstream and Vulcan Universities, most students recalled a rather powerful classroom experience in a social foundations course, and they praised the instructors in both instances. The issues and themes discussed had not been sustained through other segments and courses, however. More commonly, students recalled a hodgepodge of topics, with (in more than one instance) such diverse subjects as religion and the schools, equity, and a philosophical position such as realism, each discussed in a single session. The overwhelming tendency was to get on with what would be of rather immediate utility in the classroom. Typically, however, early childhood education students reported child-development themes running through their courses and referred to such early figures as Rousseau and Pestalozzi, invariably Montessori and Piaget, and then contemporary leaders such as Bruner, Elkind, and Zigler. Yet overall, at all levels, there were no common themes, educators, and readings in the curricula. A local professor was more likely than Dewey, Thorndike, or Piaget to be cited as influential in a student's thinking.

Data that we gathered in probing into curriculum and instruction strengthen the conclusion that the future teachers in our sample were being prepared primarily for an operational role in the classroom. We saw that mission statements regarding, for example, the role of schools and teachers in a democracy were usually missing. There was little faculty agreement on what the purposes of schools are or should be or on the present orientation of programs toward preparing teachers for such specific ends. Many admitted to stepping rather warily around controversial issues for fear of indoctrinating their students. One program chairperson took offense at the idea of some general agreement on program purpose, on the grounds that faculty members were competent, had their own beliefs, and were free to teach those beliefs as they saw fit. We found little evidence that future teachers were being introduced to the canons of inquiry by which opinions might be assessed. Indeed, evidence pointed instead to an ethos of "everyone is entitled to have his or her own opinion," the view attacked so vigorously by Allan

Bloom in his book, *The Closing of the American Mind*, referred to earlier.

To repeat, our sobering conclusion is that future teachers in the programs we visited—with the exceptions already noted—were being introduced to the profound moral and ethical issues of schooling and teaching briefly and in a desultory fashion. Again, with the exceptions noted, such encounters failed to "grab" the students intellectually. Yet, in spite of their admitted desire to get on with classroom operations, many students admitted to a regrettable omission of important matters. And the omissions were fairly obvious. My colleagues and I, on coming together to collate our field notes, expressed our concern and disappointment over the general inability of students, regardless of institutional type, to engage in intelligent, informed discussion of educational issues, even at the point where they impinged on teachers' decisions. Many students simply assumed, for example, that present differences in achievement were largely the result of innate differences in ability and that the best the school could do was to sort pupils into groups and teach to the level at hand.

Professors readily admitted the degree to which their programs were oriented to the present realities of students and classrooms. Many said that the best thing they could do for their students, considering the circumstances in schools, was to teach them to survive—and sometimes they meant sheer physical survival. This opinion was often accompanied by the commonly expressed view that inexperienced undergraduates are too young and immature for serious study of the major philosophical, value-laden issues of education.

Yet we also found an interesting dissonance between the general avoidance of the value dimensions of education and educating and some student and faculty views of what should or could be in the program. All of us, during group and individual interviews, were impressed by the degree to which many faculty members saw their students as being shortchanged and underchallenged, and they (as well as some students) put forward excellent ideas as to what should be. "*Could* be," however, was problematic, considering the lack of structure for dialogue and renewal in their school or college, the likelihood that new state rulings would undo their efforts in any case, and the probability that the norms of schooling would soon override whatever temporary success they might have with students. Not an uplifting set of perceptions! Nonetheless, these discussions with students and faculty led us to believe that the context and the conduct of teacher education today grossly underestimate the potential for productively challenging future teachers and their professors with a mission that pulls at their very highest ideals regarding the role of education, schooling, and teaching—that sense of mission that called many of them in the first place.

In Chapter One, I referred to a second wave of school reform rising in the wake of the first following release of *A Nation at Risk*. Still ongoing, it is driven by the concept of greater authority and responsibility at each school site and by rhetoric regarding school-based management, reconstruction, and renewal. Proponents urge "professional" teachers to join in effecting a wide array of changes proposed for years but rarely implemented.[24] Not surprisingly, the National Education Association and the American Federation of Teachers are strong advocates and have launched pilot efforts, as I noted earlier. Several colleagues and I have had the idea of the school as the center of change at the heart of our educational writing and other activities for several decades, as have other educators.

I still believe the most promising road to be that of uniting family and school in a context of greater decentralization of authority and responsibility and then further uniting this local effort with colleges and universities to improve both schools and teacher education. The data of this study, however, add to my conviction that this road is far more difficult and tortuous than is even hinted at in second-wave rhetoric, in part because teachers are not being prepared to walk it.

First, the dominant program ethos, as was stated earlier, is preparation for the classroom. Second, our sample revealed no clear statements of mission and purpose even suggesting that teachers have a responsibility for renewing schools. Third, teacher education presents only the briefest introduction to the problems and issues likely to be encountered by a principal and a group of teachers taking on such responsibility. (Preparation to deal with parents, for example, was placed by students in our sample near the bottom of what they acquired in their programs.) Fourth, we encountered scarcely any efforts to introduce teacher education students to the calcified problems that school reformers have addressed with little success over the years. (At best, students interviewed were only dimly aware that their preparation to teach was occurring at a time of intense interest in the reform of schools and teacher education.) Fifth, again with a few exceptions, the programs in our sample were oriented to suburban or relatively mildly urban school settings, where most participants did their student teaching. (We had hoped, and indeed expected, that urban universities would orient their curricula and teaching primarily, if not exclusively, to the urban environment, but this proved only occasionally to be the case.) Sixth, the minority teacher role models (male blacks, for example) thought to be so crucial—given the rapidly changing population demographics—appeared to be in devastatingly short supply. (Although our sample was well distributed across rural, suburban, and urban settings, the student population was 92 percent white and only 4.6 percent black, 1.1 percent Asian, and 0.9 percent Hispanic.) Seventh, programs were heavily oriented toward schools as they are. (When dissonance arose out of clear differences between, for example, the approaches to teaching mathematics taught on campus and school practices found by students during their student teaching, they were advised to do as their cooperating teachers did; what they had been taught could be used later in their own classrooms.) Eighth, adding support to the first observation in this list, it was rare to find students whose student teaching exposed them to aspects of school life beyond the classrooms to which they were assigned. (When student teachers attended parent meetings, staff meetings, and the like, it was almost invariably because the cooperating teacher either suggested or required it, not because this broader exposure was built deliberately into the program.)

In view of the above, it would be extraordinary—verging on the bizarre—for novices to come into their first teaching assignments attuned to school problems and all steamed up to do something about them. Let us put aside for the moment the suggestion that they should. Let us assume, instead, that they join their experienced colleagues in an ambience of school renewal, coming together regularly to agree on purpose, agenda, and acceptable alternatives for the school's organization, curriculum, and general conduct. Or are they socialized into a culture of staff meetings that feature little dialogue over established school ways but considerable discussion of lesser matters, and isolation from peers? Virtually all research supports the latter likelihood.

Putting aside also the frequently mentioned reasons for teachers' acceptance of the status quo in their schools—particularly lack of time specifically allocated for site-based renewal—what explains the prevalent situation? The data presented here and in Chapter Six suggest a reason rarely brought forward: The aspiring teachers we studied were not being socialized, critically enculturated, or in any other way commonly educated for and introduced to teaching as a profession (See Chapter Two for a definition of professional requirements.) Further, their preparation programs were not deliberately developing the skills of discourse, debate, analysis of conflicting views, compromise, and the like required by faculties engaged in school renewal. But students were, by almost everyone's admission, learning a good deal about how to go it alone in a classroom with a group of children or youths.

Only now are serious efforts beginning to codify the knowledge basic of teaching in schools. We are leagues away from the taxonomies of decision making around which more refined codification might occur. There is no common set of case studies, as in law, although the development of such a set would be extraordinarily useful.[25] It is virtually impossible even to predict the books that graduating teachers will have read during their courses. As our findings clearly show, we cannot be certain that all will recognize the name of John Dewey, for example—let alone lesser figures—in a list of ten highly productive scholars in the field of education. Our survey question regarding the books that had influenced students most brought out almost as many titles as there were students in the sample.

Even though education is, in the final analysis, a normative enterprise involving values, most students are at a loss to know whether a problem is best answered by data or logical argument. Even the belief that school renewal requires at least a working consensus—that is, everyone agrees to go along—is not shared. Although the moral and ethical dimensions of teaching have received attention from scholars for decades—and there has been renewed interest in recent years[26]—the programs we studied (with the exceptions noted) paid little attention to these. Many students (and regrettably, many faculty members) had little interest in or vocabulary for discourse regarding moral issues and norms.

Exacerbating this lack of common experiences (and partial lack of interest) is the plethora of semiautonomous teacher education programs on the campuses of some multipurpose universities: in schools of home economics, music, physical education and athletics, agriculture, business, and more—as well as education. In addition, prospective secondary teachers in the various subjects get most of their education in separate departments, usually coming together only for two or three courses in social foundations, educational psychology, and general methods. Some of these units appeared to us to be doing a rather good job of socializing their students as prospective teachers—but into their subject specialties, not into a common mission for all teachers. Nothing like this multiplicity exists in any of the other professions. If a second or third school of law or medicine were to spring up on a university campus, the already-established school would rise up in outrage and have it immediately closed down.

Modeling

If there ever was a time in history when our young people needed careful nurturing in schools, it is now. In our earlier work, we found that parents were primarily concerned that their children be safe at school, and attentively cared for.[27] For large numbers of children and youths, particularly those whose parents are not similarly concerned, school is (or could be) the place where they might be most assured that adults care about them. While there are highly regarded private schools, in particular, known and respected by their clientele for the strict, uncompromising standards they maintain, there is little disagreement among researchers regarding importance of the added stimulus of sensitive, supporting teachers. Although, in learning, love is not enough,[28] its absence hurts.

In general, we were impressed by the degree to which students described their relationships with faculty as positive and to which they perceived themselves to be known as individuals and the faculty to be nurturing and encouraging. At Pilgrim University, for example, it was standard for students not only to have the telephone numbers of their mentors but also to be expected to use them in times of need. One student described to me with great feeling the visits and support she received during a period of serious illness; the others in the group nodded their heads and said that this was to be expected at Pilgrim. At most of the settings, faculty members lauded their colleagues for the time and attention given to students. (Once again, the data favored small institutions or small programs in larger ones.)

It is unfortunate that the modeling of curricular and instructional practices proved to be much more spotty, the main problem being general failure on the part of the responsible planning groups to identify several major teaching methods and ensure not only field experiences with each but also exemplary use in their own classes. Again and again, students reported the use of lecturing on such subjects as inquiry methods, the use of technology, cooperative learning, and the like—without accompanying opportunities to view exemplary use or try them out under supervision. In interviews, faculty members often sheepishly or laughingly admitted that they often told students, "Do as I say, not as I do." Lack of time and appropriate resources were often given as excuses.

Students spoke appreciatively of the practical help they received in classroom practices, but as I just noted, they were rarely systematically immersed in the concepts of various instructional methods. Similarly, the programs through which they progressed were in only four or five settings models of the curriculum-planning principles described in some of their classes.

When students spoke of their mentors' modeling for them the behavior they should practice in their own classes, much of it came down to speech, dress, and personal deportment—and here the comments were usually laudatory. However, students frequently criticized the degree to which the same rhetorical admonitions about being good role models were repeated from class to class.

Students, particularly at the elementary level, were critical of boring lecture classes in the arts and sciences and the rarity of anything else; arts and sciences faculty members were rarely considered role models for teaching by education students. There were boring lecture classes in education, too, they said, but their critiques of the quality of teaching overall favored their education professors—and so it should be.

Beyond these generalizations, student reports of exemplary modeling were confined almost exclusively to what turned out to be repetitive reports on specific classes and professors: the foundations class at Legend State, with discussions led by students tied to readings; foundations courses at both Vulcan and Mainstream Universities closely tied to a professional vision of teaching; off-campus student teacher centers at Forest and Kenmore State Universities, providing a wide range of personal and professional support for students; the opportunity to observe and even participate in a campus laboratory school developed around a clearly stated set of educational propositions at Sterling College.

Methods classes, more than those in social foundations and psychology, provided variations in the teaching modes employed by instructors. They were more interactive, providing for both large- and small-group discussions as well as demonstrations. Many of the professors appeared aware of the need to provide their students with an array of models. Nonetheless, the most frequent model was of dispersing information in a lecture format. Commonly, there was little effort to connect one methods course with another so as to avoid duplication and ensure comprehensive attention to a full range of alternatives.

The prospect of providing exemplary models slipped rapidly away at the point of providing field experiences to accompany classes and first-rate student-teaching placements. Providing field experiences is a staggering challenge for institutions that prepare large numbers of teachers, especially those whose setting is rural. Almost always, the logistics are formidable. In urban areas, several institutions generally compete and often must settle for less than what is desirable. In more isolated settings, on the other hand, access to a variety of school practices necessitates extensive travel. In both kinds of settings, connecting class discussions with relevant, let alone exemplary, practice frequently becomes an unattainable dream.

In general, we give instructors in teacher education high marks for caring, for supporting students, and even for their accessibility for counseling; in these areas, their modeling was effective.

Student complaints in these areas were greatest in the large research universities, where many students said that they never got to interact with professors enjoying national reputations. Modeling of good teaching, on the other hand, was spotty, the major student complaints focusing on repetition and on failure to connect with practice. Lack of programmatic control over the selection of field settings sharply restricted the joining of theory and practice. It is fair to conclude that no program ensured the modeling, throughout its length and breadth, of the curricular and instructional principles and practices that future teachers might draw upon frequently and productively in their own later work.

Providing for Program Evaluation and Renewal

My colleagues and I are now convinced that no segment of higher education and no professional programs are as pushed, prodded, and controlled from without as are programs in the education of educators. Perhaps this phenomenon in large measure explains the common lack of a renewing drive within. On one hand, an enormous amount of time and energy on someone's part goes into responding to evaluative demands—demands that frequently require new data or a rearrangement of the old. On the other hand, frequent changes in external expectations create lethargy on the inside that is inhospitable to change and renewal. The "second wave of reform" at the K–12 level called for easing up on rules and regulations as part of a process of empowering principals and teachers to renew their schools. A similar approach to renewing the education of educators is overdue. Our data support this and similar recommendations.

Four sets of findings led us to the conclusion that there is much to be done on the inside by way of program evaluation and renewal. First, as was already noted, little was being done to square the selection and progress of students with a clear sense of mission. There were, in the programs we reviewed, no mechanisms designed to find out whether student traits desired but not perceived at the outset developed and matured during the course of a program. Without formative evaluation of the progress of cohort groups of students over successive years, there is no way to determine where students tend to be weak or strong. Consequently, program changes can be driven only by hunch, whimsy, or requirements imposed from without.

This last generalization applies only minimally to Dorsey and Lakeview, where the programs were small, the relationships between students and faculty were relatively intimate, and the faculty was in considerable agreement on its mission. Faculty members at these institutions shared impressions at regular meetings from which program revisions emerged. This was also true of the small postbaccalaureate program at Sherwood University, described earlier, and the campus course sequence at Broadmoor University.

Second, students in teacher education programs, like students in schools, were grossly underused in formative evaluation. One would think that teacher educators would go first to their students for reactions to their experiences and for suggestions for improvement, but this was done only sporadically, if at all. On every campus we visited, I questioned student groups about their involvement in program revision. Commonly, they had opportunities to evaluate specific courses and instructors (a requirement of many colleges and universities as part of the faculty review and promotion process). But it was very uncommon for them to work with a faculty planning group or respond to an evaluative questionnaire dealing with segments or the whole of a program. They rose to this opportunity in sessions with me, and proffered what I thought responsible faculty members should know. Student observations frequently squared with and confirmed the impressions of our research team.

Among the larger institutions, Mainstream University represented a partial departure from this pattern. Its students were taken somewhat seriously as useful counselors on strengths and weaknesses of programs. Similarly, Gerald University had made an effort to collect data from a largely commuting, evening-class student body. Generally, however, our sample of colleges and universities failed to gather information from students in any consistent, systematic way.

Third, there was a conspicuous absence, in all but a handful of institutions, of any clear structure for conducting processes of program renewal. Rarely did a group exercise control, let alone much influence, over *all* program components. Authority and responsibility were so extensively scattered across both individuals and groups that any impetus for broad-scale revision appeared unlikely. And any centralized authority that did exist tended to be minimized. For example, groups such as campuswide policy committees often functioned well below the overall authority they possessed on paper. Even some education deans seemed unaware of their authority in the teacher education arena. One went so far as to express his pleasure over the fact that the education of teachers was carried out in several campus schools and departments entirely outside his jurisdiction. This was evidence, he said, of widespread interest in producing teachers.

In spite of the fact that preservice programs at Pilgrim University were scattered geographically and were operated during the day at the undergraduate level and in the late afternoon and evening at the postbaccalaureate level, groups of faculty members nonetheless were substantially involved in planning and revision. They also managed to secure considerable input from students. Their cost in time and energy, in view of heavy teaching loads, was considerable.

Fourth—and here the criticism applies almost uniformly—systematic follow-up of graduates appeared to be absent in the settings we studied (just as it is in other professional education programs). Some SCDEs sent out questionnaires, but the information obtained appeared not to find its way into a renewal process in large part because no structure for such a process was in place. Many deans and heads of teacher education programs expressed a strong interest not only in gathering information from graduates to use in evaluating their programs but also in providing first-year teachers with follow-up support. But there were no budgetary provisions for either, they said. As I noted in Chapter Four, several deans in Oklahoma successfully joined forces to promote passage of a bill that authorized first-year follow-up and evaluation of graduates by their preparing institutions. Faculty members there were generally supportive of the plan, and many reported gaining useful information about their courses and programs as a consequence of visiting recent graduates in elementary and secondary school classrooms.

Three overarching problems discussed earlier are relevant to the issue of program evaluation and renewal: the general absence of a unifying mission shared by faculty and students, the perceived futility of engaging in long-term renewal because of the expectation that externally imposed requirements will prevail in any case, and the degree to which many faculty members perceive their work to be little appreciated in both the university and the public contexts. In a perverse sort of way, the ethos accompanying and resulting from these problems justifies the absence of *data-based* evaluation. Instead, program revision often results from the triumph of one opinion over others and, by its very nature, tends not to be fundamental— perhaps courses are revised, there are sometimes changes in course sequences, and student-teaching requirements may be reexamined.[29] Almost intuitively, faculty groups sidestep the exacting demands of launching data-based reconstruction of teacher education. The fact that we found a few instances of substantial ongoing renewal is a tribute to those involved, and especially to the leadership of a few individuals—usually department chairpersons or heads of teacher education.

Summary and Discussion

A considerable amount of data and accompanying discussion pertaining to programs for teachers in our representative sample of settings is spread over Chapters Five and Six and the preceding pages of Chapter Seven. This cumulative body of material adds up to some rather clear conclusions regarding the expectations put forward as reasonable and the conditions described as necessary in Chapter Two.

The range between colleges and universities closest to and farthest away from these expectations and conditions is enormous— from what can be described only as shabby to the near acceptable. At the bottom end, faculty groups had virtually given up. At the upper end, faculty members demonstrated not only the utmost in caring about the well-being of their students but also found time, even when carrying heavy teaching loads, to maintain reasonably coherent programs. The greatest weaknesses were in areas where these faculty members had little or no control.

One of the most glaring weaknesses throughout stemmed

from the common assumption that undergraduate general-education requirements provide sufficient background for future teachers. This is a dangerous assumption. A task of great magnitude—that of determining the education required to ensure that teachers will be capable of participating broadly in human discourse and that they will be intellectual role models for their students—is scarcely being addressed. We can have little confidence that the series of often-unrelated courses taken by students in their first two years of college provide "the context building resources of the educated citizen's understanding and appreciation."[30]

Nor can we have much confidence that this shortcoming is remedied in the so-called professional preparation sequence of courses. When a class that engages students in lively, thoughtful discussions about important educational issues and dilemmas is the exception rather than the rule in students' experiences, something is seriously amiss. With some exceptions, many of them already noted, these education courses were focused on specific skills and techniques—and large numbers of students, especially in elementary teacher education programs, wanted more of the same. We encountered no great student thirst for something more intellectual. Too often, the faculty view was that students either could not engage in thoughtful discussion of educational issues or had no interest in doing so. Yet my colleagues and I came away from interviews with the impression that the interests and abilities of students were too often underestimated.

We know that the educational attainments and aptitudes of future teachers vary widely. Much less is known and said about the potential of most of them for intellectual stimulation and challenge. However, because education is in the end a cultivation of the intellect, presumably intellectual challenge is what teacher education should be mostly about.

In a few—but only a few—of the settings we visited, a required course addressing the role of education and schooling in a democratic society stood out. This role of schools did not, however, drive teacher education programs. Faculty members, on questionnaires and in interviews, presented a hodgepodge of possible purposes for schools (and for their own programs). Many admitted to stepping around controversial issues for fear of indoctrinating their

students—a practice that presents the educated person as one above
or neutral toward critical debate. Worse still, at institutions of privilege some faculty members appeared to avoid ruffling the feathers of
affluent students and their parents with questions of equity and
justice in education and economics.

The place of educational foundations—that part of the curriculum viewing education from philosophical, historical, and sociological perspectives—has dropped considerably during the years
since Conant's 1963 report. A foundations course, if required, usually came early in the programs we studied; it was often devoted in
part to administrative matters pertaining to student admissions and
orientation and rarely provided threads or elements developed in
subsequent courses. As Harry Broudy, a longtime advocate of the
philosophical underpinnings of teacher education, points out,
"Foundational courses are not an intellectual luxury; . . . many of
the problems in teaching are rooted in such contexts. . . . Put into
their appropriate contexts, many educational problems cease to be
matters of technique."[31] Alas, technique has come to dominate over
all else—and for want of adequate grounding in theory, teaching is
too often reduced to mechanical procedures.

The idea of moral imperatives for teachers was virtually foreign in concept and strange in language for most of the future
teachers we interviewed. Many were less than convinced that all
students can learn; they voiced the view that they should be kind
and considerate to all, but they accepted as fact the theory that some
simply cannot learn. Students preparing to be secondary school
teachers, in particular, commonly viewed as necessary and inevitable the tracking of youths into low, middle, and high groups and
the resulting adjustments in curriculum. Few had thought much
about the moral issues posed by the intrusion of special interests
into the curriculum—special interests that banned certain books or
excluded global studies, for example. They saw their role almost
exclusively as ministering to the individual needs of a class of pupils—and they were anxious to get on with it. Large numbers ap-
proached the prospect of teaching with altruistic feelings and a
sense of being "called" to make a difference. Even so, they perceived
themselves more as adjusting to rather than seeking to change existing circumstances.

A recurring criticism of schooling addresses student passivity, rote learning, and a general absence of assignments that force students to inquire, to defend a course of action, or to generate alternative solutions. Theodore Sizer has laid down as central to school reform curricular, instructional, and evaluative initiatives designed to activate students' minds.[37] At the end of the 1985 edition of his book *Horace's Compromise,* he raises the troublesome question of whether Americans want question-askers or whether "the unchallenging mindlessness of so much of the status quo is truly acceptable: it doesn't make waves."[33]

We found little intellectual wave-making in the programs we studied. The very listening, responding to questions, and participating in teacher-directed discussions that go on in schools, according to much research, characterized almost all of most teacher education programs. As we concluded in our earlier research on schools, teachers teach as they observed and experienced teaching in schools, colleges, and universities during sixteen or seventeen years of attendance.[34] In general, students in teacher education programs did not see teaching as "deliberate action"; they did not think in terms of the ability to use knowledge to inform their actions.[35] "Instead, they seemed to be trying to squirrel away as many specific solutions and techniques as possible against the challenges to come."[36] The rush to cram it all into the limited time available in teacher education programs appeared to abort the emergence of sustained inquiry and reflection.

In the rush to cover, there is no time—and perhaps no inclination—to contemplate the need for or the nature of school reconstruction and renewal being called for in the larger social context. A program of teacher education not under continual renewal fails to convey the necessity for such. We have seen that most students focus their attention on individual classrooms, giving little thought to issues beyond their doors. They come to teaching from diverse backgrounds of preparation, sharing little with respect to mission, goals, concepts, readings, and so on. Not deliberately socialized into teaching as members of cohort groups, they come through their preparation as individuals. It is a long leap in expectations to assume that they will join colleagues in schools ready and eager to effect the changes increasingly seen as necessary. Beginning teachers are likely to take responsibility only for their individual classrooms and assume that someone else will take care of everything else. To the degree that this attitude continues, the curriculum and organization of the school as a whole will continue to go unattended and our educational system will remain stagnant and in decline.

Considering the similarities between the conduct of schooling and of teacher education programs, is it not reasonable to assume that there is a close connection between the two—that some of the circumstances of schooling owe their existence to the education of those who work in schools? Is it not equally reasonable to assume that this connection could be made far more ideal given a common mission, a moral perspective that embraces the principle that all children can learn, and both a curriculum and teaching methods to ensure that they do? University presidents, the press, and the general public should expect no less from the teacher education enterprise than Derek Bok and the *New York Times* expected of the Harvard Graduate School of Business. Teacher education makes a difference. Now it must make a much more positive difference.

Strong professions are marked by a relatively large, complex, rapidly accumulating body of professional lore requiring years of sustained study for its mastery, as well as a code of ethics designed to guide the professional behavior of practitioners. The vigor of knowledge production is so great that tensions are created for the practitioner to keep up and for licensing agencies to ensure public protection. Professional programs in strong professions respond to knowledge production and scholarly norms, keeping an eye on the validation of research in practice and the changing requirements of licensure. The pools of practice and tests for licenses are fed by the streams of relevant inquiry. Admittedly, the above is descriptive only of ideal circumstances; but it is, nonetheless, the professional model.

To the degree that the tension for practitioners and licensing agencies in seeking to keep up with and reflect knowledge production is limp, the profession is weak. To the degree that the conventions of practice and the demands of testing determine "professional" programs, these and their products are *not* professional. This does not necessarily mean, however, that knowledge production relevant to practice and licensing is nonexistent or weak. It may mean that circumstances of neglect, poor or misplaced judgment, inappropriate intervention, ignorance, or all of these factors have managed to prevent or inhibit the desired process of connecting knowledge production with professional program development.

Our studies have led us to several conclusions (and related hypotheses) supporting the proposition that teaching is a weak profession and some reasons, growing out of the foregoing brief analysis and supporting data, as to why this is so. The argument proceeds as follows. First, the various handbooks and compendia of research on teaching, some referenced in preceding chapters, convinced us that there is now a knowledge base sufficient to justify the claim that teaching warrants classification as a profession. But for an occupation to become a profession in its practice and for its practitioners to be professionals, this knowledge base must be codified and transmitted. For it to be transmitted, it must be rather readily accessible, presumably in materials and programs organized for this purpose. These, in turn, must be bona fide—that is, they must bear the stamp of scholarly effort and approval and not be the hunches and conjectures of individuals who possess political or bureaucratic authority but not professional authority.

Our second conclusion, related to the first, is that the knowledge underlying and relevant to teaching has been little codified. The process is just beginning. There are no taxonomies or hierarchies of knowledge connected to a classification of the teaching decisions in which teachers regularly engage. To some degree, this conclusion requires modification of the one above: There is a knowledge base that is potentially relevant and powerful for teaching, but it has not yet been rendered useful. It is now encapsulated in the annals of scholars and largely inaccessible to the practitioner. Indeed, it is sufficiently inaccessible to the practitioner and obscured from the layperson to cause both to question its existence.

Our third conclusion is that curriculum development in teacher education is largely absent, inadequate, primitive, or all of these. In the absence of accessible relevant knowledge and potent curricula, both the teacher educator and the teacher are left to their intuitive and practical interpretations. Because intuition is capricious and in short supply among humans, it is not surprising that both teacher educators and teachers are unduly influenced by what appears to work for them or others, has been part of their own experience as students, is well packaged and marketed, or is required by an empowered regulatory agency.

Once again, there is a great deal of blame to spread around; once again, there is little to be gained in doing so. The legacies from yesterday contribute their share of problems, as does the context of higher education in which teacher education is lodged. Because many scholars in education identify with the arts and sciences and disassociate themselves from teacher education, the body of education knowledge is little differentiated from that of the arts and sciences generally. In the research universities, in particular, many of the people conducting teacher education are connected neither to this knowledge nor to those actively engaged in producing it. In those colleges and universities where the heaviest teaching loads prevail, there is little time for either scholarly activity or curriculum development activities; in fact, it is questionable whether most faculty members are even adequately steeped in the lore they should be teaching. And in all the settings we visited, campus linkages with schools and practicing teachers were tenuous. With the whole teacher-training enterprise conducted in conditions of near-impoverishment (with respect to resources of money and faculty time), it is little wonder that teacher education is Second Hand Rose and that teaching is a not-quite profession.

The demands of state regulatory agencies, accreditation standards and procedures, and the tyranny of conventional practice have combined to impede the codification of a knowledge base and the development of curricula necessary to professional teacher education programs and the professional behavior of graduates from them. Yet the appropriate contribution of all three is essential to the emergence of a strong teaching profession. The degree to which these factors have defined not just the context but the substance of preparation programs has come close to reversing the flow of theory and knowledge into practice. Instead of scholarly productivity and knowledge codification continually fueling curriculum development, curricula overly reflect practice and prepare future teachers for prevailing conditions and circumstances. The resources, effort, creativity, and leadership needed to create the necessary productive tension between sound theory and sound practice and the integration of the two are prodigious. Meanwhile, teacher education muddles along with neither a clear sense of mission nor coherent programs.

Chapter Eight

An Agenda for Change

❖ ❖ ❖

A race preserves its vigour so long as it harbours a real
contrast between what has been and what may be; and
so long as it is nerved by the vigour to adventure
beyond the safeties of the past. Without adventure civilization is in full decay.

—Alfred North Whitehead[1]

Proposals for educational reform usually proceed from the assumption that the train is on the tracks and just needs to go faster, more
smoothly, or to new destinations—improvements that are straightforward and relatively minor. But what if that assumption is incor-
rect? If the train is derailed, the work needed is major indeed.

It can be concluded from the investigation reported in
preceding chapters that the teacher education train is *not* on the
tracks. Further, the engine is not coupled to the cars nor the cars to
one another. The board of directors is not even sure where the train
should go once it is on the tracks and coupled. Confusing signals
have demoralized many of the workers; unsure about what is expected of them, they do not know where to direct their energies in
order to be rewarded. The responsible parties need to determine

where the train is to go, connect all of its parts, charge the workers to get it moving, and provide the fuel necessary to its fast movement along the tracks.

After examining the prospectus of our study for her 1989 review of ongoing research and current proposals for teacher education reform, Sharon Feiman-Nemser wrote the following: "By studying a set of representative programs in relation to an explicit normative framework, researchers hope to generate ideas about improving teacher preparation that go beyond piecemeal programmatic changes."[2] In this chapter, we examine the gaps between our conclusions of the preceding chapters and this normative framework as laid out in the nineteen postulates of Chapter Two and point toward what is required in order to close them.

The resulting agenda will convey different meanings to different institutional settings. For example, the part of the train belonging to the liberal arts colleges that is most seriously derailed involves the back cars—those carrying future teachers into their field or practice experiences. Most of the problems afflict *all* the institutions in our sample; some much more than others.

The Postulates Revisited

The first three postulates are clustered as a group, all having to do with the place of teacher education in institutional mission, parity with other campus functions, and autonomy equivalent to that enjoyed by other professional programs on college and university campuses.

> *Postulate One.* Programs for the education of the nation's educators must be viewed by institutions offering them as a major responsibility to society and be adequately supported and promoted and vigorously advanced by the institution's top leadership.
>
> *Postulate Two.* Programs for the education of educators must enjoy parity with other campus programs as a legitimate college or university commitment and field of study and service, worthy of rewards for faculty geared to the nature of the field.

Postulate Three. Programs for the education of educators must be autonomous and secure in their borders, with clear organizational identity, constancy of budget and personnel, and decision-making authority similar to that enjoyed by the major professional schools.

Teacher education in the representative sample of colleges and universities we studied enjoyed very little of the above. The word *vigorously,* applied to supporting, promoting, and advancing the education of teachers (Postulate One), inaccurately describes existing circumstances in all of the colleges and universities. The institutions ranged from near-evisceration of teacher education to modest support, with the liberal arts colleges coming closest to providing the necessary supportive context. No institution proclaimed teacher education as its central mission. No multipurpose university held up its school or college of education as its most prized possession. Indeed, no matter how central the school of education and teacher education were in the past, by the time of our visits both had been pushed or were being pushed to the periphery.

No school or college of education in the flagship and major universities, public or private, put teacher education at the forefront as its preeminent function. In the colleges of education of the regional public universities, teacher education had not lost its centrality for faculty members, who committed their time and energies, but its importance in the reward structure had been eroding for some years. In the private regionals, teacher education frequently appeared to be caught in a kind of tug-of-war between a college of education that had lost status and a college of arts and sciences that wanted to play a stronger hand. In the liberal arts colleges (often founded with teaching at the core of their mission), the centrality of teacher education did not prevail, but neither was it overtly or implicitly downplayed.

On no campus was teacher education regarded as a highly scholarly activity, nor was there a widely held view that it was potentially highly scholarly. Rather, teacher education was commonly looked upon as a service to be provided, its scholarly component derived from courses plucked from or created out of the more discipline-oriented educational foundations: educational history, philosophy, psychology, sociology. Yet these foundations courses, in turn, have lost out in recent years to those regarded as more immediately practical. Beyond the SCDEs, the word *educational* in front of these disciplines almost automatically lowered the status of scholarly work in them; while within the SCDEs, increasing intensity in the research drumbeat was generally interpreted to favor research in education as a field of study and not research designed to shed light on the effectiveness of the teacher education program—an interpretation that was often puzzling to university-wide administrators and faculty members in the arts and sciences.

Nowhere was teacher education organized and supported as a mission in its own right. Rather, it took second place, at best, within an organized unit fitting the conventions of the institution as a whole. In the liberal arts colleges, the department of education and teacher education were almost one and the same—a situation that ignored the degree to which teacher education was thus cut off from discipline-oriented components handled by other departments. Despite its reliance on a close relationship with other academic departments, the destiny of teacher education was closely tied to the fortunes of the department of education—a department ranking near the bottom in academic standing and prestige. Its autonomy was eroded because responsibility and authority for the general-education and field components of teacher education were lodged with the arts and sciences departments and school districts, respectively.

This less-than-satisfactory situation with respect to the place, status, and autonomy of teacher education in the liberal arts colleges of our sample ballooned to decidely unsatisfactory proportions in the universities. Whereas teacher education is the central activity of departments of education, it ranges from secondary to peripheral in schools and colleges of education, according to our data. One laments the general neglect of a teacher education mission in our institutions of higher learning; one weeps over its fate in the schools and colleges of education created to nurture it.

In seeking to assure for teacher education the centrality in institutional mission, parity, and autonomy put forward in the above three postulates, there are not many levers to push and handles to turn. One would hope that boards of trustees and university

presidents would realize the importance to society of the commitment implied by the very existence of a teacher education program,
face up to the moral imperative, and decide to conduct the enterprise properly or not at all. To argue for continuing clearly unsatisfactory conditions on quantitative grounds—that is, more teachers
are needed—is to perpetuate mediocrity or worse and is un-
conscionable.

It is reasonable to assume that some responsible bodies and
individuals, already lukewarm about the appropriateness of their
institutions' involvement, will respond to a moral argument and
decide to bow out. It is equally reasonable to assume that responsible parties will rise to the challenge of doing the job right and will
ensure the basic conditions necessary to success. This latter responsibility may take the form of implementing what a substantial
number of college and university presidents have already subscribed
to in the Spring Hill Letter they signed or implementation of the
initiative put forward by the Renaissance Group (led by several
university presidents).[3] Similarly, those educational leaders responsible for the report of the Association of American Colleges might
add to the provocative stand already taken by examining the extent
to which even more is required than endorsing teacher education as
an undergraduate enterprise.[4]

Implementation of what is called for in these first three postulates would inevitably lead to much of what is called for in the
next fourteen. Rhetorical commitment, which costs little or nothing
(and is therefore more readily offered), would not. My argument
throughout is that teacher education must be elevated from its poor-
orphan status. To the inevitable question, "Will this cost more
money?" the unequivocal answer is yes. Once upon a time, humankind stood by while its members died young for want of health care.
To the question, "Did the change that has taken place cost money?"
the answer is yes—a great deal; but we consider the money well
spent. Transforming teacher education will not cost a great deal by
comparison, but it will cost.

When this fact is fully recognized, three beneficial developments could result. First, some colleges and universities—perhaps
quite a few—might decide to go out of the business of producing
teachers, just as some doctors operating proprietary medical schools

closed their doors on realizing that the new expectations for medical schools connected to universities would be costly. Second, an announced commitment to higher standards and the resources to support them should raise program quality by attracting more able faculty (and students). Third, a rising tide of institutional commitment and support is likely to lower costs in the long run. For example, students completing more rigorous programs who are then more respected and better paid are likely to remain in teaching. (The current low costs of educating a teacher are deceptive; where they are low, they are low only for the preparing institution. But because the turnover rate is very high, especially in the first three years, it is necessary to prepare five or six or more teachers to provide the length of one lifetime career. This has elevated the cost of guaranteeing teachers for our schools to that of maintaining an adequate corps of physicians.)

This hard economic reality offers a unique opportunity to states. Suppose, for example, that a state wanted to increase its financial support of teacher education—but in a way that would encourage results. It might begin by freezing all allocations for teacher education at their present levels. Further allocations—such as, for example, those assumed necessary for economic inflation or expansion—would be pooled and made available on a competitive basis, with awards going to a third or, at most, half of the state-supported colleges and universities.[5] This would be novel behavior on the part of state policymakers, but it holds promise of moving from mandated standards for all to the unleashing of creativity for purposes of putting in place conditions necessary to quality programs.[6]

The actors relevant and necessary to implementation of these first three postulates are outside of those immediately responsible for the conduct of teacher education programs: officials responsible for colleges and universities as a whole and, with respect to the concluding suggestion above, state leaders—governors, legislators, state commissions of higher education, and chief state school officers. Implementation of Postulate Four, on the other hand, is the responsibility primarily of campus officials in higher education. In my judgment, the redesign of teacher education, which must be a companion piece to commitment and resources, will not occur unless this fourth postulate is also implemented.

> *Postulate Four.* There must exist a clearly identifiable group of academic and clinical faculty members for whom teacher education is the top priority; the group must be responsible and accountable for selecting students and monitoring their progress, planning and maintaining the full scope and sequence of the curriculum, continuously evaluating and improving programs, and facilitating the entry of graduates into teaching careers.

General absence of the above group was the most serious deficiency in all programs. It was very conspicuous to observers. The fact that no such group, responsible for the whole, existed did not appear to press hard on the conscience of those in charge of the parts, however. Nobody was in a position of awareness, authority, and responsibility to assemble all the pieces. Humpty Dumpty had not fallen off the wall; he had never been there.

The situation was best in the liberal arts colleges, once again. But the teacher education faculty there had little leverage with respect to the general-education prerequisites and the school settings for practice teaching. This shortfall was not always to faculty liking and appeared to result in part from lack of financial resources;[7] yet leaders had not persisted in seeking to highlight the need for change.

When we turn to the situation in the universities in our sample, we toboggan downhill. The number of faculty members per unit of instruction increased sharply—that is, more taught only part-time in the program (even though some were full-time tenure-track education professors). In general, faculty time and energies were spread across more activities; thus the proportion given to any one declined. And the percentage of part-time appointees and of adjunct and temporary faculty members conducting teacher education increased. An increasingly large percentage of regular, full-time education faculty members was not at all involved but retained power over the program and carried voting rights regarding who would be hired to teach in it.

With growing complexity and diversity of activities in the school or college of education, then, the program of preparing teachers became increasingly fragmented. Professors of education in universities were more impotent in relation to and more separated from the undergraduate arts and sciences than such professors in the liberal arts colleges. In the major universities, they were much less likely to have any connection with student teachers. The campus-wide committees and councils commonly existing for purposes of coordination and articulation lacked the power and authority commensurate with the demands placed on them; they appeared to be pro forma.

Two disturbing generalizations emerge from these observations. First, the farther down in a university's organizational structure teacher education finds itself, the less chance it has to obtain the conditions necessary to a healthy, dynamic existence. Second, the farther down in the hierarchy teacher education finds itself, the less likely it is that it will enjoy the tender loving care of those tenure-line faculty members universities strive so hard to recruit. Who, then, speaks for teacher education? Who speaks for those who would become teachers?

Unacceptable though the conditions described above clearly are, no convincing argument for separating teacher education from universities has yet appeared. Indeed, were this to occur, something similar to a university with respect to knowledge production and dissemination would be found necessary and would emerge. Nonetheless, teacher education will not have a *congenial* university context until drastic changes occur. These will be difficult to bring off and stressful for many people. Much of what is required carries with it the certainty of threatening established ways and structures, of claiming turf already occupied, of challenging reward systems, and of granting to persons now excluded from decision making a voice equal to that of people who believe that their voice should be the only one.

Keeping teacher education within the context of universities and simultaneously creating for it first-class status is a route plagued by land mines. It will become passable to the degree that the university itself responds to the new challenges pressing in upon it. "We need to . . . arrive at a basic conception of the modern university as a metropolitan region, itself reflecting the complexity and 'messiness' of the world around it but capable of bringing to bear any part of its resources as appropriate to the knowledge needs of the society it is supposed to serve."[8] The flame is well worth the candle, and this must be recognized by a wide range of committed actors.

First, there must be a school or center of pedagogy committed solely to advancing the art and science of teaching and immersing educators in it. Second, this school or center must have its own budget, determined in negotiation at the highest level of budget approvals, and this budget must be immune to erosion by competing interests. Third, this unit must possess authority and responsibility over a student body of specified size and qualities, and over the personnel, materials, equipment, laboratries, and the like essential to the professional preparation of its members. Fourth, it must encompass the full complement of academic and clinical faculty members required for the development and renewal of a high-quality curriculum. Fifth, this school or center of pedagogy must control the specification of prerequisites for admission and, in collaboration with school officials, the educational use of practice facilities.[9]

There are many ways to provide for these minimum essentials, just as there are many ways to circumvent them while claiming that they are in place. The only protection against chicanery is the moral commitment of those in charge.

Local circumstances will lead to differences in the way the new school or center of pedagogy is fitted comfortably into the context of a college or university. The first steps will be the most difficult. Given the degree to which schools of education and their professors in the major universities have neglected teacher education, one might believe that they would appreciate having the new unit located elsewhere in the institution. This is an unlikely scenario, however. Growing public interest in better schools and in what schools of education do could make such a move politically unwise. My guess is that the interest of most schools of education in the preparation of teachers will rise in proportion to the increasing danger of losing it and becoming a lesser player in an endeavor that is becoming increasingly important to the public.

Even if a center of pedagogy is to remain in the school of education, it must nonetheless meet the minimum essentials listed above. At the simplest organizational level, this center of pedagogy, together with a center for specialized studies, could compose the school of education—each center with a director reporting directly to the dean, and each independent of the other but linked collaboratively for various mutually beneficial purposes.

The existence side-by-side of a school of education and a center of pedagogy is an alternative possibility. In Norway, an institute for teacher education exists independently of the school of education, with both its own full-time faculty and other faculty members drawn from the rest of the university on a part-time basis. The unit enjoys both considerable autonomy and its own resources for teacher education; it is not unique in Norway.[10]

Wherever it is located organizationally, the new center must deal with issues surrounding the pre-education component of professional preparation and the junior- and senior-year concentrations in subject matter and their teaching. Flexner was faced with somewhat different problems in determining the premedical curriculum in his six-year program. The freshman and sophomore years, as he saw them, were to provide the general studies of a broadly educated citizen. The next two years were to provide the sciences on which the study of medicine rests, as well as some of the more specialized subjects: pharmacology, pathology, bacteriology, anatomy, physiology, and "elementary clinic." But Flexner did not have to face the curricular demands of preparing doctors to teach subject matters to others. These subjects are not the tools of the doctor, but they are the tools of the schoolteacher.

Flexner had before him, too, the luxury of two more years for applied anatomy, preventive medicine, physical diagnosis, surgery, and the like. Decades later, teacher education enjoys no such luxury of time, in large part because of the costs associated with adding time. Thus there is a powerful argument for reexamining the present use of the undergraduate years. The arts and sciences subject matters constitute a large part of the stuff of teaching. Teachers must do more than understand them, however; they must know how to teach them.

In Chapter Seven, I paraphrased Bryan Wilson's seminal

distinction between the teacher's and other professionals' roles: "The doctor and the lawyer are applying the rules of their expertise: they are not attempting to inculcate it."[11] Pedagogy, on the other hand, includes this inculcation. But pedagogy is not something *appended* to subject matters; nor is the reverse the case. They become one in the teaching of, for example, mathematics.

The most efficacious time for mathematics and its teaching to become one is when the student is studying mathematics with a view to teaching it. The undergraduate years offer the ideal opportunity—an opportunity that could be partially recovered in the graduate years, but only to a limited degree and at greater cost. Nonetheless, the attempt to recover the undergraduate opportunity for students returning to pursue postbaccalaureate preparation to teach must be made. Indeed, experiments in endeavoring to do so may provide important insights into doing the job well at the undergraduate level.

A school or center of pedagogy inquiring into both generic and subject-specific pedagogy becomes a valuable resource for universities producing professors for higher education. The growing interest in improving teaching on campuses as well as in schools argues for a center with the necessary resources for preparing teachers of English, history, biology, or foreign languages at *any* level. The blueprint for such a comprehensive center does not yet exist, but the time is come to get to the drawing board.[12]

Another set of complex problems arises out of the need to provide exemplary practice settings—problems not resolved through building up a roster of cooperating teachers. Some of the most unacceptable shortcomings in the settings we studied were found in this part of the programs, although both students and faculty members rated student teaching highest among program components for impact.

The chasm between what is and what should be is so great that it appears to have intimidated those who should be finding ways to cross it. Several institutions we visited maintained laboratory schools, some of which appeared to be providing innovative programs around a coherent philosophy. But innovative programs are the exception rather than the rule among the university-based laboratory schools still remaining.[13] Rarely are such schools able to provide more than limited observation for future teachers. Access to other schools is necessary for student teaching.

I use the word *school* deliberately. Placement of a neophyte in a single classroom with a single cooperating teacher—the conventional way of handling student teaching—is a seriously flawed approach. It does not prepare future teachers to be stewards of entire schools—a growing expectation and a significant part of the mission of teacher education.

Rather than focusing only on the classroom, we must expand our thinking to embrace whole schools maintained jointly by school districts and universities.[14] The concept of exemplary "practice" or "teaching" schools, which I have referred to throughout, dovetails with parallel proposals: the professional-development schools recommended by the Holmes Group, the clinical schools of several experimental projects supported by grants from the Ford Foundation, and the partner schools in some of the school-university partnerships that make up the National Network for Educational Renewal. At this time of writing, all of these are in an exploratory, embryonic stage; few of the problems of control, funding, division of labor, and the like have been worked out.[15]

Flexner insisted that university-based medical schools establish full *educational* control over the necessary laboratories and clinics. He was ambivalent, in principle, about whether schools of medicine should or could "possess" their own hospitals. Practically, however, he recommended ownership—even if it resulted in immense budgetary increases over gaining and maintaining necessary educational control of a hospital belonging to other people through the uncertainties of diplomacy.[16] Most institutions followed his recommendation, although some boards and presidents of universities probably wish that their medical schools had opted for diplomacy in seeking to work out satisfactory educational arrangements with hospitals owned by others. The operation of university hospitals in conjunction with schools of medicine has been, for most institutions, a major burden. The potential costs for universities seeking to operate their own practice schools—enough to accommodate several hundred student teachers or individuals spending longer periods of time as (often paid) interns—are awesome. This is not a route they will travel.

The feasible alternative is challenging, to say the least: the collaborative selection, maintenance, and development of exemplary schools conducted in the best educational interests of children and youths, on one hand, and prospective teachers, on the other— with school and university personnel joined collegially as peers for the advancement of both. The tasks and problems line up like a long string of boxcars on a railway track waiting for the little engine that could, with the bettors lining up to say it can't.

There are not yet models operating at a level worthy of emulation—a condition of great usefulness to reform efforts. Therefore, the few exploratory ventures now under way must be supported on faith. Yet faith is an attribute of few funders. The need for what is proposed here is moving toward the forefront of attention, however, and the solution is viewed as sensible by enough opinion makers to raise our hope that this might be an idea whose time is come.

Because I believe that practice schools engaged in the simultaneous renewal of themselves and the education of teachers constitute an idea of great significance and timeliness, I devote a major part of Chapter Nine to conceptualizing one model. Lacking operating models, one must begin with the conceptual. My purpose is not to provide a blueprint but to expose the considerations, problems, and issues most likely to be confronted by pioneers engaged in developing practice schools, and to provide one of many possible designs for these schools. I realize that this model, like every component of every process proposed, will be subjected to the critical, "Yes, but. . . ." Nonetheless, I shall forge ahead.

> *Postulate Five.* The responsible group of academic and clinical faculty members described above [in Postulate Four] must have a comprehensive understanding of the aims of education and the role of schools in our society and be fully committed to selecting and preparing teachers to assume the full range of educational responsibilities required.
>
> *Postulate Six.* The responsible group of academic and clinical faculty members must seek out and select for a predetermined number of student places in the program those candidates who reveal an initial commitment to the

moral, ethical, and enculturating responsibilities to be assumed.

Again, the gap between what we found and what is stated above was enormous and disturbing. Closing it, however, is a challenge quite within the capabilities of the proposed faculty group. Faculty members whom we interviewed and who responded to the survey questions relevant to the above expressed good ideas about the role of schools in our society and the responsibilities of teachers. A significant percentage viewed their programs as preparing for missions less comprehensive than their own preferences; others saw their programs as devoid of mission. Many deplored the absence of a structure through which dialogue about the schools for which they were preparing teachers might proceed—and subsequently drive program planning and evaluation.

One of the legs on which the proposed profession of teaching stands is the unique role of schools as the only institution specifically charged with enculturating the young. If teachers are to engage successfully in this important task, *their* teachers must have a clear understanding of the history and principles of the Constitution and the Bill of Rights. Teacher educators must be very conscious of the differences between a democracy and a totalitarian state and realize what is required of a teacher in a democracy. Their awareness and understanding must be made explicit in the teacher education curriculum. Because we take our liberties too much for granted, we prepare our teachers inadequately for educating their students to be citizens.

Given the general absence of this linkage between even an ill-defined conception of the aims of education, the role of schools, and expectations for schoolteachers, on one hand, and the qualities these imply for teachers, on the other, we should not be surprised at the absence of definitive selection criteria. Not only were there no criteria tied to the moral, ethical, and enculturating responsibilities to be assumed, however; there was little evidence of established processes through which a faculty group responsible for preparing teachers might give serious attention to the selection of candidates.

Nor, in the programs we studied, was there a distinction between qualities desired in candidates at the outset and those to be developed subsequently. Even supposing it could be argued that all traits are amenable to education, teacher education programs possess neither the resources nor the time to redress severe personality disorders; and they appear ill-equipped to perform much lesser tasks. Consequently, the moral and ethical imperatives of selection require that applicants be counseled out if they fall seriously short in characteristics that are deemed important but for which there are no programmatic provisions. Failure to so counsel is morally wrong, and the consequences are costly.

I was told over and over that there are legal sand traps in the sort of selection proposed here. I agree. But the courts have been supportive of more selective professions when their criteria were comprehensive, when care went into the selection process, and when decisions were made on the basis of "best professional judgment." I was also told that we do not know how to be more than academically selective. Again, I agree—although we know more than we apply.[17] Our failure is one of omission; it is easier to use standardized tests of achievement or intellect than to look at the whole person. We can learn how to evaluate students on ethical, moral, personality, and other grounds if we seriously try, however. We should proceed experimentally. After reading the experiential and goal statements of a group of applicants and then interviewing those applicants, the responsible faculty members would reject only those about whom there is complete negative agreement. Every possible effort would be made subsequently to bring all those admitted up to a standard of quality. Initial judgments would then be juxtaposed against the relative success of students in the program.

What alarmed my colleagues and me about the selection process—or, more accurately, the near-absence of such—was the almost complete failure to "seek out" candidates, as called for in Postulate Six. Although there was ample rhetoric about the need to attract more candidates from minority pools, there was little effort to evaluate what might be the appeal of teaching to the various minority groups or to reach those pools from that perspective of appeal. Earlier, I reported the paucity of minority students in the programs we studied (except in historically black and de facto black institutions). But surely that is no surprise. Why would a student with a lifetime of experience as a member of a minority group want to extend that experience into a teacher education program dominated by the white majority?

Recruiters appear to focus rather single-mindedly on making teaching attractive as a career. And the minority students we interviewed *did* find teaching attractive; many saw it as a career that would elevate their economic status beyond what it had been and presently was. Going to college with many peers of the same race or ethnic group presented them only with the same kinds of academic problems faced by white students. Going to college or through a program dominated by white students by a ratio of fifteen or twenty to one, however, added a burden they already knew a great deal about and preferred not to perpetuate. Besides, why teach in a school system designed to advance the white race and seeking minority teachers primarily in order to blunt the charge of racism?

These are not questions we like to raise, let alone seek to answer. But until they are raised and faced, the perilous situation of our schools and teacher education programs is likely to grow worse. [18]

Our recommendation is that recruiters go much deeper down into the educational system—to community colleges, yes, but necessarily to secondary schools with well-diversified student populations as well. Encourage the creation of a Future Teachers of America club—a concept that is far from new. Recruit cohort groups in accordance with guidelines that enhance the importance of their own cultural experiences. Combine the secondary school Future Teachers of America club with one at the college level. Use students in the latter to mentor students in the former. Go to local businesses and the local branches of large corporations for incentive fellowships carrying the name of the donor company. These are only a few of the approaches that could be created out of the brainstorming of the responsible group of faculty members, their students, and members of minority groups in the surrounding community.

An early set of tasks, then, for the faculty of the proposed school or center of pedagogy is agreement on what schools are for, what teachers ideally must do, what traits are desired at the outset, and what processes of recruitment and selection are to be used. Attention then must turn to the nature of the program required for the necessary professional knowledge, skills, and attitudes for which this faculty and the students admitted will assume responsibility.

> *Postulate Seven.* Programs for the education of educators, whether elementary or secondary, must carry the responsibility to ensure that all candidates progressing through them possess or acquire the literacy and critical-thinking abilities associated with the concept of an educated person.
>
> *Postulate Eight.* Programs for the education of educators must provide extensive opportunities for future teachers to move beyond being students of organized knowledge to become teachers who inquire into both knowledge and its teaching.

We can assume that testing for basic literacy will soon be the norm for entry into teacher education programs. Such testing was already common in the colleges and universities of our sample. We heard glowing accounts of how well students were doing on these tests and of their improving grade point averages at admission. We heard much less about those students who failed to meet these standards. We also heard a good deal from faculty members about their students' being uninterested in or too immature for discussion of the major issues surrounding the role of schools and the fair treatment of students in them. We also listened to the frustrations of students who hoped to be admitted to the teacher education program—many of them first-generation college students whose earlier education had been disadvantaged—but who were blocked by the examination requirements and unhappy about the long road to teaching lying ahead.

Teacher education faculties must address two sets of problems embedded in the above—problems not appearing at first to be closely related. First, it is tempting to assume that apparent improvement in the academic qualifications of candidates translates into a good crop of new teachers and to relax attention paid to the intellectual traits desired in good teachers. This temptation must not be succumbed to. Second, this overall improvement encourages programs to ignore not only the students who fail the tests but also the consequences of their loss to teaching. The potential loss to the local public schools of those confronted with a year or more of remedial work at one rural and one urban institution in our sample is not likely to be made up by the infusion of teachers (now students at other institutions) whose academic qualifications are higher. These students will continue to seek out advantaged school districts in which to teach.

The answers to these problems lie only a little in better recruitment. They lie more significantly in more careful attention to those students already recruited and in the tubes. Our data reveal clearly that future teachers received very little attention and encouragement until they were well along toward student teaching. Some of those who came to prepare to teach failed entry tests and disappeared; some who failed were struggling financially to remain enrolled during remediation. The situation is exacerbated for low-income students from minorities. Meanwhile, university officials are looking right over these circumstances in mounting recruitment programs for those more able students, particularly from minorities, who must be "out there." Students already in the tubes are receiving precious little guidance in selecting their general studies and in becoming something more than passive course-takers.

The faculty of the proposed school or center must expand its net to gather in all of the undergraduates committed to or considering teaching. This does not mean creating new courses, although it may mean providing credit seminars (per quarter or semester) throughout the freshman and sophomore years (or accompanying the postgraduate years, for future teachers entering at that level) for purposes of reflecting on the general education in which students are participating. And it most certainly means securing the resources, financial and human, to remedy the deficiencies for some in basic literacy and to support students for more than the usual years of college when necessary. In addition, faculty must devote particular attention (perhaps in the aforementioned seminars) to the intercultural ignorance and prejudice embedded in the value systems brought to college by those who want to teach. Failure to do so allows these values to be carried, unchallenged and unexamined, into the schools.

The faculty is confronted with the task of ensuring that

future teachers are literate and thoughtful inquirers into knowledge and teaching. At the same time, every effort must be made to remedy the deficiencies of eager candidates whose backgrounds have left them disadvantaged. Universities spend millions of dollars—admittedly, primarily from gate receipts—in tutorial services for athletes. Surely our society can provide the same support for aspiring teachers.

> *Postulate Nine.* Programs for the education of educators must be characterized by a socialization process through which candidates transcend their self-oriented student preoccupations to become more other-oriented in identifying with a culture of teaching.

There are two sets of issues here. The first pertains to the socialization process itself; the second, to the nature of the culture into which future teachers are socialized. The process was weak in most of the institutions we studied, and the enculturation was, for the most part, into rather narrow, technocratic behavior focused on classrooms, not schools.

Our major recommendation is that much greater use be made of peer socialization through cohort groups (groups that stay together throughout their programs). Unlike the education programs in some other professions, the programs we looked at made scarcely any attempt to employ this approach. As was noted earlier, we did find some use of buddy systems—arrangements in which candidates well along in the program took responsibility for students in the first two years of college. However, as one-on-one arrangements, these had a limited effect. It would also make good sense to involve a number of advanced students in the freshman and sophomore seminars proposed above. The contingent of beginners would grow in size during these two years as students made up their minds about teaching as a career. We recommend that the decision to teach be finalized in the sophomore year and that formal applications be acted upon before the end of it. Students delaying a decision nonetheless would be faced with completing the full programs of studies, field experiences, and internships. This is the expectation in other professional programs; no less should be expected and required in teacher education.

The freshman and sophomore years, then, should constitute a voluntary, somewhat informal socialization process intended for those students who come to college eager to enter teaching, those who decided soon after coming, and those who are interested and undecided. Many freshmen have planned for years to become teachers; the socialization process cannot begin too soon for them. The more formal process, with courses and field experiences, should begin in the junior year. Each student should be a member of a cohort group that remains relatively intact throughout. This does not mean that all students will proceed precisely together; there will be individualized branching activities of many kinds. But they should proceed together through a core program and perhaps find themselves reassembled as, for example, a cohort group of ten interns in an elementary partner or practice school. Placement of individuals with individual teachers for experiences in only one or more single classrooms must end.

Important concomitants of this process are (1) the formal selection procedures described under the preceding postulates and (2) complete elimination of casual entry through taking and passing courses, which now characterizes the enterprise in most settings. Present procedures simply perpetuate the course taking syndrome so deeply embedded in our entire system of education. These procedures guarantee only that future teachers meet the academic demands of classes, not that they demonstrate growth in traits essential to effective teaching.

Some of what has been proposed here should be easier to attain for so-called nontraditional students enrolled in postbaccalaureate programs. Once again, however, some tough decisions must be made, one of which is the careful selection of a group admitted together at the time of the program's beginning. Admitting others for later quarters or semesters may be convenient for students but is inexcusable because it violates the coherence of well-planned programs. This cohort group must then go through a process designed to aid in the transition from being a student to being a teacher. This takes time—more time than that allotted in the programs we studied. In Chapter Nine, I propose a longer, more intensive sequence of studies designed to effect the necessary transition and ensure the requisite knowledge and skills.

The restructuring described above does not ensure these traits in all graduates, of course. But it does force attention to the need for a curriculum tied to a conception of teaching rather than to the somewhat artificial divisions of knowledge from which required courses are extracted. Stated differently, every curriculum component must be developed for its contribution to a professional curriculum, not selected merely to meet a specified content requirement. The socialization process needs to become a highly intellectual one through which students transcend their previous experience as relatively passive course-takers and become active agents in the learning of others. To some characteristics of the necessary curriculum we now turn.

> *Postulate Ten.* Programs for the education of educators must be characterized in all respects by the conditions for learning that future teachers are to establish in their own schools and classrooms.
>
> *Postulate Eleven.* Programs for the education of educators must be conducted in such a way that future teachers inquire into the nature of teaching and schooling and assume that they will do so as a natural aspect of their careers.

Most of the faculty members observed and interviewed were not adequately aware that they have a responsibility to future teachers that goes far beyond transmitting the contents of their courses. They must model what they hope these students will do as teachers. Such modeling is a powerful component of the professional curriculum, not just a mode of delivery. It is not something to leave to chance.

Consequently, the faculty of the school or center of pedagogy must come together to plan the array of teaching methods to be demonstrated in the program, the kinds of faculty-student interactions to be modeled for and replicated by their students, and the ways in which these students are to participate in evaluating the teaching they observe and the curriculum they experience. The unfolding of the results of this planning can then become part of a reflective process in which students and faculty engage and from which replanning evolves.

We found very little of this. There were instances of faculty groups—the entire faculty roster in the liberal arts colleges—so engaged, but students were commonly omitted from the process. The students interviewed did not view the educational program in which they were involved as deliberately designed to exhibit for them exemplary practices in testing, teaching, counseling, curriculum planning, or any other of the tasks in which they were to be involved later in their own teaching. What opportunities lost!

We recommend, then, that the responsible faculty plan not just a sequence of courses and field experiences but deliberate demonstration of the pedagogical procedures their students will be expected to use in the practice part of their preparation programs. (I address the conduct of this practice part later.) We recommend, further, that reflection on how this is being done—and how *well* it is being done—become a built-in component of a staff planning process in which student representatives participate. [19]

A sensitive problem rarely brought to the surface by faculty members in our discussions is the degree to which they model, usually quite unconsciously, the very values and beliefs *not* desired in schoolteachers. It will be recalled from data presented earlier that students were warm in their praise of faculty deportment. They were much less enthusiastic, however, about other areas in which they had hoped faculty members would serve as role models. Our short associations were insufficient to bring out unintended modeling in such sensitive areas as racial prejudice; yet a heated exchange in one setting told me that this interracial faculty did not normally engage in reflection on and interaction regarding individual biases and prejudices. Given the common absence of sustained program planning and evaluation, such a finding is hardly a surprise.

The kind of teamwork we are recommending might well lead naturally to considerable self-examination, especially of values and how values are conveyed in the classroom, but this process must not be left to chance. We strongly recommend for all faculty groups the same kinds of experiences in interpersonal and intercultural understanding that we recommend for their students.

What faculty members must demonstrate is a reasoned, collegial approach to the continuous improvement of the enterprise to
which they are committed. They must become self-conscious about
the modeling of it, because this is precisely the approach that
teachers must take in the renewal of the schools for which they will
assume responsibility. But even beyond this modeling, faculty
members must engage their students in inquiry that brings divergent views to the surface and helps students to realize that all opinions are not of equal value—that their validity depends on moral
and ethical norms as well as data and even reasons. Such inquiry
into faculty opinions and beliefs is no less important.

> *Postulate Twelve.* Programs for the education of educators
> must involve future teachers in the issues and dilemmas
> that emerge out of the never-ending tension between the
> rights and interests of individual parents and special-
> interest groups, on one hand, and the role of schools in
> transcending parochialism, on the other.
> *Postulate Thirteen.* Programs for the education of educators
> must be infused with understanding of and commitment
> to the moral obligation of teachers to ensure equitable
> access to and engagement in the best possible K–12 educa-
> tion for *all* children and youths.

During the last two decades, in particular, much of the controversy swirling around our schools has focused on the rights of
parents, demands of special-interest groups, and equity in regard to
access to schools and knowledge. Most of the students we interviewed appeared to be innocents with respect to these issues and
how they might deal with them as teachers. Some vaguely remembered having listened to a lecture or participated in a class discussion on related topics, but they had not thought much about them
since. They wanted to get on with practical matters of classroom
management and teaching. Most failed to translate their college
study of intellectual differences among children into a moral responsibility toward those who do not take readily to the school
environment. The concept of teachers as stewards of schools,

preserving the role of schools in a democratic society, was viewed by most as remote and abstract.

The present practice of encapsulating these issues in the topical outline of a course in the social foundations of education—worse yet, not requiring even this smattering exposure—is unsatisfactory. Much more is needed, despite the claim we heard from some faculty members that their students were too immature for serious study of these educational issues and the claim from some students that these issues were irrelevant—both dangerous claims indeed. One does not need to look far for the practical problems teachers confront in which moral issues are embedded: parents who view "global education" as virtually obscene and differ widely on sex and AIDS education; pressures for schools of choice, magnet schools, classes for the gifted, homogeneous grouping of slow learners, tests for admission to first grade, and more; decisions whether to bus or not to bus, to track or not to track, to promote or not to promote. The underlying issues of equity and excellence, the inquiry necessary to both informed opinion and reasoned discourse, and the appropriate role for schools and teachers in this discourse should be themes that appear and reappear throughout the entire preparation program.

After grappling with this issue of moral discourse required of teachers in the schools in year-long seminars with very able teachers preparing to be school principals, I am convinced that the necessary educating cannot be accomplished in lecture-type courses and with the conventional reading list.[20] These graduate students and I agreed that carefully prepared case studies were necessary, augmented by field observations and by short, student-prepared cases derived from their teaching internships—all accompanied by intensive dicussion and relevant reading. We concluded that issues pertaining to school and teacher responsibilities in a political democracy, the rights of parents and children, the teacher as professional, the right to learn, and similar topics should be introduced early in preparation programs and revisited throughout.

We strongly recommend the careful development of case studies not only for the above components of the curriculum but also for several others. These should be well prepared using videotaped incidents and computer simulations by a professional team of educators and technical experts, probably as a commercial venture. The ability to deal with the complexities of conducting schools would be very much enhanced in teachers who came through preparation programs organized in part around a commonly encountered set of case studies.[21]

> *Postulate Fourteen.* Programs for the education of educators must involve future teachers not only in understanding schools as they are but in alternatives, the assumptions underlying alternatives, and how to effect needed changes in school organization, pupil grouping, curriculum, and more.

Again, most of the students interviewed—all engaged in, about to begin, or just beyond student teaching—were largely innocents in regard to the above matters. They were strangely detached from the school reform ethos of their community, state, and nation.

I am not about to suggest that prospective teachers be prepared to be experts in school change and reform. That is too ambitious a goal. Rather, they need an orientation to schools engaged in renewal of sufficient intensity to impress upon them the view that schools can and must change and that much of the process will ultimately be in their hands. They also require group experiences in making real decisions, formulating plans for change, evaluating progress, and the like.

Consideration of curricular, organizational, and evaluative alternatives is appropriate for college and university classes and related field observations. Some of the rest must be obtained on-site—in exemplary social studies programs, team-taught schools within schools, classes organized into cooperative learning groups instead of by homogeneous achievement levels, and more. Finally, they must become junior members of school faculties engaged in the renewal process. The conventional practice of assigning a student teacher to a cooperating teacher and a classroom—a practice suggesting that classroom duties are the sum total of a teacher's job—falls far short of what is required.

Clearly, the partner, practice, or professional-development school emerges once again as a necessary component. Each group of neophytes should join such a partner school as interns who are in every way members (albeit junior members) of the faculty. At this culminating stage of preparation, they should be able to contribute to the school's well-being not only through student teaching but also through participation in the renewal process.

Part of the overall intent of any teacher education program ought to be to develop in each future teacher the view that change is necessary and possible and that he or she carries into a school a commitment to its betterment. This requires that students be exposed to alternatives and their supporting rationale and that they experience the demands and rewards of working constructively in a team enterprise. To the relative inwardness of being a good student must be added the self-transcendence required of each caring, responsible team member in a renewing school.

> *Postulate Fifteen.* Programs for the education of educators must assure for each candidate the availability of a wide array of laboratory settings for observation, hands-on experiences, and exemplary schools for internships and residencies; they must admit no more students to their programs than can be assured these quality experiences.

The strong professions admit to preparation programs only the number of candidates for whom the necessary resources are available. Any increase in enrollment is accompanied by increases in faculty size, facilities and equipment, laboratories, and the accommodations provided by resident sites. This balancing is almost nonexistent in teacher education. Applicants are generally (but not always) admitted with some attention to the availability of faculty, but the notion of rationing the intake in relation to the laboratory resources available is almost unheard of.

Indeed, rationing the intake for any reason contradicts common practice, past and present. Teacher education has been for many institutions a convenient "cash-cow." Nearly every student who applies is run through programs set up by some colleges and universities to meet minimum certification requirements. This behavior will not be stopped easily.

Part of the problem is created on the outside. A state legislature might pass down a directive such as "Every qualified applicant must be admitted" without giving thought to its impact on some other directive—one admonishing colleges and universities to improve quality, for example. Much of the rest of the problem stems from the persistence of the established mentoring model: run the candidates through the required courses (increase class size if necessary) and then find cooperating teachers willing to take them. The need for sheer numbers of cooperating teachers overshadows the importance of getting good ones. Many of the arrangements for student teaching are disgraceful. Yet it is difficult to get out of doing the job cheaply and inadequately—and many teacher educators would not quarrel with the use of these adverbs—without simply saying, "No more students." "No more" is easily translated into lack of sympathy for a potential teacher shortage.

Nonetheless, the time for "no more" is come. Teaching is a hands-on occupation: Teachers interact with individuals and groups, manipulate materials, demonstrate the trip of a jumbo jet around the world, comfort a child. It is a hands-on *profession* to the degree that hands-on activities are guided by an informed head.[22] Very little in preparation programs is driven by such a conception— especially the very large part controlled and conducted by the arts and sciences. The next time a colleague tells me that teachers need preparation only in the subjects they are to teach, I will suggest to him or her a sentence of several weeks in a classroom of twenty-five six-year-olds.[23]

As was stated earlier, little in the way of laboratory resources—particularly of an exemplary sort—is available for either observation or hands-on experience. Universities and their teacher education programs stand apart from the schools—different levels of a common educational system—too often with considerable tension between the two.[24]

The proposed school or center of pedagogy must have ready access to surrounding schools for observation of troublesome problems, short-term linkages of aspiring teachers with both individuals and groups of children or youths, experiences with school or district curriculum committees, and narrow-range innovative projects. Participation in alternative and magnet schools and in the practice or partner schools described earlier is also desirable. In *A Place Called*

School, I suggested the possibility of "key schools"—schools engaged in truly innovative projects. [25] Although these would not normally accept interns, they would be opened up periodically to both preservice and in-service teacher observers prior to and during a period of deliberate dissemination. This concept is being developed in the BYU–Public School Partnership; professors from Brigham Young University are near-full-time residents in schools designated by districts in the partnership.

For the above close relationship between teacher education programs and schools to be implemented, several ground-breaking developments are necessary. First, of course, the center of pedagogy must work out, from the beginning, collaborative agreements regarding the range of essential laboratory settings needed and conditions of access to them. Second, state funds must be allocated according to formulas that provide additional funding for the most intensively used school settings and for the reciprocal responsibilities carried by school and university personnel. (Some, but not all, of the necessary funds will come as a result of allocating present funds differently, and some of the reciprocal responsibilities can be funded as quid pro quo arrangements between schools and universities.) Third, flexible ways must be found for crediting faculty members for their work in schools or with teacher novices and interns, as appropriate. "Crediting" must encompass both the teaching and service load carried and rewards in the merit and promotion system. These three conditions appear rather obvious, perhaps, but they will not be easily attained.

Once a close working relationship has been established between campus and schools, teacher educators must do what they are so reluctant to do: Adjust the intake of students to the availability of these laboratory resources. They must toughen up in regard to limits on admission and straighten up in regard to their moral promises to students. Here is what we pledge (they must say): observations connected with the subject matter of each course, accompanied by discussion; individually arranged visits to settings of your choice; observations and hands-on experiences with at least six different methods of teaching; a year-long induction into school practice, at least half of that as a member of a cohort group assigned to a practice school, accompanied by theory-related-to-practice seminars—and more (details to be specified). The most able, dedicated candidates will want to shop around until they are satisfied that a given program offers this much and that there is truth in its advertising.

One critically important element in the capstone experience as a junior faculty member in a partner school—an element discussed as relevant to previous postulates as well—is embedded in the concept of the teacher as steward of the school. The typical student-teaching model—a neophyte working with an experienced cooperating teacher—almost always proceeds as though the rest of the school did not exist. Consequently, the future teacher is screened off from the larger context. Worse, teacher educators do not have to confront and deal with the whole of what teachers face—especially teachers who take seriously their role as stewards. For example, teacher educators fail to see and reflect on the degree to which the continuing output of teachers who do not speak a relevant second language (Spanish, for example) and who have little or no multicultural experience and empathy perpetuates the very conditions that school reform must radically change.

Centers of pedagogy must thus include multiracial, multiethnic schools. Assigning to them groups made up of only white interns would bring into sharp relief the necessity, referred to earlier in this chapter, of recruiting minority students. And although the input of future teachers is to be controlled quantitatively as well as qualitatively, those admitted must still reflect the diverse population and needs of communities. The faculty can no longer continue admitting from a narrowly defined pool of applicants, merely *hoping* for greater diversity. It must recruit groups of students as if each would become the staff of real schools enrolling children and youths of all races and creeds. There must be no *one* model of the American teacher.

> *Postulate Sixteen.* Programs for the education of educators must engage future teachers in the problems and dilemmas arising out of the inevitable conflicts and incongruities between what works or is accepted in practice and the research and theory supporting other options.

The integrity and coherence of even the most carefully planned and conducted teacher education programs are frequently violated at the point where students leave the domains over which the university has authority and enter those over which the school district prevails. It is unfair to dichotomize these domains by labeling one as dominated by scholarly authority and the other as dominated by practice authority, because many schoolteachers operate from a base of knowledge and practice that carries with it legitimate scholarly authority. But there are many intrusions into practice, some initiated by administrative edict and district policy, that have no scholarly legitimacy whatsoever. In Chapter Four, I referred to a district that required teachers and student teachers to adhere to a model of teaching reading having dubious merit and to a state that set lesson-planning requirements for first-year teachers that propelled a kind of political intrusion into the contents of teacher education courses. It is pretentious to describe an occupation as a profession if it is driven by conventions and conveniences of practice, on one hand, and arbitrary policies designed for political expediency, on the other.

The blame for teachers' teaching according to practices both observed over the years and arbitrarily prescribed must not be brought down exclusively on their preparation programs, of course. But neither should teacher educators be wholly spared. Their sins are primarily ones of timidity and omission. Rather than perpetuating the status quo, they should seek arrangements whereby student interns, cooperating teachers in the schools, and supervising teachers from the college campus come together in an atmosphere of dialogue. The rule of administrative authority would then be replaced by mutual learning. This high level of collaboration can best be achieved in partner schools where only practices supported by research and honed in successful experience prevail. Under no circumstances should student teachers be placed in settings where they have no recourse but to scrap what they have just learned in favor of opposing school requirements.

There are in-between measures, most of them based rather simply on a true collegial relationship between those from the schools and those from the university who together plan and conduct the teacher education program. We found few such measures to commend as exemplary in our sample, although there were encouraging collaborations in a few settings. The goal is to join theory and practice in every component of a future teacher's preparation. The first step—which happens to be an early step in creating a center of pedagogy—is to bring together as one faculty all those individuals who will be participating in the program's creation and conduct. This requires the earlier or simultaneous ground-breaking steps described above. It can be done without them, but disillusionment will then set in early (as it so often does when educators add one more good thing to their schedules without taking anything out of them).

The recommended approach, then, is not to teach future teachers how to adjust to realities beyond their control, although some preparation for adjustment is in order. Rather, it is to create an environment designed to promote frank discussion among faculty members about how to structure and maintain the program so that students do not become chameleons adjusting to circumstances instead of developing a consistent, defensible philosophy of education.

> *Postulate Seventeen.* Programs for educating educators must establish linkages with graduates for purposes of both evaluating and revising these programs and easing the critical early years of transition into teaching.

Our data show that faculty members and deans were favorably disposed toward maintaining close connections with their graduates, especially during their first year of teaching, although not many did so. They rarely mentioned the potential use of this follow-up relationship for redesigning programs, however. They spoke almost exclusively of providing support during the time when beginners confront problems they had not anticipated.

It is difficult for academics to shed the teacher-pupil model and to regard their former students as colleagues in a two-way process of evaluation, yet that is exactly what must happen. Teacher educators must get beyond the routine of surveying graduates (done only sporadically in the colleges and universities in our sample) and instead adopt continuing assessments designed for program renewal. I believe that a good deal of this could be done within present budgets. Work has a way of using up all available time. Thus getting the needed time is, in part, a matter of rearranging priorities. Securing and using feedback from graduates should be high on the schedule of priorities. The information is crucial, and the process provides legitimate scholarly work for both students and faculty members.

Maintaining close connections with graduates for support purposes—the process of "easing the critical early years of transition into teaching"—is perhaps a more complex matter. First, it requires collaboration between supplier and employer. Second, it requires reciprocity between and among settings in different parts of the country. (Teachers prepared in Maine sometimes begin teaching in Idaho.) Third, it requires the time of mentors, supervisors, and helpers; and time costs money. The desire of teacher educators in most of the settings we studied to provide follow-up assistance was frustrated by lack of funds.

The necessity for a variety of services to support beginning teachers and for collaboration between school districts and teacher-preparing institutions is relatively obvious. What is *not* so obvious, although it has been exposed again and again by school reformers and innovators, is that schools and the occupation of teaching are conducted in ways that are ill-suited to collegial support of any kind. Solid research, insightful literary portrayals, and poignant biographical accounts have revealed the isolation of teachers encapsulated in anachronistic school structures carried over from the nineteenth century.[26] These structures have withstood the onslaughts of successive reform eras. And this study suggests that the go-it-alone ethos has its roots in teacher education programs.

One of the most promising proposals for school restructuring—one often recommended—involves redesigning the school's educational delivery system into teams made up of experienced, beginning, and apprentice teachers (and supported by an array of electronically driven instructional systems). This team and a group of students, some replacing departing ones each year, would stay together for several years in a nongraded structure. Surely partner schools embraced by the new centers of pedagogy will implement these long-standing recommendations and, in so doing, create school structures hospitable to beginning teachers.

> *Postulate Eighteen.* Programs for the education of educators, in order to be vital and renewing, must be free from curricular specifications by licensing agencies and restrained only by enlightened, professionally driven requirements for accreditation.
> *Postulate Nineteen.* Programs for the education of educators must be protected from the vagaries of supply and demand by state policies that allow neither backdoor "emergency" programs nor temporary teaching licenses.

A license attests that someone meets standards designed to protect the public; a certificate attests to satisfactory completion of a preparation program; accreditation attests that a program meets conditions deemed necessary by the profession. The three together, attended to separately, provide the best assurance we now have that a teacher is competent. With these three sets of requirements met, certification by the National Board for Professional Teaching Standards would provide the capstone.

The legacies described in Chapter Three have left states confused over their regulatory role. With this hand, they specify requirements for teaching certificates; with the other, they grant temporary licenses to persons not holding certificates. State intrusion into college and university curricula suggest that the state is vigilant with respect to the quality of teachers for our schools. State waivers of these curricular intrusions in times of teacher shortage suggest that the state is empathetic in regard to local needs. Together, however, these internally contradictory behaviors drive down quality. Further, they ensure shortages of teachers except when the economy is depressed and a decline in the quality of candidates when the economy is thriving.

To stop this self-perpetuating malaise, the process of setting standards must be separated from that of enforcing standards, and both of these must be separated from the state's responsibilities for ensuring a supply of qualified teachers.[27] Further, the state must get out of the business of regulating the teacher preparation curriculum. The California Commission on the Teaching Profession prefaced its recommendations that the training of teachers be deregulated with the following statement: "The state currently prescribes in detail the courses and other experiences required for a teaching license, something it does not do for other professions that require far more academic training, such as medicine and law. Such rigid requirements tend to stifle innovation in developing teacher education curricula, they fail to prepare teachers adequately for the classroom experience, and they offer no assurance that individuals meeting the requirements are, in fact, ready to teach."[28]

Instead of rigidly prescribing the details of teacher education, states should give to teacher educators the full authority they need to create exemplary teacher education programs and then hold those educators responsible. The recommendations of this book will not go far if states continue to specify curricula and simultaneously open wide the gates under pressures of teacher shortage and political intervention.

Concluding Comments

Why the foregoing postulates and not others? In Chapter Two, I defined a *postulate* as an *essential* presupposition or premise in a train of reasoning. My colleagues and I viewed as essential those conditions of teacher education that transcend the immediate. In other words, the conditions essential now will be equally essential years from now. Salaries enter significantly as one of several major factors in attracting able people into teaching. They are not included in a postulate, however, because salaries will be less of an issue in the future if our society takes seriously the crisis in schooling. We believe that full implementation of the postulates would dispose citizens toward awarding higher status and financial rewards to teaching and teachers.

Even though each postulate must stand the test of long-term relevance, we could have chosen fewer or more. We tried to strike a balance: to provide direction without confining the options. The nineteen are not equally relevant to all actors, of course. Although the parties most responsible are identified in the foregoing discussion, let us now connect actors to the major themes.

The first three postulates are designed to ensure a secure, semiautonomous place for teacher education in higher education. This it never has enjoyed. To leave teacher education to the collective goodwill of the arts and sciences, the college of education, and the schools is to ensure the opposite: its continued ill-health.

The key actors in seeking to ensure identity and autonomy equivalent to other professional schools and programs are those responsible for the institutions as a whole—boards of trustees, presidents, provosts. They cannot alone guarantee the consistency of budget and personnel, but they are in pivotal positions with respect to finding both public or private sources.

Likewise, boards of trustees, presidents, and provosts are the key actors in creating the recommended school or center of pedagogy (Postulate Four). The chairperson or dean of education lacks authority over the components to be brought together and may not be able to overcome faculty resistance to a possibly unwanted development.

All else follows from the creation of this center, with its own identity, budget, academic and clinical faculty, and authority over mission, student recruitment and selection, curriculum, and more. The limitations are the usual ones related to human purpose and capability. Postulates Five through Seventeen state the conditions to be established.

The two concluding postulates take us to state capitals, where a regulatory model differing radically from that of the past must prevail. The state should set standards for individuals seeking licenses but deregulate the processes of attaining them. The balance of state attention should go toward creating the conditions likely to attract able people into teaching and keep them there.

What Follows

This book might well end here. Chapter Eight serves as a summary of the themes developed from data presented in the preceding chapters. It serves also to highlight the gap between the picture of conditions and circumstances emerging from our sample of settings studied and alternatives that are supposedly more exemplary. Further, Chapter Eight defines a comprehensive agenda of improvement and points to the key actors for carrying it forward.

At least two essential elements are missing, however. First, the pieces of this agenda need to be integrated into a comprehensive whole. Second, there needs to be some attention given to the human problems that should be taken into account as the agenda is carried out. Both elements are conditioned significantly by local circumstances—so significantly, indeed, that there can be no prescription or formula equally applicable in all settings. Nonetheless, there are features common to processes of educational change that focus on institutions: threats to the security of individuals who perceive that they will probably be called on to behave in ways different from those with which they have grown comfortable; jousting over turf that will now be shared or shared differently; increased work loads caused by phasing out the old and phasing in the new simultaneously; rules and regulations to be changed; almost constant ambiguity; and so on. These, more than the absence of good ideas, explain why nonevents are so often the consequence of supposed reform.

I have chosen to address the two missing elements—integration of the pieces and processes of effecting change and renewal—in a fable about a fictitious regional public university with a clearly recognizable history—of transformation from normal school to university. It represents the type of institution producing the largest percentage of the nation's teachers. I have included an array of (fictitious) characters necessary for significant change. Had I selected a private liberal arts college or a major public or private university, the fable would have developed somewhat differently— but the differences would have been more of degree than of kind.

Although the whole is fiction, it is based on the real-life experience of seeking to effect institutional and programmatic change and will be recognizable, therefore, to those who have engaged seriously in similar endeavors. Those now in positions of leadership who have not previously been so engaged should anticipate many of the problems and difficulties described, although probably in different guise.

Most of the substantive themes developed in preceding chapters are revisited. However, I have chosen to pay major attention to structures and infrastructures and to the sociopolitical processes of shaping them, since these are the elements so commonly neglected in proposals for educational reform. What follows is intended to encourage, not prescribe, steps toward the fundamental redesign of programs for the preparation of this nation's teachers.

Chapter Nine

Renewal at Northern State University: A Fable

❖   ❖   ❖

It may be that one of the many reasons some people have contributed to the utopian literature, and why millions today and in the distant past have been avid readers of these descriptions, is that it permits one to bypass the realities of the creation of new settings and societies. What these literary utopias have in common is that they were brought into existence by an act of controlled fantasy, and they avoid the evils of creation by a process analogous to the belief in virginal birth.

—*Seymour D. Sarason*[1]

It should suffice for now to say that if the history of medical education has any lesson for us, it is that the problem of pedagogical knowledge is not the lack of knowledge so much as the lack of will to institutionalize an effective program of pedagogical education.

—*B. Othanel Smith*[2]

Dr. Harriet Bryan had been casually scanning the "positions available" section of the *The Chronicle of Higher Education* en route to

307

page 68B and the End Paper there that interested her. She most certainly was not looking for another job. Her drive, verve, and especially flair for teaching had been recognized at Meridale, the small liberal arts college where she had become, in record time, a full professor and chair of the department of education. Nonetheless, the position advertised had caught her eye: dean of the school of education, Northern State University.

The more she inquired into Northern over succeeding weeks, the more interested she became. The university's normal-school beginnings, strong commitment to the region, emphasis on liberal studies, and apparent connectedness to surrounding schools (if the mission statement in a document she found in the library at Meridale could be believed) fit in nicely with Harriet Bryan's perceptions of the right context for her.[3] By the time of her interview as one of six finalists, she had become so interested that she began to fear losing out. She had been overjoyed when the post was offered to her.

Northern's New Dean

From May to September 1988, when she became Dean Bryan, Harriet grew a lot clearer on many of the facts of academic life at Northern State University and on the many faces of these "facts." Until the late 1950s, when the institution became Northern State College, it had been a teachers' college—and a good one at that. Even as it broadened its scope, its teachers' college image remained, to the increasing discontent of some faculty members and trustees.

Then, in 1969, controversy had swirled around the upcoming appointment of a new president to replace the longtime, much-respected president—a man who had been a local high school teacher and principal before becoming a professor of education and who employed to the institution's advantage with the legislature his down-home, somewhat folksy approach to explaining what "his" college was all about. The board had debated long and hard the qualifications of the two finalists: a teacher educator of considerable visibility as a scholar in the field of education, and a Rhodes Scholar currently serving as associate provost in a major private university. The trustees chose the latter, but not unanimously. The chairman, in particular, backed by powerful members of the arts and sciences faculty, had argued convincingly that the appointment of Thomas Medford would hasten the passage to full university status.

The dream of a scholarly mecca did not work out as envisioned. Although the gentle-mannered, somewhat austere President Medford was not easily understood by most legislators, they approved the "university" designation in 1972—but with clear restraints. Northern State University, along with five other regionals, was to be in the second tier below "State," as it usually was called, the flagship "world-class" university. The granting of the doctorate, for example, was to be reserved solely to State. The course toward greatness at Northern was shifted further by outside factors. Because of the rapid growth of higher education in the 1960s and early 1970s, together with a shortage of doctoral-level candidates in some fields, competition for faculty posts was intense. Northern found itself having to settle for those who had not made the final cut at places already enjoying first-class standing, including the nearby flagship state university. Then the state economy, university budgets, and enrollments had all faltered in the second half of the 1970s and had continued to sag until shortly before Dean Bryan's arrival.

When Harriet Bryan arrived at Northern in September 1988, some things had improved, but deep scars from past wounds remained. In 1985, Provost Lee had succeeded a provost who had savaged the budget of the school of education during a period of declining enrollment and had so touted publication in refereed journals that faculty members had virtually withdrawn from services to the geographical area that they had once served generously. The impact on field experiences and student teaching had been severe; even now, faculty members often participated only at token levels. Yet despite the emphasis on scholarly work, there was relatively little evidence to point to Northern's being a major player in competing for grants and contracts. Faculty members were quite active in giving papers at scholarly meetings, but their writings were not widely cited in the works of leading scholars in the various fields. Once one probed beneath the outer shell of Northern, it was in many ways the kind of place it had been twenty years before—except that the administrative messages being internalized caused faculty members to feel less good about what they did each day and caused students to feel that the institution existed only secondarily for them. These feelings were somewhat more intensively experienced by students and faculty members in the school of education. Simultaneously, the outer shell suggested a university in transition from whatever it was before to something not yet clearly envisioned.

Nothing Ventured, Nothing Gained

Harriet Bryan learned a lot more that first year at Northern, and a good deal of it puzzled her. Although the description of the job she held, written by a faculty recruitment committee, spoke highly of leadership (in fact, it implied that the new dean should be able to walk on water), she soon discovered that expectations for leadership ranked well below other things—particularly being easily accessible to deal with faculty members' needs and problems. She found no plans for the future of the school of education beyond those stated for the most recent review by the National Council for Accreditation of Teacher Education—and most of those words sounded to her like boilerplate. There were at hand virtually no data regarding previous requests for faculty additions, projections of anticipated retirements, current teaching loads, agreements with school districts regarding numbers and kinds of cooperating teachers needed to staff student teaching, and so on. Nor were there any ad hoc faculty committees at work on issues and problems; there were only standing committees on routine matters of maintenance and administration.

At the beginning of the 1989 winter quarter—the second quarter after her arrival—Dean Bryan sent a questionnaire to all education faculty members regarding their activities and preferences in teaching, research, and service. Much to her surprise, this elicited sharp questioning at the next faculty meeting of the school of education. Was there some significance to her listing *teaching* first on the form? What did she mean by *research?* By *service* did she have something more in mind than accepting membership on university and school committees? What about consulting? Time ran out, but the discussion had not. There was a request—seconded by many— that the next faculty meeting be devoted to the same topic.

What surprised and somewhat disturbed Dean Bryan was the

vehemence of the discussions. Quite a few faculty members had challenged her apparent decision to put teaching highest among her priorities. Actually, she had not even thought about her ordering of teaching, research, and service on the questionnaire; she *always* put them in that order. But why the faculty concern? She had heard a great many complaints about the pressure to publish in her first few months on campus. What she gradually came to realize during the early spring of 1989 was that, though unintentionally, she was stirring up the issue of priorities once again. Painful though the shift to an increasing research emphasis had been, faculty members had been struggling to align the new rhetoric of expectations with at least an appearance of conformity to them; they had been endeavoring not so much to adjust their behavior to expectations as to adapt to the appearance of what these expectations implied. Or, to put the matter another way, they were in the process of creating a culture that flattened out and absorbed unsettling intrusions while giving the appearance of responding to them. And now Harriet Bryan—in all fairness, innocently—appeared to be injecting once again the importance of teaching—the very ingredient the new appearances downplayed. Sometimes change itself is more threatening than the substance of that change.

It is worth noting that this faculty, after a rather long period of institutional evolution—during which stated expectations were often out of sync with ongoing reality—was responding very much as most public school faculties respond to successive eras of imposed reform: They nullify the impact by wrapping the school culture around each intrusion so as to minimize its impact. Unfortunately, potentially helpful as well as potenitally negative changes are thereby eviscerated.

Dean Bryan tried to make it clear to the education faculty in those 1989 faculty meetings that her innocently prepared questionnaire had been intended only as a first attempt to rectify the lack of information and that her colleagues should expect to see similar efforts during the coming year. She also made it clear, however, that she did have strong views about the importance of teaching—especially in a school of education—and about research directed toward the improvement of teaching and teacher education.

During the summer, she took a step that would be announced in writing at the beginning of the fall quarter and discussed at the first faculty meeting of the 1989-90 academic year: appointment of the Committee of Ten, with herself as chair. Because she had sought counsel in many quarters, there was widespread speculation—not all positive—regarding her plans and intentions before she announced them. She had been encouraged by Provost Lee, however, who had told her that appointment of ad hoc committees was well within her authority and had pledged his support.

There were no surprises in the letters of invitation to the other nine committee members: a teacher, a middle school principal, and a deputy superintendent selected from the three school districts with which the school of education worked most closely; representatives (one from each) of the state teachers' association, the office of state superintendent of schools, and the office of the governor (his education aide); a faculty member from the school of education, one from the college of arts and sciences, and the associate provost. Dean Bryan explained the general nature of the written charge: to "look into" all aspects of the operation of the school of education—particularly its preservice teacher education programs—and its local and state context with a view to determining strengths, weaknesses, needs, and areas for change. Nothing in the school's present operation was to be regarded as off limits. But the committee's authority was confined to the identification of issues, problems, strengths, and weaknesses, and to recommendations. It could recommend to Dean Bryan the creation of additional task forces and committees to report to it and could request the compilation of various kinds of data, but it had no authority to act or implement.

Needless to say, there was a considerable uproar over the fact that the school of education was represented by only one faculty member (the elected chair of the faculty for the previous year) and Dean Bryan. She countered by saying that she wanted as many constituencies as possible represented while still keeping the group small—small enough to sit comfortably about the table in the conference room next to her office. Further, she urged the faculty to use faculty meetings during the year to address the same kinds of topics and to feed ideas generated at these meetings to the committee. The committee's work was intended to be comprehensive, to extend throughout the entire academic year (with periodic weekend retreats), and to culminate in a two-day, all-school faculty retreat near the end of the 1990 spring quarter. President Scott had provided $5,000 in support of the committee's work, and Dean Bryan had used this as leverage in securing $3,000 from each of the participating constituencies. Thus she had a kitty totaling $23,000—a solid beginning, she thought.

Succeeding months proved to be bumpy. Faculty members derived both intended and unintended messages from the creation of the committee—most of them unfavorable. Dean Bryan's predecessor had been entrepreneurial in his administrative style, simultaneously supporting consulting with schools, the never-ending faculty search for grants, and teaching geared as closely as possible to faculty preferences. Some members of the faculty had been uneasy with the alliance with school districts that the dean had apparently engineered shortly after publication of *A Nation at Risk*. The membership of the Committee of Ten more than five years later stirred these concerns once again. Dean Bryan would have preferred that faculty members address their misgivings head on, but there was more restlessness and informal conversation outside of meetings than real dialogue in them.

What troubled her most was fear that she had initiated more than could be brought off, especially in the time period initially designated. Even as 1990 was being ushered in, the committee was still circling the agenda. Members were more accustomed to tackling specific problems; the breadth of their charge caused them (properly but dysfunctionally) to see everything as related to everything else. They could not agree on a good entry point.

Dean Bryan had always been a risk-taker. A colleague at Meridale had referred to her affectionately as "in love with the sweet tragedy of lost causes."[4] Recalling those words had always amused and energized her. This time, however, she had felt as though a valley of depression was closing in around her.

Dean Bryan Goes to Chicago

Dean Harriet Bryan had not initially planned to attend the annual meeting of the American Association of Colleges for

Teacher Education (AACTE), but the 1990 conference theme enticed her: "Doing or Being Done To." In conference promotional material, both the program chair and the current AACTE president called for teacher educators to be proactive. In February 1990, Dean Bryan was feeling done to rather than doing. Teacher educators were once again being placed by critics in the villain's role. She was tired of being the target of criticism she considered unfair. Yet she was not at all sure that the criticism was *entirely* unfair. For the first time in her eighteen-year career in higher education, Dean Bryan felt daunted in the face of increasingly discouraging circumstances. She wanted to change her mood to one of doing. At the eleventh hour, Dean Bryan told Bill Parr, director of teacher education and associate dean of the school of education, and two other colleagues that she would be joining them in Chicago.

Over the course of the several days of the annual AACTE meeting, some things came together for her in a disturbing but highly motivating way. The messages of the several general session speakers meshed as though the speakers had together planned their addresses. The disconnectedness of the component parts of teacher education programs described by the principal investigator in a just-completed study fit all too well and all too uncomfortably her institution back home in Somerville—as it did, she learned afterward in casual conversations, the programs represented by many fellow deans. Another speaker, although cautiously optimistic, addressed the recalcitrant problems of school reform and urged school-based and university-based educators to come together to create schools and prepare teachers for schools *other* than those we have. Dean Bryan was intrigued by the third speaker's advocacy of a five-part general-education curriculum for future elementary school teachers and reacted sympathetically to his strong appeal for all teachers to be literate in a second language. A fourth speaker appealed for much closer collaboration between universities and schools, for better research on pedagogy, and for teachers to understand the larger social context and to work toward collaboration between schools and homes in the education of the young.

A recurring theme of the conference—the social dynamite represented by a neglected third of the nation's people—surfaced again and again. There was a tone of urgency, of the need to act rather than wait for others to act. "Business as usual won't get *this* job done," said another of the general session speakers.

Dean Bryan was ready for Mary Catherine Bateson's near-poetic prose near the end of the conference. Bateson spoke first of connectedness and the degree to which most of us are not closely connected to the world around us—or even, for that matter, to the people closest to us. She went on to discuss teaching and testing, noting how the latter often disconnects teacher and student from what is most important.

Bateson's was the kind of address that encouraged reflection in its listeners—reflection that connected things not quite linked before. On one hand, Harriet Bryan's thoughts went to all the old bromides for reforming schools that had been prescribed still more times during the 1980s, and to how ineffectual they had been in dealing with the problems now overwhelming the schools—problems requiring the direct social, economic, and political action to which all the speakers had referred. Her blood began to boil (yet again) when she thought about the simplistic notions for reforming teacher education that had been dredged up over and over since the 1890s and that were being dusted off and paraded once again in state policymaking arenas.

On the other hand, Dr. Bateson's address reaffirmed for Dean Bryan so much of what she deeply believed to be the essence of educating—the essence being ignored or corrupted by the degree to which education and schooling were being called upon to be instrumental to inappropriate ends. "We set ourselves up to be disappointed," she thought. "Teachers are not processors of raw materials. They serve to help all children connect with one another and our world."

A Visit with President Rosemary Scott

On the return flight from Chicago, what Dean Bryan had heard and subsequently discussed with fellow conferees was still churning in her mind. The AACTE meeting had fallen short of being a born-again experience, but it had served to pull her out of the valley of depression. She realized that, lately, her *job* seemed more and more to be getting in the way of her *work*, and she had not been laughing much. She decided that it was time for another chat with President Rosemary Scott.

On the following Thursday afternoon, Dean Bryan found herself departing from the script she tried to follow in the precious moments she spent every six weeks or so with the businesslike president, now in her third year at Northern. Harriet Bryan had been President Scott's first appointment to a deanship; no woman had held either the presidency or the deanship previously. The gist of what Harriet had to say was that she still believed the teacher education program at Northern to be one of the best, if not *the* best, in the state. "But . . . ," she hesitated, "we do a little better than others what we shouldn't be doing in the first place: We do a great job of turning out teachers to maintain schools that should no longer exist."

If President Scott was disappointed in the content of Dean Bryan's outpouring, she did not show it. With a few well-chosen questions, she teased out the core of discontent. This boiled down to essentially four concerns. Harriet perceived a disconnectedness in the total education of future teachers—in part, she said, because of the lack of a clear mission. She believed that the mission of the undergraduate college of arts and sciences was not adequately built into the teacher education program and, indeed, that this college was not itself living up to the stated mission. She saw the school of education she headed as splintered by a vague and inadequate sense of priorities. Finally, although relations with surrounding schools were good, the quality of field experiences and student teaching left much to be desired.

"Are these matters being addressed by your committee?" President Scott asked.

"Yes and no," replied Dean Bryan. "We seem to get *almost* up to them. Then somebody says that we're talking about the cart and not the horse. Pretty soon, we're off in a field looking for the horse."

"Do you expect there to be some rather fundamental changes recommended by the committee?"

"Until a few days ago, I would have said, 'Perhaps yes, perhaps no.' But now I'm convinced that there will be because there *must* be. I think I see what I didn't see before: Our central business has always been teacher education, and it still is. We've allowed ourselves to be diverted by less important matters, most of them attached to the preferences of individual faculty members."

"Then let me make a suggestion," President Scott said. "Your committee is going to come up against the observation someday, by someone, that you can't change teacher education *fundamentally* and keep the existing programs afloat. Because you seem confident that a major overhaul is called for, why don't you simply declare a date for closing admission to existing programs?"

"Do I have that authority?" asked Dean Bryan.

"I believe you do. But I'll take the responsibility. After all, if the changes prove to be minor, nothing will be lost. You simply announce the details of the new program in time to maintain a steady flow of students from the old to the new. So what shall I announce, and when?"

"The sooner the better. I suggest you explain that work under way is expected to lead to some changes in Northern's approach to the education of teachers, and that consequently, the last class in the present postbaccalaureate program will enter for the 1991–92 academic year. Early that year, we would announce the program to be in place for 1992–93, with whatever the changes might be."

"And what about the undergraduate program?" President Scott asked.

"That's more troublesome, because students make up their minds to be teachers at so many points along the way. But I think that the basic message would be the same. Freshmen admitted in the fall of 1991 (the class of 1995) would be the last under the present program. All others already in the tubes at that time would know that they would need to complete requirements for certification by the end of the 1994–95 academic year. I suppose we would have to take care of any stragglers through the following year, but this wouldn't cause any undue problems."

"Then it's done," said the president. "I'd appreciate your preparing an initial draft of the announcement, and I'll see to it that it gets into all the appropriate documents and, before the end of spring quarter, to the press. Meanwhile, you'll probably have some explanatory work to do."

Dean Bryan was still trying to get used to the idea. "Just like that," was all she could say.

"Just like that. After all, what we're doing could scarcely be called bold. Even if you end up changing only a couple of courses, you will have protected the chance of doing something significant. Goodness knows, Harriet, we don't seem to get that chance very often."

Creating a New Setting

The amazing thing about creating a new setting out of an existing one is that the more successful the undertaking, the less distinct and noticeable the changes. What happens, of course, is that the values and "world view" of those most deeply involved undergo profound changes along the way. One's opinions at the outset may have been very different than after the change, but so was the setting; the two were probably more in sync than not. When the setting and one's values change together over time, the two remain considerably in sync. Hence, there is in successful change no excessive jarring for those attempting to move things along. Ironically, it is often those who were most out of sync in the first place who did not want change, and they may remain out of sync and resistant to change when it begins to occur around them. This phenomenon requires deep study.

Sarason made the following observation: "The decision to create a new and independent setting usually reflects two considerations: the opinion that the existing settings are inadequate for one or another reason and, independent of this, the awareness that the conflicts that emerged in the process of arriving at a decision were of such strength and quality as to make a new and independent setting the desirable possibility."[5]

In Quest of an Agenda

A good many things seemed to fall into place for Dean Bryan as she prepared for the next meeting of the Committee of Ten. She wondered why things had been so unclear and disconnected before. She had failed to see, for example, that the school of education was organized around the idea that there are several distinct branches of knowledge, each being advanced by the scholarly work of the faculty. Yet most faculty members spent their time teaching in programs that cut across these divisions. "We should be organized to support the *functions* we carry out," she thought. The data gathered to date had revealed that most of the faculty members spent most of their time teaching present and future practitioners. They were not part of a research institute; nor did the divisions into which they were organized encompass the full breadth of the problems they should be addressing through research.

Surprisingly, the committee seemed to have little difficulty with the direction of her thinking. They had been seeking an appropriate entry point for their comprehensive task. Obviously, teacher education was it; the horse had caught up with the cart. The proposed announcement regarding termination of existing programs brought no objections from committee members. In fact, it seemed to remove a cloud that had been on the horizon. Committee members plunged enthusiastically into suggestions for creating and staffing the task forces proposed by Dean Bryan as the first step in the design of the new program—task forces on mission; organization (of the school of education); faculty and program; student recruitment, selection, and socialization; cooperating schools and practice sites; state context; family and community. The representation of school and university people clearly should vary, they agreed, according to the nature of each task force.

A sudden, paralyzing awareness set in as the meeting drew to a close: The committee had taken nearly six months to get to this point of decisiveness and activity, and much of their progress was simply the result of what Harriet Bryan had experienced and done since the previous meeting. How were they now—efficiently and diplomatically—to convince and orchestrate all the faculty members, schoolteachers, principals, superintendents, and others who had come into the picture during discussion of the task forces? The committee members felt weary.

The deputy superintendent of the Susqua Valley School District stirred them to life again with a suggestion. He proposed that the committee should not assign to its members the duty of chairing the proposed task forces. Instead, it should define for itself a support and liaison role and should devote immediate attention to two matters: first, selecting chairs from outside its own membership and developing guidelines to be used by chairs in selecting task-force members; second, planning for a late-spring or early-summer workshop designed to encourage dialogue of persons representing all constituencies around the task-force topics and elicit suggestions for the work of each. The workshop would take the place of the late-spring meeting that had been announced the previous fall. His colleagues agreed unanimously.

These seemingly routine matters occupied a good deal of the committee's time during its spring meetings. But the extended timeline, along with members' increasing comfort with the committee's redefined role, provided some luxury of reflection. Members read selected books and reports on teacher education and led discussions of them during time deliberately set aside for this purpose. And then Dr. Peter Junger asked to meet with them.

In 1984, while deputy superintendent of the Hawthorne Ridge School District, he had joined with counterparts in two other districts in seeking closer collaborations with Northern State, to which Harriet Bryan's predecessor had responded favorably. Except for some cross-district communication and a few joint projects with the university, not much had come of the collaboration, however. Since then, most of those then involved had moved on or retired— and without institutionalizing the concept of close school-university connections. In 1987, Junger had taken on the demanding tasks of the Somerville superintendency. Now, nearly three years later, he was still very much respected, in spite of the degree to which he had shaken many established ways. People listened when he spoke.

He had taken an active role in supporting Dean Bryan's conception of the Committee of Ten and in the selection of the teacher representative from his district, by far the largest in the area. Junger had followed the committee's work closely and sensed that the time was ripe for another attempt at collaboration.

Unlike many of his colleagues, Junger set aside an hour early each morning for reading; lately, he had been reading about growing national interest in professional-development, key, clinical, teaching, practice, or partner schools (as they were variously called) for preservice teacher education. He was intrigued by the concept but skeptical of his ability to support such a school in the Somerville district without a closer relationship with the university. One morning he read a paper on school-university partnerships that seemed to offer a solution. Unlike most partnership proposals, which tended to place the university in a somewhat avuncular relationship to the schools, the collaboration proposed here was to be two-way. The writer described, for example, the successful mutual development of a new program for the preparation of school principals in which school personnel served as equals with university professors in all aspects of planning and implementation. This, it seemed to Peter Junger, was an idea whose time was come. He asked for and quickly got a hearing with the Committee of Ten.

He proposed the creation of a school-university partnership to embrace Northern State and the five surrounding school districts. This time, however, there was to be more than a meeting of superintendents and the dean, a verbal agreement, and a handshake. There would be a set of formal agreements, financial commitments from each of the partner institutions, a budget, and at least a part-time director—all signed off on by the five superintendents and President Scott. Dr. Junger agreed to serve on a small committee to draw up a document outlining the nature of the mutual commitment. He suggested that first, however, President Scott should call a meeting to be attended by her or Provost Lee (or both) and the superintendents. Peter Junger admitted that he had already discussed the idea with two other superintendents, and he offered to call the others. Finally, he suggested that Dean Bryan confer with Dr. Scott, but she thought it better for Dr. Junger to visit with the president himself.

Spring quarter went by all too quickly. The task forces were created, but each managed only two or three meetings. Peter Junger found himself up against the problem of calendars—and the unexpected interest of superintendents of two districts located well beyond "greater" Somerville. President Scott was thus unable to convene the group until the second Saturday in June—just a week before commencement.

She invited, in addition to the seven superintendents, Provost Lee, Dean Bryan, and Dean Shirley Cochrane of the arts and sciences college. Perhaps it was just as well that there was, as yet, no

document proposing a formal agreement. Without the structure
that such a document would have imposed, the discussion roved
rather freely over possibilities. Peter Junger and Harriet Bryan
found themselves talking more often than they preferred, but they
proved to be the ones most familiar with developments pertaining
to school-university partnerships. Harriet realized that she should
have requested the participation of Professor Ted Anderson of the
school of education, who had recently participated in a conference
on school-university partnerships at the University of Washington.
The group agreed that Anderson, Junger, and Associate Provost
Gerald would be asked to draw up an agreement, share it with the
others, and present it for approval and signatures at a meeting tentatively scheduled for July 20, 1990.

Perhaps it was just as well, too, that the task forces had done
little by the time of the workshop held the last weekend of June. It
proved to be a look-ahead affair; there was yet nothing to be approved. The Committee of Ten wisely decided to focus on input to
the task forces. Committee members realized, not long before the
workshop, that only three of the seven school districts involved in
the school-university partnership proposal were represented in the
task forces. The other four districts had been used only sporadically
for student teaching and observations of classes; and this was, after
all, an effort focused on the redesign of teacher education. It was
decided, however, because both the partnership and the teacher education effort were embryonic and overlapped in part, that the workshop should seek to advance both.

This turned out to be a fortuitous decision. Each of the seven
districts was invited to send individuals representing different levels
of leadership: teachers, principals, central office personnel, and the
superintendent. Five members of the arts and sciences faculty and
twelve from the school of education, in addition to those already
serving on task forces, accepted invitations. The others had plans to
be elsewhere; the dates conflicted with many people's plans to teach
summer school, travel, or do research.

The package of materials sent in advance to the 122 prospective participants included reports of the Holmes Group, the National Board for Professional Teaching Standards, Project 30 (of the
American Association of Colleges for Teacher Education), and the

Association of American Colleges (on undergraduate preparation programs for teachers); several articles and a book on school-university partnerships; and articles on the reform of teacher education, including reports on a recent comprehensive study. Mindful of the special needs and interests of school personnel, the committee assembled a small library of recent books on school reform; multiple copies of several of these were also ordered by the university's bookstore.

So far as could be determined, virtually everyone came away from the workshop with the realization that something was stirring, that there was a prospect of relationships between schools and the university that had not hitherto existed, and that some things were going to be different. And the task forces were given more ideas than they could use. Serendipity proved to be the most important factor at work. Teachers, for example, found themselves talking face-to-face—even arguing—with their superintendent, seen before only at a distance (usually on a speaker's platform). Workshop planners had thought that it would be just great to stimulate cross-district and school-to-university dialogue. More important and powerful, apparently, had been the opportunity for people of differing responsibilities in the same district to talk with one another. And university professors found themselves talking with virtual strangers who turned out to be colleagues in the same building. Most important, the groundwork was laid for more tightly coupling the university-based and school-based components of a new teacher education program in the making.

An Agenda Takes Shape

Summer is not the best time for endeavors requiring continuity, especially when the meshing of two sets of differing institutional cultures is required. Yet three matters of significance transpired between June 15 and September 15, 1990. First, Northern State University announced that all undergraduates seeking to complete teaching credential programs then in place had to do so by the end of the 1995 spring quarter; all freshmen admitted to Northern in the fall of 1990 would be guaranteed admission to and completion of the program, provided they met all requirements to graduate by June 1995 (a period of five years). The announcement included a warning to students planning to enter Northern as freshmen in the fall of 1991. They would not be assured of five years for completion; they, too, would have to graduate in the spring of 1995, so they would have only four years to finish. Summer-school attendance might be necessary, should they schedule programs carelessly or need to make up deficiencies. Similarly, the last class admitted to the one-year postbaccalaureate program would enter in the fall of 1991.

Second, on July 20, the seven school district superintendents and the president of Northern State signed an agreement, previously approved by their respective boards, to create and maintain for a five-year-period (subject to renewal) the Susqua Valley School-University Partnership for Educational Renewal. Third, enough members of the Committee of Ten and of the seven task forces were able to meet with sufficient frequency to develop initial drafts for the design of what they hoped would be a collaborative teacher education program involving several of the partnership districts and the university.

The Partnership Agreement. The school-university partnership agreement adopted in July was fashioned by the small committee after the mission statement of an organization called the National Network for Educational Renewal (NNER), with adaptations where appropriate—a mission statement accepted by the fourteen members of the NNER, each a school-university partnership, in 1986 or subsequently. The collaborating school districts and university (in some instances, several universities) in each partnership of the NNER had agreed to work together on three overarching goals:

1. To promote exemplary performance by universities in their role of educating educators.
2. To promote exemplary performance by schools in their role of educating the nation's young people.
3. To promote constructive collaboration between schools (and their districts) and universities in assuring exemplary performance of overlapping mutual self-interests.[6]

To this third goal, the committee added the following: "especially the simultaneous renewal of schools and the education of workers for them."

The committee had met with a great many people from both schools and the university in seeking to build an agenda for the proposed partnership. The question addressed to schoolteachers and administrators was, "In what areas of work and responsibility might the participation of university personnel be useful?" The question to university professors and administrators simply substituted "school personnel" for "university personnel." At first, there were difficulties in moving the dialogue beyond the conventional and traditional. Teachers said that they wanted help with discipline problems, their use of time, various subject areas of the curriculum, research findings—all the things that they were accustomed to requesting of their districts' in-service education coordinators. The university people were similarly conventional: They thought it would be nice to get easier access to groups of students for their research. The committee soon became tough-minded in setting the ground rules: "Anything you're getting now is ruled out," they said. "We're talking about schools and universities working together to make their institutions more effective—perhaps quite different than they are now. We're not talking about staff development and in-service education of individuals; these go on without institutional collaboration."

They encountered a good deal of reluctance. School people were skeptical about genuine, helpful university involvement. "Professors come out and talk about their research. They don't get engaged in our problems." One school principal used expletives in describing his experience with and expectations for professors of educational administration. Some of the professors interviewed were no less severe in their views of what school people wanted. "If we don't tell them what to do next Monday morning, their eyes glaze over," said a professor in the field of curriculum development. Nevertheless, most took the questioning seriously and offered suggestions that ultimately came together in an agenda that could readily be viewed as embracing overlapping self-interests. (See Exhibit 1, below.)

Exhibit 1. The Susqua Valley School-University Partnership: A Substantive Agenda.

1. The development of school curricula that reflect the very best analyses and projections of what young people need in order to be effective citizens, workers, parents, and individuals.
2. Equal access for all to these curricula.
3. Instructional practices designed to encompass all students and carried out by teachers who care.
4. The restructuring of schools to ensure sequential, integrated learning in the most important domains of knowledge and knowing; a drastic reduction in students' alienation; a substantial increase in the personalization of learning in more familylike groupings; and establishment of an atmosphere of fairness to all—of human decency, if you will.
5. Cultivation of a talent in each student, whether in the core school subjects, the arts, athletics, or some area of technology.
6. Emphasis on students' ability to demonstrate competence through actual performance, with special attention to synthesis of knowledge, skills, and sensitivities (with correspondingly less attention to norm-referenced scores on standardized achievement tests).
7. Emphasis on the intellectual purposes of schools in all of their aspects and on the student as learner and worker rather than as passive recipient of information delivered by teachers.
8. A substantial shift of staff-development dollars from district-determined activities to site-based activities designed to foster continuous school renewal.
9. The creation of exemplary teaching sites in which future teachers are educated—sites that demonstrate both the best we know about how schools should function and the best we know about how to maintain them in a renewing mode.
10. The creation of internships and residencies for educational specialists (including administrators) through which these professionals may observe and gain experience with the best possible educational practices.
11. The creation and utilization of opportunities to promote in the community a continuing dialogue about what education is and why it has more to do with the general welfare of both individuals and society than just preparation for jobs.

In compiling their agenda, the committee borrowed freely, especially from the principles espoused by the Coalition of Essential Schools and again the mission statement of the NNER. After all, they reasoned, both programs had by the summer of 1990 a considerable track record—one dating back to the immediate aftermath of *A Nation at Risk*. But the topics included in the proposed agenda were matters that had come up rather frequently in their own discussions and in conversations with other school and university personnel; committee members now felt strongly about them. They regarded the sources used as both corroborative of and contributing to the language used.

They wrapped up their document with some recommendations for a governance structure and financial support. After considerable discussion, they included the figure of $7,500 for each of the seven districts—a total of $52,500—for the first year, this amount to be reconsidered after a year. President Scott's suggestion regarding the university's first-year contribution was unanimously accepted: payment of up to $20,000 (plus benefits, if appropriate) for a part-time director to be selected by a committee representing both the districts and the university. Candidates for the position were suggested to the search committee almost before it was formed: recently retired individuals from the schools or the university, an advanced doctoral candidate at the flagship state university, or someone already employed in the districts or at Northern State University whose work load might be reduced to accommodate the demands of the partnership.

There appeared to be satisfaction with the final agreement on all sides. The commitments made on July 20 advanced Peter Junger's initial proposal of a few months before well beyond even his most optimistic expectations. Once again, people in different parts of the same educational enterprise found that they could talk productively together and plan what had not even been envisioned earlier.

The Task Forces. The task-force activities had not moved forward as smoothly; nor was the agenda as clear, even as the fall quarter rolled around. What its members and those of the Committee of Ten increasingly realized was that they were tangled in thickets of words—thickets not encountered by the partnership committee. Creating exemplary school sites for educating future teachers, for example, sounded sensible indeed. But how? Prickly issues soon came popping out like thorns on the bushes of the thickets: How are these schools to be staffed? Where do the university teacher educators come into the picture? Who makes decisions? Who pays? The articles in the educational literature were virtually mute on such issues. Indeed, they made the creation of such schools sound so natural and easy, partly because most were about intentions rather than accomplishments. And the issue of professional-development or practice schools was only one of a host of nettlesome matters to be dealt with.

Despite these difficulties, and although meetings had been sporadically scheduled and not fully attended, an interesting set of proposals was beginning to emerge. As one member put it, "With poor meeting attendance, there are fewer of us to argue."

Although the school districts had been represented at the June workshop, most individual schools were not represented at all on the various task forces. Thus for most teachers and principals, the workshop, the subsequent solidification of a partnership agreement, and especially the work of the Committee of Ten were non-events. There was, when school personnel returned for the 1990-91 year, a Susqua Valley School-University Partnership, but their lives were not yet affected by it. The size and bureaucratized structure of these school systems (like school systems everywhere) created a peculiar disjuncture between high-level events that appeared to be pregnant with promising consequences and the daily lives of those who work in classrooms.

For university personnel, on the other hand, creation of the partnership, the work of the task forces, and the work of the Committee of Ten were events worthy of note, if only because decision making in the university was assumed to be participatory. There had not yet been full faculty participation, however. The fall quarter at Northern—particularly in the school of education—began quietly. Yet the stillness appeared—to Dean Bryan, at least—to be somewhat ominous.

The 1990-91 Academic Year Unfolds

There is one sure way to appear successful as a dean for a few years: Challenge nothing and support everyone. One other thing is for sure: It takes from five to ten years for a dean to bring about major accomplishments. On the other hand, it takes only three or four years for the "support everyone and challenge nothing" deans to use up campus goodwill, at which point they generally begin seeking other jobs. Harriet Bryan was in for the long haul, although her commitment was sorely pressed during the first five or six months of her third year. What kept her going then was a fundamental belief in the goodwill of most people, confidence that keeping the issues on the table until everyone had an opportunity to address them would lead to good resolutions, and awareness that only a very few people are ornery out of sheer cussedness rather than out of the fear of change and demands that they feel unable to face. Academe, she knew, is a tough place—something that is little known and understood on the outside. One depends heavily on colleagues in seeking insight into the importance of what one does. These colleagues, in turn, depend heavily for their sense of worth on a culture that is parsimonious in doling out mutual support and commendation.

The agenda of faculty meetings in the school of education was constructed jointly by Dean Bryan and the elected chair of the faculty (Tom Rivers) after routine circulation of a request to the faculty for items. These two agreed that a portion of each meeting would be devoted to reports from task forces and, when appropriate, the Committee of Ten.

The report of the task force on cooperating schools and practice sites at the October meeting raised some eyebrows over the proposal that student teachers be assigned together in cohort groups to a few carefully selected partner schools rather than individually to cooperating teachers in many schools. After the report, some concerns were expressed by various faculty members regarding the political implications of using just a few schools instead of spreading the student-teaching contingent widely across the schools of three nearby districts (and more remote ones as needed). But this idea had been discussed before, so it was not unduly jolting. Besides, it was the first faculty meeting of the year—a time for pleasant exchanges and congeniality.

The November meeting, on the other hand, was tense. The task force on organization presented its preliminary thinking on a unit to be devoted exclusively and virtually autonomously to teacher education, with its own clearly defined student body, faculty, and budget. The faculty was to be representative of the school of education, the arts and sciences, and the schools. This task-force report, juxtaposed against the October report on student teaching, caused alarm. Something very different from present ways and structures was being suggested in these two reports, but the specifics were apparently being held back. For example, what would be the role of teachers in these partner schools regarding the conduct of teacher education? What was the university giving up and what would it get in return? These and other questions had been raised in the task forces and discussed extensively by the Committee of Ten, and answers were not yet forthcoming. Unfortunately, task-force and committee members began to appear not forthcoming as well, even in the eyes of generally supportive faculty members.

The dam broke at the December meeting, following what appeared initially to be a routine progress report: that of the task force on student recruitment, selection, and socialization. The task-force chair reported that they were giving serious thought to requiring a second language for all prospective teachers. Because the Latino population, particularly in the schools of Somerville, was increasing rapidly, they thought it best that this language be Spanish. To ensure fluency (not just a reading knowledge), the task force was considering immersion of students and faculty alike. There was silence, then a few giggles, and then several simultaneous negative explosions. (There were, too, several expressions of enthusiasm and of congratulations to the task force, but these were more subdued.) A few matters of business were then attended to and the meeting was adjourned.

A Call on President Scott. Harriet Bryan knew that the issue of faculty priorities she had triggered unwittingly during the previous year had not been laid to rest. It couldn't be, given the mixed signals with respect to institutional mission that she was increasingly receiving. Although President Scott always sounded convincing when talking about Northern's responsibility to the region, her own academic credentials were impressive and she traveled in prestigious intellectual circles. Further, nearly all of the faculty members who were recognized in her annual reports were in the arts and sciences and had been singled out for their scholarly accomplishments. What was President Scott's mission for Northern? Dean Bryan's ordering of teaching, research, and service could put the school of education out of step with the rest of the university—her confessed innocence in this wording notwithstanding. Dean Bryan anticipated that, at some point in the restructuring now under way, a small but powerful group of faculty members would use her own words to blunt the change process.

Things did not work out exactly that way. Dean Bryan had to some degree misinterpreted the recent faculty silence on this issue, perhaps becoming mildly paranoiac regarding its meaning. Further, she had allowed her faith in the basic goodness of most people to slip a little. She had, of course, stirred up a fear of change now being exacerbated by the present state of ambiguity in task-force plans for change, so some reaction was to be expected.

After the December meeting, a very senior member of the education faculty requested a hearing with President Scott for himself and three colleagues. The president's secretary always probed a bit regarding the purpose of an appointment, but this time she learned only enough to tell President Scott that four members of the school of education wanted to talk with her about "some concerns they had with the work of the Committee of Ten." Even this small admission may have been a strategic error on the part of the senior faculty member, however. After all, although Dean Bryan had drafted the letter of invitation, President Scott had signed it.

When the faculty members were seated in her office, President Scott explained the unexpected presence of Provost Lee. She assumed, she said, that this was a matter pertaining to one of the units reporting directly to the provost. The normal channel to the president was through the provost, if he did not provide satisfaction. She had thought it expedient simply to skip standard procedures and so had asked Provost Lee to join them. (The implication that normal channels had been bypassed was not lost on the faculty members.)

Two of the four appeared somewhat embarrassed to be there and remained silent most of the time. The initiator of the meeting spoke with some passion about "the dismantling of carefully established relations with schools"—largely put together by him in the 1970s and early 1980s, when he had been associate dean for teacher education, something unknown to President Scott. Although the Cooperating Teachers Club he had organized had faded away by the mid 1980s, its former members still constituted the core of the cooperating teacher network. Shifting to a small group of partner schools was a politically strategic error, he felt, and not good for the university's image. This image, he added, had already slipped from where it had once been.

His fellow spokesperson, a midcareer scholar with an impressive record of publications, shifted the focus from the work of the task forces and the Committee of Ten to Dean Bryan. He compared her negatively to her predecessor in regard to seeking research funds and faulted her for putting teacher education at the forefront of her developmental agenda. One of the two silent colleagues nodded.

Provost Lee thought for a moment and then put a few questions to the faculty members—questions that they thought were somewhat misdirected: He asked the second speaker about his views on the cooperating teacher education network (the issue raised by the *first* speaker) and asked the teacher educator about his views on Dean Bryan's support for research. He then asked the other two—the silent two—about their colleagues. Had they talked with others about these problems?

"Yes, and they seemed to agree—at least they didn't *dis*-agree," responded one.

"Did you suggest that they join you at this meeting?" Provost Lee asked.

"Yes, but they seemed to think that the four of us would be enough."

Then Dr. Lee turned to the teacher educator. "Has the Committee of Ten made any decisions yet, or any recommendations to the faculty?"

"Not that I know of," he said.

"But I assume that you've voiced your views regarding the changes being proposed with respect to student teaching?"

"Of course," the faculty member responded emphatically.

"Good," said Provost Lee. "You made a very significant contribution to it, and it's important that you keep your views before the committee as it pushes toward recommendations."

"Are you here to ask anything of me?" interjected President Scott.

"Yes," replied the second spokesperson. "We believe that there should be an early review of Dean Bryan's stewardship of the school of education."

"If my estimate is correct, Dr. Lee will be appointing a committee next year to engage throughout the following year in the five-year cycle of reviewing Harriet Bryan's performance. We have a lot at stake in the work now progressing under her leadership. To review her now, out of the normal cycle, would be to send the wrong signals. Further, how well all this is coming out will be valuable information for the review committee. I've heard no outpouring of dissatisfaction regarding Dean Bryan's leadership; indeed, I've heard just the opposite. Were we to disrupt what has been put in motion by conforming to your request, we would have to hold you accountable, to a considerable degree, for the consequences, whatever they might be. I do appreciate your concern for the school's welfare, however. Presumably, you will continue to argue vigorously for what you believe is right."

And that was that.

A Slight Shift in Procedures. Word of the meeting got around, although not in any formal settings (not even in meetings of the task forces). In response to rumors, however, Tom Rivers (chair of the education faculty) suggested to Harriet Bryan a change in format for winter-quarter faculty meetings.

"It seems to me," he said, "that the verbal reports coming to us are not yet sufficiently fleshed out to provide real alternatives for debate. As a result, we're simply stimulating everyone's worst fantasies. We need to lower the level of ambiguity. Also, there's a lot of normal business to be attended to that's being neglected."

Dean Bryan agreed with him on a new procedure—one close to what he had already discussed with several colleagues. The task forces would confine their progress reports to interaction with the Committee of Ten. The committee, in turn, would send to Tom Rivers a brief written summary of matters as committee members neared the recommendation stage. He would send these to all faculty members and request written input. Similarly, summaries of matters likely to be of concern to the constituencies represented on the Committee of Ten might go to relevant groups, at the discretion of the committee.

The timing of this decision was good. A retreat for the chairs of the task forces and members of the Committee of Ten had already been scheduled for the first weekend in January. They would be discussing written progress reports of the task forces at that time— reports that, under the new agreement, Tom Rivers would send to the faculty. The committee was also considering a series of meetings with the various constituent groups to take place in May, dependent on agreement at the January retreat that preparation of a comprehensive report during the interval was feasible.

The revised plan worked well. A few faculty members took advantage of the opportunity to write their suggestions, although these were as often as not addressed to topics not appearing to be on the agenda. The issue of Spanish for all brought forth a response from almost everyone, with "no" or "need to think more about this" dominating over "yes" responses. Although nearly all the statements sent in on all issues were signed—and some of these were strongly critical of the direction emerging in regard to three or four matters—several of the most harsh were anonymous.

At the January faculty meeting, Tom Rivers announced that the May meeting would be unusual: Devoted to a report of the Committee of Ten, it would begin at 1:00 P.M. on Friday, May 17, and continue (attendance voluntary) until not later than 3:00 P.M. on Saturday. Faculty members would be guests of the committee for Friday dinner and Saturday lunch.

Then, during a three-day retreat between winter and spring quarters, committee members (augmented by task-force chairs) assembled the several pieces of their report and turned it over to a small subcommittee for cutting and editing. In a mood of celebration, they named it "Northern Lights." What follows is a very much abbreviated version. Because creating the blueprint for a new unit in pedagogy had proved to be so controversial and pivotal—and promised to remain so—this section was placed first in the report. The editorial committee departed somewhat from the structure represented by the seven task forces in producing the whole, sometimes combining their reports into new combinations of topics.

"Northern Lights": A Proposal

Our proposal, although still tentative in many respects, puts forward some significant changes for the way Northern State University and three collaborating school districts intend to conduct the teacher education enterprise. Although participation of four additional districts in the Susqua Valley School-University Partnership may lead to a later expansion in the number of participating districts, we view our proposal as involving exclusively Northern State University and the Somerville, Susqua Valley, and Hawthorne Ridge School Districts. Collaboration among several but not all members of the partnership for specific purposes appears to us to be entirely in the spirit of the umbrella-like structure for school-university collaboration intended in the creation of that partnership. We realize fully that the specifics of what follows are recommendations only, requiring for their implementation action by the relevant parties. It must be remembered that our charge at the outset was focused on the school of education, with particular attention to teacher education within the university and in cooperating schools.

We recommend that the school of education be divided into two units: the Center of Pedagogy and the Center for Specialized Studies, each to be headed by a faculty member (carrying a reduced load of teaching) who will report directly to the dean. Each center will enjoy autonomous status and have its own budget and allocation of full-time-equivalent (FTE) faculty. It is expected that the two will work closely together in mutually supportive roles and, when appropriate, share faculty.

This recommendation removes the school's overall administrators from direct management of programs. We recommend that the dean of the school of education be assisted by two associate deans, each with schoolwide responsibility: one for the "people" side—both students and faculty members—and one for business, finance, and facilities. We urge that all three deans engage moderately in teaching, especially in the core elements of programs.

The Smith Center of Pedagogy

Our planning processes have been enlightened not only by the materials read commonly in last summer's workshop but also by

A Design for a School of Pedagogy. Its principal author, B. Othanel Smith, was scholar-in-residence at Northern for the 1975 spring quarter and mentor to three of Northern's professors during his long tenure as a member of the faculty of the University of Illinois. We are all saddened by his recent death. In appreciation of his contributions to educational thought and practice, we have recommended to President Scott that the proposed pedagogical center be named the Smith Center of Pedagogy.[7]

In designing the center, we have studied growth and demographic changes projected for our area over the next decade, as well as university projections and plans. University trustees plan to cap enrollment at 15,000 students; the growth since 1980 has been from just under 10,000 to 14,566. Enrollment in the school of education declined between 1968 and 1985, steadied in 1986, and has risen since then to nearly 800 (student FTE). Some 600 of these are in preservice teacher education programs: 502 at the undergraduate level and 95 in the postbaccalaureate one-year credential sequence. The remaining 186 are experienced teachers seeking master's degrees in such fields as early childhood education, special education, elementary and secondary education, and school administration.

The faculty of 55 FTE divides itself roughly into thirds: one-third teaching exclusively in the undergraduate program, one-third teaching exclusively in graduate programs, and the rest distributed across both. Of these, usually 3.0 FTE are left open, to be filled as needed with part-time, interim, and adjunct faculty members who assist in the two teacher education programs.

Our inquiries led to the conclusion that there is very little prospect of increasing the size of this faculty in the immediate future. But the school of education must join with the rest of the university in capping enrollment; in fact, we recommend the option of cutting back somewhat with no loss in faculty size. Given the number of experienced teachers in the area, we consider it ill-advised to cut back on the graduate program; we propose that it be capped at 200 students (up slightly from the present level). Given the fact that graduate programs are presently conducted almost entirely through formal classes, with little accompanying field work, 13 faculty FTE, plus 1.5 FTE in teaching assistants (3 at .5 each) should be sufficient, especially since faculty responsibility for the required master's projects is spread rather widely across the school. (We assume that there will be a later study of master's degree offerings; we did not assume attention to these to be in our charge.)

As is detailed in Table A, we recommend for the fall of 1992 the introduction of two new preservice teacher education programs, one requiring up to five years for completion, and the other, at the postbaccalaureate level, requiring up to two years. The first is projected to generate a first class of 1997 consisting of 105 individuals well prepared to teach; the second should graduate up to 60 by 1996. Because of the student load that will be generated at the points of overlap between present and new programs, we strongly advise beginning the postbaccalaureate program in the fall of 1992 with only 20 students, increasing to 40 in 1993, and then moving to a full class of 60 in 1994.

Table A requires some explanation. The 502 students shown as enrolled this year and the 500 for next year (the last year for entering freshmen who intend to complete the present progam) are concentrated for teacher education primarily in their junior and senior years and, to a lesser degree, in either the sophomore or an extended senior year. (Some students, mostly those preparing to teach at the elementary level, take one or two additional quarters to complete their work.) We estimate that there will still be up to 500 of these in the tubes during 1992–93 but that enrollment will decline with subsequent graduations. Because we think that it may be necessary to honor some stragglers claiming a grandfather clause beyond the one announced, we have projected 50 enrollees through the 1995–96 academic year.

We realize that the proposed reduced production of preservice teachers is not fully offset by the projected increase at the inservice master's degree level. We argue, however, that improvement in quality requires either cutting numbers or increasing faculty size, and the latter is not a viable alternative. As we shall see in a section below, the programmatic changes recommended do not reduce the numbers of students to be cared for at any given time, even when estimates of dropouts are included; in fact, they appear to increase. The 80 identified for the first year of this program, 1992–93, will be freshmen with declared intentions of preparing to teach. They will proceed as a cohort group and in subdivisions of a dozen or so, each

Table A. Projected Enrollments, Smith Center of Pedagogy, 1990–2000.

	1990–91	1991–92	1992–93	1993–94	1994–95	1995–96	1996–97	1997–98	1998–99	1999–2000
Existing Undergraduate	502	500	500	300	200	50				
Existing Postbaccalaureate	95	100								
New Undergraduate	Planning									
Class of 1997			80	95	110	108	105			
Class of 1998				100	110	120	116	110		
Class of 1999					100	110	120	116	110	
Class of 2000						100	110	120	116	110
Class of 2001							100	110	120	116
Class of 2002								100	110	120
Class of 2003									100	110
Class of 2004										100
Total Student FTE	597	600	580	495	520	488	551	556	556	556
New Postbaccalaureate	Planning									
Class of 1994			20	18						
Class of 1995				40	36					
Class of 1996					60	54				
Class of 1997						60	54			
Class of 1998							60	54		
Class of 1999								60	54	
Class of 2000									60	54
Class of 2001										60
Total Student FTE	597	600	600	553	616	602	665	670	670	670

such subgroup with a faculty adviser. They will meet regularly throughout their freshman and sophomore years for purposes of preliminary induction into the demands, expectations, and moral responsibilities of teaching. Faculty members assuming these responsibilities will be credited with teaching hours and have their teaching loads in other areas reduced by from three to five hours per quarter. (More details below.) We anticipate that this cohort group of 80 will be augmented by as many as 30 more who will decide to teach during their freshman or sophomore year. The plan is built on the assumption that each group will reach its maximum size in the junior year and then decline a little as students are advised out or decide to drop out. The estimated size of each graduating class assumes some attrition from the junior-year high point in enrollment.

The faculty of the Smith Center responsible for these students is projected to be 37 FTE. We recommend the addition of 4.5 FTE for post-master's degree teaching assistants (9 at .5 FTE each). The major potential source of these assistants is described below.

Mission

Early in its work, the task force on the mission of the Smith Center of Pedagogy joined with an interdistrict committee that has been working with two professors from Northern on the task of determining school indicators of excellence and equity.[8] An abbreviated version of the resulting mission statement for the Center appears in Exhibit A, below. It has been substantially revised from the first draft as a result of helpful suggestions submitted to us during recent months.

Faculty Mix and Transition

A survey of all faculty members in the school of education provided useful information in planning for a transition from existing teacher education programs to new ones. First, we needed to know more about faculty members' plans for retirement, especially with the pending removal of age ceilings. It turned out that more intend to retire in the next few years than might have been estimated

Exhibit A. Mission of the Smith Center of Pedagogy.

The Smith Center of Pedagogy, embracing Northern State University and the Susqua Valley, Hawthorne Ridge, and Somerville School Districts, is committed to preparing schoolteachers in and for exemplary schools characterized by equity and excellence.

Excellence is indicated by conditions, practices, and outcomes in schools that are associated with high levels of learning for most students in all valued goal areas of the common curriculum.

Equity is indicated when there are no systematic differences in the distribution of those conditions, practices, and outcomes based upon such variables as race, ethnicity, religion, sex, and economic status.

Working Assumptions

1. There are no systematic differences in human learning potential other than those attributable to individual variation itself.
2. Schooling environments can be created within which most students can achieve high levels of learning with respect to a valued, common curriculum.
3. A working consensus can be reached on a quality common curriculum that does not limit creative implementation at local levels but that still leaves no question of educational commitment and responsiblity of the state and district.
4. Information on the quality of schooling may include but must not be limited to scores on standardized achievement tests; the educational conditions, practices, and outcomes all must be evaluated in order to assess the quality of schooling; and information pertaining to excellence must include both qualitative and quantitative approaches to explaining and understanding what goes on in schools.
5. Teachers for such schools must understand the role of schools in our democratic society and be fully sensitive to the moral responsibilities they carry in seeking to enculturate the young critically into this society.
6. Teachers must possess the knowledge and skills necessary to maximally developing the capacities of children and youths to be effective parents, citizens, workers, and humane individuals. These attributes are acquired primarily through rigorous study in coherent programs of general, liberal studies.
7. Teachers' ability to relate effectively to all students and to exercise sound and humane moral judgment in helping them learn is honed primarily in programs of pedagogical studies and in socialization with peers and faculty members over a relatively long period of time.
8. Teachers are the primary stewards of our schools. They must be well versed in what this stewardship demands and in the processes of working with colleagues, parents, and the community in ensuring that their schools be both exemplary and renewing. They must be sensitive to the moral and ethical dimensions involved in seeking to deal honestly and

Exhibit A. Mission of the Smith Center of Pedagogy, Cont'd.

---

fairly with differing, strongly held beliefs among colleagues and within the community.

The Smith Center of Pedagogy is dedicated to the above mission and to sustaining dialogue directed not only to its critique and revision but also to its pursuit.

---

solely from distributions of chronological age. Twenty-three members of the faculty expect to retire within ten years; fourteen, within five years. We urge that recruitment to fill these slots be tied closely to the needs of new programs.

Planning the new program while phasing out the present one creates undue burdens on the faculty. Consequently, we recommend "borrowing" from future retirements—that is, several faculty members to replace persons scheduled to retire would be recruited a year or two in advance of those retirements instead of on the usual replacement schedule. Dean Bryan is currently engaged in discussions with Provost Lee about various configurations of faculty allocations to free up some faculty members next year for intensive planning and to ease the transition from present to new programs. Unfortunately, Dr. Lee is making plans for his own retirement next year and is reluctant to make firm promises. Consequently, President Scott is being kept well informed, and she has not closed the door on some advance borrowing on at least next year's retirements. Unfortunately, there will be little savings from this year's. The recruitment now drawing to a close will replace a full professor with an assistant professor, for a savings of about $15,000 in salary and benefits. But the professorship to be vacated this June by retiring Associate Dean Parr has already been filled at the full professor level with the appointment of Dr. Ricardo Montes. Provost Lee has specified that next year's three retirees must be replaced at the assistant professor level. The anticipated savings in salary and benefits is conservatively estimated at $40,000.

The next two years will be the toughest ones in the restructuring process. Thus we have encouraged Dean Bryan to request 3.0 additional faculty FTE for the next two years. To compensate, the first three positions vacated by retirees after the 1992–93 year would be "returned" to the president's office and not replaced. The additional costs of this faculty increase come to approximately $110,000 for 1991–1992 and $80,000 for 1992–93. President Scott understands the need but can make no promises. Even in a university of this size, with its budget somewhat enhanced recently, there is little flexibility. The improved budget has whetted the appetites of other schools and departments. For the moment, the matter is on hold.

We have worked closely with the governing board of the Susqua Valley School-University Partnership in seeking state funds for site-based school renewal. Governor James Stewart has been persuaded to include in his education package for the 1992 legislative session a two-part proposal: one for a statewide competition open to any school district and the other for a competition open only to districts heavily involved in a college's or university's teacher education program. The first would provide for up to forty "schools of the future"; the second, for up to twenty partner schools in 1992, thirty in 1993, and forty in 1994, joined with universities for purposes of teacher education (no more than ten per university). The funding for each school in the first group will be $50,000, subject to renewal for five years, depending on legislative approval. Funding for the second group is to be up to 8 percent of each school's annual budget, once again subject to legislative renewal. With the three districts used most extensively for teacher education already in a formal partnership with Northern, we view our situation as already advantaged in the competition, should the governor's proposals be funded.

We shall not detail here the data from another part of the faculty survey that sought to determine preferences in teaching and, consequently, in allocation to one of the two new centers. More faculty members than anticipated stated their preference for full-time preservice teacher education and the Smith Center—about 40 percent. Twenty percent chose full-time commitment to the Center for Specialized Studies. The remainder preferred to divide their time between the two.

We recommend a 60 percent or more time allocation to one or the other center, giving faculty members a home base and the right to vote in that center. (All faculty members with total appointments of 50 percent or more have the right, of course, to vote on schoolwide matters.) Faculty members should have the privilege, we believe, of distributing the remaining percentage of their time according to interest and programmatic need.

Because the curriculum calls for a much closer working relationship between education and the arts and sciences, we recommend that some of the resources needed to ensure that the center will not have to beg for help be built into the allocation of faculty FTE. We propose that approximately 5.0 FTE—in addition to those already utilized in the arts and sciences college for teacher education (approximately 3.0 FTE)—be reserved for purposes of staffing the program. These FTEs will be filled, for the most part, on a fractional basis (involved arts and sciences faculty members currently participate half-time or less in teacher education). Given a total center allocation of 37 FTE, the 8.0 FTE used to ensure an arts and sciences contribution to content-specific pedagogy—for example, in cooperation with education faculty members specializing in various aspects of teaching—is a significant portion. Attention must be given to the matter of voting rights attached to these 8.0 FTE.

We envision for the future, then, a Smith Center faculty made up of personnel from the existing school of education, from the arts and sciences departments most closely related to the curricula of the schools and teacher education, and from partner schools that provide the center's laboratory facilities. Many important decisions must be made before the class of 1997 enrolls in September 1992.

It is our hope that negotiations with State, now under way, will lead to a joint doctorate in pedagogy, with Northern providing a significant part of the clinical/practice component. Such a program would provide a major source of our teaching assistants, referred to above, and we envision that many of its graduates would be among the teacher educators of tomorrow.

Students and Program

We recommend an annual intake to the Smith Center of 100 freshmen and 60 candidates for the postbaccalaureate program. The latter group will be composed primarily of individuals coming out of other lines of employment, but there will also be some recent graduates of four-year colleges. All will have made the decision to

prepare to teach. Those in the former group will also have declared
such an intention. Students not so declaring will be given the
opportunity to do so at any time during their first five quarters of
study—until near the end of the winter quarter of their sophomore
year, when a formal application of admission must be made. There
will be no later point of admission. Individuals deciding to become
teachers while in their junior or senior year will have the opportunity to apply later for the postbaccalaureate program.

The Undergraduate Program. We now address the undergraduate program in some detail. All freshmen and sophomores
expressing an interest in teaching will be advised to enroll in a series
of seminars collectively titled "An Introduction to Teaching,"
which will count as a lower-division course elective. These seminar
groups of not more than fifteen students will visit schools and various other educational and social agencies in the community and
engage in discussion and a modest amount of reading. All seminar
sections will come together at least once each quarter for social
gatherings and more formal programs (panel discussions, sympo-
sia, speakers, and so on). (Note: The three-hour maximum credit
registration for the lower-division seminar and the accompanying
teaching credit each quarter for faculty members involved is designed to recognize the faculty work load involved, not to cut into
the general-education curriculum of future teachers.)

The seminars will be voluntary. However, our recent study of
freshmen and sophomores now enrolled at Northern suggests that
at least 200 are strongly interested in teaching and would be interested in enrolling in such seminars, perhaps on a continuing basis.
In view of the fact that we are recommending that each class selected
(after the smaller initial class of 1997) be limited to 120, at its maximum level in the junior year, there could be as many as two applicants for each place. Consequently, we believe that most students
interested in teaching careers will want to enroll voluntarily in the
seminars—partly to make up their minds and partly to enhance
their chances of being selected as teacher education candidates.

Students will be given the opportunity to take at any time in
their freshman or sophomore year the test in basic knowledge and
skills to be required for all prospective teachers. We recommend a

significant augmentation in the tutoring services provided at Northern so as to ensure passage of this test for those students whose educational backgrounds have disadvantaged them. For students who pass this test and apply for admission, a screening process going beyond the necessary academic prerequisites (both specific course areas and grades) will take place during the spring quarter of their sophomore year. Special consideration will be given to the following: proficiency in English and one other language common to the region, understanding of teachers' moral responsibilities in a system of compulsory schooling, cross-cultural experience indicative of an ability to work successfully with members of different racial and ethnic groups, relevant work with children or adolescents and social agencies (particularly those focused on families and community enhancement), strength of character, and commitment to the profession of teaching.⁰ Letters of recommendation and a written statement of the candidate's self-appraisal for teaching will be required, and all candidates will be interviewed in person. Obviously, there is much work still to do in seeking to design an effective screening process.

The 120 students selected will then move as a cohort group, subdivided into smaller groups, through a three-year preparation program that will combine from the beginning four major components: subject matter concentration in a discipline or division of knowledge (such as the social sciences); field experiences in small groups (no more than fifteen students) accompanied by discussion and reading, and including in the third year at least five months of full-time teaching (except for a day each week for other class- and school-related activities); a three-year sequence, closely tied to the planned sequence of field experiences, dealing with historical, philosophical (particularly moral and ethical), social, and psychological (both cognitive and developmental) dimensions of education and schooling, with the third year focused directly on the nature and practice of teaching; and a five-part upper-division general-education program of integrated studies designed to provide a global, environmental, economic, political, and multicultural perspective. This fourth component should be planned as the equivalent of 25 quarter-hours of traditional coursework. Each of the other three components is to be the equivalent of from 35 to 40 quarter-hours, the whole adding up over the three years to the equivalent of 135 quarter hours. However, we recommend that a combination of field work and related seminars replace the conventional course structure for a large part of the curriculum.

We have outlined a five-year program (with required studies and field work concentrated in the last three years) that is, in actuality, only a quarter or two beyond the current mode for elementary school teachers and even many secondary school teachers. Indeed, many who enroll for only one less quarter, particularly in the former group, are not at all happy about the scheduling problems and lack of adequate advising along the way. Further, their programs are crowded and often haphazard. Students become credit-takers; they reflect little on what it means to be making the transition from student to teacher. We believe that our recommendations, if adopted, will result in a coherent program for those large percentages of students who decide before coming to college or early in their college years that they want to become teachers.

Because we regard all of the above requirements to be prerequisite to status as a qualified teacher, we recommend that completion be rewarded with a professional bachelor's degree in teaching. The precise designation of that degree has not yet been determined, but we urge Northern State University to explore the possibility of granting a uniquely *teaching* degree—a bachelor's degree in pedagogy. Because this is not a graduate program or a graduate degree, candidates will not be required to be admitted to the graduate division following their completion of a bachelor of arts or science degree. At the core of this recommendation is our belief that the curriculum must be seamless, coherent, and completely free of the dissonance created by artificial distinctions of courses labeled "graduate" or "undergraduate." Another advantage of our recommendation is that it clears the way to restore meaning to the master's degree. Current one-year, preservice, postbaccalaureate programs leading, for example, to the MAT constitute little or nothing more than undergraduate studies, field experiences, and student teaching comparable to what Northern and many other universities now provide in undergraduate preservice teacher education.[10]

It is important to understand fully the implications of the foregoing. On completing all undergraduate requirements—com-

monly after four years of study and 180 quarter-hours of credit—
each candidate would be awarded the B.A. or B.S. degree. The second baccalaureate, a degree in pedagogy, would be awarded on the
candidate's completion of the full five-year teacher education program. Candidates beginning at the postbaccalaureate level would
also receive the bachelor's degree in pedagogy, normally after two
years of study and teaching experiences.

The Postbaccalaureate Program. We are unable to justify the
current one-year postbaccalaureate certification program. Many of
those applying present college credentials that go back twenty or
more years. The experiences that they have had in other work and
their present motivation to teach are assets, but these do not out-
weigh their need for refresher studies in the subjects they plan to
teach. Most have not taken all of the pre-education liberal studies
we will recommend for undergraduates, and hardly any are knowledgeable in the five-part upper-division general-education program
we are recommending for teachers. Nor do we believe that postbaccalaureate students' exposure to schools and their preservice experiences in them should be any less than is required in the five-year
program. In addition, the undergraduates now entering teacher education at Northern generally have better grades than do most applying in the postbaccalaureate contingent. Finally, we do not
believe that completion of a shorter program with essentially the
same curricular requirements should lead to a master's rather than a
bachelor's degree.

Consequently, we recommend the following:

1. The same admission requirements we are recommending for
   undergraduates.
2. The same curricular requirements we are recommending for
   undergraduates.
3. The opportunity to examine out of general-education requirements, including the five-part upper-division sequence (an option we hope to open to undergraduates at a later date).
4. The opportunity to demonstrate competence in a discipline or
   divisional major through examination.

5. Some shortening of field experiences in recognition of previous alternative community service or work.
6. The same full year of experiences in partner schools, with accompanying seminars and up to five months of teaching.
7. A bachelor's degree in teaching following satisfactory completion of the program.
8. A reduction in the size of each year's cohort group from the present 100 to 60 in recognition of these increased expectations and of the fact that the overlap of two such groups will produce a student load of 120 FTE (less dropouts) by the 1995–96 academic year.

We estimate that most enrolling in this program will require two years for its completion, but very able individuals may be able to complete it in a shorter period of time. Our thoughts in planning to date have led us to the conclusion that the year spent primarily in schools should be rewarded by a stipend for all coming through either of the two preservice programs. Curricula are planned so that individuals will be knowledgeable about schools and will have had hands-on experiences. They will be assets to schools during the residency portion and should be given modest pay. Members of the Committee of Ten have met with the governor and the education committees of the legislature regarding this recommendation.

Student Mix. The mission statements of the Susqua Valley School-University Partnership and the Smith Center for Pedagogy make clear commitments to equity. Our earlier statements on student selection stress multicultural experiences and the importance of a second language. We insist that the rhetoric be followed by a strong recruitment program designed to attract a supply of teachers reflecting the growing diversity of population in the region.

Less than 10 percent of our current enrollees in teacher education are of minorities. In contrast, enrollment in the primary grades of the Somerville School District will be from 15 to 18 percent black and approximately 30 percent Latino by the end of the decade. The rise of both groups in the enrollments of neighboring school districts will be significant as well, although the percentages will be lower than in Somerville. Enrollment of Asian students varies from 5 to 12 percent across districts and is also growing. The small percentage of Native Americans in the region's schools is predicted to remain stable. Increasing percentages of students from all racial groups are impoverished, itinerant, and homeless.

We recommend that recruitment programs designed to attract minorities into teaching extend downward into the secondary schools. Future Teachers of America clubs, at the high school level, for example, should be created with recruitment active among minorities. The field work of future teachers enrolled at Northern should include service to these clubs (along with other kinds of school and community activity), and club members should be invited to special socialization functions at Northern. High school seniors and juniors at nonaffiliated schools should become significantly involved in the activities of the partner schools.

The intent of our recommendations is to ensure diversity in the groups coming into Northern's teacher education programs comparable to the diversity of student enrollments in the surrounding schools. Present practices of depending on well-qualified minorities to be attracted to teaching careers without special encouragement and support are short-sighted and ineffective. We doubt that improved recruitment and retention of minorities will be feasible without substantial financial support, however. Additional money is required to provide remediation for candidates whose economic and educational backgrounds handicap them in their efforts to pass the required test in basic knowledge and skills.

Partner Schools and Laboratory Settings

By now, individuals reading this proposal should be aware that we are recommending a teacher education entity profoundly different from what now exists. The proposed Smith Center of Pedagogy is not merely a new configuration within the existing school of education—something that stops at the edge of the campus of Northern State University and then reaches out in a begging posture for use of laboratory sites made available (and subject to withdrawal) at the whim of schools and school districts.

No, Smith Center includes partner schools that provide a significant component of the center's teacher education programs—

schools operated for teacher education purposes jointly by the district and the university. Teacher education programs will not be restricted to the use of partner schools, however; they will stretch, as is the case now, into all the school districts of the Susqua Valley School-University Partnership. But visiting various schools as a field experience is a different matter than interning for a time as a junior faculty member in a partner school.

Figure A portrays what we have in mind in terms of Smith Center's shared educational control over all components of preservice teacher education: from general-education prerequisites, to specialized subject-matter requirements, to a theory-practice component connecting field experiences and actual teaching, to the intellectual foundations of educating and teaching. It is a new setting that gains from the public schools, supported by tax dollars, the laboratories and clinics never built into and sorely needed in the teacher education enterprise. The laboratory school concept comes into its own not as an appendage but as an integral part of the whole. There must be a sufficient number of designated, renewing partner schools to accommodate internships for all students admitted to teacher education. The concept, once implemented, offers the promise of breaking the regulatory stranglehold of unchallenged conventional practice to which future teachers now must submit during the critical phase of student teaching. Further, properly implemented, it promises to bring teacher educators out of the university and into school settings, where they will work with school-based colleagues in renewing schools and educating new teachers.[11]

Of course, the programmatic area where Northern State and, for example, the Somerville School District overlap is proportionately much smaller for both than is shown in Figure A. The intent of the figure is to show the nature of activities shared in the turf represented where the two circles overlap. Both the district and the university continue to retain large amounts of unshared, autonomous territory.

It is essential to remember that the faculty of the Smith Center is to consist of three groups conventionally separated: several faculty members from the arts and sciences (mostly dividing their time between an academic department and the center), a much larger number from the school of education (spending 60 percent

Figure A. Site-Based School Renewal and the Simultaneous Education of Educators: A Collaborative Program of Northern State University and Three Neighboring School Districts Through the Smith Center of Pedagogy.

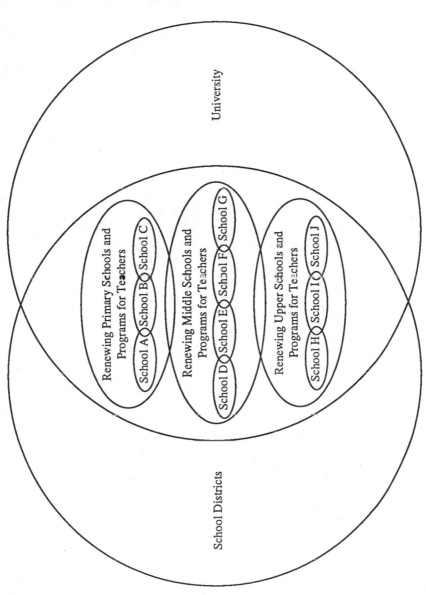

time or more in the center), and selected teachers from the partner schools (dividing their time between a class of children or adolescents and novice teachers). All will share in planning the whole of a program, not a piece of it. We anticipate that, in time, it will become increasingly difficult to sort out the differing home-base appointments of faculty members.

To repeat, the faculty is not to be restricted to partner schools in seeking to provide a full range of field experiences for students. It is important that future teachers visit schools in disarray, special schools of various kinds, and exemplary programs not currently available in partner schools. Creation of the Susqua Valley School-University Partnership is a welcome development that should ease access to facilities beyond the partner schools.

Family and Community

We have relatively little to report regarding the work undertaken by the task force on family and community, not because the group has done little but because this arena is so important, complex, and transitional. There is so much to learn that most of our time has been spent doing our homework.

We have had to come to grips with a new conception of family. Children in nontraditional families will soon outnumber those in traditional families (with a married adult couple of opposite sexes) even in this region, where we have lagged somewhat behind the rest of the nation in changing demographics. Even routine practices of registering students in schools have not caught up with the changes, to the detriment of the homeless and itinerant in particular. There is an urgent need to link educational facilities to families at an earlier age of the children and to involve families much more in school affairs. We are not now preparing teachers to deal with changing family and community circumstances.

We have no recommendations to make at this time, but we do have a growing laundry list of needs. At the top of this list is the necessity of effecting much closer collaboration among all those groups and agencies now dealing with a piece of the problem—but rarely with anything resembling the whole. Some of our time has been spent in looking into current university involvement in family-related issues. We were surprised at the number of faculty members from several departments (and other units) now directly involved in service, training, and research directed to family and community conditions.

It appears to us at this point that the Smith Center may not be the vehicle best suited for bringing these faculty members together or for effecting the necessary collaboration among agencies and groups. Our immediate next step is to bring into conference the relevant people from inside the university with at least one other individual on the outside with whom they work closely. We doubt that we will have more to report before the winter or spring of 1992, after we have had time to consider what we hope will come out of such a conference.

State Context

We know exactly what we want from the state in regard to its teacher-credentialing role but have only a progress report to include at this time. The charge of the State Commission on the Teaching Profession, appointed last year, is to address recruitment, salaries, and working conditions of teachers. The commission is now endeavoring to decide whether to include or ignore teacher education in its work.

We have recommended to the commission that it not get involved in the whole of teacher education but that it take a stand on two matters. First, teacher education curricula should be deregulated: The state should withdraw completely from what it should not do and is incompetent to do. That is, the state should distinguish between the necessary and appropriate standards it sets for licensing and enforces through tests for occupational entry (similar to the bar exam in law) on one hand, and the curricular requirements most likely to produce a competent teacher—which should not be set by the state—on the other. With deregulation, teacher-preparing institutions will be encouraged to be creative and competitive in designing their programs. Currently, they simply conform to a standard, unimaginative model determined by the state.

Second, the practice of issuing temporary licenses to teach should be abolished—and never reinstated, whatever the crisis. The state is inconsistent and self-contradictory in determining the curricular requirements for a teaching certificate and then waiving them when it feels like it. People interested in becoming teachers but not sure of that goal—particularly college graduates—should be given appointments to teach (perhaps as members of teaching teams in partner schools) but should not be certified. Then, should they decide on teaching as a career, they should be guided into regular programs.

These two recommendations are in the hands of the commission, which expects to decide in the fall on the extent of its involvement in matters pertaining to teacher education. We recommend for the Smith Center no certification programs alternative to those recommended above. Faculty energies should go into renewing these and not into creating other routes. Of particular importance is the creation of innovative ways for future teachers to obtain a variety of educational experiences and even to progress through programs at differing rates of speed.

Concluding Statement

The Smith Center of Pedagogy proposed here seeks to combine the ideal liberal arts college and the ideal teachers' college, with the latter encompassing access to ideal school circumstances for internships and residencies. The energies of the faculty, representing all of these component parts, are to be devoted to two preservice teacher education programs: a five-year program for those students who make up their minds early to be teachers, and a two-year program designed primarily for older individuals coming from other lines of work. The shorter time for those in the latter group is based on the premise that, because much of what these students studied as undergraduates is applicable, they should have the opportunity to test out of various requirements.

The first two years of the five are to be taken up largely by a pre-education core curriculum very similar to that recommended by the National Endowment for the Humanities,[12] with studies added in comparative religion, government, art appreciation, and American history. The introductory seminars (with accompanying field experiences), "An Introduction to Teaching," are voluntary but strongly recommended. The upper-division years add to general education with a five-part sequence designed to provide a global, environmental, economic, political, and multicultural perspective and to extend the integration of educational theory and practice already begun informally and voluntarily in the lower division. Students do not seek admission to graduate school on completing their first bachelor's degree but proceed immediately toward the professional baccalaureate in a final year that is primarily field-based, with accompanying reading and reflection. The same general sequence characterizes the postbaccalaureate program, and again admission to graduate school is not required; this program, too, culminates in a professional bachelor's degree in teaching.

It must be understood that students enrolled in these two programs will come together for some major components. For example, there will be only one version of the five-part general-education sequence for teachers. Similarly, the groups will be combined for their internships in partner schools. Such combinations are both economical in their use of faculty time and good for these students, who are otherwise separated by age and experience. They will not enroll together, however, in the small seminars characterizing both programs.

The major laboratory settings—the partner schools—are considered to be component parts of the Smith Center under the educational control of a faculty employed by both the collaborating school districts and the university. Inquiry into schooling, learning, teaching, and teacher education is a normal part of the activity of this diverse faculty group. Scholarly work is, then, an expectation—but in conjunction with teaching and program development rather than separate from it. There is to be considerable flexibility in the balance among teaching, research, and service in the work load and reward structure of individual faculty members.

We see, then, that what is proposed seeks to take care of the major charges leveled against the ways teachers are now educated. Future teachers in these two programs—unlike those in our existing programs, who are left largely to their own devices with respect to curricular choices—will be guided to enjoy a broad general education, depth of understanding in a discipline or broad field of studies, and knowledge about their cultural context and the larger world in which they live. Instead of courses in educational foundations and methods divorced from practice, these subjects will be encountered largely in field settings and discussed as encountered. Field experiences are to be planned in a sequence, with readings designed to deepen meaning and understanding. Instead of simply adapting to schools as they generally function, novices are to be regarded as part of a faculty team engaged in redesigning their school settings. Their apprenticeships are to be whole schools, families, and communities, not merely to individual teachers and classrooms.

The most significant characteristic of the proposed Smith Center is a unified faculty embracing the several parts of the teacher education program. Its members are responsible for the whole; there is no other group to blame for deficiencies and shortcomings or to commend for excellence. Similarly, there is an identifiable student body from entry to completion. Faculty and students are to be engaged together in ongoing inquiry—not only about education, schools, learning, and teaching, but also about the programs of which they are a part and the continuing improvement of these programs. A significant part of this inquiry is to be directed toward partner schools—how to make them most effective for students and, therefore, good places for educating teachers.

We recognize the magnitude of our recommendations and the exercise of human will required to implement them. Consequently, we urge the allocation of additional resources during the years immediately ahead so that the work begun will move forward with two cohort groups—one of freshmen and one of college graduates, both of which will begin in the fall of 1992. We look forward to celebrating the granting of their degrees in pedagogy in June 1994 and June 1997.

We conclude this report with a different version of Figure A. Again the circles representing school districts and the university overlap, creating the ellipse of common turf depicted in Figure B. In this ellipse, we have identified just a few of the major tasks that must be tackled by the faculty group representing all of the major components of the Smith Center of Pedagogy.

These tasks are daunting, but they are not wildly utopian. Indeed, seen from some perspectives, they are quite modest. They are daunting largely because they call upon us all to give up now

Figure B. Major Tasks for the Smith Center of Pedagogy for the Coming Year and Beyond.

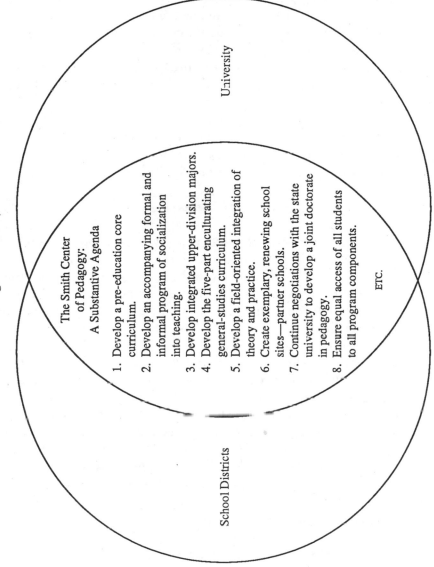

University

School Districts

The Smith Center
of Pedagogy:
A Substantive Agenda

1. Develop a pre-education core curriculum.
2. Develop an accompanying formal and informal program of socialization into teaching.
3. Develop integrated upper-division majors.
4. Develop the five-part enculturating general-studies curriculum.
5. Develop a field-oriented integration of theory and practice.
6. Create exemplary, renewing school sites—partner schools.
7. Continue negotiations with the state university to develop a joint doctorate in pedagogy.
8. Ensure equal access of all students to all program components.

ETC.

what ultimately must be to a considerable degree given up anyway: our tyrannous pursuit of individual gain and of turf jealously guarded. "What we fear above all, and what keeps the new world powerless to be born, is that if we give up our dream of private success for a more genuinely integrated societal community, we will be abandoning our separation and individuation, collapsing into dependence and tyranny. What we find hard to see is that it is the extreme fragmentation of the modern world that really threatens our individuation; that what is best in our separation and individuation, our sense of dignity and autonomy as persons, requires a new integration if it is to be sustained."[13]

Six Eventful Years: 1991–1997

The "Northern Lights" proposal, above, was essentially a report on work in progress, not a blueprint for actions to be taken by others. The agenda proposed was for the Smith Center of Pedagogy, but that entity did not yet and might not ever exist. And so, after some self-congratulation, the Committee of Ten and its task forces picked up the work again. Just a little of what subsequently transpired is described below.

By the beginning of the 1991–92 academic year, over half of those faculty members who perceived their work to be encompassed by the proposed Smith Center had been more than peripherally involved in its conception. They were not about to see its creation aborted by detractors now. Most internal objections were blunted as they bumped up against the interests of faculty members who were now advocates. Many of those voicing objections were becoming increasingly comfortable with the idea of confining their time to the Center for Specialized Studies and no longer being called upon to "service" the teacher education programs.

The Smith Center Comes into Existence

The Smith Center of Pedagogy, housed in the education building, was dedicated on May 27, 1992. The local newspapers gave the dedication more press than expected, heralding the center's announced mission as a bold breakthrough in "the mossbound conduct of teacher education." The *Somerville Herald* praised the university for its increasingly active role in the growing problems of the schools, and noted the significance of Governor Stewart's initiative for "partner schools" and "schools for tomorrow" (earlier endorsed by the newspaper), approved and funded during the most recent legislative sessions. An article elsewhere in the paper noted that 19 percent of the eighty students (the class of 1997) admitted for the fall were from minorities, whereas minority enrollment in the past had not exceeded 10 percent.

Then, in June, Ola Lauton of *Education Week* mentioned the Smith Center of Pedagogy in a front-page story. She had been following an initiative in the reform of teacher education—the Coalition of Exemplary Settings for Teacher Education (CESTE)—since its beginnings early in 1991. She listed the Smith Center as one of five new settings added by CESTE to the previous six "for its outstanding approach to redesigning the education of educators for tomorrow's schools." The criteria employed by the coalition in the selection process included not only status as a semiautonomous unit devoted exclusively to pedagogy and the preparation of teachers but also a top-priority commitment by the university, close collaboration with school districts that included the designation of professional-development schools, and a supportive state infrastructure.

Dean Harriet Bryan, Director Ricardo Montes, President Rosemary Scott, and their colleagues were overjoyed. The grant of $35,000 accompanying selection of the Smith Center to CESTE was welcome, but the recognition for several years of hard work and unfailing will was more so. And additional benefits came with membership in CESTE: A hub had been set up to assist member programs with matters common to all—matters that were now part of the center's agenda: designing curricula, developing case studies to be used in seminars, and working toward renewing partner schools, in particular. In addition, of course, there were benefits to be obtained through interacting with other members of the coalition. All of the settings so far selected to form CESTE had come to benefit financially through a plan whereby funds from private foundations were used to leverage state money on a matching basis. Communication with Governor Stewart's office had already been established by the founders of CESTE before the Smith Center was invited to become a member.

Harriet Bryan and her colleagues had fallen in love with a cause that was neither lost nor easy. The five-year Alpha class of 1997 and the two-year Beta class of 1994 were launched on schedule in September 1992. Students in the latter had good reason to regard themselves as guinea pigs. They were not fully aware of the degree to which the faculty members who conducted the screening interviews relied on intuition, but they realized early on that much of the curriculum emerged as they progressed, on a weekly and even daily basis. The lumpy uncertainty of the curriculum, particularly in regard to field experiences, was more than offset, however, by the degree to which these individuals, most in their thirties and forties, were involved in the entire process, as colleagues rather than as students.

The faculty had greater luxury of time in setting up the five-year program, because its first two years involved only the field and socialization experiences of "An Introduction to Teaching." The intensive curriculum was still down the road a piece. Consequently, these younger students had a much smoother time of it, so far as a reasonably coherent curriculum was concerned.

Beta 1994 fared well nonetheless. Eighteen of the initial cohort group of twenty successfully completed the program—precisely conforming to the "Northern Lights" prediction. Subsequent Beta classes also did well; their percentages of successful completion slightly exceeded predictions. The high retention rate was believed to be partly a result of very careful selection from the large number of applicants.

Although 80 freshmen were tentatively admitted to Alpha 1997, several changed their minds before the final selection process took place in the spring of 1994. Other freshmen and sophomores made up their minds to prepare for teaching, however, swelling the cohort to 109 candidates, all of whom looked very promising. Ten were lost to the program during the succeeding three years, several following counseling regarding their suitability for careers in teaching. Ninety-nine remained to participate in the commencement ceremonies of 1997.

Redesigning the Faculty Reward System

Heavy faculty involvement in the restructuring process had exacerbated the troublesome issue of faculty members' work priorities. The task force on faculty and program had devoted some time to this issue during the 1991–92 academic year, but Provost Lee had made it clear that recommendations would have to await his successor. Just before the Smith Center came into being, Northern's board of trustees announced the appointment of Dr. Sherwood Thompson, an alumnus who had gone on to a distinguished career as a biophysicist. The *Somerville Herald* quoted President Rosemary Scott: "We are exceedingly pleased about Dr. Thompson's joining us. His decision to leave a professorship at the University of California, Berkeley, is indicative of his commitment to assist Northern State University in its continuing drive toward excellence." Several campus experts on Sherwood Thompson emerged during the next few days, and their opinions were unanimous: The soft, qualitative research stuff would clearly be out.

The newly appointed director of the Smith Center, Dr. Ricardo Montes, chaired the small subcommittee that called on Provost Thompson to discuss faculty work priorities early in November 1992. Thompson had done his homework regarding the work of the Committee of Ten and the mission of the center, thanks in part to the briefing by Associate Provost Gerald.

Provost Thompson proved to be very open to the notion of recognizing a wide range of scholarly work, at the same time noting the difficulty of setting comparable standards of excellence for all fields. He offered the opinion that much of what was being published in journals was of little value and that some fields, including engineering and education, appeared increasingly to publish material that was either irrelevant or inaccessible to practitioners. He noted that education had been delinquent in providing review committees with criteria on which to judge the scholarly work of professors and added that he needed guidance regarding, for example, the grounds he should use in reviewing the promotion recommendations of Dean Bryan.

The remainder of the session had gone less well, at least according to those reporting back to the Committee of Ten and the task force on faculty and program. "This university is centrally committed to teaching, of course," Provost Thompson had said, "but I doubt that the poor teachers on this campus are trying very hard to improve—or, for that matter, are being encouraged and given help to become good. I understand that professors here are required to submit student evaluations of only one class each year. Does that mean that they can get student evaluations of all classes and then throw out the worst? And are students ever surveyed independent of the classes they take in order to secure their views of teaching here? I just don't trust the present evaluation system."

Dr. Thompson's reaction to the proposal that faculty supervision of students in the field and faculty work in partner schools be evaluated and rewarded was ambivalent. Rewarding such activities seemed appropriate, yet he regarded as simplistic and untrustworthy for evaluation purposes the letters of commendation that faculty members sometimes received from school personnel—lauding, for example, "Professor Jones for his wonderful presentation to our faculty." He noted, however, that the schools of business and law in the University of California system have been quite successful in writing criteria emphasizing professional performance and getting them recognized as appropriate.

In general, task-force and committee members were encouraged to continue with their work; clearly, the door had been left open. They recognized, however, the need to be very precise in wording recommended criteria for rewarding teaching, service, and scholarly work and to provide specific examples of approved (and perhaps even disapproved) activity in each area.

Like many regional universities, Northern State had no campuswide academic review committee. Instead, each unit had its own. The dean of each had full authority to act on this committee's recommendations for salary increases based on merit (which were then reported to the provost); but all recommendations for promotions were forwarded to the provost, with an accompanying statement of the dean's agreement or disagreement with committee recommendations. Halfway through his first year, Provost Thompson sought advice from the Council of the Academic Senate in regard to the appointment of a campuswide committee to review this procedure.

In April 1993, Dean Bryan conveyed to Provost Thompson her own committee's report on promotion criteria for the school of education, which had been reviewed twice by the faculty before its approval. She was somewhat surprised that Dr. Thompson did not announce a delay in his consideration of the criteria, pending his review of the university-wide process. Instead, he announced that he would get back to her with a response within ten days. His parting comment, after briefly perusing the document, was that he thought it would be useful as he examined campus practices more generally.

The criteria recommended were approved, with only a few changes, for the school of education (both centers) for the 1993–94 review process. A new criterion—involvement and quality of involvement in program renewal (including the field and partner school portion)—had been added to the standard three (teaching, scholarship, and service). In addition, the scope of evaluating teaching was broadened to include all associations with students, both formal and informal (students would be called upon to evaluate all of their instructors for a given year in April of that year); and the service criterion was broadened to include service to the university, the cooperating schools, the community (including other schools), and the profession.

The major problem facing the committee as it drafted the report (and the whole education faculty as it sought to approve the report) had been with the criterion for scholarship. There had been little objection among education faculty members to broadening the scope of acceptable research, but the circumstances of its publication caused much discussion. How is equity to be ensured when the several specialties in education vary widely in the number and types of journals available to faculty members? And although there had been no difficulty in agreeing that educational historians and philosophers rarely report data requiring statistical analyses, debate arose over the legitimacy of conceptual pieces and how to judge their value. There was debate over collaboration as well: Coauthoring of articles represented a desired colleagueship, but perhaps multiple-authored work should receive only fractional credit?

These issues and more were far from settled in the document finally sent on to the provost. But they had been opened up in a rather wholesome fashion, clearing the air somewhat with respect to expectations. Use of a point system for publication in different kinds of journals had been avoided, as had been penalties for collaborative reports of work. Most important, there was stress on quality—importance of the problem, relevance of methodology, clarity of prose, creativity and originality—over quantity. Indeed, the report closed with a recommendation that faculty members report work in progress, not only in forums throughout the year organized for that purpose but also in writing, as part of the folio to be reviewed.

The accompanying discussions probably had only a limited effect on faculty biases and prejudices regarding the relative significance of what colleagues were doing and should do. Nonetheless, many matters not normally discussed and often constituting the downside of university culture were brought out into the open. Most faculty members learned something about the scholarly interests of colleagues and probably became more tolerant—perhaps even appreciative—of the varied talents and activities required to educate future teachers well and to advance the pursuit and dissemination of knowledge.

A Subtle Change in the Rhetoric of Mission

People close to Northern State University might have noticed an interesting change in the introductory pages of the 1993–94 general catalogue. For some years, it had begun: "Northern State is a metropolitan university of 15,000 students [a figure revised annually] that reaches out . . . ," etc. Now, however, this statement was preceded by the following:

> *History and Mission.* The education provided for students at Northern State University, whatever their field of specialty and career aspirations, is built around a core of general studies in the arts, humanities, and social and natural sciences. From arrival to departure, students assume responsibility for their own learning in curricula carefully designed to ensure that their intellectual encounters will be rewarding. The faculty is here to assist in this learning and to see

to it that the opportunities to learn are equitably distributed. This perspective guides the educational process outside of the liberal arts core as well as within it,
whether the specialized field be environmental studies,
journalism, business, architecture, or education.

Northern State University began as a normal
school, offering its first courses in 1899. It evolved into
a degree-granting institution in 1931, a teachers' college in 1938, a state college in 1958, and a university in
1972. At Northern, we believe that the university's
continuing commitment to the education of educators
for the schools is best fulfilled in a setting infused with
the best of the liberal arts, on one hand, and closely
linked to the elementary and secondary schools, on the
other. Similarly, preparation in the other professions
for which programs are offered is enriched by both the
intellectual climate of the campus and close linkages
with the resources of the region.

This new statement on history and mission was followed by
what had been included in the general catalogue in previous years.
The change in rhetoric had not resulted directly from the work of
the Committee of Ten. But it had played a part, largely through the
initiative of the associate provost—one of its members—in stimulating institutionwide study of priorities. The new mission statement
was a product of this ongoing effort.

The Joint Doctorate

Progress toward a joint doctorate in pedagogy (D.Paed.) with
the flagship state university proved to be fraught with complications. There were concerns within both universities about the first
such joint venture in the state being in the field of education—and a
branch of it for which no prerequisite degree had previously been
offered. There were fears in the legislature that approval would set a
precedent and encourage a plethora of such arrangements.

Nonetheless, the degree was approved in the fall of 1993, and
the first candidates appeared at State a year later. Members of the

joint committee representing Northern's interests participated in the orientation session. It was intended that enrollment in the program would be kept small. Thanks to a grant from a corporate foundation, ten teaching assistantships (the internship component at Northern) were available on a competitive basis.

Aquí Se Habla Español

The issue of a second language had been left to simmer on a back burner after boiling over during the 1990–91 academic year. Those faculty members most opposed braced themselves for the matter to boil once again following the appointment of Professor Montes as director of the Smith Center in 1992. But Dr. Montes, though interested in the language issue, was much too wise to risk a divisive confrontation. He was a patient man to begin with; he had learned even greater patience the hard way as an administrator in a California state university, after moving from New Mexico.

He focused his attention elsewhere initially. He put a great deal of time and energy into the announced recruitment program, for example—especially in helping secondary schools in the school-university partnership create Future Teachers of America clubs. Success with this, he believed, lay in first recruiting a small nucleus of club members from each major minority group, which then served to support younger students in each school. The first induction into teaching for a member of a club was to serve as a mentor to younger students, including the provision of tutoring to boys and girls in middle and elementary schools.

Simultaneously, he and his colleagues in the Smith Center were making critical decisions about the curricula of future teachers coming into the new programs. All were to have field experiences in schools of diverse populations; all were to spend up to half of the internship component in a multiracial, multi-ethnic partner school. All of the small cohort clusters were to be integrated in proportion to the diversity of each class—diversity that was to become much greater for the class of 1999 than for the class of 1997, for example.

But Director Montes had not forgotten his interest in language. As he looked at those early projections of each successive class moving through the Smith Center's five-year program against a backdrop of projections regarding enrollment diversity (dependent on successful implementation of the recruitment plan), he realized that by 1994 or 1995, faculty members responsible for field experiences would be going with their students into schools where some children would be just beginning to learn English. The largest proportion of these would be speaking Spanish as their first language.

Ricardo Montes foresaw that the growing need of future teachers to deal with the language problem would serve in a couple of years as the vehicle to spur the faculty to action. And by 1995 it did. The process was not unlike what had already occurred with respect to computers: Teachers had had to keep up with their students. It was much easier to get agreement on the second-language question in the spring of 1995 than it had been in 1990, because all members of the Smith Center faculty were now caught up in the problem. Those in the Center for Specialized Studies were still dealing with a more traditional graduate student body and were not yet confronted with it. Soon, however, they would be.

Smith Center's growing enrollment of Spanish-speaking students (and the addition of Spanish-speaking faculty members, some in partner schools) accelerated development of a plan to immerse all faculty members, as well as students, in the language, free of charge and without academic credit. Throughout the academic year, faculty members came together in Spanish-speaking sessions and tutorials and worked side by side with Spanish-speaking colleagues and students in the schools. Most became quite proficient in the language over the course of the year, and subsequently. A somewhat parallel program in English was made available to ensure that all graduates of the center would be excellent role models in the nation's first language. The whole went into effect for the 1995–96 academic year, which meant that the class of 2000 would be bilingual. For faculty members scheduling retirement for June 2000 or earlier, the program was optional.

Commencement, 1997

June 14, 1997, has come—a day of celebration on the campus of Northern State University. The first Alpha class and the fourth

Beta class of the Smith Center of Pedagogy will receive the bachelor of pedagogy (B.Paed.) degree in the university-wide commencement ceremonies to begin at 1:30 P.M.

An announcement of the previous week had cast a shadow over the event, while simultaneously reminding all those responsible for creating the center of the quietly supportive role that President Scott had played. She would be leaving in December, after more than a decade of effective service to Northern State University, to head the newly created Walker Foundation. (Margaret and Allen Walker had left a substantial estate to be devoted primarily to enhancing the role of universities in seeking to better the human condition in metropolitan areas.) Anticipating her departure, Dr. Scott broke with her own policy in accepting the invitation to be commencement speaker. It is anticipated that she will make some mention of the fact that this former normal school, just two years away from its centennial, is a quarter of a century old as a university.

But the focus today is the Smith Center of Pedagogy and graduation of its first full class: the ninety-nine students who make up Alpha '97—the initially casual designation that stuck—and the fifty-seven who make up Beta '97. Most of the former were admitted to Northern State in the 1992 fall quarter and were joined by others admitted to the teacher education program during the subsequent two years. This, then, is the first class to complete the five-year program. The Beta group was preceded, however, by Beta '94, '95, and '96. All 112 graduates of the previous three Beta classes were invited to today's ceremony, and many are in attendance.

Each of those graduating on this beautiful Saturday already holds a bachelor of arts or bachelor of science degree. Today each will receive the professional bachelor of pedagogy degree (B.Paed.). Because the founders of the Smith Center looked to the past and elsewhere for the *concept* of a first-level professional teaching degree, they also looked to the Latin *paedagōgus* and Greek *paidagōgos* in naming the degree B.Paed. By choosing to make this professional degree a bachelor's degree, they made it clear that the master's degree would be restored to its earlier meaning and used solely to indicate advanced status as a master teacher, specialist, or school principal; while the doctor of pedagogy (D.Paed.), offered in collaboration with the flagship state university, would be reserved for the most advanced level of theoretical and clinical competence. It is anticipated that three or four of the dozen D.Paed. candidates currently enrolled—all employed by the Smith Center on a part-time basis—will complete the doctoral requirements by the following June.

Peter Junger Reminisces

Ola Lauton of *Education Week* had attended the preceding two weeks of parallel commencements that included the graduation of first classes from several of the members of the Coalition of Exemplary Settings for Teacher Education. Now she was on Northern's campus to complete her research. Her story was scheduled to appear in the final issue of volume 16. Her first appointment of the day was in the Student Union with Peter Junger, still going strong as superintendent of the Somerville School District. She was then due at Dean Bryan's office. Dr. Junger was waiting for her. They got quickly into Ola Lauton's agenda.

"You've been part of the whole of what is significant about today, having been in on the beginning. What's been most important to you directly, personally and professionally, about what's transpired over the past half-dozen years or so?"

"It's not easy to sort out any one thing. But let's just say that we've been given permission to deviate from the norm—even to create new norms."

"And what has this enabled you to do?"

"Well, all seventeen of our middle schools are well along toward almost complete redesign. Each is divided into smaller units—'houses' that vary in size but enroll about 150 students; most are multi-aged and nongraded. Each has approximately the same core curriculum, but each team of teachers responsible for a house has considerable freedom in selecting approaches to it. There's no set period of time for each component, and no bells ring; the length and scheduling of blocks of time vary. There's a rotating schoolwide schedule one day each week—for classes geared to special interests and the development of individual talents. Each class on these days contains students from several or even all houses. By staggering these days throughout the week for the whole—Tuesday for one school and Wednesday for another, for example—we make more efficient use of districtwide and community resources."

"What's the reasoning behind all this?"

"The research coming out in the 1980s pointed to increased alienation and feelings of anonymity among members of this age group—feelings probably exacerbated by jumping suddenly from largely self-contained classes in elementary schools to seven-period days and seven different teachers in junior high schools."

"What helped most, the Susqua Valley School-University Partnership or the Smith Center?"

"Both. We were getting several partner schools and several schools for the future off and running simultaneously in the early 1990s."

"Could you have succeeded without the center and the partnership?"

"My earlier experiences tell me no. I tried to support similar changes in one forward-looking school when I was deputy superintendent of the Hawthorne Ridge District, but we were just too much alone; the school was looked on as a funny farm. Now, with both the center and the partnership, there's a supportive infrastructure; and parents feel more comfortable knowing that the university is closely involved."

"Other places have made pretty good progress with this concept, some at the senior high level. Is there anything in which your district is a pioneer?" Ola asked.

"We may not be the only pioneers in the 4-4-4 plan that caught my attention early in the 1980s, but we must be among the earliest. The 4-4-4 plan, as you probably know, consists of a primary, a middle, and an upper school, each for four years. Students begin at age four, progress through the three schools, and normally graduate from the upper school at the age of sixteen. Implementing the plan encourages—indeed, demands—a complete restructuring of schools. By the end of the 1980s, I was getting pretty tired of all the high-level talk about restructuring our schools and then measuring them the next day to see how much they had changed. That sort of thing destroys schools. I came to the conclusion that tomorrow's schools are the ones we have now. You create the new by beginning today at the bottom, at the very beginning. This is what was behind my interest in seeing a school-university partnership get started."

"I don't get it."

"Well," replied Peter, "it's that permission thing again, and the creation of a climate that makes innovation not only legitimate but expected—the norm, if you will. When I came to Somerville, the district was on a binge of closing down small schools and busing the kids somewhere else. Meanwhile, the president and the governors of at least half the states were talking about poor kids, most of them minorities, being disadvantaged in getting a start in school, and being at risk. I figured that the time would come when they had to put some money where their mouths were, and I wanted to be ready to catch some of it."

"And you were?"

"It was a natural, really. We proposed to start a partner school from scratch. Instead of closing down another small elementary school, we opened up the one most recently closed and brought the kids back. First of all, though, we got some construction money from the state, added a little to it, redesigned a corner of the school, and announced the beginning of a class for twenty boys and girls of low-income families who would become four in June, July, or August of . . . 1993, I guess it was."

"You make it all sound easy and quick," Ola interrupted, "and yet you're up to 1993 and don't have the school open by that time. Why so long?"

"Your question brings to mind some of the nonsense being tossed around in that restructuring talk of the late 1980s and early 1990s. You don't just pull a school apart and put it back together in some neat new configuration. Schools are *people* places, not pencil factories. They connect with many different individuals and groups. Ideas are the easy part, yet it took us over two years just to lay the groundwork even though we pretty much knew from the beginning where we were heading. Goodness knows, there was plenty of good stuff in the educational literature to guide us. By the way, I haven't heard that word *restructuring* for quite a while. What happened to it?"

"I think it died from abuse."

"Anyway, last week we graduated fourteen of those twenty little boys and girls admitted to the Dewey Primary School nearly four years ago. Six others are age-and-sex replacements for six who moved on. They'll all celebrate their eighth birthdays this summer. We've added a new cohort each year; next September, twenty four-year-olds will come into Dewey Primary to build enrollment back to eighty again. There are no grade levels in Dewey; that helps us to keep admission flexible and enrollment stable. From here on out, we'll simply build new schools-within-the-school; each at maximum size will enroll eighty youngsters and have a staff of four regular teachers and two interns from Northern."

"This is where you connect with the Smith Center?"

"Yes, except that you don't quite use the right words. Dewey Primary School and Dewey Middle School are *part* of the center," Peter replied. "However, schools in the district connect much more broadly than this. Each of our partner schools has a cohort of ten or twelve interns. Two years ago, the center's new program for school principals came into being. Each of our partner schools has an intern principal. He or she and the teaching interns commonly come together as though they were the faculty of that school, dealing with its problems and future. Commonly, too, a faculty member of the partner school and another of the university participate in these seminars (simulated faculty meetings, if you will)."

"That's something I've got to explore in greater depth. What happens now to the graduating class?"

"They become the first in the new Dewey Middle School; they'll push a class of those now enrolled in the present junior high into Dewey Secondary School, which, in time, will be the new Dewey Upper School. You see, it takes a long time to restructure— pardon the word—a school. Our first graduating class from Dewey Primary will graduate from Dewey Middle in 2001 and from Dewey Upper School in 2005. They'll be sixteen years old by then."

"I don't have time to ask you what happens to kids graduating from high school at age sixteen who are out of sync with everybody else."

"They won't be. We've got some great planning going on in the partnership that includes people from the business world and the community colleges. And we're no longer alone in what we're doing. In fact, we've got seven other centers like this already started just in our own district. These kids won't be out of sync, although quite a few others may be out of sync with them."

"This sounds very much like the transition process that's been going on overall in the Smith Center of Pedagogy," said Ola thoughtfully.

"Precisely. Designing a new program or school to replace what now exists is just like redesigning a house while the present residents go on living in it. You don't just throw these people out into the streets."

"But doesn't effecting change this way take longer and cost more?"

"I don't know what base you're using in talking about 'more' and 'longer,'" Peter responded. "Six or seven years may appear to be a long time to replace a worn-out teacher education program or create a new unit of schooling, but the graduation days at Dewey Primary last week and here today testify to a restructuring accomplished. Research reported a half-dozen years ago showed that not much had changed in teacher education in thirty years and perhaps longer. Researchers on schools reported nonevents and noted that 'nothing changes but the appearance of change.' Seymour Sarason used almost these exact words in a book he wrote in the early 1970s and revised with the same conclusions in the early 1980s. Then, as you know, he produced another in the early 1990s, effectively arguing that the failure of school reform in the 1980s was entirely predictable.[14] You ask about cost? It appears to me that the burden of proof regarding educational reform rests with short-term tinkering."

"I agree, when we mean by *costs* those of human frustration and disappointment. What I've been following here and in several other settings where teacher education is being completely overhauled has revealed enormous satisfaction among those involved. I'm sure I would find the same thing at Dewey Primary. But what about the costs in dollars?"

"Education appears to be the one area of human enterprise where we anticipate—indeed, demand—an entirely new model, with vastly improved output, and completely reject the notion of start-up costs. The corporate sector insists on the application of business principles to the reform of schools but completely overlooks the most basic of competitive business assumptions—namely, the need to invest capital today in the models that probably won't appear for five or six years. Look, for example, at the development schedule of Boeing's future aircraft. Present models must be kept flying while millions of dollars are being poured into what's on the drawing board or only beginning to go into production. The costs of both must be sustained simultaneously. And then Boeing's customers have the added advantage of selling off old planes to help pay for new ones. We in education have no such alternatives available.''

"Are you saying that the continuing reform of schooling and teacher education requires these double costs?" Ola asked.

"No. The added costs are only up front for a few years. But it's absolute folly—funny, if it weren't so dangerous—to think that a new model of schooling or teacher education can be brought into existence while the old one continues to take care of those now in it, all with the same actors and at no additional cost. Once all the new and necessary conditions are in place, we are in a position to know how parsimoniously or generously we wish to support them. That's a matter of deciding among values—our priorities and life-styles.''

"You've been very helpful. I must get over to Harriet Bryan's office. She must be feeling very good on this beautiful morning about what the day symbolizes.''

Harriet Bryan Reflects

Indeed she was. Dean Bryan was alternately gazing abstractedly at the part of the campus framed by her window and equally abstractedly reviewing the short statement she would make at the special eleven o'clock hooding ceremony for school of education graduates. The review was overkill, she knew, but the words she had so painstakingly spoken into her word processor and then rearranged as they appeared before her helped her to order her reflections. She looked out to the campus and back to the printed words, but her brain failed to process much of what her eyes observed.

The nine years at Northern had gone by quickly, and yet the span of experiences belied their brevity. She thought about how difficult it had been at first, about how hostile and even sadistic some faculty members had been. The early confrontation over her ordering of the words *teaching, research,* and *service* was not the last—over either that issue or others. The visit paid by colleagues on President Scott in 1990 had been the last, but several colleagues had tormented her in other ways. She marveled at the degree to which she now valued several of those who had been her most severe critics in the early days. There were still a few she did not trust; they were the ones most prone to tell her about the behind-the-back criticism of others, although she made it clear that she did not want to hear it.

She realized that the seemingly endless process of getting at least a working consensus before moving ahead had been the most difficult, frustrating, and yet gratifying, part. Next to that had been the endless explaining—always from the beginning—to a constantly changing parade of university, school, community, state, and organizational actors. Ideas had come more easily with time and from many sources, getting better and better as they were worked over by different interested, affected individuals and groups. The unexpected move to create the Susqua Valley School-University Partnership had eased in many ways the ground-breaking tasks of carving the Smith Center of Pedagogy out of the existing school of education. The schedule set forth in the "Northern Lights" proposal had simply unfolded in successive cycles of revision over the years, as though preordained. "This must be what is meant by miracles," she thought. Some of the most significant happenings had been serendipitous.

Dean Bryan's reflections turned to unfinished business. The faculty reward system would never get settled. "It's another of those grey cat problems," she thought. "Just when you think it's finished, it comes crawling back." And the joint doctorate with State requires a lot of polishing. Trying to mesh two bureaucracies is fraught with complications.

"In the end, it's 'the way we've always done things' that gets most in the way. I can't believe all the hours we've spent trying to get away from three credits for three hours of instruction per week over a twelve-week quarter. The old system just doesn't fit with a program organized around long-term themes and field experiences integrated into a curriculum. Why does the new so often have to bend to fit what exists—even when there's much dissatisfaction with the way things are?" she asked herself.

Harriet Bryan's reveries were interrupted by a knock on her office door.

Postscript

Although everything that goes before in this chapter is a fable, most of the events are known to me. I trust that the descriptions reflect realities experienced by readers who have tried to change settings or create new ones. The major actors are prototypes of people I know and have known.

The ten-year period portrayed for effecting significant change in such conservative, tradition-bound institutions as schools and universities is, I think, realistic. Perhaps it is overly optimistic, including more serendipity than one might reasonably expect. But at least the narrative avoids that opiate, the idle contemplation of utopias.

The fable does assume an extraordinary commitment, the exercise of great will, a supportive infrastructure, and the infusion of dollars. What is required pales, however, before the commitment, will, resources, and plan of action that must be brought to bear over an even longer period of time if the educational goals for the *nation*, now being proposed in high places and already being described by pundits as utopian, are to be realized. The scary part is the present absence of so much as a glimpse of what will be required by humans to achieve even partially the goals of readiness for school, literacy, competence in mathematics and science, responsible citizenship, much higher rates of graduation from high school, and professional teachers to do the necessary teaching.

Two caveats come to mind. The first is contained in a quote from a little book recently sent by a friend: "Excellence cannot be parachuted into schools; it must be built from within."[15] Similarly, excellence cannot be parachuted into teacher education; it must be built from within. The second is in a quote from a book I wrote following an in-depth study of a sample of schools in the United States around 1980—schools that are, I suspect, little different today. But the circumstances surrounding them are vastly different.

"Futurists have a tantalizing way of describing the year 2001 as though being there has little to do with getting there. The future simply arrives full-blown. But it is the succession of days and years between now and then that will determine what life will be like—"[16] and what we will do with each of those days and years.

Teachers for Our Nation's Schools reports an in-depth study of a sample of teacher-preparing settings in the United States near the end of the decade preceding the one we are in. We do not know whether replication of the study toward the end of this century would reveal fundamental or only marginal differences in the conditions and circumstances I have described in earlier chapters. If little is done, if only halting steps are taken, if we become bemused in contemplating utopias, it is certain that conditions will be markedly worse—perhaps catastrophically so. There are two things we can be sure of: The world will be very different, and the circumstances of our lives will be largely a product of our commissions and omissions during the remaining days of the intervening years. My, how these years flew for Harriet Bryan. May our own be as well spent.

Notes

❖ ❖ ❖

Chapter One

1. R. M. Hutchins, "The Great Anti-School Campaign," in *The Great Ideas Today* (Chicago: Encyclopaedia Britannica, 1972), p. 155.
2. L. A. Cremin, *Popular Education and Its Discontents* (New York: Harper & Row, 1990), p. *viii.*
3. This was the commitment of the Council of Chief State School Officers in 1989. See Council of Chief State School Officers, *Assuming School Success for Students at Risk: A Council Policy Statement* (Washington, D.C.: Council of Chief State School Officers, 1987)
4. Torsten Husén wrote the following: "Let me suggest that the most serious problem faced by schools on both sides of the Atlantic is the rise of a new educational underclass." See T. Husén, "Are Standards in U.S. Schools Really Lagging Behind Those in Other Countries?" *Phi Delta Kappan*, 1983, *40*, 461. Bowles and Gintis bluntly located the educational problem in an economic context of inequality, not the other way around, as so many business, political, and educational leaders in the United States are prone to do: "Hence we believe—indeed, it follows logically from our analysis—that an equal and liberating educational system can only emerge from a broad-based movement dedicated to the transformation of economic life." See S. Bowles and H. Gintis, *Schooling in Capitalist America* (New York: Basic Books, 1976), p. 266.
5. S. B. Sarason, K. S. Davidson, and B. Blatt, *The Preparation of Teachers: An Unstudied Problem in Education*, rev. ed. (Cambridge, Mass.: Brookline Books, 1986).

6. See J. B. Conant, *The American High School Today* (New York: McGraw-Hill, 1959); and J. B. Conant, *The Comprehensive High School* (New York: McGraw-Hill, 1967). The first was followed four years later by J. B. Conant, *The Education of American Teachers* (New York: McGraw-Hill, 1963).

7. J. B. Conant, *Slums and Suburbs* (New York: McGraw-Hill, 1961).

8. R. R. Edmonds, "Programs of School Improvement: An Overview," paper presented at the NIE Invitational Conference on "Research on Teaching: Implications for Practice," Warrenton, Va., Feb. 1982.

9. See J. S. Coleman, *Equality of Educational Opportunity* (Washington, D.C.: Government Printing Office, 1966); and C. Jencks and others, *Inequality* (New York: Harper & Row, 1972).

10. See J. Oakes, *Keeping Track: How Schools Structure Inequality* (New Haven, Conn.: Yale University Press, 1985).

11. The first to catch widespread attention was that of the National Commission on Excellence in Education, *A Nation at Risk* (Washington, D.C.: Government Printing Office, 1983), which warned of a rising tide of mediocrity in our schools. Three years later, a report of the National Governors' Association linked the quality of schools in the United States to the nation's declining economic productivity; see *Time for Results* (Washington, D.C.: National Governors' Association Publication Office, 1986). At the beginning of the 1990s, considerable political debate surrounded a report challenging the assumption that the United States spends more dollars on its K-12 schools than other industrialized countries and should expect more return; see L. Mishel and M. E. Rasell, *Shortchanging Education: How U.S. Spending on Grades K-12 Lags Behind Other Industrial Nations* (Washington, D.C.: Economic Policy Institute, 1990). Hundreds of other reports appeared between 1983 and 1990; most of these focused on individual states, but some examined the relatively poor showing of U.S. students when compared to counterparts in other industrialized countries.

12. See J. Ogbu, "Overcoming Racial Barriers to Equal Access," in J. I. Goodlad and P. Keating (eds.), *Access to Knowledge: An Agenda for Our Nation's Schools* (New York: College Entrance Examination Board, 1990).

13. Lambert's work demonstrated that this end can be achieved without loss in either language through "total immersion" instructional programs. See W. E. Lambert and G. R. Tucker, *Bilingual Education of Children: The Saint Lambert Experiment* (Rowley, Mass.: Newbury House, 1972).

14. See V. O. Pang, "Ethnic Prejudice: Still Alive and Hurtful," *Harvard Educational Review*, 1988, *58*, 378; and G. Jackson and C. Cosca, "The Inequality of Educational Opportunity in the Southwest: An Observational Study of Ethnically Mixed Classrooms," *American Educational Research Journal*, 1974, *11*, 219-229.

15. E. W. Gordon, "Toward an Understanding of Educational Equity," in *Equal Opportunity Review*, 1976, ERIC Clearinghouse on Urban Education, p. 2.

16. H.H.L. Kitano, *The Japanese Americans: Evolution of a Subculture* (Englewood Cliffs, N.J.: Prentice-Hall, 1969).

17. S. Sue and D. W. Sue, "MMPI Comparisons Between Asian-American and Non-Asian Students Utilizing a Student Psychiatric Clinic," *Journal of Counseling Psychology,* 1974, *21,* 423-427; and L. Onoda, "Personality Characteristics and Attitudes Toward Achievement Among Mainland High Achieving and Underachieving Japanese-American *Sanseis*," *Journal of Educational Psychology,* 1976, *68,* 151-156.

18. For further discussion, see V. O. Pang, "Test Anxiety and Math Achievement: The Relationship to Parental Values in Asian American and White American Middle School Children," paper presented at the annual meeting of the American Educational Research Association, San Francisco, Mar. 1989; and S. B. Sarason and others, *Anxiety in Elementary School Children* (New York: Wiley, 1960).

19. P. Schrag, "End of the Impossible Dream," *Saturday Review,* Sept. 1970, p. 68.

20. Gordon, "Toward an Understanding of Educational Equity," p. 2.

21. T. R. Sizer, "Taking School Reform Seriously," in *Preparing Schools for the 1990s: An Essay Collection* (New York: Metropolitan Life Insurance Company, 1989), p. 79.

22. Calvin Frazier, former Commissioner of Education for Colorado, and I were on the speakers' platform at a conference of school-board members and administrators about six months after release of *A Nation at Risk.* He asked for a show of hands to signify how many had taken the initiative to call or had themselves been called to meetings designed to discuss the recommendations of the report. Only a few hands were raised.

23. This is essentially what was said by many teachers surveyed in the late 1980s. See Carnegie Foundation for the Advancement of Teaching, *Report Card on School Reform* (Princeton, N.J.: Carnegie Foundation for the Advancement of Teaching, 1988); and Metropolitan Life Survey, *The American Teacher 1989* (New York: Harris and Associates, 1989). Earlier, Philip Jackson had provided a detailed account of what it takes as a teacher to make hundreds of decisions each day in constantly demanding classroom circumstances; there is no energy left over for planning and conducting fundamental changes in these circumstances. See P. W. Jackson, *Life in Classrooms* (New York: Holt, Rinehart & Winston, 1968).

24. For an analysis of the immediately preceding context, see M. W. Kirst, *Who Controls Our Schools* (Stanford, Calif.: Stanford Alumni Association, 1984); for the views of a corporate executive, see D. T. Kearns and D. P. Doyle, *Winning the Brain Race* (San Francisco: ICS Press, 1988).

25. See E. House, *The Politics of Educational Innovation* (Berkeley, Calif.: McCutchan, 1974); and S. B. Sarason, *The Culture of the School and the Problem of Change* (Newton, Mass.: Allyn & Bacon, 1971 [rev. 1982]).

26. See particularly two reports of a change strategy focused on individ-

ual schools and their networking in the League of Cooperating
Schools in Southern California: M. M. Bentzen and Associates,
Changing Schools: The Magic Feather Principle (New York:
McGraw-Hill, 1974); and J. I. Goodlad, *The Dynamics of Educa-
tional Change* (New York: McGraw-Hill, 1975). For a detailed ac-
count of the conditions necessary for renewal to become a natural way
of life in a school, see B. R. Joyce, R. H. Hersh, and M. McKibben,
The Structure of School Improvement (New York: Longman, 1983).
A school seeking to break with convention and renew itself often finds
itself to be a fragile culture in a hostile environment. See L. M. Smith,
Anatomy of Educational Innovation (New York: Wiley, 1971); and
L. M. Smith, J. P. Prunty, D. C. Dwyer, and P. F. Kleine, *The Fate of
an Innovative School* (New York: Falmer Press, 1987).

27.   T. R. Sizer, *Horace's Compromise: The Dilemma of the American
High School* (Boston: Houghton Mifflin, 1984 [rev. 1985]).

28.   For more information on all three initiatives, see C. Livingston and S.
Castle (eds.), *Teachers and Research in Action* (Washington, D.C.:
NEA Professional Library, 1989); M. Levine (ed.), *Professional Prac-
tice Schools: Building a Model*, Monograph no. 1 (Washington, D.C.:
American Federation of Teachers Center for Restructuring, 1988); and
W. G. Spady, "Organizing for Results: The Basis of Authentic Re-
structuring and Reform," *Educational Leadership*, 1988, *46* (2), 4–8.

29.   K. A. Sirotnik, "The School as the Center of Change," in T. J. Sergio-
vanni and J. H. Moore (eds.), *Schooling for Tomorrow: Directing
Reform to Issues That Count* (Newton, Mass.: Allyn & Bacon, 1989).

30.   H. Judge, *American Graduate Schools of Education* (New York: Ford
Foundation, 1982).

31.   Holmes Group, *Tomorrow's Teachers: A Report of the Holmes
Group* (East Lansing, Mich.: Holmes Group, 1986). A later report
made a clear connection in recognizing the need not just to link
teacher education and schools but to ensure good professional-
development schools through joint school and university effort. See
*The Holmes Group, Work in Progress: The Holmes Group One Year
On* (East Lansing, Mich.: Holmes Group [501 Erickson Hall] 1989).

32.   Carnegie Forum on Education and the Economy, *A Nation Prepared:
Teachers for the 21st Century* (Washington, D.C.: Carnegie Forum on
Education and the Economy, 1986).

33.   J. S. Johnston, Jr., J. R. Spalding, R. Paden, and A. Ziffren, *Those
Who Can* (Washington, D.C.: Association of American Colleges,
1989).

34.   M. C. Reynolds (ed.), *Knowledge Base for the Beginning Teacher*
(Elmsford, N.Y.: Pergamon Press, 1989); W. R. Houston (ed.), *Handbook of Research on Teacher Education* (New York: Macmillan,
1990).

35.   These were the goals the president brought from the so-called Education Summit (of governors) held in early fall 1989.

36.   See T. F. Green, *Predicting the Behavior of the Educational System*
(Syracuse, N.Y.: Syracuse University Press, 1980).

37.   Cremin, *Popular Education and Its Discontents*, pp. 59 and *ix*.

38. International Association for the Evaluation of Educational Achievement, *The Underachieving Curriculum* (Champaign, Ill.: Stipes, 1987).

39. Husén, "Are Standards in U.S. Schools Really Lagging Behind Those in Other Countries?" p. 456.

40. E. D. Hirsch, Jr., *Cultural Literacy* (Boston: Houghton Mifflin, 1987).

41. These data are drawn from H. L. Hodgkinson, *The Same Client: The Demographics of Education and Service Delivery Systems* (Washington, D.C.: Institute for Educational Leadership, 1989). Hodgkinson is doing this nation a tremendous service in continuing to keep these compelling statistics updated and before us, and in continuing to remind us of the relationship between what they portend and our ambitions for universal K–12 education.

42. A. N. Whitehead, *The Aims of Education and Other Essays* (New York: Macmillan, 1929), p. 22.

43. J. I. Goodlad, *A Place Called School* (New York: McGraw-Hill, 1984), p. 361.

44. Three published in 1983 and 1984 were in substantial agreement and received widespread rhetorical attention: E. L. Boyer, *High School* (New York: Harper & Row, 1983); J. I. Goodlad, *A Place Called School* (New York: McGraw-Hill, 1984); and T. R. Sizer, *Horace's Compromise* (Boston: Houghton Mifflin, 1984). The books by Boyer and Sizer addressed the secondary level; Goodlad examined both elementary and secondary schools; the statements regarding elementary schools are based on the research conducted by him and his colleagues.

45. See, especially, the introduction in the 1987 edition of J. I. Goodlad and R. H. Anderson, *The Nongraded Elementary School* (New York: Harcourt Brace Jovanovich, 1959 [rev. 1963]; and New York: Teachers College Press [repr. 1987]).

46. For an overview, see L. A. Shepard and M. L. Smith (eds.), *Flunking Grades: Research and Policies on Retention* (New York: Falmer Press, 1989).

47. The work of B. S. Bloom and J. B. Carroll is seminal here. In the 1960s, Bloom's book on the importance of early intervention spawned an array of studies alerting educators to the need to keep students engaged in subject matter for all while remedying the deficiencies of the slowest before they become overwhelming. See B. S. Bloom, *Stability and Change in Human Characteristics* (New York: Wiley, 1964); and B. S. Bloom, *All Our Children Learning* (New York: McGraw-Hill, 1981). Bloom drew upon a model of the components of school learning developed by Carroll; see J. B. Carroll, "A Model of School Learning," *Teachers College Record*, 1963, *64*, 723–731. Carroll revisited the model more than a quarter-century later and concluded that most of its aspects have been confirmed by research; see J. B. Carroll, "The Carroll Model: A 25-Year Retrospective and Prospective View," *Educational Researcher*, 1989, *18*, 26–31.

48. K. A. Sirotnik, "What You See Is What You Get: Consistency, Persis-

tency, and Mediocrity in Classrooms," *Harvard Educational Review*, 1983, *53*, 16–31.

49. For a detailed account of life in classrooms throughout the continuum of schooling, see M. F. Klein, *Curriculum Reform in the Elementary School* (New York: Teachers College Press, 1989); K. A. Tye, *The Junior High* (Lanham, Md.: University Press of America, 1985); and B. B. Tye, *Multiple Realities: A Study of 13 American High Schools* (Lanham, Md.: University Press of America, 1985).

50. A. G. Powell, E. Farrar, and D. K. Cohen, *The Shopping Mall High School* (Boston: Houghton Mifflin, 1984). For a way out, see M. J. Adler, *The Paideia Proposal* (New York: Macmillan, 1982).

51. See L. Cuban, *How Teachers Taught: Constancy and Change in American Classrooms, 1890–1980* (New York: Longman, 1984).

52. L. M. McNeil, *Contradictions of Control: School Structure and School Knowledge* (New York: Routledge, Chapman, & Hall, 1986).

53. Z. Su, "Teacher Education Reform in the United States (1890–1986)," Occasional Paper no. 3 (Seattle: Center for Educational Renewal, College of Education, University of Washington, 1986).

54. L. Stedman and C. F. Kaestle, "The Test Score Decline Is Over: Now What?" *Phi Delta Kappan*, 1985, *67*, 204–210.

55. G. J. Clifford and J. W. Guthrie, *Ed School* (Chicago: University of Chicago Press, 1988); J. I. Goodlad, R. Soder, and K. A. Sirotnik (eds.), *Places Where Teachers Are Taught* (San Francisco: Jossey-Bass, 1990); K. R. Howey and N. L. Zimpher, *Profiles of Preservice Teacher Education* (Albany: State University of New York Press, 1989); and D. Warren (ed.), *American Teachers: Histories of a Profession at Work* (New York: Macmillan, 1989).

56. Some of the lessons learned are reported in R. Soder, "Professionalizing the Profession," Occasional Paper no. 4 (Seattle: Center for Educational Renewal, College of Education, University of Washington, 1986).

57. J. I. Goodlad, "Linking Schools and Universities: Symbiotic Partnerships," Occasional Paper no. 1 (Seattle: Center for Educational Renewal, College of Education, University of Washington, 1986 [rev. 1987]).

58. J. B. Conant, *Two Modes of Thought* (New York: Trident Press, 1964), p. 30.

59. See K. A. Sirotnik and J. I. Goodlad (eds.), *School-University Partnerships in Action* (New York: Teachers College Press, 1988); C. M. Frazier, "An Analysis of a Social Experiment: School-University Partnerships in 1988," Occasional Paper no. 6 (Seattle: Center for Educational Renewal, College of Education, University of Washington, 1988); J. I. Goodlad, "The National Network for Educational Renewal: Past, Present, Future," Occasional Paper no. 7 (Seattle: Center for Educational Renewal, College of Education, University of Washington, 1988); and C. Wilson, R. Clark, and P. Heckman, "Breaking New Ground: Reflections on the School-University Partnerships in the National Network for Educational Renewal," Occasional Paper

no. 8 (Seattle: Center for Educational Renewal, College of Education, University of Washington, 1989).

60. H. S. Pritchett, "Introduction," in A. Flexner, *Medical Education in the United States and Canada* (New York: Carnegie Foundation for the Advancement of Teaching, 1910).

61. A. Flexner, *Medical Education in the United States and Canada* (New York: Carnegie Foundation for the Advancement of Teaching, 1910).

62. K. M. Ludmerer, *Learning to Heal: The Development of American Medical Education* (New York: Basic Books, 1985).

63. For a comprehensive review of the research methods, see K. A. Sirotnik, "Studying the Education of Educators: Methodology," Technical Report no. 2 (Seattle: Center for Educational Renewal, College of Education, University of Washington, 1989).

64. The twenty-nine case histories form the basis of a book providing a historical perspective on teacher-preparing colleges and universities. See J. I. Goodlad, R. Soder, and K. A. Sirotnik (eds.), *Places Where Teachers Are Taught* (San Francisco: Jossey-Bass, 1990).

65. *A Classification of Institutions of Higher Education* (Princeton, N.J.: Carnegie Foundation for the Advancement of Teaching, 1987).

66. Lightfoot introduced the concept of portraiture to schooling in seeking to describe and analyze a sample of secondary schools; see S. L. Lightfoot, *The Good High School* (New York: Basic Books, 1983).

67. W. Chance, *The Best of Educations: Reforming America's Public Schools in the 1980's* (Chicago: John D. and Catherine T. MacArthur Foundation, 1986), p. 178.

Chapter Two

1. Alexander Pope, letter to William Fortescue, 23 Sept. 1725, in G. Sherburn (ed.), *The Correspondence of Alexander Pope*, Vol. 2 (Oxford: Clarendon Press, 1956), p. 323.

2. It is encouraging to note the effort of thirty-seven college and university presidents (and others who joined later) to turn this shameful situation around. Their concerns and commitments, pulled together by President Donald Kennedy of Stanford following their gathering at the Spring Hill Conference Center near Minneapolis, were addressed not only to themselves but also to fellow presidents nationwide. See "The Letter: 37 Presidents Write . . . ," American Association for Higher Education *Bulletin*, 1987, *40* (3), 10–13. Likewise, the later creation of the Renaissance Group, led by several university presidents, for purposes of furthering their institutions' commitment to teacher education, is encouraging.

3. R. E. Slavin, "PET and the Pendulum: Faddism in Education and How to Stop It," *Phi Delta Kappan*, 1989, *70*, 752–758.

4. Philip Jackson has pointed out that pedagogy is a relatively new requirement for elementary and secondary teachers; see P. W. Jack-

son, *The Practice of Teaching* (New York: Teachers College Press, 1986), p. 5.

5. R. A. Gibboney, "A Critique of Madeline Hunter's Teaching Model from Dewey's Perspectives," *Educational Leadership*, 1987, *44* (5), 46–50.

6. For a far-reaching discussion of the relationships between privatization and educational choice—of school, program, course, or teacher—see M. Lieberman, *Privatization and Educational Choice* (New York: St. Martin's Press, 1989).

7. The more we pursued this line of reasoning, the more we found ourselves in moral and ethical domains. The moral dimensions of teaching and teacher education emerged as of such great importance in our total inquiry that we decided to pursue them in their own right. With the financial support of the MacArthur Foundation, we were able to commission several papers and to put them together with our own in a separate volume: J. I. Goodlad, R. Soder, and K. A. Sirotnik (eds.), *The Moral Dimensions of Teaching* (San Francisco: Jossey-Bass, 1990). What follows here is abstracted primarily from chap. 1 of that volume.

8. M. J. Adler, *We Hold These Truths* (New York: Macmillan, 1987).

9. G. D Fenstermacher, "Some Moral Considerations of Teaching as a Profession," in *The Moral Dimensions of Teaching*, p. 132.

10. See E. L. Boyer, *High School* (New York: Harper & Row, 1983), chap. 3; and J. I. Goodlad, *A Place Called School* (New York: McGraw-Hill, 1984), chap. 2.

11. See K. E. Boulding, *The World as a Total System* (Beverly Hills, Calif.: Sage, 1985). For a translation of these systems into the subject matters of school curricula, see J. I. Goodlad, "The Learner at the World's Center," *Social Education*, 1986, *50* (6), 424–436.

12. D. H. Kerr, "Authority and Responsibility in Public Schooling," in J. I. Goodlad (ed.), *Ecology of School Renewal*, Eighty-Sixth Yearbook of the National Society for the Study of Education, part 1 (Chicago: University of Chicago Press, 1986), p. 24.

13. Kerr, "Authority and Responsibility in Public Schooling," p. 23.

14. J. I. Goodlad, "Equality of Educational Opportunity: A Values Perspective," in *Equality of Opportunity Reconsidered: Values in Education for Tomorrow*, proceedings of the Third European Colloquy for Directors of National Research Institutions in Education, Hamburg, Germany, Sept. 1978 (Lisse, the Netherlands: Swets & Zeitlinger, 1979).

15. See, for example, D. C. Berliner and B. V. Rosenshine (eds.), *Talks to Teachers* (New York: Random House, 1987); V. Richardson-Koehler (ed.), *Educators' Handbook: A Research Perspective* (New York: Longman, 1987); L. Shulman, "Those Who Understand: Knowledge Growth in Teaching," *Educational Researcher*, 1986, *15* (2), 4–14; and M. C. Wittrock (ed.), *Handbook of Research on Teaching* (New York: Macmillan, 1986).

16. T. R. Sizer, *Places for Learning, Places for Joy* (Cambridge, Mass.: Harvard University Press, 1973).

Chapter Three

1. J. Herbst, *And Sadly Teach* (Madison: University of Wisconsin Press, 1989), p. 197.
2. For an account of their beginnings in different regions of the country, see J. Herbst, "Teacher Preparation in the Nineteenth Century," in D. Warren (ed.), *American Teachers: Histories of a Profession at Work* (New York: Macmillan, 1989), pp. 213–236.
3. These necessary conditions of identity, autonomy, homogeneity of student populations and programs, and secure boundaries or borders are derived in part from the analysis of R. Soder, "Status Matters," Technical Report no. 4 (Seattle: Center for Educational Renewal, College of Education, University of Washington, 1989).
4. R. J. Altenbaugh and K. Underwood, "The Evolution of Normal Schools," in J. I. Goodlad, R. Soder, and K. A. Sirotnik (eds.), *Places Where Teachers Are Taught* (San Francisco: Jossey-Bass, 1990). The work of Altenbaugh and Underwood was exceedingly useful to me in my attempt to understand the nineteenth-century beginnings of teacher education.
5. The first documented attempt to create such a school appears to have occurred in Vermont in 1823. Horace Mann is credited with founding the first public normal school in Lexington, Mass., in 1839. A particularly useful account is that of M. L. Borrowman (ed.), *Teacher Education in America: A Documentary History* (New York: Teachers College Press, 1965).
6. P. Woodring, "The Development of Teacher Education," in K. Ryan (ed.), *Teacher Education*, Seventy-Fourth Yearbook of the National Society for the Study of Education, part 2 (Chicago: University of Chicago Press, 1975), p. 9.
7. For a definitive treatment of the ideas of Johann F. Herbart and their impact, see H. B. Dunkel, *Herbart and Herbartianism* (Chicago: University of Chicago Press, 1970).
8. Herbst sounds an appropriate warning regarding the common view of normal schools as a one-dimensional institutional development. See J. Herbst, "Nineteenth-Century Normal Schools in the United States: A Fresh Look," *History of Education*, 1980, *9*, 219–227.
9. Herbst, "Nineteenth-Century Normal Schools in the United States," p. 223.
10. G. J. Clifford and J. W. Guthrie, *Ed School* (Chicago: University of Chicago Press, 1988), pp. 4–5.
11. A notable exception is the University of California, Los Angeles, once a normal school and then the southern branch of the University of California, Berkeley, before coming into its own as a sister campus among those constituting the University of California system.
12. Clifford and Guthrie, *Ed School*.
13. H. Judge, *American Graduate Schools of Education* (New York: Ford Foundation, 1982).

14. A. Cartter, "The Cartter Report on the Leading Schools of Education, Law, and Business," *Change*, 1977, *9*, 44–48.

15. A. Flexner, *Medical Education in the United States and Canada* (New York: Carnegie Foundation for the Advancement of Teaching, 1910).

16. A personal anecdote emphasizes this point. In the late 1960s, I was invited, for reasons that escape me, to lunch in the UCLA Faculty Center with a small group of geophysicists. One was being queried about the current activities of a brilliant colleague now devoting a large part of his time to science education and the education of science teachers. On learning that this pursuit was increasingly consuming his time, they shook their heads as though lamenting the demise of an old friend. Fifteen years later, I listened to an almost identical conversation among several professors of education from major universities. A distinguished scholar was reporting the recent decision of a brilliant younger colleague, who had just agreed to take over the university's small teacher education program. The shaking of heads in unison among this small group of education professors reminded me of the parallel episode with geophysicsts.

17. In a major research university, it is often difficult to retain the focus on the needs of the teacher education program when the selection committee must be attuned to the demands of research and the requirements of affirmative action as well.

18. It is difficult to sort out the numbers of teachers produced in private liberal arts colleges from those produced in private institutions generally. States differ widely. Minnesota, with large numbers of small private colleges, increased production from about 20 percent in 1972 to over 30 percent in 1988 for the private group as a whole.

19. This omission has been in large part rectified by C. Burgess, "Abiding by the 'Rule of Birds': Teaching Teachers in Small Liberal Arts Colleges," in Goodlad, Soder, and Sirotnik (eds.), *Places Where Teachers Are Taught*.

20. Carnegie Foundation for the Advancement of Teaching, *A Classification of Institutions of Higher Education* (Princeton, N.J.: Carnegie Foundation for the Advancement of Teaching, 1987).

21. In the early 1960s, Conant wrote the following: "The professors of education, for their part, found that their own convictions coincided with those of state department and public school personnel, and realized, too, that their source of greatest support was outside the university faculty; as a result, they were more careful to cultivate the outside group." See J. B. Conant, *The Education of American Teachers* (New York: McGraw-Hill, 1963), p. 11.

22. Among top executives, President Donald Kennedy of Stanford University and Chancellor Ira Michael Heyman of the University of California's Berkeley campus have called for increased attention to the schools and those who staff them.

23. Listed in the 1987 edition of the Carnegie Foundation's *A Classification of Institutions of Higher Education*, p. 5.

24. See R. Soder, "Studying the Education of Educators: What We Can Learn from Other Professions," *Phi Delta Kappan*, 1988, *70*, 299–305.

25. Two chapters of a companion book are particularly useful in sorting out and understanding the state context. See L. Eisenmann, "The Influence of Bureaucracy and Markets: Teacher Education in Pennsylvania" (chap. 7), and K. Cruikshank, "Centralization, Competition, and Racism: Teacher Education in Georgia," (chap. 8), in Goodlad, Soder, and Sirotnik (eds.), *Places Where Teachers Are Taught.*

26. A proposal made frequently in speeches during his tenure.

27. J. Herbst, "Teacher Preparation in the Nineteenth Century: Institutions and Purposes," in Warren (ed.), *American Teachers: Histories of a Profession at Work*, p. 217.

28. Herbst goes so far as to say that it was the normal schools rather than the land-grant colleges that brought higher education to the people. Herbst, "Teacher Preparation in the Nineteenth Century: Institutions and Purposes," p. 231.

29. Another illustrative anecdote: When I was director of the Division of Teacher Education at Emory University in Atlanta in the mid 1950s, my response regarding whether or not a graduate's course in psychology met the "knowledge of the learning process" requirements was all that was needed for John Medlin, the director of teacher certification for Georgia, to make a decision.

30. J. B. Conant, *The Education of American Teachers* (New York: McGraw-Hill, 1963), p. 15.

31. See J. I. Goodlad, "The Occupation of Teaching in Schools," in J. I. Goodlad, R. Soder, and K. A. Sirotnik (eds.), *The Moral Dimensions of Teaching* (San Francisco: Jossey-Bass, 1990), pp. 7–8.

32. California Commission on the Teaching Profession, *Who Will Teach Our Children?* (Sacramento: California Commission on the Teaching Profession, 1985). Conant made a similar recommendation, arguing that competition among a number of models would invigorate the institutions. See Conant, *The Education of American Teachers*, p. 60.

33. R. W. Clark, "School/University Relations: Partnerships and Networks," Occasional Paper no. 2 (Seattle: Center for Educational Renewal, College of Education, University of Washington, 1986).

34. See J. I. Goodlad, *School Curriculum Reform in the United States* (New York: Fund for the Advancement of Education, 1964); and J. I. Goodlad (with R. von Stoephasius and M. F. Klein), *The Changing School Curriculum* (New York: Fund for the Advancement of Education, 1966).

35. W. Johnson, "Teachers and Teacher Training in the Twentieth Century," in Warren (ed.), *American Teachers: Histories of a Professional at Work*, p. 244.

36. Cronbach is far too wise to have believed more than three decades ago that his proposal for tightening up studies into the relations between selected variables and student outcomes was to become an all-encompassing model for educational research. Indeed, nearly twenty years later, he cautioned those following it against the danger of ignoring the influence of significant variables not included in the model. See L. J. Cronbach, "The Two Disciplines of Scientific Psy-

chology," *American Psychologist*, 1957, *12*, 671–684; and L. J. Cronbach, "Beyond the Two Disciplines of Scientific Psychology," *American Psychologist*, 1975, *30*, 116–127.

37. Johnson, "Teachers and Teacher Training in the Twentieth Century," p. 244.

38. C. L. Bosk, *Forgive and Remember: Managing Medical Failure* (Chicago: University of Chicago Press, 1979), p. 86.

39. Johnson, "Teachers and Teacher Training in the Twentieth Century," pp. 250–251.

40. V. Richardson-Koehler, "Barriers to the Effective Supervision of Student Teaching: A Field of Study," *Journal of Teacher Education*, 1988, *39* (2), 28–34.

41. See, for example, L. J. Cronbach and P. Suppes (eds.), *Research for Tomorrow's Schools* (New York: Macmillan, 1969); V. Richardson-Koehler (ed.), *Educators' Handbook: A Research Perspective* (New York: Longman, 1987); P. Suppes (ed.), *Impact of Research on Education* (Washington, D.C.: National Academy of Education, 1978); and R.M.W. Travers, *How Research Has Changed American Schools* (Kalamazoo, Mich.: Mythos Press, 1983).

42. J. Dewey, *The Sources of a Science of Education* (New York: Horace Liveright, 1929), p. 33.

43. R. M. Hutchins, *The Higher Learning in America* (New Haven, Conn.: Yale University Press, 1936), p. 114.

44. J. Dewey, "The Relation of Theory to Practice in Education," in Charles A. McMurry, (ed.), *The Relation of Theory to Practice in the Education of Teachers*, Third Yearbook of the National Society for the Scientific Study of Education (Chicago: University of Chicago Press, 1904), p. 10.

45. Clifford and Guthrie, *Ed School.* See chap. 8 in particular.

46. B. R. Clark, "Schools of Education: The Academic Professional Seesaw," *Change*, 1989, *21*, 62.

47. Johnson, "Teachers and Teacher Training in the Twentieth Century," p. 245.

48. G. D Fenstermacher included this observation in a presentation to state legislators soon after becoming dean of the college of education at the University of Arizona.

49. Holmes Group, *Tomorrow's Teachers, A Report of the Holmes Group* (East Lansing, Mich.: Holmes Group, 1986). With considerable expansion of the group into a much broader array of institutions, this position has been substantially modified.

50. Carnegie Forum on Education and the Economy, *A Nation Prepared: Teachers for the 21st Century* (Washington, D.C.: Carnegie Forum on Education and the Economy, 1986).

51. S. B. Sarason, K. S. Davidson, and B. Blatt, *The Preparation of Teachers: An Unstudied Problem in Education* (New York: Wiley, 1962; and Cambridge, Mass.: Brookline Books, 1986 [rev.]).

Chapter Four

1. I. M. Heyman, memo to the Academic Senate, University of California, Berkeley, Jan. 13, 1982, p. 4.
2. J. I. Goodlad, R. Soder, and K. A. Sirotnik, (eds.), *Places Where Teachers Are Taught* (San Francisco: Jossey-Bass, 1990).
3. E. L. Boyer, *College: The Undergraduate Experience in America* (New York: Harper & Row, 1987).
4. B. R. Clark, *The Academic Life* (Princeton, N.J.: Carnegie Foundation for the Advancement of Teaching, 1987).
5. The Carnegie Policy Series, published from 1967 to 1979, consisted of 37 policy reports by the Carnegie Commission on Higher Education and the subsequent Carnegie Council on Policy Studies in Higher Education, 128 sponsored research reports, and a few reprints and related items, for a total of over 170 publications, under the direction of Clark Kerr as chair and director. The major areas of concern for these reports and monographs included greater social justice via higher education, development of high skills and new knowledge, effectiveness in use of resources, quality and integrity of academic programs, adequacy of governance, sources of financial support, and purposes and performance of higher education.
    Commission works were published by McGraw-Hill, and Council publications came from Jossey-Bass. Summaries of the Carnegie Commission's policy reports are found in *A Digest of Reports of the Carnegie Commission on Higher Education* (New York: McGraw-Hill, 1974), and summaries of research reports are in *Sponsored Research of the Carnegie Commission on Higher Education* (New York: McGraw-Hill, 1975). Summaries of works of the Carnegie Council are contained in *The Carnegie Council on Policy Studies in Higher Education: A Summary of Reports and Recommendations* (San Francisco: Jossey-Bass, 1980), which also lists all publications of both the Commission and the Council.
6. G. J. Clifford and J. W. Guthrie, *Ed School* (Chicago: University of Chicago Press, 1988).
7. B. R. Clark, *The Academic Life*, p. xxi.
8. Greater attention to teaching is being stimulated, also, by harsh criticism from within the academic community. See, for example, P. Smith, *Killing the Spirit* (New York: Viking, 1990).
9. I. Edman, *Arts and the Man* (New York: Norton, 1928), p. 15.
10. The University of Chicago provides a stunning example of an institution with a clear mission that, under the leadership of Robert M. Hutchins, demonstrated that the institution did not require a football team to enhance its reputation. See H. S. Ashmore, *Unseasonable Truths: The Life of Robert Maynard Hutchins* (Boston: Little, Brown, 1989).
11. Given the enthusiasm with which this president embraced this mission, it is perhaps overly cynical to wonder about the degree to which he was responding to a policy decision that had recently declared this

university to have prime responsibility for teacher education in the state's plan for higher education.

12. Apparently, there has been a somewhat low level of awareness of this turnover rate among higher education officials, who expressed surprise over figures reported for 1987–88 and 1988–89: 17 percent for presidents (considerably higher than the twenty-five-year average of nearly 11 percent for presidents in our sample); and 24 percent for provosts (slightly higher than our quarter-century average of 21 percent but identical with our 1987–88 figures of 24 percent). See D. E. Blum, "24-Pct. Turnover Rate Found for Administrators; Some Officials Are Surprised by Survey Results," *The Chronicle of Higher Education*, Mar. 1989, *29*, pp. A13–A14.

13. H. H. Gerth and C. W. Mills (eds.), *From Max Weber: Essays in Sociology* (New York: Oxford University Press, 1958).

14. J. M. Burns, *Leadership* (New York: Harper & Row, 1978), p. 4.

15. L. G. Bolman and T. E. Deal, *Modern Approaches to Understanding and Managing Organizations* (San Francisco: Jossey-Bass, 1984), pp. 149–150.

16. T. J. Peters and R. H. Waterman, Jr., *In Search of Excellence* (New York: Harper & Row, 1982), p. 82.

17. For a short attempt at clarification, see J. I. Goodlad, "Keeping the Gates," *AACTE Briefs*, 1989, *10* (6), 3, 9.

18. Currently, a colleague on one of our two visiting teams, Phyllis Edmundson, is seeking to compare our list of necessary conditions and NCATE standards; see her "NCATE Accreditation and the Study of the Education of Educators: A Comparison," Working Paper (Seattle: Center for Educational Renewal, College of Education, University of Washington, 1988).

19. L. M. McNeil, *Contradictions of Control: School Structure and School Knowledge* (New York: Routledge, Chapman, & Hall, 1986).

Chapter Five

1. D. Light, Jr., "Introduction: The Structure of the Academic Professions," *Sociology of Education*, 1974, *47*, 17.

2. For both survey and interview questions, see K. A. Sirotnik, "Studying the Education of Educators: Methodology," Technical Report no. 2 (Seattle: Center for Educational Renewal, College of Education, University of Washington, 1989).

3. Earlier, I cited the view of Hutchins, who relegated the professional schools—which he associated with vocationalism—to the status of institutions outside the academic core of his ideal university. See. R. M. Hutchins, *The Higher Learning in America* (New Haven: Yale University Press, 1936), pp. 114–115. Flexner was a little more generous: "Of the professional faculties, a clear case can, I think, be made out for law, and medicine; not for denominational religion, which involves a bias, hardly perhaps for education, certainly not at all for

business, journalism, domestic 'science,' or library 'science.' " See A. Flexner, *Universities: American, German, English* (New York: Oxford University Press, 1930), p. 29.

4. N. Glazer, "The Schools of the Minor Professions," *Minerva*, 1974, *12* (3), 346–364.

5. D. F. Machell, "A Discourse on Professional Melancholia," position paper (Danbury, Conn.: Western Connecticut State University, 1988).

6. A. Kojève, "Tyranny and Wisdom," in Leo Strauss. *On Tyranny* (Ithaca: Cornell University Press, 1968), p. 172, footnote 6.

7. W. Pfaff, *Barbarian Sentiments* (New York: Hill and Wang, 1989), p. 132.

8. T. R. Sizer, *High School Reform and the Reform of Teacher Education*, ninth annual DeGarmo Lecture (Minneapolis: University of Minnesota, 1984), p. 8.

9. R. W. Clark, "School/University Relations: Partnerships and Networks," Occasional Paper no. 2 (Seattle: Center for Educational Renewal, College of Education, University of Washington, 1986).

10. K. A. Sirotnik and J. I. Goodlad (eds.), *School-University Partnerships in Action: Concepts, Cases, and Concerns* (New York: Teachers College Press, 1988).

11. See, for example, Carnegie Forum on Education and the Economy, *A Nation Prepared: Teachers for the 21st Century* (New York: Carnegie Corporation, 1986); Holmes Group, *Tomorrow's Teachers* (East Lansing, Mich.: Holmes Group, 1986); Southern Regional Education Board, *Changing the Education of Teachers* (Atlanta: Southern Regional Education Board, 1988); and Holmes Group, *Tomorrow's Schools: Principles for the Design of Professional Development Schools* (East Lansing, Mich.: Holmes Group, 1990).

12. P. A. Graham, "An Exciting and Challenging Year," *Harvard Graduate School of Education Association Bulletin*, 1983, *28* (1), 2–3.

13. J. I. Goodlad, "Linking Schools and Universities: Symbiotic Partnerships," Occasional Paper no. 1 (Seattle: Center for Educational Renewal, College of Education, University of Washington, 1986 [rev. 1987]).

14. N. D. Theobald, "The Financing and Governance of Professional Development or Partner Schools," Occasional Paper no. 10 (Seattle: Center for Educational Renewal, College of Education, University of Washington, 1990).

15. In our travels, we found that individuals had interpreted "five-year programs" in two different ways: either as fifth-year programs (involving a single postbaccalaureate year) or as five-year programs (including two years of general education, two years of specialized studies, and a postbaccalaureate year). Consequently, this item should be discarded because of the confusion in interpretation.

16. It is difficult to weight all the factors entering into this action. The specific response was directed toward the announced prerequisites for eligibility to take the board's examination. But AACTE had already gone on record as opposing another aspect of the board's work: an effort to secure substantial sole-source funding from Congress. Our

data suggest a more general and pervasive rejection by teacher educators of national board certification as a strategy for enhancing teaching as a profession.

17.   J. Herbst, *And Sadly Teach* (Madison, Wis.: University of Wisconsin Press, 1989).

Chapter Six

1.   From *Die Bauleute* [The builders] in *Franz Rosenzweig: His Life and Thought*, 2nd rev. ed., presented by N. N. Glatzer (New York: Schocken, 1976), p. 237.

2.   A. Flexner, *Medical Education in the United States and Canada* (New York: Carnegie Foundation for the Advancement of Teaching, 1910), p. 26.

3.   Flexner, *Medical Education in the United States and Canada*, p. 26.

4.   National Board for Professional Teaching Standards, *Toward High and Rigorous Standards for the Teaching Profession* (Detroit and Washington: National Board for Professional Teaching Standards, 1989), p. 49.

5.   D. H. Kerr, "Teaching Competence and Teacher Education in the United States," *Teachers College Record*, 1983, *84*, 525–552.

6.   J. B. Conant, *The Education of American Teachers* (New York: McGraw-Hill, 1963), p. 114.

7.   D. C. Lortie, *Schoolteacher* (Chicago: University of Chicago Press, 1975), pp. 60–65.

8.   The considerable influence of this earlier experience with teachers is documented in F. F. Fuller and O. H. Brown, "Becoming a Teacher," in K. Ryan (ed.), *Teacher Education*, Seventy-Fourth Yearbook of the National Society for the Study of Education, part 2 (Chicago: University of Chicago Press, 1975), pp. 25–52.

9.   H. S. Becker, B. Geer, E. C. Hughes, and A. L. Strauss, *Boys in White* (Chicago: University of Chicago Press, 1961).

10.   Lortie, *Schoolteacher*.

11.   K. A. Tye, "Changing Our Schools: The Realities," Technical Report no. 30 (Los Angeles: A Study of Schooling, Laboratory in School and Community Education, University of California, 1981).

12.   J. I. Goodlad, *A Place Called School* (New York: McGraw-Hill, 1984).

13.   Z. Su, "Exploring the Moral Socialization of Teachers: Factors Related to the Development of Beliefs, Attitudes, and Values in Teacher Candidates," Technical Report no. 7 (Seattle: Center for Educational Renewal, College of Education, University of Washington, 1989).

14.   T. S. Popkewitz, *Teacher Education as a Process of Socialization: The Social Distribution of Knowledge*, Teacher Corps, United States Office of Education, Technical Report no. 18 (Madison: University of Wisconsin, CMTI Impact Study Team, 1975).

15.   See, for example, R. J. Friebus, "Agents of Socialization Involved in Student Teaching," *Journal of Educational Research*, 1977, *70*, 263–

268; A. H. Karmos and C. M. Jacko, "The Role of Significant Others During the Student Teaching Experience," *Journal of Teacher Education*, 1977, *28*, 51–55; and K. M. Zeichner, "Key Processes in the Socialization of Student Teachers: Limitations and Consequences of Oversocialized Conceptions of Teacher Socialization," paper presented at the annual meeting of the American Educational Research Association, Boston, Mass., Apr. 1980.

16.   An important distinction between *curriculum* and *program* is made in K. R. Howey and N. L. Zimpher, *Profiles of Preservice Teacher Education* (Albany: State University of New York Press, 1989), chap. 8. Whereas a curriculum can be and usually is a specification for courses, Howey and Zimpher perceive a program to be coherent with respect to the fit of its component parts, all aligned toward a conception of schoolteaching. I use the word *program* more loosely here but work toward specification that is in close agreement with that of Howey and Zimpher. (See particularly my Chapter Seven.)

17.   Howey and Zimpher, *Profiles of Preservice Teacher Education*, pp. 248–249.

18.   R. Hofstadter, *Anti-Intellectualism in American Life* (New York: Knopf, 1963).

19.   National Endowment for the Humanities, *50 Hours: A Core Curriculum for College Students* (Washington, D.C.: National Endowment for the Humanities, 1989).

20.   E. L. Boyer, *High School* (New York: Harper & Row, 1983), chap. 2.

21.   L. Stedman and C. F. Kaestle, "The Test Score Decline Is Over: Now What?" *Phi Delta Kappan*, 1985, *67*, 204–210.

22.   K. A. Sirotnik, "What You See Is What You Get: Consistency, Persistency, and Mediocrity in Classrooms," *Harvard Educational Review*, 1983, *53*, 16–31.

23.   D. A. Schön, *Educating the Reflective Practitioner: Toward a New Design for Teaching and Learning in the Professions* (San Francisco: Jossey-Bass, 1987).

24.   As part of our effort to conceptualize the study, we wrote to a rather large sample of school superintendents to gauge their views regarding the quality of teacher education programs in their states. The responses were exceedingly diverse and sometimes contradictory (with a given college or university receiving both very high and very low ratings). No clear patterns emerged. If employers of teachers disagree on the strength of nearby teacher-preparing institutions, we should not be surprised to find that future teachers do not always discriminate clearly among these institutions on the basis of program quality.

Chapter Seven

1.   A. Einstein, *Ideas and Opinions* (New York: Crown, 1955), p. 108.

2.   D. Bok, "The President's Report," *John Harvard's Journal*, May–June 1979 (entire issue).

3. B. R. Gifford, "Prestige and Education: The Missing Link in School Reform," *The Review of Education*, 1984, *10*, 187.

4. Gifford, "Prestige and Education: The Missing Link in School Reform," p. 188.

5. Gifford, "Prestige and Education: The Missing Link in School Reform," p. 192.

6. Gifford, "Prestige and Education: The Missing Link in School Reform," p. 193.

7. R. Soder, "Faculty Work in the Institutional Context," Technical Report no. 3 (Seattle: Center for Educational Renewal, College of Education, University of Washington, 1989), p. 93.

8. This commitment would be the natural, tangible follow-through on the part of the several hundred college and university presidents who have up to this date of writing signed the so-called Spring Hill or Kennedy letter referred to earlier.

9. In the long journey toward credibility for teacher education programs, this prima facie, commonsense evidence may be more persuasive with the public than is recent supportive research favorable to teachers with pedagogical studies in their preparation backgrounds. See, for example, D. C. Berliner, "The Development of Expertise in Pedagogy," Charles W. Hunt Memorial Lecture presented at the annual meeting of the American Association of Colleges for Teacher Education, New Orleans, Feb. 17–20, 1988; and P. L. Grossman and A. E. Richert, "Unacknowledged Knowledge Growth: A Reexamination of the Effects of Teacher Education," *Teaching and Teacher Education*, 1988, *4* (1), 53–62.

10. In endeavoring to describe conditions and circumstances, we recognized that there are multiple realities depending on the perceptions of the beholders. We were guided in our efforts by the multilevel curriculum framework developed by J. I. Goodlad, M. F. Klein, and K. A. Tye, "The Domains of Curriculum and Their Study," in J. I. Goodlad and Associates, *Curriculum Inquiry* (New York: McGraw-Hill, 1979), pp. 43–76.

11. K. Ryan, "The Moral Education of Teachers," in K. Ryan and G. McLean (eds.), *Character Development in Schools and Beyond* (New York: Praeger, 1987), chap. 14.

12. For a historical overview of the concept of general education, closely linked to views of teacher education, see M. L. Borrowman, *The Liberal and Technical in Teacher Education* (New York: Teachers College Press, 1956). For a comprehensive view of the knowledge domains to be included in general studies at the baccalaureate level, see Report of the Harvard Committee, *General Education in a Free Society* (Cambridge, Mass.: Harvard University Press, 1945). For a relatively recent account of the undergraduate program, see especially part 3 of E. L. Boyer, *College: The Undergraduate Experience in America* (New York: Harper & Row, 1987). See also G. E. Miller, *The Meaning of General Education* (New York: Teachers College Press, 1988).

13. Z. Su, "Teacher Education Reform in the United States (1890–1986),"

Occasional Paper no. 3 (Seattle: Center for Educational Renewal, College of Education, University of Washington), 1986.

14. Edmundson, "The Curriculum in Teacher Education," p. 32.

15. B. R. Wilson, "The Teacher's Role: A Sociological Analysis," *British Journal of Sociology*, 1962, *13*, 23.

16. D. H. Kerr, "Authority and Responsibility in Public Schooling," in J. I. Goodlad (ed.), *The Ecology of School Renewal*, Eighty-Sixth Yearbook of the National Society for the Study of Education, part 1 (Chicago: Chicago University Press, 1987), p. 24.

17. This pattern was established early in the normal schools. Even as late as 1900, no real entrance requirements were in effect in these schools. Further, reports Eisenmann, "Any student with a rudimentary command of common school material could present himself or herself at the school during any point in the term, and the professors would have to carve out time to place that student in a program." See L. Eisenmann, "The Influence of Bureaucracy and Markets: Teacher Education in Pennsylvania" in J. I. Goodlad, R. Soder, and K. A. Sirotnik (eds.), *Places Where Teachers Are Taught* (San Francisco: Jossey-Bass, 1990).

18. For more information, see the brochure prepared by the College Studies Board Executive Committee (Hazard Adams, director), College Studies Program, University of Washington, Seattle, 1989–90.

19. For an analysis of efforts to develop such an understanding in teachers and their students, see J. I. Goodlad, *School Curriculum Reform in the United States* (New York: Fund for the Advancement of Education, 1964); and J. I. Goodlad (with R. von Stoephasius and M. F. Klein), *The Changing School Curriculum* (New York: Fund for the Advancement of Education, 1966).

20. This turf problem hides a more serious one—the common assumption that the contents of a subject field and methods of teaching it bear little relation to each other.

21. It is interesting to note that laboratory schools, once so central to teacher education and still present on nine of the campuses we visited, faded rather quietly and in large numbers from the educational scene during the 1960s and 1970s. Their immediate faculties and parents of children enrolled were the most voluble protesters of their demise. Now, years later, professional-development schools connected with universities are being proposed as a natural, virtually unopposed answer to the need for better regulated settings in which teacher education students can gain field and student-teaching experiences. But movement toward them proceeds slowly and without apparent urgency.

22. J. S. Bruner, *The Process of Education* (New York: Vintage Books, 1960), p. 33.

23. L. Shulman, "Those Who Understand: Knowledge Growth in Teaching," presidential address at the annual meeting of the American Educational Research Association, Chicago, Mar. 31–Apr. 4, 1985.

24. See, for example, Task Force on Teaching as a Profession, *A Nation Prepared: Teachers for the 21st Century* (New York: Carnegie Forum

on Education and the Economy, 1986); and National Board for Professional Teaching Standards, *Toward High and Rigorous Standards for the Teaching Profession* (Detroit and Washington: National Board for Professional Teaching Standards, 1989).

25. Some efforts to develop case studies addressing issues and problems in teaching are now under way. See, for example, H. S. Broudy, "The Case for Case Studies in Teacher Education," project description (Indiana: Coalition of Teacher Education Programs, 1985); and T. J. Kowalski, R. A. Weaver, and K. T. Henson, *Case Studies in Teaching* (with an accompanying instructor's manual) (New York: Longman, 1990).

26. See, for example, J. Dewey, *Moral Principles in Education* (Boston: Houghton Mifflin, 1909); J. Piaget, *The Moral Judgment of the Child* (New York: Macmillan, 1965); K. Ryan, "Teacher Education and Moral Education," *Journal of Teacher Education,* 1988, *39,* 18–23; S. M. Hauerwas, "The Morality of Teaching," in A. L. DeNeef, C.D.W. Goodwin, and E. S. McCrate (eds.), *The Academic's Handbook* (Durham, N.C.: Duke University Press, 1988); and J. I. Goodlad, R. Soder, and K. A. Sirotnik, (eds.), *The Moral Dimensions of Teaching* (San Francisco: Jossey-Bass, 1990).

27. J. I. Goodlad, *A Place Called School* (New York: McGraw-Hill, 1984), chaps. 3 and 8.

28. B. Bettelheim, *Love Is Not Enough* (Glencoe, Ill.: Free Press, 1950).

29. And so it has been for quite a long time. See J. I. Goodlad, "The Reconstruction of Teacher Education," *Teachers College Record,* 1970, *72,* 61–72.

30. H. S. Broudy, "Variations in Search of a Theme," *Journal of Educational Thought,* 1985, *19* (1), 37.

31. Broudy, "Variations in Search of a Theme," p. 37.

32. See, in particular, his afterword in T. R. Sizer, *Horace's Compromise,* rev. ed. (Boston: Houghton Mifflin, 1985), pp. 222–236.

33. Sizer, *Horace's Compromise,* p. 237.

34. See particularly chaps. 4 and 6 of Goodlad, *A Place Called School.*

35. H. Barnes, "Structuring Knowledge for Beginning Teaching," in M. C. Reynolds (ed.), *Knowledge Base for the Beginning Teacher* (Elmsford, N.Y.: Pergamon Press, 1989), p. 19.

36. Edmundson, "The Curriculum in Teacher Education," p. 141.

Chapter Eight

1. A. N. Whitehead, *Adventures of Ideas* (New York: Macmillan, 1933), p. 360.

2. S. Feiman-Nemser, *Teacher Preparation: Structural and Conceptual Alternatives.* Issue Paper no. 89-5 (East Lansing, Mich.: National Center for Research on Teacher Education, Michigan State University, 1989), p. 36.

3. Regarding the letter that emerged from the Spring Hill Conference,

see "The Letter: 37 Presidents Write . . . ," *American Association for Higher Education Bulletin*, 1989, *40* (3), 10–13. Subsequently, several hundred college and university presidents signed it. Regarding the mission of the Renaissance Group, see its *Teachers for the New World: A Statement of Principles* (Cedar Falls: University of Northern Iowa, 1989).

4. J. S. Johnston, Jr., and Associates, *Those Who Can: Undergraduate Programs to Prepare Arts and Sciences Majors for Teaching* (Washington, D.C.: American Association of Colleges, 1989). See also *Consortium for Excellence in Teacher Education*, published by the Consortium in 1989 (place of publication not given).

5. This idea did not stem from me. It emerged out of the discussion of a small committee working with the National Advisory Board to the Center for Educational Renewal—a committee that has taken on responsibility for planning how the recommendations of this report might be implemented.

6. There have been some attempts by state coordinating agencies in higher education to allocate among public colleges and universities responsibility for various functions, including teacher education. The few attempts that have focused on teacher education have not enjoyed marked success, primarily because of apparent reluctance to curtail teacher education in some institutions and to make the tough budget-ary decisions in a charged political context.

7. Education deans have often been called upon to do more with less. See J. Geiger, "Education Deans as Collaborative Leaders," *Journal of Teacher Education*, 1989, *40*, 4.

8. E. A. Lynton and S. E. Elman, *New Priorities for the University: Meeting Society's Needs for Applied Knowledge and Competent Individuals* (San Francisco: Jossey-Bass, 1987), p. 4.

9. The BYU–Public School Partnership, one of more than a dozen such partnerships constituting the National Network for Educational Renewal, is in the process of developing different kinds of such collaborative arrangements for different purposes: partner schools for the development of innovative practices, teacher education schools for student teaching, and focus schools for exemplary programs in various components of schools (to be used also for teacher education programs).

10. This information was obtained from Professor Rolf Grankvist, Rector of the Teacher-Training Institute, University of Trondheim, Norway.

11. B. R. Wilson, "The Teacher's Role: A Sociological Analysis," *British Journal of Sociology*, 1962, *13*, 23.

12. Over 70 percent of faculty members surveyed in 1989 said that their interests lie in teaching; 62 percent agreed that teaching effectiveness should be the primary criterion for promotion. See Carnegie Foundation for the Advancement of Teaching, *The Condition of the Professoriate* (Princeton, N.J.: Carnegie Foundation for the Advancement of Teaching, 1989), pp. 43, 45.

13. J. I. Goodlad, "How Laboratory Schools Go Awry," *UCLA Educator*, 1980, *21* (2), 47–53. While John Dewey saw his laboratory school at the

University of Chicago as a vehicle for teachers to become inquirers into education, schooling, and teaching (J. Dewey, *Studies in Logical Theory* [Chicago: University of Chicago Press, 1903]), most university-based laboratory schools have been unclear about their mission—a factor contributing significantly to the demise of many.

14. For a discussion of the collaborative relationship proposed, see J. I. Goodlad, "The National Network for Educational Renewal: Past, Present, Future," Occasional Paper no. 7 (Seattle: Center for Educational Renewal, College of Education, University of Washington, 1988).

15. In the Center for Educational Renewal, we attempted to assess the developmental status of professional-development schools in the United States. The results were very disappointing; the gap between rhetoric and reality was found to be great. See F. Brainard, "Professional Development Schools: Status as of 1989," Occasional Paper no 9 (Seattle: Center for Educational Renewal, College of Education, University of Washington, 1989). Simultaneously, we initiated an effort to anticipate some of the funding and governance issues likely to be confronted by those seriously attempting to establish and maintain such schools. See N. D. Theobald, "The Financing and Governance of Professional Development or Partner Schools," Occasional Paper no. 10 (Seattle: Center for Educational Renewal, College of Education, University of Washington, 1990).

16. A. Flexner, *Medical Education in the United States and Canada* (New York: Carnegie Foundation for the Advancement of Teaching, 1910), p. 128.

17. Readers are directed to the comprehensive treatment of the selection process by M. Scriven, "Teacher Selection," in J. Millman and L. Darling-Hammond (eds.), *Teacher Education* (Newbury Park, Calif.: Sage, 1990), pp. 76–103.

18. See L. S. Miller, "Nation-Building and Education," *Education Week*, May 14, 1986, pp. 52, 42. See also Quality Education for Minorities Project, *Education That Works: An Action Plan for the Education of Minorities* (Cambridge, Mass.: MIT Press, 1990).

19. This is essentially the process now ongoing in the Danforth Principal Preparation Program at the University of Washington. The group meeting at intervals consists of the faculty, representatives from the present group of experienced teachers enrolled, some mentor principals, and district representatives who help select nominees for the program.

20. We focused entirely on the drafts of chapters in J. I. Goodlad, R. Soder, and K. A. Sirotnik (eds.), *The Moral Dimensions of Teaching* (San Francisco: Jossey-Bass, 1990), and short written accounts of situations encountered by these graduate students in the schools where they served as interns. Because this was a cohort group with considerable opportunity for informal interaction, the seminar was part of a rather carefully planned curriculum, and there were frequent planning and evaluating sessions designed to integrate the whole, the total experience appeared to be quite effective.

21. As was stated earlier, this idea did not originate with me. At this time, several teacher educators are engaged in developing case materials. My fear is that they will lack the dollars and time necessary to the first-rate creativity and technical expertise required.

22. Schön's concept of reflection-in-action is particularly relevant. For further development, see D. A. Schön, *The Reflective Practitioner: How Professionals Think in Action* (New York: Basic Books, 1982). Particularly relevant to teacher education is his *Educating the Reflective Practitioner: Toward a New Design for Teaching and Learning in the Professions* (San Francisco: Jossey-Bass, 1987).

23. In the Corinne A. Seeds University Elementary School at UCLA, my colleagues and I had access to a rich array of campus resources. Frequently, professors offered their services to provide a missing curriculum piece (for example, in foreign languages) or to test out some hunch about teaching. We welcomed this and benefited from it occasionally. More often, however, the volunteer complained about the behavior of the children and requested that one of our regular teachers be on hand to quell disturbances. There were apparently to be no human intrusions into the purity of what was being taught! The need for all who teach to have some help confirmed Madeline Hunter's (the principal at this time) decision to create a theory-into-practice teaching model. This has been found useful by many teachers, widely praised by administrators confronted by pressure to improve instruction, and condemned by a good many teacher educators who view the model as simplistic, atheoretical, and not grounded in research. (One critic labeled it "Madeline Hunter's Mud Hut," because he viewed it as lacking a sound theoretical framework.) We begin to see here the unfortunate gap between a campus-based push for a solid conceptual or theoretical base and the school-based reliance on what appears to work. The need to unite the two is not yet being widely met, but a useful debate has found its way into the literature. For example, see R. A. Gibboney, "A Critique of Madeline Hunter's Teaching Model from Dewey's Perspective," *Educational Leadership*, 1987, *44* (5), 46–50; M. Hunter, "Beyond Rereading Dewey: What's Next? A Response to Gibboney," *Educational Leadership*, 1987, *44* (5), 51–53; and R. A. Gibboney, "The Vagaries of Turtle Research: Gibboney Replies," *Educational Leadership*, 1987, *44* (5), 54. See also R. E. Slavin, "PET and the Pendulum: Faddism in Education and How to Stop It," *Phi Delta Kappan*, 1989, *70* (10), 752–758.

24. A good deal of such tension has surfaced in the school-university partnerships constituting the National Network for Educational Renewal. We have found it possible to get to a level of productive collaboration, but the road to it has usually been bumpy. The schools generally have less difficulty than the universities letting the other into their affairs. University professors are accustomed to serving as consultants to schools; there has been little of the reverse. The concept of working together on matters of mutual interest is not easily assimilated. See K. A. Sirotnik and J. I. Goodlad (eds.), *School-University*

Partnerships in Action: Concepts, Cases, and Concerns (New York: Teachers College Press, 1988).

25. J. I. Goodlad, *A Place Called School* (New York: McGraw-Hill, 1984), pp. 301–310.

26. Excellent examples of each genre are D. C. Lortie, *Schoolteacher* (Chicago: University of Chicago Press, 1975); T. Kidder, *Among Schoolchildren* (Boston: Houghton Mifflin, 1989); and S. Ashton-Warner, *Teacher* (London: Virago, 1963).

27. Relevant here are the analyses and accompanying recommendations of D. Scannell, D. G. Andersen, and H. Gideonse, *Who Sets the Standards?* (Washington, D.C.: Association of Colleges and Schools of Education in State Universities and Land Grant Colleges and Affiliated Private Universities, 1989).

28. California Commission on the Teaching Profession, *Who Will Teach Our Children?* (Sacramento: California Commission on the Teaching Profession, 1985).

Chapter Nine

1. S. B. Sarason, *The Creation of Settings and the Future Societies* (San Francisco: Jossey-Bass, 1972), p. 6.

2. B. O. Smith, *A Design for a School of Pedagogy* (Washington, D.C.: U.S. Department of Education, 1980), p. 18.

3. In creating the fictitious Northern State University, I had in mind two existing regional public universities—one in a town of about 50,000 residents and the other in a city of over 500,000—and bits and pieces of other colleges and universities. Both of the two major settings were established as normal schools near the end of the nineteenth century. I placed Northern in an urban setting of less than 350,000 residents—approximately the size of Albuquerque, New Mexico—about eighty miles from the imaginary small-town site of the state's land-grant university (also fictitious).

4. I came across this artfully crafted little gem of a thought in a short piece by David Brewster, editor-in-chief of the *Seattle Weekly;* see D. Brewster, "Gill and Gigantism," *Seattle Weekly,* Feb. 28, 1990, p. 7.

5. Sarason, *The Creation of Settings and the Future Societies,* p. 31.

6. Taken (and slightly reworded) from J. I. Goodlad, "Linking Schools and Universities: Symbiotic Partnerships," Occasional Paper no. 1 (Seattle: Center for Educational Renewal, College of Education, University of Washington, 1986 [rev. 1987]), pp. 28–29.

7. In memory and in recognition of the work of B. Othanel Smith, principal author of *A Design for a School of Pedagogy.* I am indebted to Bunnie Smith and those who worked with him for ideas that have been neglected for too long. I am indebted, also, to Seymour B. Sarason for insights into the processes and problems of creating new settings; see his *The Creation of Settings and the Future Societies.*

8. I am indebted to the Inquiry Group, "Indicators of Equity and Excel-

lence," unpublished progress report of the Equity and Excellence Task Force, Puget Sound Educational Consortium, University of Washington, 1989. See also K. A. Sirotnik, "Equal Access to Quality in Public Schooling: Issues in the Assessment of Equity and Excellence," in J. I. Goodlad and P. Keating (eds.), *Access to Knowledge: An Agenda for Our Nation's Schools* (New York: College Entrance Examination Board, 1990), pp. 159–185; and J. I. Goodlad, "The Occupation of Teaching in Schools," in J. I. Goodlad, R. Soder, and K. A. Sirotnik (eds.), *The Moral Dimensions of Teaching* (San Francisco: Jossey-Bass, 1990), pp. 3–34.

9. I have adapted these criteria from those announced by the College of Education, University of Arizona, in the spring of 1989. Subsequently, minority enrollment in teacher education increased in the fall of 1989 to 29 percent, in contrast to a minority enrollment of 12 percent in the fall of 1988.

10. The MAT appears to have been the inspiration of James B. Conant and Francis Keppel when they were, respectively, president and dean of the graduate school of education at Harvard University. Neither had a high regard for the education courses normally constituting a considerable portion of teacher preparation programs; both highly valued guided experience for the novice. There is some evidence that Conant, late in his career, worried somewhat about the degree to which this plan confused and cheapened the meaning of the master's degree.

11. Holmes Group, *Tomorrow's Schools: Principles for the Design of Professional Development Schools* (East Lansing, Mich.: Holmes Group, 1990).

12. National Endowment for the Humanities, *50 Hours: A Core Curriculum for College Students* (Washington, D.C.: National Endowment for the Humanities, 1989).

13. R. N. Bellah and others, *Habits of the Heart* (New York: Harper & Row, 1985), p. 286.

14. S. B. Sarason, *The Predictable Failure of Educational Reform: Can We Change Course Before It's Too Late?* (San Francisco: Jossey-Bass, 1990).

15. W. E. Nothdurft, *SchoolWorks* (Washington, D.C.: German Marshall Fund of the United States, 1989), p. 91.

16. J. I. Goodlad, *A Place Called School* (New York: McGraw-Hill, 1984), p. 321.

Appendixes

❖   ❖   ❖

A. Technical Reports

B. Commissioned Papers

C. Occasional Papers

D. The Center for
   Educational Renewal

APPENDIX A: TECHNICAL REPORTS

The following technical reports were published by the Center for Educational Renewal during the Study of the Education of Educators. Most of these provided collations and analyses of data drawn upon in Chapters One through Nine of *Teachers for Our Nation's Schools.*

Technical Report #	Author(s)	Title
1	John I. Goodlad, Kenneth A. Sirotnik, and Roger Soder	Studying the Education of Educators
2	Kenneth A. Sirotnik	Studying the Education of Educators: Methodology
3	Roger Soder	Faculty Work in the Institutional Context
4	Roger Soder	Status Matters: Observations on Issues of Status in Schools, Colleges, and Departments of Education
5	Roger Soder	Faculty Views of Schooling, Schools, Teaching, and Preparing Teachers: A Summary of the Study of Education of Educators Questionnaire Data
6	Phyllis J. Edmundson	The Curriculum in Teacher Education
7	Zhixin Su	Exploring the Moral Socialization of Teachers: Factors Related to the Development of Beliefs, Attitudes, and Values in Teacher Candidates
8	Roger Soder	Students and Faculty in Teacher Education: Views and Observations
9	Michael C. Reed	Leadership, Commitment, and Mission in American Teacher Education: The Need for Culturally Attuned Organizational Change
10	Sharon Field	The Special Field of Special Education

APPENDIX B: COMMISSIONED PAPERS

In seeking to develop the conceptual underpinnings of the Study of the Education of Educators, the Center for Educational Renewal commissioned scholarly papers from the individuals listed below. Most of these became chapters in two companion volumes edited by John I. Goodlad, Roger Soder, and Kenneth A. Sirotnik: *The Moral Dimensions of Teaching* (Jossey-Bass, 1990), and *Places Where Teachers Are Taught* (Jossey-Bass, 1990).

Richard J. Altenbaugh, Northern Illinois University
Barbara Beatty, Wellesley College
Barry L. Bull, University of Minnesota
Charles Burgess, University of Washington
Christopher M. Clark, Michigan State University
Kathleen Cruikshank, University of Wisconsin, Madison
Linda Eisenmann, Radcliffe College
Walter Feinberg, University of Illinois, Urbana-Champaign
Gary D Fenstermacher, University of Arizona
John I. Goodlad, University of Washington
Irving G. Hendrick, University of California, Riverside
Jurgen Herbst, University of Wisconsin, Madison
Robert A. Levin, Carnegie-Mellon University
Kenneth A. Sirotnik, University of Washington
Hugh Sockett, George Mason University
Roger Soder, University of Washington
Kenneth A. Strike, Cornell University
Bruce R. Thomas, consultant, Chicago, Illinois
Kathleen Underwood, University of Texas, Arlington

APPENDIX C: OCCASIONAL PAPERS

In advancing its agenda, the Center for Educational Renewal published a series of occasional papers over the several years that the Study of the Education of Educators was in progress. Authors and titles are as follows.

Occasional Paper #	Author(s)	Title
1	John I. Goodlad	Linking Schools and Universities: Symbiotic Partnerships
2	Richard W. Clark	School/University Relations: Partnerships and Networks
3	Zhixin Su	Teacher Education Reform in the United States (1890–1986)
4	Roger Soder	Professionalizing the Profession: Notes on the Future of Teaching
5	Kenneth A. Sirotnik	The School as the Center of Change
6	Calvin M. Frazier	An Analysis of a Social Experiment: School-University Partnerships in 1988
7	John I. Goodlad	The National Network for Educational Renewal: Past, Present, Future
8	Carol Wilson, Richard Clark, and Paul Heckman	Breaking New Ground: Reflections on the School-University Partnerships in the National Network for Educational Renewal
9	Frank Brainard	Professional Development Schools: Status as of 1989
10	Neil D. Theobald	The Financing and Governance of Professional Development or Partner Schools
11	Donald L. Ernst	The Contexts of Policy and Policy Making in Teacher Education

APPENDIX D: THE CENTER FOR EDUCATIONAL RENEWAL

The Center for Educational Renewal was founded in September 1985 for purposes of promoting the simultaneous renewal of schools and education of those who work in them. During the intervening years, this work has been advanced by a dedicated staff and an array of advisers, grouped below in three broad categories.

Center Personnel

The full-time staff of the center is and has been small, usually numbering only four or five individuals at any given time. Consequently, it has relied heavily on people employed on a part-time basis or for only brief periods: students at various levels of preparation, postgraduate research associates, specialists in several educational fields, educators on leave from other institutions, and so on. Those commissioned for special tasks but not in the employ of the center are not included below.

Frank Brainard	Jean Melton
Karin Cathey	Kim Newell
Richard Clark	Kathleen Olson
Jan DeLacy	Jason Osgood
Phyllis Edmundson	Carol Reed
Don Ernst	Michael Reed
Art Gallagher	Kjell-Jon Rye
John Goodlad	Teresa Scott
Patricia Ann Hamill	Candice Smith
Jill Hearne	Roger Soder
Paul Heckman	Kenneth Sirotnik
Pamela Keating	Zhixin Su
Lembi Kongas	Joan Waiss
Deborah Kremen	Carol Wilson
Craig Landon	Shana Windsor
Scott McClelland	Jordis Young
Paula McMannon	

National Advisory Board

The Center for Educational Renewal has benefited from the advice of a panel of distinguished people who constitute its National Advisory Board:

Betty Castor, commissioner, Florida Department of Education
Bill Clinton, Governor of Arkansas
David Imig, executive director, American Association of Colleges for Teacher Education
Arthur Jefferson, superintendent, Detroit Public Schools
Leeda Marting, consultant, New York City
Frank Newman, president, Education Commission of the States
Robert O'Neil, president, University of Virginia
Thomas W. Porter, Jr., vice-chairman, Security Pacific Bank
Bambi Cardenas Ramirez, commissioner, U.S. Civil Rights Commission
Irving Richardson, teacher, Freeport Public Schools, Maine
Sophie Sa, executive director, Matsushita Foundation, Inc.
Theodore Sizer, chairman, Coalition of Essential Schools, Brown University
Suzanne Soo Hoo, principal, Carver Elementary School, ABC Unified School District, California
Gerald Tirozzi, commissioner, Connecticut Department of Education
Blenda Wilson, chancellor, University of Michigan, Dearborn

Advisers

At several critical junctures in its work, the Center for Educational Renewal sought the advice of people in fields of expertise such as medical education, educational policy, sociology, the history of education, and so on. They included:

Robert Abbott, University of Washington
Robert H. Anderson, Pedamorphosis, Inc.
Richard Andrews, University of Wyoming

Elizabeth Ashburn, Office of Educational Research and
    Improvement, U.S. Department of Education
Jack Beal, University of Washington
Patrick Callan, Education Commission of the States
James I. Doi, University of Washington
Ellis Evans, University of Washington
Joni Finney, Education Commission of the States
Calvin Frazier, University of Denver
Allen Glenn, University of Washington
Patricia Graham, Harvard University
Edward Gross, University of Washington
Francis Hunkins, University of Washington
William Johnson, University of Maryland, Baltimore County
Carl Kaestle, University of Wisconsin, Madison
Donna Kerr, University of Washington
Alan Klockars, University of Washington
David Madsen, University of Washington
Kathy Mueller, University of Washington
Charles Odegaard, University of Washington
Roger Olstad, University of Washington
Theodore Phillips, University of Washington
Seymour Sarason, Yale University
Stephanie Shea, University of Washington
Gary Sykes, Michigan State University
David Tyack, Stanford University

Index

❖ ❖ ❖

413